Architectures and Frameworks for Developing and Applying Blockchain Technology

Nansi Shi
Logic International Consultants, Singapore

A volume in the Advances in Systems Analysis, Software Engineering, and High Performance Computing (ASASEHPC) Book Series

Published in the United States of America by
    IGI Global
    Engineering Science Reference (an imprint of IGI Global)
    701 E. Chocolate Avenue
    Hershey PA, USA 17033
    Tel: 717-533-8845
    Fax: 717-533-8661
    E-mail: cust@igi-global.com
    Web site: http://www.igi-global.com

Library of Congress Cataloging-in-Publication Data

Names: Shi, Nansi, 1953- editor.
Title: Architectures and frameworks for developing and applying blockchain
    technology / Nansi Shi, editor.
Description: Hershey, PA : Engineering Science Reference, 2020. | Includes
    bibliographical references.
Identifiers: LCCN 2018060063| ISBN 9781522592570 (hardcover) | ISBN
    9781522592594 (ebook) | ISBN 9781522592587 (softcover)
Subjects: LCSH: Blockchains (Databases) | Software architecture.
Classification: LCC QA76.9.B56 A73 2020 | DDC 005.1/2--dc23 LC record available at https://lccn.loc.gov/2018060063

This book is published in the IGI Global book series Advances in Systems Analysis, Software Engineering, and High Performance Computing (ASASEHPC) (ISSN: 2327-3453; eISSN: 2327-3461)

British Cataloguing in Publication Data
A Cataloguing in Publication record for this book is available from the British Library.

For electronic access to this publication, please contact: eresources@igi-global.com.

Advances in Systems Analysis, Software Engineering, and High Performance Computing (ASASEHPC) Book Series

Vijayan Sugumaran
Oakland University, USA

ISSN:2327-3453
EISSN:2327-3461

MISSION

The theory and practice of computing applications and distributed systems has emerged as one of the key areas of research driving innovations in business, engineering, and science. The fields of software engineering, systems analysis, and high performance computing offer a wide range of applications and solutions in solving computational problems for any modern organization.

The **Advances in Systems Analysis, Software Engineering, and High Performance Computing (ASASEHPC) Book Series** brings together research in the areas of distributed computing, systems and software engineering, high performance computing, and service science. This collection of publications is useful for academics, researchers, and practitioners seeking the latest practices and knowledge in this field.

COVERAGE

- Computer System Analysis
- Software Engineering
- Parallel Architectures
- Enterprise Information Systems
- Computer Graphics
- Performance Modelling
- Storage Systems
- Human-Computer Interaction
- Network Management
- Virtual Data Systems

IGI Global is currently accepting manuscripts for publication within this series. To submit a proposal for a volume in this series, please contact our Acquisition Editors at Acquisitions@igi-global.com or visit: http://www.igi-global.com/publish/.

Titles in this Series

For a list of additional titles in this series, please visit: www.igi-global.com/book-series

Cyber-Physical Systems for Social Applications
Maya Dimitrova (Bulgarian Academy of Sciences, Bulgaria) and Hiroaki Wagatsuma (Kyushu Institute of Technology, Japan)
Engineering Science Reference • copyright 2019 • 440pp • H/C (ISBN: 9781522578796) • US $265.00 (our price)

Integrating the Internet of Things Into Software Engineering Practices
D. Jeya Mala (Thiagarajar College of Engineering, India)
Engineering Science Reference • copyright 2019 • 293pp • H/C (ISBN: 9781522577904) • US $215.00 (our price)

Analyzing the Role of Risk Mitigation and Monitoring in Software Development
Rohit Kumar (Chandigarh University, India) Anjali Tayal (Infosys Technologies, India) and Sargam Kapil (C-DAC, India)
Engineering Science Reference • copyright 2018 • 308pp • H/C (ISBN: 9781522560296) • US $225.00 (our price)

Handbook of Research on Pattern Engineering System Development for Big Data Analytics
Vivek Tiwari (International Institute of Information Technology, India) Ramjeevan Singh Thakur (Maulana Azad National Institute of Technology, India) Basant Tiwari (Hawassa University, Ethiopia) and Shailendra Gupta (AISECT University, India)
Engineering Science Reference • copyright 2018 • 396pp • H/C (ISBN: 9781522538707) • US $320.00 (our price)

Incorporating Nature-Inspired Paradigms in Computational Applications
Mehdi Khosrow-Pour, D.B.A. (Information Resources Management Association, USA)
Engineering Science Reference • copyright 2018 • 385pp • H/C (ISBN: 9781522550204) • US $195.00 (our price)

Innovations in Software-Defined Networking and Network Functions Virtualization
Ankur Dumka (University of Petroleum and Energy Studies, India)
Engineering Science Reference • copyright 2018 • 364pp • H/C (ISBN: 9781522536406) • US $235.00 (our price)

Advances in System Dynamics and Control
Ahmad Taher Azar (Benha University, Egypt) and Sundarapandian Vaidyanathan (Vel Tech University, India)
Engineering Science Reference • copyright 2018 • 680pp • H/C (ISBN: 9781522540779) • US $235.00 (our price)

Green Computing Strategies for Competitive Advantage and Business Sustainability
Mehdi Khosrow-Pour, D.B.A. (Information Resources Management Association, USA)
Business Science Reference • copyright 2018 • 324pp • H/C (ISBN: 9781522550174) • US $185.00 (our price)

701 East Chocolate Avenue, Hershey, PA 17033, USA
Tel: 717-533-8845 x100 • Fax: 717-533-8661
E-Mail: cust@igi-global.com • www.igi-global.com

Table of Contents

Detailed Table of Contents

A typical example of a distributed process is trade finance where data and documents are transferred between multiple companies including importers, exporters, carriers, and banks. Blockchain is seen as a potential decentralized technology that can be used to automate such processes. However, there are also other competing technologies such as managed file transfers, messaging, and WebAPIs that may also be suitable for automating similar distributed processes. In this chapter, a decision framework is proposed to assist the solution architect in deciding the technology best suited to support decentralized control of a distributed business process where there are multiple companies involved. The framework takes as input the different areas of concern such as data, processing, governance, technical, and the pros and cons of the technologies in addressing these areas of concerns and provides a method to analyze and highlight the best technology for any process in question. Two example processes, trade finance and price distribution, are used to show the application of the framework.

Managing today's highly dispersed and intertwined supply chain in order to maximize the overall organizational benefit by leveraging partner competencies is a herculean task and one that is of ever-growing importance in a highly competitive and truly globalized market. Information technology in the form of point-of-sale data, materials requirement planning software, and enterprise-wide systems have often been leveraged to assist with this. However, with the proliferation of data, storing, managing, and analyzing data on a large scale is a challenge. Blockchains provide numerous benefits such as data transparency, immutability, and traceability that are so critical in building a cohesive cyberinfrastructure that facilitates cooperation and collaboration among supply chain partners. This chapter examines the characteristics of blockchain that make it suitable for supply chains and explore how the benefits afforded by blockchain can be leveraged to enhance value creation while optimizing the supply chain.

Chapter 3

Jorge Tarifa-Fernández, University of Almería, Spain
María Pilar Casado-Belmonte, University of Almería, Spain
María J. Martínez-Romero, University of Almería, Spain

The accounting information system could be improved by blockchain technology, but some potential risk could arise. Thus, it is worth considering such risks. The accounting research and academic literature regarding the impact of this technology on the accounting system are in an initial stage of this emergent field. The purpose of this chapter is to go a step further on this topic and to spur additional research regarding accounting and blockchain technology. The contribution of this study is twofold. On the one hand, it shows the main technologies comprising blockchain and their main consequences understood as sources of improvement. On the other hand, it assesses said effects applied to different processes of the accounting information system. Not only does this work show implications for the accounting profession, but the effects on the primary stakeholders are also brought to light.

Chapter 4

Rajalakshmi Krishnamurthi, Jaypee Institute of Information Technology, India
Tuhina Shree, Jaypee Institute of Information Technology, India

Blockchain is the world's most trusted service. It serves as a ledger that allows transaction to take place in a decentralized manner. There are so many applications based on blockchain technology, including those covering numerous fields like financial services, non-financial services, internet of things (IoT), and so on. Blockchain combines a distributed database and decentralized ledger without the need of verification by central authority. This chapter surveys the different consensus algorithms, blockchain challenges, and their scope. There are still many challenges of this technology, such as scalability and security problems, waiting to be overcome. The consensus algorithms of blockchain are proof of work (POW), proof of stake (POS), ripple protocol consensus algorithm (RPCA), delegated proof of stake (dPOS), stellar consensus protocol (SCP), and proof of importance (POI). This chapter discusses the core concept of blockchain and some mining techniques, consensus problems, and consensus algorithms and comparison algorithms on the basis of performance.

Chapter 5

Tarek Taha Kandil, Helwan University, UAE
Shereen Nassar, Heriot-Watt University, UK
Mohamed Taysir, Drakon Tech Solutions, Egypt

Blockchain technology starts to reconfigure all aspects of society to make it clear and beneficial for the legal system. The chapter introduces "The Blockchain Revolution" in categories 1.0, 2.0, and 3.0; in the form of analyzing the use of the technology that is being applied in new innovative business models, Blockchain 1.0 starts with the creation of the first blockchain and the introduction of the technology in the "Bitcoin Whitepaper," the crypto-currency model, via Bitcoin's application in services related to cash, payments, and transfers. Blockchain 2.0 starts with the indication that using smart contracts on blockchains will be available via the development of syntax (i.e., "solidity" that would enable developers to create solutions with blockchain technology at the backend). The chapter explores the feature of the new disruptive business models-based blockchain technology as a new approach in delivering business products and services. In the chapter, the authors explore the new technologies raised in different fields of business.

Chapter 6

Erginbay Uğurlu, Istanbul Aydın University, Turkey
Yusuf Muratoğlu, Hitit University, Turkey

Two of the important topics concerning scientists and governments are blockchain and climate change. After the paper of Satoshi Nakamoto, blockchains became a global phenomenon. After its usage for cryptocurrencies, blockchain is starting to be used for digital protocols and smart contracts. Blockchain technology is used in many sectors, such as banking, finance, car leasing, entertainment, energy, etc. Climate change leads to global warming, which means the long-term warming of the planet. Therefore, governments have made an effort to decrease global warming or keep it stable. One of the mitigation ways of global warming is to use renewable energy. Solar energy is one of the most used types of renewable energy sources, and also blockchain technology is widely used in this sector. In this chapter, the authors investigate the use of blockchain technology in the solar energy sector.

Chapter 7

Edward Lehner, Bronx Community College, USA
John R. Ziegler, Bronx Community College, USA

This chapter conceptualizes a process for cryptocurrency to diversify traditional methods of higher education funding in the United States. Cryptocurrency funding augments traditional revenue streams and shifts the discussion of education costs from expenses to a more robust conversation about innovative avenues to wealth generation as a potential solution to fund the mission of American higher education. This chapter acknowledges the central concerns of higher education funding as it explores these arguments as legacy discourses rooted in career preparation, accessibility and affordability, and arguments about the need for a broad-based education vs. more technical skills training. Further, an alternative model to current higher education funding models is presented, and if deployed, this asset class could help to serve education needs by funding research, students, and the academy through an illustrated conceptual framework for funding.

Chapter 8

Edward Lehner, Bronx Community College, USA
John R. Ziegler, Bronx Community College, USA
Louis Carter, Best Practice Institute, USA

This chapter builds on the body of work that has depicted cryptocurrency as a model for science and higher education funding. To that end, this work examines the degree to which one or more cryptocurrencies would need to be adopted and achieve a network effect prior to implementation of such a funding model. Empirical data from three different cryptocurrencies were examined. The current work deploys generalized autoregressive conditional heteroskedasticity (GARCH) to analyze stochastic volatility.

This work contends that the examined coins are likely overdistributed and too volatile, thereby limiting the wealth generation possibilities for funding science or higher education. Additionally, based on the GARCH analysis, this work highlights that cryptocurrency pricing metrics and valuation models, to this point, may be insufficiently complex to persuade institutional investors to seriously allocate capital to this ecosphere.

Chapter 9

Charu Virmani, Manav Rachna International Institute of Research and Studies, India
Dimple Juneja Gupta, Poornima University, India
Tanu Choudhary, Manav Rachna International Institute of Research and Studies, India

Blockchain is a shared and distributed ledger across an open or private processing system that expedites the process of recording transactions and data management in a business network. It empowers the design of decentralized transactions, smart contracts, and intelligent assets that can be managed over internet. It formulates the revolutionary decision-making governance systems with more egalitarian users, and autonomous organizations that can control over internet without any third-party involved. This disruptive technology has tremendous opportunities that open the doors to detract the power from centralized authorities in the sphere of communications, business, and even politics or law. This chapter outlines an introduction to the blockchain technologies and its decentralized architecture, especially from the perspective of challenges and limitations. The objective is to explore the current research topics, benefits, and drawbacks of blockchain. The study explores its potential applications for business and future directions that is all set to transfigure the digital world.

Chapter 10

Shantanu Kumar Rahut, East West University, Bangladesh
Razwan Ahmed Tanvir, East West University, Bangladesh
Sharfi Rahman, East West University, Bangladesh
Shamim Akhter, East West University, Bangladesh

In general, peer reviewing is known as an inspection of a work that is completed by one or more qualified people from the same profession and from the relevant field to make the work more error-free, readable, presentable, and adjustable according to the pre-published requirements and also considered as the primary metric for publishing a research paper, accepting research grants, or selecting award nominees. However, many recent publications are pointing to the biasness and mistreatment in the peer-review process. Thus, the scientific community is involved to generate ideas to advance the reviewing process including standardizing procedures and protocols, blind and electronic reviewing, rigorous methods in reviewer selection, rewarding reviewers, providing detailed feedback or checklist to reviewers, etc. In this chapter, the authors propose a decentralized and anonymous scientific peer-reviewing system using blockchain technology. This system will integrate all the above concern issues and eliminate the bias or trust issues interconnected with the peer-reviewing process.

Chapter 11

Usha B. Ajay, BMS Institute of Technology and Management, India
Sangeetha K. Nanjundaswamy, Jagadguru Sri Shivarathreeshwara Academy of Technical Education, India

Privacy protection is one of the basic needs for supporting a good interaction in a globally interconnected society. It is important not just for business and government but also to a huge and increasing body of electronic or online societies. In such situations, a traditional digital ledger storage systems seems more centralized. Security of traditional digital ledger system has always been a greater concern when considered for implementing at a huge scale. When such sensitive data is at stake, there should be nothing doubtable about the system's strength to secure data and withhold itself against any potential attacks. Blockchain is one way through which such potential security issues can be solved. A blockchain, actually block chain, is basically a continuously increasing list of records, which are called blocks; these blocks are linked and secured mainly using cryptography. Every block typically has a cryptographic hash of the block previous to it, along with a timestamp and data of the transaction.

Chapter 12

Dhanalakshmi Senthilkumar, Malla Reddy Engineering College (Autonomous), India

Blockchain has been created in the process of development in bitcoin. It's a singly linked list of block, with each block containing a number of transactions and each list in the blocks using with cryptographic functions. The cryptographic hash function contains the hash of the previous block, timestamp, and transaction ID. Blockchain services include the authentication, confidentiality, integrity, data and resource provenance, and privacy and access control lists technologies. The authentication provider authenticates decentralized database with transactions in private-public key pair. This key-pair is used in the transport layer security with the entire network. The network legitimizes the transaction after that and adds the transaction to the blockchain. A sequence of blocks in blockchain holds the complete record of transactions like a public ledger. The integrity data written in the blockchain cannot be altered subsequently. By limiting access to the information in confidentiality, only authorized users can access the information, so that information is also protected.

Preface

INTRODUCTION: AN OVERVIEW OF THE SUBJECT MATTER

Blockchain is a global phenomenon. From the computer science and technological perspective, blockchain technology is one type of distributed computing and database systems with the idea of decentralization realised on modern global data networks. From the angle of social science, on other hand, the blockchain is an evolution or evolution that has been revolutionary changing or impacting the economics and, becoming strategic practices for industries and whole society. Blockchain, indicated as a typical disruptive technology, enables numerous benefits such as data transparency, immutability and traceability that are very critical in building a cohesive cyberinfrastructure that facilitates cooperation and collaboration among different organizations. No doubt, such a disruptive technology has tremendous opportunities to detract the power from centralized authorities and, will usher in new models for economies and marketplaces, communications, governance, identification, and more.

OBJECTIVE OF THE BOOK

While blockchain is still in its nascent stages, there is considerable research that needs to be done to resolve the issues, challenges and even misunderstandings.

This book aims to provide a better understanding about the global phenomenon via presenting collective recent researches, focusing on blockchain architectures and frameworks for developing of blockchain-enabled systems based on both perspectives of computer science and social science. The motivation is that architectures will help people to understand main features and revolution roadmap of blockchain technology structurally, while frameworks will provide guidelines for organizations to select, assess and design their strategic applications with the technology.

As a double-edged sword, the disruptive technology can improve many information systems while arise risks and impacts. The research and academic literature regarding the impact of blockchain technology on the system will be reviewed, and the limitations, risks, challenges and impacts for applying blockchain technology will be analyzed and identified in this book.

TARGET AUDIENCE AND READERSHIP

This book targets to those audiences, who are working on, intending to, benefiting from, or simply interesting in applying blockchain technology for organizations' objectives or even themselves, through providing comprehensive knowledge architectures and frameworks contributed by global researches.

As this book collects global perspectives from across a broad range of academic and industries, so ultimately, the audiences are consists of (but not limited): researchers who intend to conduct further study for challenges; practitioners from public and private sectors in which blockchain technology had been applied or will be applied for their business usage; government bodies who are going to set up policies and rules to govern the disruptive technology and related social concerns; and educators who may use the presented finings as teaching materials. It is also good for individual who is just interested in knowing the technology.

Researchers may find there are considerable the challenges and issues to harness the disruptive technology from this book because blockchain is still in its nascent stages. Huge research efforts, therefore, need to be done to address the issues such as redundancy, complexity, energy and resource consumption, security flaws etc. Moreover, standards and good practices need to be formalized for universal adoption.

Practitioners, may refer to some workable cases or projects shared in the book, regarding blockchain technology applications like supplier chain, account information systems, trade finance, price distribution, decentralized system, distributed process, solar energy, paper peer-reviewing, higher education funding, bank data certification, etc. Although there are differences in various areas, people can view those cases and experiences as guidelines in designing and deploying blockchain-based applications.

THE CHAPTERS

As this book is devoted to a very diverse range of topics contributed by many professionals and academics, it is felt necessary to provide a bird's eye view of the contents of the chapters. The following paragraphs, therefore, provide a briefing into each chapter individually.

Chapter 1, "A Decision Framework for Decentralized Control of Distributed Processes: Is Blockchain the Only Solution?" argues that although blockchain is a decentralized technology for automating distributed processes, there are also other competing technologies may also be suitable for automating similar distributed processes. A decision framework, therefore, is proposed by the authors to assist the architects to evaluate the various distributed processing technologies and choose the most suitable technology to support decentralised control of distributed processes for the given business scenario where multiple parties are involved. The framework takes as input the different areas of concern such as data, processing, governance and technical, the pros and cons of the technologies in addressing these areas of concerns and, provides a method to analyze and highlight the best technology for any process in question. In additional, this chapter presents two example processes, trade finance and price distribution, for assisting readers to obtain a better understanding of the framework.

Chapter 2, "Blockchains for Value Creation and Supply Chain Optimization," examines the architecture and main characteristics of blockchain technology that is suitable for supply chains and, explores how the benefits afforded by blockchain can be leveraged to create value by optimizing the supply chain. This chapter delves into blockchain infrastructure and enabled applications in various business and government sectors based on the examined the requirements and challenges involved in employing this technology. Although this chapter focuses on the supply chain, the outcomes of this study will benefit many organizations since they are more or less involved in today's highly dispersed and inter-twinned supply chain. This study concludes that blockchain technology can be leveraged for enhanced value creation and supply chain optimization through its affordances of immutability, traceability, and transparency, with informed decision-making and careful implementation.

Chapter 3, "Perspectives and Challenges of Blockchain Technology in the Accountability of Financial Information," argues that the accounting information systems could be improved by applying blockchain technology albeit some potential risk could arise. This chapter examines the main technologies comprising blockchain and their main consequences, important theoretical frameworks, understood as sources of improvement. In addition, this study assesses effects applied on different processes of the accounting information systems. As the outcomes of this study, not only show implications for the accounting professions, but the effects on the primary stakeholders are also brought to light.

Chapter 4, "A Brief Analysis of Blockchain Algorithms and Its Challenges," surveys about the various consensus algorithm, including Proof of Work (POW), Proof of Stake (POS), Ripple Protocol Consensus Algorithm (RPCA), Delegated Proof of Stake (dPOS), Stellar Consensus Protocol (SCP), and Proof of Importance (POI). This study first sees core architecture and concept of blockchain and some mining techniques, and then discusses consensus problems and consensus algorithms. Following the discussion, the authors compared those consensus algorithms of blockchain in terms of the theoretical aspects of the algorithms, as well as analyzed advantages and disadvantages on a basis of essential properties of blockchain. Focused on public blockchain, this study indicates many limitations of blockchain, such as redundancy, complexity, energy and resource consumption, security flaws etc.

Chapter 5, "Blockchain Technology: A Review of the Contemporary Disruptive Business," concludes the key milestones in the blockchain revolution roadmap, with the common adopted categories - namely Blockchain 1.0, Blockchain 2.0 and Blockchain 3.0. From architecture perspective, this chapter analyze the use of the blockchain technologies that are being applied in new innovative business models. Based on the description of blockchain revolution, this chapter explores the feature of the new disruptive business models based-blockchain as a new approach in delivering business values, and probes into the new technologies raised in different fields of businesses, like FINTECH, Real Estates based smart contracts, healthcare and wellbeing, etc. In end, this chapter identifies some important challenges the contemporary industry shall face until it can achieve global reach.

Chapter 6, "Blockchain Technology in Solar Energy," reports an investigation regarding the use of blockchain technology in the solar energy sector, which is one of the most used types of renewable energy sources to mitigate the climate change and global warming. The contributions of the chapter to the book are providing knowledge of blockchain technology and blockchain usage in solar energy production. While the second section discusses the fundamentals of smart grid and solar energy, the third section focuses on blockchain applications in solar energy production smart-grid systems and, shows a few cases that indicate the blockchain technology is widely used in solar energy sector effectively. Although this chapter focuses on blockchain applications in solar energy sector, the approaches and experiences presented will benefit other industry sectors in applying blockchain to create business value.

Chapter 7, "Paradise Found: The Disruption and Diversification of Funding in Higher Education," conceptualizes a process for cryptocurrency to diversify traditional methods of higher education funding in the United States. This is because cryptocurrency funding augments traditional revenue streams and shifts the discussion of education costs from expenses to a more robust conversation about innovative avenues to wealth generation as a potential solution to fund the mission of American higher education.

In short, this chapter discusses (1) higher education as a human right and its alignment with career outcomes; (2) careerism, technological disruption, and a call for new funding models; (3) cryptocurrency as wealth generator and enacting disruption of higher education funding; and (4) coin farming, revenue stream, how it works, and a model to embrace technological, disruptive wealth generation based on cryptocurrency to serve education needs through an illustrated conceptual framework for funding. Readers in other type of funding business may adopt or refer the framework for their funding systems.

Chapter 8, "A Call for Second Generation Cryptocurrency Valuation Metrics," builds on the body of work that has depicted cryptocurrency as a model for science and higher education funding, and examines the degree to which one or more cryptocurrencies would need to be adopted and achieve a network effect prior to implement a funding model. The current work deploys generalized autoregressive conditional heteroskedasticity (GARCH) to analyze stochastic volatility. Based on the GARCH analysis, this work examines cryptocurrency volatility and pricing metrics, specifically on Bitcoin, Dash, and PIVX. Furthermore, this work highlights that cryptocurrency pricing metrics and valuation models may be insufficiently complex to persuade institutional investors to seriously allocate capital to this ecosphere. The Metrics and GARCH presented in this chapter, even though are used for science and higher education funding, will be useful for other industry sectors in cryptocurrency valuation.

Chapter 9, "Blockchain 2.0: An Edge Over Technologies," outlines an introduction to the blockchain technologies and blockchain decentralized architecture, especially from the perspective of challenges and limitations. This study explores the current research topics, benefits and drawbacks of blockchain, and delves potential blockchain-enabled applications in different industry sectors for business and future directions that is all set to transfigure the digital world. Furthermore, this chapter identifies the key limitations like scalability, integration with legacy systems, initial costs and public perception. The outcomes of this exploration presented, may enlighten views of organizations who intend to apply blockchain for enhancing their decentralized business processes.

Chapter 10, "Scientific Paper Peer-Reviewing System With Blockchain, IPFS, and Smart Contract," proposes a framework for decentralized and anonymous scientific paper peer-reviewing system after inspects existing peer reviewing systems. Aimed to address the existing problems in present system to deliver a transparent and unbiased peer-reviewing process, this proposed framework integrates the cutting-edge technologies, including Blockchain and Inter Planetary File System (IPFS) and Smart Contract, in order to improve the existing peer-reviewing process. Within this framework, decentralized Blockchain technology is integrated with the peer-reviewing process to ensure the elimination of central authority; IPFS is used for file sharing process; and the Smart Contract is applied for communication through transactions between various actors of the system so that the system can be autonomous and unbiased. This framework works toward a scientific paper peer-reviewing system that will provide anonymity, decentralization and transparency. It is not difficult to see the framework can be applied to other business processes which require anonymity, decentralization and transparency

In Chapter 11, "Bank Data Certification and Repurposing Using Blockchain," the authors report a project to implement a system with following features: Retaining anonymity of the user's identity and the data created; Demonstrate data ownership without revealing actual data; Document time-stamping and immutable recording; Provide a means to hold a token of monetary value in return for the data provided; Real time validation and certification of consumer data; Provide a user-friendly ownership validation and storage system and cut the cost of any central authority. This chapter describes how consensus protocols are the key factor in deciding the adoption of decentralized applications to the masses and, argues that blockchain is one way through which many information security and privacy protection issues, including those in traditional digital ledger systems, can be solved or mitigated. The experiences in implementing such a bank system, may be used for other finical organizations.

The final chapter, Chapter 12, "Data Confidential, Integrity, and Authentication," describes the blockchain architecture, revolution road and various blockchain technologies. This chapter discusses the information security concerns, in terms of Confidentiality and Integrity and Authentication. The discussion can be used as a reference for organizations to apply blockchain for their business processes while the data is critical resources for their success or survive.

CONCLUSION

This book collects 12 chapters, contributed by professionals from worldwide, reporting high-level academic research outcomes for architecture and framework for developing and/or applying blockchain technology strategically in different sectors in the digitalized world, including government body, private company and academic organizations. This book provides evidence-based insights into the technology, architecture, framework, model and security. It appeals to both researchers and practitioners in the field of blockchain technology and application, no matter they are working in public or private sectors, like architect, strategist, system developer, and even social workers.

Several architectures and frameworks proposed assist the solution architects or government body in deciding the technologies best suited to support their objectives for distributed business processes where there are multiple companies involved.

Although some chapters in this book provide practical insights and models that are instrumental in getting business value from blockchain, the overall conclusion should be no 'silver bullet' in achieving business objectives from blockchain technology. This book, therefore, may not appeal to those seeking 'quick fixes' to the problems since that is not objective of this book, and quick fixes are not always a realistic option. In short, a long-term view is required to deliver short-term solutions.

Acknowledgment

Credit for the successful accomplishment of this book is due to many people's contributions and assistances. It is my pleasure to acknowledge with gratitude the insights and excellent contributions provided by all the authors.

I would like to acknowledge all of reviewers who supported and contributed me in this project.

Special thanks also go to the all the staff at IGI Global, particularly to Jan Travers and Jordan Tepper.

Finally, I would like to express my deepest gratitude to my family members for their love and support throughout this project.

Nansi Shi
Logic International Consultants, Singapore
April 19, 2019

Chapter 1
A Decision Framework for Decentralized Control of Distributed Processes:
Is Blockchain the Only Solution?

Paul Robert Griffin
Singapore Management University, Singapore

Alan Megargel
Singapore Management University, Singapore

Venky R. Shankararaman
Singapore Management University, Singapore

ABSTRACT

A typical example of a distributed process is trade finance where data and documents are transferred between multiple companies including importers, exporters, carriers, and banks. Blockchain is seen as a potential decentralized technology that can be used to automate such processes. However, there are also other competing technologies such as managed file transfers, messaging, and WebAPIs that may also be suitable for automating similar distributed processes. In this chapter, a decision framework is proposed to assist the solution architect in deciding the technology best suited to support decentralized control of a distributed business process where there are multiple companies involved. The framework takes as input the different areas of concern such as data, processing, governance, technical, and the pros and cons of the technologies in addressing these areas of concerns and provides a method to analyze and highlight the best technology for any process in question. Two example processes, trade finance and price distribution, are used to show the application of the framework.

DOI: 10.4018/978-1-5225-9257-0.ch001

INTRODUCTION

Many critical business processes span across multiple companies or legal entities. These processes often have to be in real-time and can contain large data volumes. Furthermore, data and documents have to be passed back and forth during the process. Such distributed business processes require the cooperation across a network of companies where documents are exchanged between them. For example, in the international trade finance process, exporters, importers, carriers and banks are involved in the financing of goods being manufactured, shipped and received in different countries. The whole end-to-end process involves multiple banks to lend money and act as escrow throughout the process, and data and documents are created in one company and transmitted to another company to be processed before being sent again to another company. Traditionally, such processes have been manually executed through the exchange of physical documents.

Over the last decade, such processes have been automated partially or fully by leveraging various technologies. There are two approaches to automation; centralized or decentralized. In centralized processing, the process is controlled by a single system that manages the logic controlling the flow of documents across the multiple entities. In decentralized processing, each entity in the process manages the flow by applying logic that is local to that entity.

A business process system, such as an Enterprise Resource Planning (ERP) system, containing the process flow logic and data store capable of storing all the documents in one place is an example technology that can support centralized processing.

Decentralized processing has been achieved through technologies such as managed file transfers (MFT), messaging (managed e.g. MQ and unmanaged e.g. Email) and Open API/web services. These technologies can be used to support synchronous or asynchronous communication. However, a key requirement is that for each transmission of data, the different organizations in the business process must agree on the data specification, output formats and input validation and each organization needs to store the data separately in their own data stores. This can very easily lead to inconsistencies and also open up opportunities for illegal data manipulation and committing fraud. In order to mitigate these challenges, over the last five years, organizations have started seriously exploring the use of blockchain or Distributed Ledger Technology (DLT) to manage multi-party real-time business processes. With a blockchain, the different enterprises involved in the process can write entries into a record of information and, as a community, can control how the record of information is validated. The key advantage of DLT is that it eliminates the need to separately validate and store data as a consensus network provides constant validation, synchronisation and immutable storage. Furthermore, Smart Contracts in DLTs provide trusted shared processing capabilities.

All these technologies have their strengths and weaknesses. For example, blockchain maintains consensus of the data on the blockchain but all participants on a blockchain have access to the data on the blockchain. Open API/web services, also referred as Web APIs, can be accessed easily but have limited data volumes. And MFT can handle large volumes securely but involve significant effort to set up. For some inter-company processes such as trade finance, a blockchain may be more useful, enabling companies to easily access the shared data and update it as necessary in real-time. Alternatively, by considering the distribution of public stock pricing information, there is only a need for a trusted source of the pricing information which is then consumed by many companies. For this, a Web API pull mechanism may be a good solution.

Hence, the solution architect has to choose the right technology for the given business problem. In this chapter we propose a decision framework to help the architect evaluate the various distributed processing technologies and choose the most suitable technology for the given business scenario. Additionally, using two worked examples, trade finance and a price distribution process, we describe how the framework can be applied in a real world context. In the proposed framework, the areas of concern that need to be carefully considered for the potential usage of any technology for decentralised solutions are categorized as *data, processing, governance* and *technical. Data* includes privacy, ownership, external sources and volumes; *processing* is concerned with speed, parallelism, efficiency; *governance* looks at trust, incentives, on-boarding and regulations, and *technical* considers legacy systems, allowed technology stacks and complexity of infrastructure (Figure 1).

With the advent of digitisation, organisations are now considering how to re-engineer current solutions to improve customer service, reduce costs and exploit new technologies. This is an ideal time to consider the best architectural approach for critical business processes, many of which will be inter-company. The proposed framework which helps to analyse decentralised processes and highlight the best technology fit, is a useful tool for solution architects and business process managers.

The rest of the chapter is structured as follows. Section 2 describes the need and problems in distributed business processes explaining the background of why and how companies exchange data, and the business concerns associated with such processes. There are many end to end business processes that span multiple companies and a case study for trade finance is used to highlight organisational boundaries and discuss the needs for data security, validation and reconciliation at each boundary. Section 3 describes an approach to automate the trade finance process using centralized control and the challenges associated with this approach. Section 4 provides an overview of common technologies used for decentralised networks that help to overcome the challenges associated with centralized control. The technologies are: Managed file transfers (MFT), Messaging (e.g. MQ, Email), Open API/web services, and public and private blockchains. Section 5 examines the main areas of concern that need to be considered when providing a decentralised solution for a distributed process. These are categorised into data, processing, governance and technical where data includes privacy, volumes, ownership and external data; processing includes speed and parallelism. Section 6 describes the decision framework for decentralization showing how the areas of concern for the different technologies for a given business process can be scored to identify the most suitable technology for that specific business process. Section 7 applies the framework to two real world business processes to highlight the strengths and weaknesses of the different technologies

Figure 1. The main areas of concern in the decentralisation decision framework

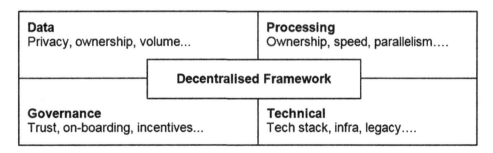

for the chosen processes. Section 8 summarises the key contribution of this chapter and provides some suggestions on the application of the decision framework along with potential extensions to the framework. This chapter focuses on technology and, does not consider social implications of decentralisation.

DISTRIBUTED BUSINESS PROCESSES ACROSS ORGANISATIONAL BOUNDARIES

Distributed business processes exist within industry ecosystems, across organizational boundaries, where there is no centralised control of the end-to-end business process (Klen et al., 2001; Camarinha-Matos, 2001).

Following are two common examples of distributed business processes.

Producer-Consumer Process

The basic process steps are; a) the consumer sends a request for quotation to the producer for a given product and quantity to be delivered by a given date, b) the producer sends a quotation to the consumer including the price and the payment terms, c) the consumer sends a purchase order to the producer referencing the quotation, d) the producer sends an invoice to the consumer referencing the purchase order, e) the producer delivers the product to the consumer by the agreed upon date, and f) the consumer initiates payment to the producer according to the agreed upon payment terms.

Supplier-Manufacturer-Distributor + Bank Process

This business process expands on the Producer-Consumer pattern within a larger supply chain. There is a Producer-Consumer relationship and associated business process interaction between both the Supplier-Manufacturer and the Manufacturer-Distributor legs of the supply chain. The complexity is amplified when the manufacturer has a relationship with multiple suppliers and multiple distributors (Lamoureux & Evans, 2011). To ensure cash flow across the supply chain ecosystem, a bank provides financing to all parties involved, anchored around the creditworthiness and industry strength of the manufacturer (Bryant & Camerinelli, 2012). The basic process steps for receivables financing are; a) the producer sends an invoice (receivable) to the bank, b) the bank notifies the consumer, c) the bank credits the producer's account with the face value of the invoice minus charges and interest, d) on the maturity date of the invoice, the consumer makes payment to the bank for the full face value of the invoice (Pandian, 2013).

In the above cases, the processing logic is distributed amongst all the parties involved, with the understanding that each party will fulfil their part of the process within an agreed set of rules. Business processes involve business data and the parties involved must share data. Sharing data can be problematic from both business and technology perspectives, and requires a certain degree of trust between parties (Greiner et al., 2007).

By further examining the above mentioned distributed business process patterns, a number of concerns can be identified and summarised as follows:

- Business Exceptions. What happens, for example, when the delivered product does not meet specifications or quality requirements? Is the product returned? Or is the product accepted at a lower price?
- Timeliness. What happens if the product is delivered late? Is a discount applied? What happens if the payment is late? Is there any penalty imposed?
- Information Exchange. What happens when the information on a document is entered incorrectly by the originator or is misinterpreted by the recipient? What if a document is lost or is sent to the wrong party?
- Confidentiality. What if business sensitive information like pricing, quantity, producer details or consumer details fall into the wrong hands, eg; a competitor who might use the information to gain advantage?
- Fraud. What if a business deal is transacted by someone other than an authorised party? What if there is collusion between parties with the intent to launder money?
- Governance. Who makes decisions about all of the above within an industry ecosystem where there is no centralised control of the end-to-end business process?

Case Study of a Distributed Business Process: Manual Trade Finance Process

The traditional trade finance process has been done the same way for hundreds of years, with ancient terms like "Bill of Lading" and "Bill of Exchange" still in use today (Ivarsson, 2012). Due to the distance and transportation time between the origin and destination of goods traded, there exists a certain amount of risk for both sides of the trade (Broens, 2014). From the seller's point of view, there is a risk that the buyer will not make payment, and therefore the best arrangement for the seller is to be paid in advance of dispatching the goods. From the buyer's point of view, there is a risk that the goods delivered might be lost or damaged, and therefore the best arrangement for the buyer is to make payment only after receiving the goods. Both of these payment arrangements cannot co-exist for the same trade, so the compromise solution was to implement a Letter of Credit process (Dixon et al., 1999).

In the Letter of Credit process, banks act as trusted intermediaries to ensure the flow of trade documents from the exporter to the importer, and to ensure the flow of payments from the importer to the exporter. Figure 2 illustrates the traditional Letter of Credit process involving seven different parties, a distributed business process that cuts across organisational boundaries.

The process steps illustrated in Figure 2 are described as follows:

1. Apply for Letter of Credit (LC). In the situation where the Exporter is unsure about the trustworthiness of the Importer to make payment, then the Exporter will ask the Importer to apply for an LC. The LC Issuing Bank is then obliged to initiate payment upon receipt and verification of the trade documents (see steps 10 and 11).
2. Issue LC. The Issuing Bank prepares the LC in accordance with the commercial arrangement between the Importer and Exporter, including such details as; quantity, delivery details, payment terms, and required documents to be presented by the Exporter. The Issuing Bank then forwards the LC to the Advising Bank.
3. Advise LC. The Advising Bank forwards the LC to the Exporter. This event triggers the Exporter to: a) start preparing the goods for shipment, and b) start preparing the required trade documents.

Figure 2. Traditional letter of credit document and payment flows

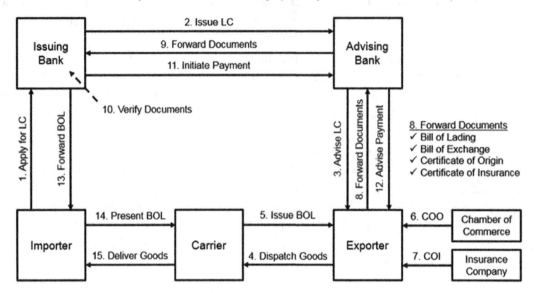

4. Dispatch Goods. The Exporter dispatches the goods onto the Carrier. Note: The "Carrier" in international trade is most always an ocean-going vessel.

5. Issue Bill of Lading (BOL). The Carrier issues a BOL to the Exporter. The BOL is a negotiable instrument, and it serves three purposes: (i) it is a receipt for the goods shipped; (ii) it evidences the contract of carriage; and (iii) it serves as a document of title (i.e. ownership) (Gehrke, 2001).

6. Issue Certificate of Origin (COO). The local Chamber of Commerce issues a COO to the Exporter, authenticating that the goods were produced in the Exporters country. The COO provides evidence to the Importer's government as to whether or not to impose import tariffs on the goods, as per their international trade policy.

7. Issue Certificate of Insurance (COI). The Exporter's Insurance Company issues a COI to the Exporter, authenticating that the Exporter has purchased cargo insurance to cover any lost or damaged goods during transit.

8. Forward Documents. The Exporter forwards the trade documents to the Advising Bank, including a Bill of Exchange (BOE). The BOE is a negotiable instrument that binds the drawee to pay a fixed sum of money to the drawer either immediately (a sight bill) or at a predetermined date (a term bill) (Gehrke, 2001).

9. Forward Documents. The Advising Bank forwards the trade documents to the Issuing Bank. This event triggers the Issuing bank to start verifying the documents.

10. Verify Documents. The Issuing Bank verifies that the trade documents meet the requirements as specified in the LC. This is a manually intensive activity which is typically done at the bank's Trade Finance Operations (TFO) regional processing centre. The skill requires domain knowledge about trade finance laws and practices.

11. Initiate Payment. Once the Issuing Bank has verified the trade documents, they accept the BOE as the drawee. If it is a site bill, they initiate an immediate payment to the BOE drawer, via the Advising Bank. If it is a term bill, say 90 days, then the bill becomes negotiable and can be sold at a discount onto a secondary market.

12. Advise Payment. The Advising Bank advises the Exporter on the acceptance of the BOE. If it is a site bill, the payment to the Exporter is immediate. If it is a term bill, the Exporter may sell the BOE at a discount onto a secondary market in order to generate immediate cash flow, perhaps to fund further business or to settle debts.
13. Forward BOL. The Issuing Bank forwards the BOL to the Importer. The Importer, now in possession of the original BOL, becomes the owner of the goods. At this point, the goods are still at sea, typically several weeks away.
14. Present BOL. When the goods arrive at the port, the Importer presents the original BOL to the Carrier, to show proof of ownership.
15. Deliver Goods. The Carrier delivers the goods to the Importer.

Concerns With the Manual Trade Finance Process

The high cost of running error-prone paper-based traditional trade finance operations is a main concern for banks (McMyn & Sim, 2017), and this cost is forwarded on to customers as higher fees and charges. Much of this cost is attributed to the processing of physical documents, especially the Bill of Lading. Dematerialisation the Bill of Lading is a challenge due to the lack of international standards and differences in local jurisdictional treatment of electronic forms of title documents used to establish legal ownership of goods (Dixon et al., 1999).

Fraud is another concern. A type of invoice fraud occurs whenever a fake Bill of Lading is presented to the Issuing Bank which then initiates payment for non-existent goods (Islam & Ahamed, 2008). Another type of fraud exists whenever there is collusion between the Importer and Exporter with the intent to launder money, for example pricing razor blades at $1000 each in order to transfer illegally obtained money from the Importer's country to the Exporter's country. In the traditional paper-based process, these types of fraud can only be uncovered by skilled bank officers with domain knowledge about trade finance laws and practices (Alavi, 2016).

CENTRALIZED PROCESSING: AUTOMATING THE TRADE FINANCE PROCESS

Due to banks' concerns over the high cost of running traditional trade finance operations, as well as concerns over Trade Finance related fraud and money laundering, there have been several attempts from companies to develop and implement centralised trade finance processing capability. Dematerialisation of trade documents, in particular the Bill of Lading which serves as the Title of goods, is central to these solutions. Notable trade finance dematerialisation and centralised processing providers include; Bolero, ESS-CargoDocs, and Smart L/C (Calatayud et al., 2018).

In a centralised trade finance process, the Central Processing System (CPS) acts as trusted intermediary to: a) maintain trade documents stored in electronic form, b) maintain a Title Registry which stores the electronic form of the Bill of Lading, c) perform automated verification of trade documents against the LC, and d) orchestrate the end-to-end trade finance process (Calatayud et al., 2018; Ivarsson, 2012). Figure 3 illustrates a centralised Letter of Credit process involving seven different parties. This is an example of a centralised business process that cuts across organisational boundaries.

The process steps illustrated in Figure 3 are described as follows:

Figure 3. Centralised letter of credit processing

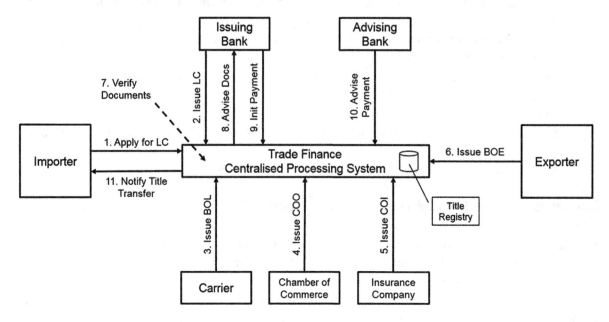

1. Apply for Letter of Credit (LC). An electronic form of the LC application is registered into the Central Processing System (CPS) and made available to the Issuing Bank.
2. Issue LC. The Issuing Bank prepares an electronic form of the LC which is then registered into the CPS and made available to the Exporter.
3. Issue Bill of Lading (BOL). The Carrier prepares an electronic form of the BOL which is then registered into the CPS Title Registry.
4. Issue Certificate of Origin (COE). The Chamber of Commerce prepares an electronic form of the COE.
5. Issue Certificate of Insurance (COI). The Insurance Company prepares an electronic form of the COI.
6. Issue Bill of Exchange (BOE). The Exporter prepares an electronic form of the BOE.
7. Verify Documents. The CPS verifies that the trade documents meet the requirements as specified in the LC. The automated process verifies the trade documents (BOL, BOE, COO, and COI) against the LC, based on a set of rules.
8. Advise Documents. The CPS advises the Issuing Bank on status of the document verification. The Issuing Bank may repeat or reconcile the document verification.
9. Initiate Payment. The Issuing Bank initiates payment upon electronic acceptance of the BOE and registers the payment instruction into the CPS.
10. Advise Payment. The Advising Bank advises the Exporter on the acceptance of the BOE, via the CPS. If it is a site bill, the payment to the Exporter is immediate. If it is a term bill, the Exporter may sell the BOE at a discount onto a secondary market.
11. Notify Title Transfer. The CPS notifies the Importer that the Title of the goods (ie; the BOL) has been transferred to the Importer. This authorises the Importer to take delivery of the goods once the Carrier arrives at the port.

Concerns With Centralised Trade Finance Process

These centralised solutions promise to reduce the cost of banks' trade finance operations due to paperless automated processing and also reduce their dependency on skilled bank officers with domain knowledge about trade finance laws and practices (Civelek, 2015). However, the dematerialisation and global acceptance of an electronic form of the Bill of Lading remains to be a challenge due to the lack of international standards and differences in local in-country jurisdictional treatment of electronic forms and signatures. Therefore, the adoption of such solutions by all parties is problematic in regions where the paper-based Bill of Lading is the only accepted legal title of goods (Civelek, 2018).

Concerns over any centralised processing system include; performance and reliability, confidentiality and control over the title registry, and information security. Furthermore, for centralised processing to work, all parties involved must participate and invest in the technology required to scan, digitise and exchange electronic documents, including businesses located in remote rural areas such as in the Asia-Pacific region. Asia-Pacific has recently become the biggest international trading region in the world, with the highest usage of Letter of Credit as a trade finance instrument (Lopez, 2015), and so technology adoption as well as local jurisdictional treatment of electronic documents in this region is a concern for centralising trade finance processes (Jessel & DiCaprio, 2018).

By further examining the above mentioned centralised control of the automated business process use case, a number of business and technology related concerns can be identified and summarised as follows:

- Throughput. What would happen if the central processing systems become overloaded? What would be the business impact due to delayed processing?
- Resilience. Central processing systems are potentially a single-point-of-failure. What would be the impact to the industry ecosystem if there occurred a central system outage?
- Technology Standards. Having a shared central processing system implies that all the parties involved need to comply with an agreed upon set of system interaction protocols, and may require technology upgrades. Who decides? Who pays?
- Confidentiality. What if business sensitive information like transaction values or volumes, or transaction counterparty details fall into the wrong hands, e.g.; a competitor who might use the information to gain advantage?
- Information Security. What if hackers gain access to the central processing system? What damage could they cause? How could this be prevented?
- Regulations. Having a shared central processing system implies that all parties involved need to follow a set of policies which constrain the usage of the system. How is compliance audited? What would be the penalties for non-compliance?

OVERVIEW OF TECHNOLOGIES USED IN DECENTRALISED NETWORKS

Given the concerns with centralized control of a distributed process discussed in the previous section, a number of technologies can be considered that can support decentralized control of a distributed process.

Electronic communication between companies has been occurring since the inception of the telephone network in the early 1900's with ticker tapes and then further enhanced with packet switching networks in the 1980's. After the internet became more common and secure in the 1990's, electronic communications became much more sophisticated going beyond FTP and HTTP (and secure versions SFTP and HTTPS) protocols. FTP has matured into managed file transfer (MFT) for high volume and highly secure point to point data transfers (Skybakmoe, 2011). Messaging technologies have also been evolving over the years and has seen widespread adoption within distributes business processes. These messaging technologies include Message Oriented Middleware (MOM) systems using protocols such as IBM MQ and JMS, and messaging through email using SMTP protocol (Shankararaman & Megargel, 2013). Web APIs (application programming interfaces) have matured over the past 10 years, and recently banking institutions are opening up their data and processing capabilities with Open Banking APIs (Boyd & Medjao, 2016). And finally, blockchain, the new kid on the block, promises wide data synchronisation and platforms to execute code that is trusted between companies (Henshall, 2018).

This section gives a brief overview of these technologies and describe the key advantages and disadvantages for each.

Managed File Transfers (MFT)

Managed file transfers (MFT) have evolved from FTP and SFTP to become a secure method for the transfer of large data sets. FTP is one of the original data transfer protocols used on the internet from the 1970's and is still common today. The main drawback is that the data is transferred in plain text and so SFTP was introduced to encrypt the data payloads. This also solved another problem with FTP, in that it did not ensure that all the data is sent. The SFTP protocol includes a hash check that ensures all data is transferred correctly.

However, company security typically includes firewalls around the internal networks that stop external traffic coming directly to internal machines in a trusted zone. Most commonly there are gateway servers in a DMZ (demilitarised zone) that connect to the internet and connect to internal machines providing an extra layer of protection.

MFT (Skybakmoe, 2011) takes SFTP to a new level by adding in a secure connection from a gateway server in the DMZ to a transfer server in the trusted zone with proprietary security algorithms. The transfers are scheduled by an automation server to move data from the transfer server to internal machines and network drives (Figure 4).

The advantage of MFT is that it provides very controlled point to point data transfers with highly secure encryption. Data volumes can be large and the data transfers are guaranteed and monitored.

The disadvantage of MFT is that each endpoint has to be configured and set up in the system. Licensing is expensive, transfers are scheduled only, and there is no sharing of processing.

Messaging

Messaging systems are similar to email where messages are sent to another party or broadcast parties and remain in a queue until they are processed. Messaging systems can be 'send and forget' or can have guaranteed receipts. Messaging systems have also been in existence for many years, with the SMTP protocol one of the first to be used on the internet, and continue today in many forms e.g. MQ, JMS, email, chat, etc. (Shankararaman & Megargel, 2013). Interbank messaging, SWIFT, has also gained wide acceptance for interbank transactions (Scott & Zachariad, 2014). Figure 5 shows an example architecture in the Trade Finance process. As seen in the figure, different types of messaging protocols are used for the various interactions within the distributed business process. There is no sharing of processing and

Figure 4. Example MFT technology process

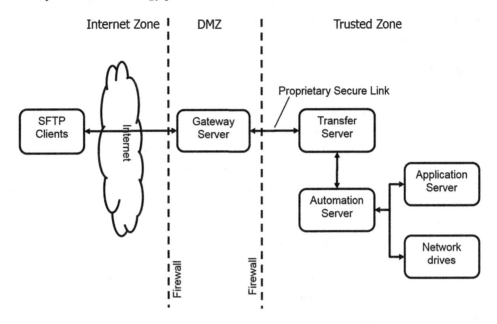

each enterprise has to manage their data and process logic. Usually, such exchange of information over messaging systems is standardized through the use of industry specific protocols, for example, OFX protocol is the standard for two-way exchange of financial data.

Messaging can be performed synchronously but most often is used asynchronously. There is often a limit to the data size sent and the queue length.

Figure 5. Example Messaging Technology in Trade Finance Process

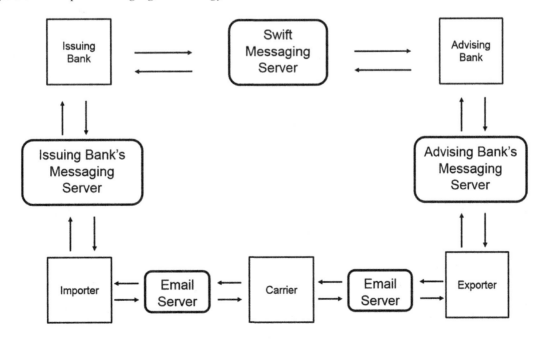

The advantage of messaging is that it can transfer many data packages which may happen at any time and in varying volumes. The queuing mechanisms ensure all the messages are processed, but when they are processed depends on the volume.

Open API/Web Services

Application programming interfaces (APIs) have been around for decades as a way of abstracting the complexity of IT systems from the programmers that want to focus on developing application functionality and not be concerned about how the underlying systems work. For example, the common operating system Microsoft Windows exposed an API for drawing the frames for the GUI (graphical user interface) elements. On top of the basic Windows API, developers then created libraries of components that other developers could call, further easing the development of applications.

At the start of the new millennium the same idea was applied to internet web applications and standards were produced to expose a programming interface for web applications (Richardson & Amundsen, 2013). Included in the standard were methods to advertise the structure of the interface. Figure 6 shows an example architecture of Web APIs in the Trade Finance process. The APIs can be invoked over the synchronous HTTPS protocol. Some example APIs in the Trade Finance process include; notify_title_ transfer, apply_lc, initiate_payment, etc.

The advantage of web APIs is that the interface is discoverable, and the code behind is hidden.

The disadvantage of web APIs is that the quantity of data transferred is limited. If the function call is synchronous then the application may have to wait and the user experience may deteriorate, and if asynchronous then care must be taken if there is a later failure to get the data and to alert the user/system.

Web APIs cannot be trusted beyond the trust in the company as they do not reveal the code behind and the interface may change without notice.

Figure 6. Example web API technology in trade finance process

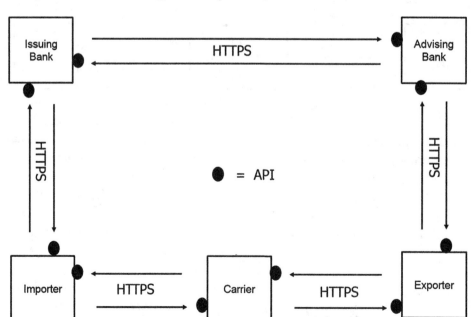

Public and Private Blockchains

Blockchains were invented by 'Satoshi Nakamoto' in 2008 (Nakamoto, 2008) to create a monetary system outside of the usual banking system by introducing an electronic currency called 'bitcoin'. Soon after, other cryptocurrencies (as these are now called) were created for similar but different purposes and then interest in the underlying blockchain technology emerged as a general method to distribute data with all the parties (called 'nodes') always remaining in agreement (called 'consensus') and the data is never able to be changed (called 'immutable'). As program code is also really just data, it can also be stored on a blockchain and then becomes agreed and immutable (Economist, 2015).

A typical blockchain will store all transaction data in each node. All nodes will connect to other nodes forming a network sending each other transactions. Some of these nodes (often called 'miners') will validate the transactions, put the transactions into blocks and then attempt to have their block put onto the blockchain and validate other blocks from other miners. Once a block is agreed and put on the blockchain it cannot be modified.

There now exists public blockchains that distribute data that anyone on the internet can download and process e.g. Ethereum, Stellar, etc and private blockchains that only invited parties can join such as R3 Corda, Hyperledger Fabric, etc. Private blockchains often have different types of specialised nodes run by different organisations such as for notary, security, transaction ordering, etc. As the parties involved in private blockchains can be trusted the robustness of the consensus protocol used is often reduced leading to faster throughputs and higher volumes. Further details of how blockchains work are assumed to be in other chapters of this book and can be found in many resources in books and online.

Figure 7 shows a how a private blockchain may be used for a simplified trade finance process where the participants in the process (exporter, importer, carrier and banks) will integrate their current systems to a decentralised application (dApp) via a software connector to their own node. The node is part of the DLT network and will ensure consistency of data and expose the dApp functions to the connector software.

The advantages are continuously synchronised data and program code for all nodes in the blockchain network that cannot be modified once verified and stored in the DLT.

The disadvantages are that the data payloads size is limited, the speed of consensus limits the transaction processing speed, and governance is more complicated than in centralised options.

AREAS OF CONCERN WHEN PROVIDING A DECENTRALISED SOLUTION

With the availability of a number of different technologies that can support decentralized processing of a distributed process, the onus is on the solution architect to select the most appropriate technology for a robust decentralized solution. This section expands on the four areas of concern presented in Figure 1 (Data, Processing, Technical, and Governance) with generic functional and non-functional requirements or needs, and guiding principles for providing such a robust cross-organisational business process solution.

DECISION FRAMEWORK FOR DECENTRALISATION

To provide the best service to a customer the underlying business processes must be; a) as efficient and robust as possible, b) efficient so that the customer receives what they are paying for as fast and as

Figure 7. Example blockchain technology in trade finance process. Note that although the DLT platform is shown as a separate box, it exists virtually in all the nodes in the network.

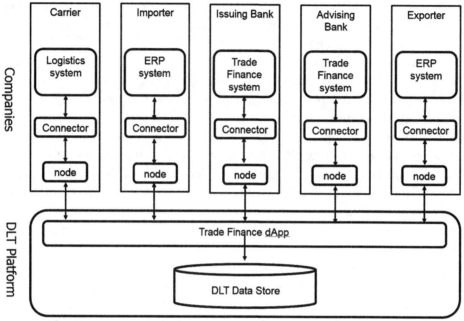

cheap as possible, and c) robust at a quality that is above expectations. Companies that provide the best services at the lowest cost will thrive.

In order to have the best underlying business processes, the supporting technology must also be the best suited for the work. Whilst most technology in use today has organically grown from what was available in the past, it is now time for many companies in the digitisation process to review and re-architect the technologies in use. There are many types of business processes and many decentralization technologies available now with the main ones discussed in Section 4. In this section, we present a decision framework to help the architect select the most appropriate decentralization technology based on the four areas of concern for a specific business process.

The act of going through the decision process will also help to highlight the risks and issues with the solution that can further drive a better change.

The scores given in the worked examples that follow are for illustration only. The emphasis of this section is not on the correctness of the actual scores but on the methodology that should be followed for evaluating the most suitable technology solution. It is up to the user of this framework to score each item according to their own rationale and within the context of their own business scenario.

Mapping Technology to Business Need

Firstly, each type of decentralised technology under consideration is given a value indicating its strength for each key area of concern.

Table 1. Areas of concern for a decentralized process solution

Areas of Concern	Element	Description
Data	Data Privacy	• Data-in-transit should be encrypted both on the payload and on the channel. • Data-at-rest (persisted data) should be encrypted. • Users should be authenticated using a digital signature or two-factor-authentication. • Data used in the business process should only be accessed by authorised parties. • The business process should be invoked only by authorised parties.
Data	Data Volumes	• The processing system should be scalable to handle any required data volume (transmitted payload size). • The transmission of large data volumes should be allowed to be done synchronously or asynchronously from the involved parties' perspective.
Processing	Speed	• The response time of interactions between the involved parties and the processing system should be near real-time. • The time between processing steps should be minimised as to not cause any bottleneck in the end-to-end process.
Processing	Throughput (Parallelism)	• The processing system should be scalable to handle any required throughput. • The processing system should be horizontally scalable as demand increases.
Technical	Legacy Systems	• Industry standards (such as web services) should be followed by the involved parties, such that their respective legacy systems can be more easily adapted and integrated with the shared business process infrastructure.
Technical	IT Support (and solution considerations)	• Data used in the business process should be backed-up / archived. • There should be a possibility for a single point of control for the end-to-end business process. • The business process should handle business exceptions according to a set of rules. • The business process execution should be traceable. • Each instance of the business process should be state-full and persisted as required. • There should be no single-point-of-failure in the infrastructure (servers & networks). • Process and Business data should be replicated at runtime. • The business process should be designed and tested using standards-based tools. • The business process rules should be authored and managed separately.
Governance	Ownership	• Only data relevant to the business process should be shared by the involved parties. • Only data authorised by the involved parties should be used in the business process. • Data used in the business process should be traceable. • Data used in the business process should be immutable.
Governance	Trust (How decisions are made, which instil trust between involved parties)	• There should be a decision-making body which represents all involved parties. • There should be decisions on the data, processing, and technical standards. • There should be decisions on the operating rules of the business process. • There should be decisions on incentives for the adoption of the business process. • There should be decisions on pricing for the use of the business process. • There should be a framework for arbitrating disputes between involved parties. • There should be a framework for negotiating through jurisdictional roadblocks. • There should be a platform for generating awareness and building trust.

The score given to each technology for each business area of concern is from 1 to 5 where 1 is the least useful and 5 is the most. The examples below provide example scores with some reasoning. The scores and reasons will differ by implementation of a technology and will also change as technology evolves.

Data Privacy

In most business processes there is sensitive data involved that requires to be transferred, processed and stored. At the very least this may be personal data that is regulated under various Personal Data Protections Acts (PDPA) or General Data Protection Regulation (GDPA) rules. Companies that run afoul of

Table 2. Example scores for data privacy with reasoning

Decentralization Technologies	Privacy Score	Comment
MFT	5	Point to point data transfers use proprietary encryption leading to higher security and MFT solutions employ mature security management tools. Data is stored internally.
Messaging	3	Point to point data transfers can use proprietary encryption leading to higher security. Data is finally stored internally but may reside in the queues accessible to other parties until the queue is clear.
Web API	3	Data is only vulnerable during transit point to point between the parties. However, common encryption protocols are used and expose the same risks as any internet transfer. Data is stored internally.
DLT	2	Data in a DLT is shared amongst the nodes in the network. The data can be encrypted but there is always a risk of data leakage. Most private DLT platforms have mechanisms to keep sensitive data out of the DLT only providing links and verification codes in the DLT.

these acts risk monetary and reputational losses that can cause bankruptcy. It is also worth noting that data must conform to a data management life cycle that includes deletion after a certain period.

Data Volumes

In the world of big data a high volume is in terabytes (TB) but it is now quite common to have data transfers of MB or even GB as part of a transaction which needs to be processed. Depending on the business process it may be necessary for the technologies involved to be able to transfer, process and store large volumes are high rates for long periods.

Speed

Transaction times can be sensitive for some business processes such as stock trading whereas for other business processes that happen on a longer timescale, for example daily batch cycles, speed is less important.

Parallelism

This is the ease of scalability and level of throughput of the technology.

Table 3. Example scores for data volume with reasoning

Decentralization Technologies	Volume Score	Comment
MFT	5	The transfer protocols are designed to ensure robust transfer of large datasets.
Messaging	4	Large datasets can be transferred but queue management is critical to ensure queues are not blocked by large data volumes.
Web API	2	Large data volumes slow the use of web APIs and are sensitive to connection issues.
DLT	2	The consensus mechanisms for DLT are sensitive to data volumes and large data is often stored off chain with a link and verification codes stored in the DLT.

Table 4. Example scores for processing speed with reasoning

Decentralization Technologies	Speed Score	Comment
MFT	3	Data transfer speeds will be high but processing speed is limited by the local systems.
Messaging	2	Data transfer speed depends on queue depth and processing speed is limited by local systems.
Web API	3	Calls over the internet are limited by the transfer protocols as well as application processing times.
DLT	1	Current consensus protocols limit transaction rates to 10's or 100's per second.

Table 5. Example scores for throughput with reasoning

Decentralization Technologies	Throughput Score	Comment
MFT	3	Throughput can be increased by adding and configuring more servers.
Messaging	4	Throughput can be increased by adding and configuring more subscribers.
Web API	3	Throughput can be increased by adding and configuring more servers.
DLT	5	Easy to scale by adding more nodes. Maintaining consensus can be affected.

Ownership

With shared data and processing in decentralisation it is important to decide the governance model to: connect to a new party, service levels to be provided, and mechanisms to ensure the service level and the course of action if a level is not met. One key aspect of governance is the ownership of the data and processing.

Trust

The extent to which the technology ensures trust within an inherent non-trustworthy business network.

Table 6. Example scores for ownership with reasoning

Decentralization Technologies	Governance Score	Comment
MFT	3	The provider of the data implicitly owns the data and any processing. SLAs will need to be explicitly agreed.
Messaging	3	The provider of the data implicitly owns the data and any processing. SLAs will need to be explicitly agreed.
Web API	3	The provider of the API implicitly owns the data and the processing. SLAs can be built into the API definitions.
DLT	2	Ownership is not implemented implicitly in DLT platforms but most enterprise platforms provide methods to make ownership explicit.

Table 7. Example scores for trust with reasoning

Decentralization Technologies	Trust Score	Comment
MFT	2	There is no implicit verification of the quality of the data and processing is all internal.
Messaging	2	There is no implicit verification of the quality of the data and processing is all internal.
Web API	3	Data is defined in the API and can often be automatically validated. Processing is internal and the party must be trusted.
DLT	5	Data and processing is shared and immutable. Trust is implicit.

Legacy

Ease of integrating with legacy systems.

Support

Ease of maintaining the systems.

Compiling all the above into Table 10 provides the overall relative strengths of each technology in addressing the areas of concerns.

Table 8. Example scores for legacy with reasoning

Decentralization Technologies	Legacy Score	Comment
MFT	2	Integration with legacy systems has to be developed. Some legacy systems already use FTP.
Messaging	3	Some integration common already.
Web API	4	Integration common already.
DLT	1	All integration with legacy systems has to be developed.

Table 9. Example scores for support with reasoning

Decentralization Technologies	Support Score	Comment
MFT	2	End points in other organisations need to be maintained
Messaging	3	Common tools can be used for maintenance
Web API	3	Common tools can be used for maintenance
DLT	2	Node owners need to agree on how to maintain versions.

Table 10. The relative strength of technologies in addressing the areas of concerns for a decentralised business process

Areas of Concerns	MFT	Messaging	Web API	DLT
data privacy	5	3	3	2
data volumes	5	4	2	2
speed	3	2	3	1
parallelism	3	4	3	4
ownership	3	3	3	2
trust	2	2	2	5
legacy systems	2	3	4	1
IT support	2	3	3	2

Business Process Needs

Every business process is unique and there is no one-size fits all for how important the areas of concerns are for a specific business process. For example, in one process data privacy concerns will be more important compared to data volume concerns.

A business process may be analysed with respect to the concerns for that process and a weightage assigned for each concern. Table 11 describes each concern and provides a range of weightage that can be allocated for that concern.

Table 11. Weightage matrix for each area of concern

Areas of Concerns	Description	Importance Range
data privacy	How sensitive the data is that needs to be decentralised	1 = no sensitive data involved 5 = bankruptcy if data leaked
data volumes	The size of the data that is being decentralised	1 = few kB 5 = TB
ownership	How clear is the owner of the data and the data processing	1 = simple e.g. peer or strong hierarchy 5 = complex e.g. multiple hierarchies with multi-levels
trust	How important is it to be able to trust the other parties.	1 = no trust is required 5 = trust between parties is paramount
speed	Transaction rates	1 = slow transaction rates 5 = high transaction rates
parallelism	How much of the process can be performed in parallel	1 = parallel would not help 5 = a lot of the process can be performed in parallel
legacy systems	How much of the process has to use legacy systems	1 = little of the process uses legacy systems 5 = there is a high dependency on legacy systems
IT support	The criticality of supporting the process	1 = support is not critical 5 = support must be fast and constant

Putting It Together

For the purpose of this exercise, we will use the weightage given in Table 12. In practice, the specific business process or its sub-processes must be analysed and weightage allocated for each areas of concern.

Combining the data from Table 10 and Table 12, the relative technology strength scores for each area of concern are calculated are multiplied with the weightage for that area of concern and the total scores for each decentralization technology is determined as shown in Table 13.

From Table 13, for the purpose of the exercise, the most suitable decentralization technology is MFT. In the next section we describe the application of the decision framework for trade finance and price distribution processes.

APPLYING THE DECISION FRAMEWORK

Two example case studies are provided of real intercompany process scenarios for trade finance (HSBC, 2018) and stock price distribution (Thomson Reuters, 2018). Trade finance involves many companies

Table 12. Example weightage matrix for each area of concern

Areas of Concerns	Example Weightage Score
data privacy	5
data volumes	4
speed	1
parallelism	5
ownership	3
trust	2
legacy systems	4
IT support	3

Table 13. The total score for each technology for the given business process

Element	MFT	Messaging	Web API	DLT
data privacy	5x5=25	3x5=15	3x5=15	2x5=10
data volumes	5x4=20	4x4=16	2x4=8	2x4=8
speed	3x1=3	2x1=2	3x1=3	1x1=1
parallelism	3x5=15	4x5=20	3x5=15	4x5=20
ownership	3x3=9	2x3=6	4x3=12	2x3=6
trust	2x2=4	2x2=4	3x2=6	5x2=10
legacy systems	2x4=8	3x4=12	4x4=16	1x4=4
IT support	2x3=6	3x3=9	4x3=12	2x3=6
TOTAL	**90**	**84**	**84**	**62**

which must work together to ensure a successful delivery of goods from the source company to the destination involving multiple shipping companies and financial institutions. Price distribution is a process that is owned by one company but used by many companies in their financial processes. The framework is applied to the processes in the case studies to provide worked examples of the usage of the framework in those scenarios highlighting the strengths of a technology for the process and providing an indication of the optimal solution.

Further to bringing greater attention to the pros and cons associated with the adoption of a decentralised technology, insights are gained in using the framework which helps make the design, management, and monitoring of a decentralised system more effective. The decentralised framework can also help in impact analysis of current architectural changes, digitisation planning and governance analysis of complex inter-organisational processes.

It is also likely that some steps in the process have different levels of importance to the areas of concern and the framework can be applied to the process steps to create a mixture of systems optimising the final best super-system for maximum efficiency and minimum risk. This is outside the scope of this work but mention is made where appropriate.

Trade Finance

The business process of trade finance Letter of Credit Document and Payment Flows as described in the case study in Section 1 (Figure. 2), will now be inspected with the aim of determining the most appropriate decentralization technology to use and highlighting pros and cons of the technologies as applicable to this case.

The process consists of five main parties (importer, exporter, issuing bank, advising bank and carrier) with two minor parties (chamber of commerce and an insurance company). All these parties need to work together efficiently to ensure a good service to the end customer who is likely to be a customer of the importer (not shown).

The process is obviously decentralised as there is no controlling party and although the steps are presented linearly in the traditional way, there are only some steps that are dependent on previous ones.

Each area of concern will now be analysed for this case and weightage score given with the reasoning behind.

The combination of the weightage (Table 14) and the technology strength (Table 10) for each area of concern results in overall scores as shown in Table 15. The final highest score (Table 15) gives an indication of the optimal system for the trade finance business process.

From the Table 15 it can be seen that DLT has the overall highest score. This can be attributed to the higher values for ownership and trust. This is because trust amongst the parties is very important due to the lack of knowledge of the parties as a result of their geographical separation. Also, it can be seen that data volumes and speed are not critical.

With further introspection, it can be seen that for each area of concern there are varying needs, for example in trade finance process, data privacy is not important for the shipment tracking but is for the costs involved. Therefore, a final solution might also introduce a secure web API for the cost details keeping the data out of a shared DLT.

Table 14. Examples of the weightage score for each area of concern for a trade finance process

Areas of Concern	Weightage Score (1-5)	Reason
data privacy	2	Some details such as the costs of the goods are private between certain parties but other details such as shipment tracking can be available to all parties.
data volumes	1	The size of the documents and number of transaction data is small.
speed	1	Hourly updates are sufficient for this process.
parallelism	4	Some parts of the processing can be performed in parallel, for example steps 2 and 3 and steps 8 and 9 could be one step.
ownership	2	There is one leading bank in the process but otherwise it is peer to peer in the consortium of parties involved.
trust	5	Trust is important as parties are not well known to each other but there are contracts in place between some parties.
legacy systems	2	There is likely to be some integration to legacy systems for example for shipping details but most of the process can be performed stand-alone.
IT support	2	Support is required for the overall solution but as the processing is slow it is not critical.

Table 15. The final score for each technology for trade finance process

Trade Finance Example	MFT	Messaging	Web API	DLT
data privacy	10	6	6	4
data volumes	5	4	2	2
ownership	3	2	3	1
trust	12	16	12	20
speed	6	6	6	4
parallelism	10	10	15	25
legacy systems	4	6	8	2
IT support	4	6	6	4
TOTAL	54	56	58	62

Price Distribution

In contrast to the trade finance process above, another common process where multiple parties are involved is gathering price information on various assets such as foreign exchange conversion rates (Figure 8). The process consists of five main parties in the example shown, one producer (publisher) of the information and four consumers (subscribers). In practice there could be thousands of consumers. The process is centralised in terms of processing in the publisher but the distribution is decentralised to many subscribers.

Each area of concern can be analysed for this case and a weightage score given with the reasoning behind it as shown in Table 16.

Figure 8. Publishing FX price information to multiple subscribers

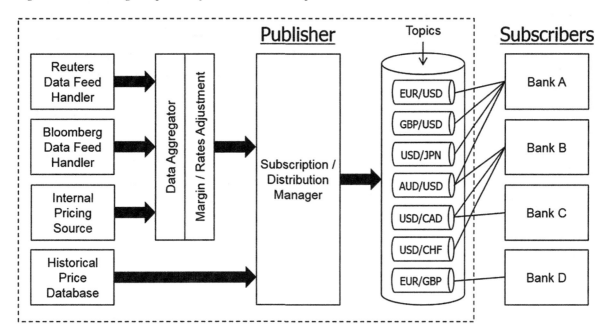

Table 16. Examples of the weightage score for each area of concern for a price distribution process

Price Distribution 1-5	Importance Score	Reason
data privacy	1	The data is not sensitive but may be a paid service and requires access control.
data volumes	5	Some subscribers may require large amounts of price data frequently.
ownership	1	Simple, the publisher owns the data.
trust	1	Subscribers must trust the publisher but not each other.
speed	4	Some subscribers may need fast price updates.
parallelism	5	All subscribers require the data at the same time as the other subscribers.
legacy systems	3	The subscribers are likely to connect to their legacy systems.
IT support	5	Support will likely be critical at certain times of the day for their internal processes.

The combination of the weightage (Table 16) and the technology strength (Table 10) for each area of concern results in overall scores as shown in Table 17. The final highest score (Table 17) gives an indication of the optimal system for the trade finance business process.

From Table 17 it can be seen that messaging has the overall highest score due to its support for parallelism enabling a lot of subscribers, which is usually the case in the price distribution scenario. Another alternative is MFT which could also offer a good solution as it can handle high volumes. Also, note that implementing a DLT is not scored highly as shared processing and trust of DLT is not required in this case.

Table 17. The final score for each technology for price distribution process

Price Distribution	MFT	Messaging	Web API	DLT
data privacy	5	3	3	2
data volumes	25	20	10	10
ownership complexity	12	8	12	4
trust	15	20	15	25
speed	3	3	3	2
parallelism	2	2	3	5
legacy systems	6	9	12	3
IT support	10	15	15	10
TOTAL	78	80	73	61

CONCLUSION

A distributed process spans across a network of enterprises and is often executed in real-time where data and documents are passed back and forth during the whole process. There are a number of decentralisation technologies that can support the automated implementation of such a distributed process. Often, due to lack of guidance, and purely based on hype, the wrong technology is chosen thus leading to solutions that do not effectively support the requirements of the business. The main contribution of this chapter is a decision framework that can help the solution architect evaluate the various distributed processing technologies and choose the most suitable technology for the given business process. This chapter identifies four areas of concerns that need to be carefully considered for the potential usage of any technology for decentralised solutions namely; data, processing, governance and technical. The example walk-through of applications of this framework for two distinct business processes provides clarity on how the framework can be used. However, the authors would like to highlight that the scores allocated for each technology for the different areas of concern may be debatable. The value of the decision framework and its application is not on the absolute scores used in the example but the methodology that needs to be followed. Hence the reader should use their own judgment in their business environment to modify these scores appropriately. It must also be noted that technologies are bound to evolve and their strengths and weaknesses with regard to particular areas of concern will also change. Additionally, new technologies will emerge which need to be added to the framework.

The current decision framework treats the distributed process as one whole end-to-end process, and thus the technologies are evaluated against the areas of concern considering this end-to-end process. However, in reality, the end-to-end process can be decomposed into multiple sub-processes. Each sub-process will have its unique requirements that may warrant a specific technology for that sub-process leading to the possibility that the end-to-end process has multiple technologies with each sub-process implemented using one technology. Future work will be directed at extending the framework to support multiple sub processes within an end-to-end process. Since this is a conceptual paper, a follow-up paper in this research area will further develop the framework within an industry context in order to study the successes and challenges of an actual implementation of the framework.

REFERENCES

Alavi, H. (2016). Mitigating the Risk of Fraud in Documentary Letters of Credit. *Baltic Journal of European Studies*, *6*(1), 139–156. doi:10.1515/bjes-2016-0006

Bolero. (2018). *Company Overview*. Retrieved from http://www.bolero.net/home/company-overview/

Boyd, M., & Medjao, M. (2016). Banking APIs: State of the Market. *Axway*. Retrieved from https://static.openbankproject.com/bnpp/BANKING-APIS-2016.pdf

Broens, H. (2014). *The Impact of the Financial Crisis of 2008 on Corporate Trade Finance*. Academic Press.

Bryant, C., & Camerinelli, E. (2012). *Supply chain finance*. Academic Press.

Calatayud, A., Carlan, V., Sys, C., & Vanelslander, T. (2018). *Digital Innovation in Maritime Supply Chains: Experiences from Northwestern Europe* (No. IDB-DP-00577). Inter-American Development Bank.

Camarinha-Matos, L. M. (2001). Execution system for distributed business processes in a virtual enterprise. *Future Generation Computer Systems*, *17*(8), 1009–1021. doi:10.1016/S0167-739X(01)00044-9

Civelek, M.E., & Özalp, A. (2018). *Blockchain Technology and Final Challenges for Paperless Foreign Trade*. Academic Press.

Civelek, M.E., Uca, N., & Çemberci, M. (2015). *eUCP and electronic commerce investments: e-signature and paperless foreign trade*. Academic Press.

Dixon, M., Glasson, B., & Network, E. C. (1999). Electronic Payment Systems for International Trade. *Western Australian Workshop on Information Systems Research*.

Duran, R. E. (2013). *Financial Services Technology: Processes, Architecture, and Solutions*. Cengage Learning.

Economist. (2015). The great chain of being sure about things. *Economist*. Retrieved from https://www.economist.com/briefing/2015/10/31/the-great-chain-of-being-sure-about-things

Gehrke, F. (2001). *New Attempts at Electronic Documentation in Transport Bolero–The end of the experiment, the beginning of the future* (Unpublished Masters Dissertation). University of Cape Town.

Greiner, U., Lippe, S., Kahl, T., Ziemann, J., & Jäkel, F. W. (2007). Designing and implementing cross-organizational business processes-description and application of a modelling framework. In *Enterprise Interoperability* (pp. 137–147). London: Springer. doi:10.1007/978-1-84628-714-5_13

Henshall, A. (2018). *An Introduction to Blockchain: The Potential for Process Management and Beyond*. Retrieved from https://www.process.st/introduction-to-blockchain/

HSBC. (2018). *HSBC and ING execute groundbreaking live trade finance transaction on R3's Corda Blockchain platform*. Retrieved from https://www.hsbc.com/news-and-insight/media-resources/media-releases/2018/hsbc-trade-blockchain-transaction-press-release

Islam, S., & Ahamed, S. (2008). *Preventing Letter of Credit Fraud*. Academic Press.

Ivarsson, M. (2012). *World Wide Trade, a manual affair. A study of the current position of the electronic bill of lading*. Academic Press.

Jessel, B., & DiCaprio, A. (2018). Can blockchain make trade finance more inclusive? *Journal of Financial Transformation, 47*, 35–50.

Klen, A. A. P., Rabelo, R. J., Ferreira, A. C., & Spinosa, L. M. (2001). Managing distributed business processes in the virtual enterprise. *Journal of Intelligent Manufacturing, 12*(2), 185–197. doi:10.1023/A:1011256711648

Lamoureux, J.F., & Evans, T. (2011). *Supply chain finance: a new means to support the competitiveness and resilience of global value chains*. Academic Press.

Lopez, C. (2015). *Trade Finance: A Catalyst for Asian Growth*. Academic Press.

McMyn, A., & Sim, M. (2017). *R3 Reports with Hogan Lovells*. Academic Press.

Nakamoto, S. (2008). *Bitcoin: A Peer-to-Peer Electronic Cash System*. Retrieved from https://bitcoin.org/bitcoin.pdf

Pandian, D. R. (2013). An analysis of effective financial supply chain management. *International Journal of Advanced Research in Management and Social Sciences, 2*, 18.

Richardson, L. & Amundsen, M. (2013). *RESTful Web APIs: Services for a Changing World*. O'Reilly Press.

Scott, S. V., & Zachariadis, M. (2014). SWIFT. Routledge Press.

Shankararaman, V., & Megargel, A. (2013). Enterprise Integration: Architectural Approaches". 01/2013. In *Service-driven Approaches to Architecture and Enterprise Integration*. Hershey, PA: Information Science Reference.

Skybakmoe, T. (2011). *What MFT Is, and How It Applies to You. Gartner Report, June 2011, ID G00214111*. Gartner.

Thomson Reuters. (2018). *Thomson Reuters Knowledge Direct API*. Retrieved from https://financial.thomsonreuters.com/content/dam/openweb/documents/pdf/financial/knowledge-direct-digital-solutions.pdf

KEY TERMS AND DEFINITIONS

Blockchain: A digitized, decentralized, and distributed ledger of immutable records that are linked chronologically using cryptography.

Centralized Control: A process control mechanism where one node (e.g., company) or a separate entity controls the logic of the flow of documents across the different nodes in a distributed process.

Decentralized Control: A process control mechanism that is distributed across the different nodes (e.g., companies) in a distributed process.

Decentralized Ledger Technology (DLT): A superset of technologies that have the same characteristics of blockchain (e.g., consensus and data immutability) but does not necessarily store data in linked blocks.

Distributed Process: A business process that involves a number of activities executed in different companies leading to an exchange of documents back and forth across these companies.

Managed File Transfer Protocol (MFTP): An enhanced software that is based on FTP that manages the secure transfer of data from one computer to another through a network, usually the internet.

Messaging-Oriented Middleware (MOM): Software platform that provides the means to transport messages between business applications using a number of interaction patterns.

Web APIs: An application programming interface that exposes functionality so that the functionality can be invoked by other applications without having to know the details of how the functionality is implemented.

Chapter 2
Blockchains for Value Creation and Supply Chain Optimization

Arun N. Nambiar
California State University – Fresno, USA

ABSTRACT

Managing today's highly dispersed and intertwined supply chain in order to maximize the overall organizational benefit by leveraging partner competencies is a herculean task and one that is of ever-growing importance in a highly competitive and truly globalized market. Information technology in the form of point-of-sale data, materials requirement planning software, and enterprise-wide systems have often been leveraged to assist with this. However, with the proliferation of data, storing, managing, and analyzing data on a large scale is a challenge. Blockchains provide numerous benefits such as data transparency, immutability, and traceability that are so critical in building a cohesive cyberinfrastructure that facilitates cooperation and collaboration among supply chain partners. This chapter examines the characteristics of blockchain that make it suitable for supply chains and explore how the benefits afforded by blockchain can be leveraged to enhance value creation while optimizing the supply chain.

INTRODUCTION

In today's globalized world, companies world over are increasingly focusing on their own core competencies while relying on specialized third-party vendors for other tasks that help bring the product or service to the market. For example, Apple focuses on the design of its products while outsourcing manufacturing and assembly. This trend combined with the affordances of modern technology has resulted in companies collaborating with a diverse group of partners from around the world. This has engendered a supply chain behemoth that is complex, highly intertwined and geographically very distributed. As a result, supply chain management has been growing in importance in today's manufacturing and production arena.

Another effect of globalization is the opening of markets thereby providing companies access to customers around the world. This has led to stiff competition often driving down prices much to the relish of customers. However, in order to stay competitive on cost, product features and responsiveness, companies need to be able to leverage the strengths of all its partners to maximize output with minimum resources. Hence supply chain optimization for enhanced value creation has become indispensable.

DOI: 10.4018/978-1-5225-9257-0.ch002

Blockchain is defined as a distributed public ledger that maintains a record of all transactions in an encrypted form and is distributed across a peer network. The system does not allow any part of the information to be deleted either intentionally or unintentionally thus ensuring data security. Blockchain represents a paradigm shift in building a secure cyber infrastructure. Traditionally, cybersecurity has been accomplished by housing servers behind firewalls and multiple levels of encryption. However, the problem with such a system is that it makes the system a vulnerable target to intrusions due to a single point of failure. In blockchains, digital information is stored on multiple geographically dispersed peer locations and in an encrypted form that requires significant computing power to break.

The invention of blockchain and its growing prominence is said to be the next biggest thing after the Internet that has the power to effect sweeping transformations in almost all industries ranging from agriculture to utilities (Mougayar, 2016). It has been suggested that blockchains will store more than 10 percent of the global GDP by the year 2027 (Carson, Romanelli, Walsh and Zhumaev, 2018). Moreover, venture capitalists are also showing significant interest in start-ups that deal with this technology by providing financial backing to these companies. Bitcoin is one popular application of this technology. Here, the underlying blockchain technology is used for harnessing and accumulating cryptocurrency.

Blockchain affords the benefits of providing a secure cyberinfrastructure that connects all partners on the supply chain that facilitates increased cooperation and collaboration resulting in increased value creation. This chapter delves into blockchain and its applications in various industries while examining the requirements and challenges involved in employing this technology.

BACKGROUND

Blockchain is a technology that Satoshi Nakamoto (which is probably a pseudonym for a person or a group of people) invented to facilitate sharing of digital information while ensuring data security. The original premise of the technology (Nakamoto, 2008) dealt with cryptocurrency. However, since then, blockchain has found application in numerous realms for a wide variety of purposes. Before diving into the applications, it helps to examine the foundations of a typical blockchain.

Basics of Blockchain

Blockchain has been defined as a distributed ledger that maintains a record of transactions between entities on the network. When an entity wants to establish a transaction with another entity on the network, the initiator announces the intent on the network. This intent is propagated throughout the network and when everyone approves the transaction takes place and is recorded with all its details into a block. This block is added to the existing chain of blocks and is communicated to all nodes on the network so that every node has a copy of the entire chain. For each transaction, both the initiator and the recipient create what is known as wallet that identifies them with the transaction. The wallets change for each transaction irrespective of the initiator and recipient in order to protect privacy. There are two broad categories of blockchains depending on the access viz. permissionless blockchains and permissioned blockchains. Bitcoins and Ethereum (see below) are examples of permissionless blockchains where anyone can join the network if they are able to solve certain cryptographic problem. Permissioned blockchains restrict access to certain users and hence is more controlled. Most organizations implementing blockchains would want to implement some form of the permissioned blockchain so that only authorized users have access.

Ethereum is a platform that purports to facilitate smart contracts (Giancaspro, 2017) between stakeholders without the usual interaction and relying solely on the trustworthiness of blockchain technology. Smart contracts include automatic initiation of transactions based on pre-established conditions thus improving efficiencies by lowering transaction costs and reducing lead times.

Since blockchain is essentially a network of users interacting with each other and the system by adding blocks, it is useful to consider the value of the network in terms of Metcalfe's law (Metcalfe, 2013) according to which the value of the network increases multifold as more and more users join the network. It has been shown (Alabi, 2017) that blockchain networks in the area of cryptocurrency tend to agree with Metcalfe's law which brings to fore the next challenge in blockchain technology.

The key benefit of the blockchain technology is disintermediation where entities can interact with one another without the need for an intermediator. Similar models are becoming common today in other areas such as hotels, and taxis. The AirBnB model that has gained so much popularity does away with the hospitality company as an intermediary. People can rent out their excess space to customers directly. Similarly, websites such as Amazon and Etsy allow individuals to sell their wares directly to the customer without having to go through the hassle of registering themselves as a company and having to establish all the trappings that goes with a typical company. Blockchain purports to do just that in the case of transactions and data exchange.

Another important benefit of blockchain is the element of trust the technology provides its users regarding data fidelity and security. By design, blockchains require more than a majority of users to agree to change information stored and due to the remoteness of majority of users on the blockchain going rogue, data is considered fairly secure. Moreover, with the use of smart contracts to automate processes without intermediaries, the need for trust is purportedly negated. This trust or rather trust-free (Hawlitschek, Notheisen, and Teubner, 2018) environment that the technology affords has led to it being called "the trust machine" by The Economist(Anonymous, 2015).

Blockchain Architecture

The underlying premise of the blockchain technology is a shared distributed architecture where data is shared between constituents of the network. There are four possibilities in this architecture based on access to the network and permissions accorded to its members. The network may be implemented as public where anyone can choose to join the network and access data stored or as private where access to the network is controlled through authorization. In each of these categories, the access to data can be based on permissions where only certain groups of users have the authority to contribute to the system while others can only read data from the system. The scalability of the blockchain architecture depends on the choice of these parameters. On one end of the spectrum, the private system with permissions to control access provides maximum scalability while public systems with no permissions provide least scalability (Carson et al, 2018).

Blockchain Requirements

The requirements for an effective blockchain network can be broadly divided into four main categories (Biktimirov, Domashev, Cherkashin and Shcherbakov, 2017):

1. **Data:** The raison d'etre of blockchains is to share data and hence it is imperative to have sufficient data available on the system to make it meaningful and useful. This requirement is often linked with the fourth requirement of trust.
2. **Technology:** This includes the technology to store and link various blocks along with the computing power to process them. Since blockchains rely on the network to ensure transparency and immutability, it is essential that the constituents of the network have the necessary capacity to carry out various tasks critical to the smooth and seamless functioning of the blockchain.
3. **Architectural Design:** Since blockchain technology allows for highly customized implementations based on the needs of the organization, an appropriate architecture that is designed to fulfil those needs is indispensable at the early stages of implementation itself. This includes permissions, access, encryption standards, and company-specific rules and regulations which in turn may be based on much wider and generic regulations.
4. **Trust:** This is perhaps the most important requirement and, in some sense, the most important hurdle for companies to overcome as they embark upon blockchain implementations. Without the mutual trust between partners, each constituent would be reluctant to share data despite all the affordances of blockchain technology such as immutability, fidelity, and encryption. This requires adoption of a cooperative mindset as research shows that collaboration yields improved yields and results.

Figure 1 below shows the requirements as being foundational support on which the edifice of blockchain is built.

Figure 1. Blockchain requirements

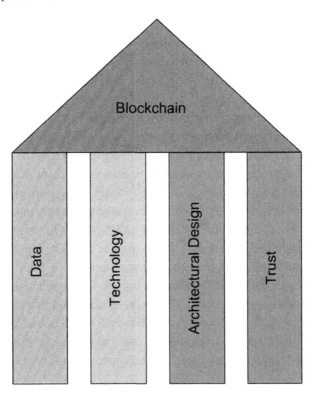

Blockchain Challenges

The underlying design of the blockchain technology that provides its transparency and immutability can pose challenges in terms of time and processing power required to complete transactions. The size and bandwidth required for implementing blockchains would significantly increase as the network grows and this poses challenges on the number of transactions that the blockchain can support (Yii-Huumo, Ko, Choi, Park, and Smolander, 2018).

Another important challenge in blockchain technology is the energy usage. Since every transaction on blockchain has to be approved by everyone on the network and the approval process requires a complex has computation, the entire process is very energy intensive so much so that it is argued that the technology is not sustainable in the long run (Malmo, 2017; Deetman, 2016). However, there has been focus on improving the efficiency of the process by examining parameters such as economic efficiency (value of system), operational efficiency (value of voluntary transaction fee) and service efficiency (number of transactions validated) in relation to the power consumed especially as it pertains to bitcoin (Cocco, Pinna, and Marchesi, 2017). The same analysis can be easily extended to the entire blockchain and it is imperative that these studies be conducted in order to make the technology environmentally sustainable.

A third challenge is the design of the blockchain (Conte de Leon, Antonius, Stalick, Ananth, Jillepalli, Haney and Sheldon. 2017) with appropriate level of cryptographic hash functions and processing algorithms which provide the affordances of blockchain such as its practical immutability and security. While blockchain is generally considered highly secure, there is a remote possibility of what is known as the 51 percent attack where if majority of the nodes on the blockchain come to consensus and decide to go rogue or if a malicious agent takes control of the 51 percent of the nodes (Efanov and Roschin, 2018). There has also been some discussion (Dinh, Liu, Zhang, Chen, Ooi, and Wang, 2018) about possible design considerations such as decoupling the various aspects of the blockchain such as its storage layer, consensus layer and the execution layer and sharing data across the network instead of each node storing a replica of the entire data to improve performance. Moreover, despite the use of cryptography, it is possible that hackers can gain access to restricted information about users if appropriate communication protocols are not employed (Henry, Herzberg, and Kate, 2018).

A fourth challenge strikes at the heart of blockchain technology - its data security and fidelity. Blockchain technology uses a consensus approach to determine if transactions are permitted on its network. While blockchain is generally Byzantine-tolerant in that a few rogue elements cannot necessarily take siege of the network, this really depends on the implementation of its consensus algorithm. On the Internet, even though data transfers seem almost instantaneous, there is an ever-so-slight lag in the delivery of packets of data from source to recipient. This makes the system an asynchronous one where it is practically impossible to arrive at a pure consensus on the network. Hence, implementations often rely on a time-predicated system (Gramoli, 2017) where parties wait for a predetermined time to see if there are any objections to the proposed transaction and once the time lapses, it is assumed that consensus was reached with a probability. Assuming that the probability is fairly high, it is safe to consider blockchains to be highly secure and the data stored on it to be immutable. However, there still remains a slight probability that things might go south. Moreover, as more and more companies jump on to the blockchain bandwagon, the networks might potentially be small and hence easily taken over by malicious agents using this loophole. Another aspect related to data fidelity is the blockchain technology often only guarantees the fidelity of the transaction and not the signature of the sender and receiver. This flaw is called malleability attack where the malicious agent can alter the signatures to make it seem as if the transaction was not successful (Yii-Huumo, Ko, Choi, Park, and Smolander, 2018).

Figure 2 summarizes the challenges involved in this technology.

APPLICATIONS OF BLOCKCHAIN

Blockchain technology has been applied in a wide range of areas for a variety of purposes all of which require data security and traceability. Figure 3 shows some of the different areas in which blockchains have been applied.

Figure 2. Blockchain challenges

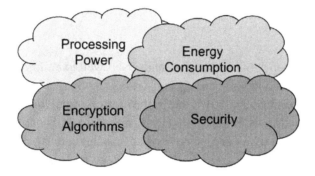

Figure 3. Blockchain applications

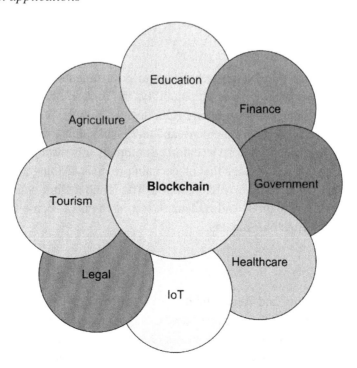

Agriculture

Blockchain technology has potential application in improving traceability in the food supply chain (Ahmed, 2017) through the use of unique digital signatures that improve traceability. This is a significant benefit that helps identify the origins of a particular crop which in turn helps contain disease outbreaks through informed and well-directed recalls.

Education

Due to the immutable record of transactions that blockchain technology creates, it has been proposed to employ this technology to ensure traceability and safeguard research from plagiarism through the development of multichain (Extance, 2017) to provide a medium to share research findings and experimental data without the fear of data being corrupted while fostering more research.

Finance Sector

The immutability and permanency of blockchains lends itself well to building trust both inward looking among stakeholders and outward looking among consumers and market in general. This trust is critical especially in the financial sector (Beck, 2018) due to the erosion of public faith in the system following the aftermath of 2008 financial crisis. Blockchains have been heralded as being transformative in financial record-keeping so much so that many executives in the financial sector believe that not implementing blockchain technology could put them at a disadvantage as the technology becomes more widespread (Carlozo, 2017). It has been estimated (Cocco, Pinna, and Marchesi, 20117) that blockchain technology could save the finance sector more than 70 percent of its financial reporting costs and more than 50 percent of its operational cost through optimized and transparent processes.

Government

Intellectual property protection poses a huge challenge to governments and companies alike. Blockchains provide numerous advantages such as immutability, and traceability that can be put to effective use in storing and protecting intellectual property (Gurkaynak, Yilmaz, Yesilaltay and Bengi, 2018). Blockchains can also be used for registering patents and trademarks thus lower enforcement costs since copyright, trademark and licensing rights can be enforced automatically through smart contracts without human intervention. Another big advantage that blockchain provides is doing away with middlemen in such registration processes which hitherto often required offices and institutional setups to accomplish. Moreover, policing copyright violations and trademark infringements become easier due to real-time access of the information through blockchains.

Healthcare

The Health Insurance Portability and Accountability Act (HIPAA) of 1996 sets forth numerous rules regarding patient privacy protection through restricted access of patient healthcare records. Cloud-based solutions have enabled the healthcare sector to build in redundancies and avoid single point of failure. However, cloud-based systems become more prone to data breaches since data is residing on the cloud in some location and is accessed over the Internet as opposed to being housed on an internal server that is not necessarily connected to the outside world. Moreover, with more and more medical devices being connected through the IoT framework (see below), the devices themselves are prone to being taken over by malicious agents. Hence, data security is of utmost concern in the healthcare sector. It might be tempting to restrict access and keep data behind the proverbial vaulted doors. However, access to non-identifiable patient data is critical to further research into the efficacy of drugs and treatments. HealthChain (Anonymous, 2017) is an application based on blockchain technology that purports to leverage the technology's inherent advantages of transparency, security and fidelity to protect patient health information and simultaneously providing access to authorized agents while complying with HIPAA. Systems such as MedRec and DokChain (Conn, 2016) are being developed that purport to create a patient-centric healthcare information system with smart contracts that automatically trigger notifications and permissions that control access to data.

Internet of Things (IoT)

In the recent years, there has been a proliferation of Internet of Things (IoT) devices in the market that has resulted in renewed focus on the vulnerability of these systems to intrusions and the security of data. However, in order to develop security frameworks, it is imperative to have access to datasets pertaining to existing IoT systems and there is a general reluctance to share such data due to security and data integrity concerns. Blockchains have been proposed (Banerjee, Lee, and Choo, 2018) to facilitate a data-sharing venue without the usual pitfalls of data security and misuse. Today's world is seeing more and more applications in the shared economy domain such as AirBnB and Uber. IoT and blockchains can be leveraged to build shared economy applications in the digital world for purposes such as payments, foreign transactions and digital rights management in a peer-to-peer way without intermediaries (Huckle, Bhattacharya, White and Beloff, 2016).

Legal

Since all transactions on a blockchain network are time-stamped and practically tamper-proof, this can act as evidence in legal battles (Gurkaynak, et al, 2018). Moreover, through the use of smart contracts, disputes between parties on the blockchain can easily be resolved by providing neutral entities access for arbitration. This would help lower legal costs in settling some of the more common issues.

Tourism

The benefits of blockchain technology can be leveraged in the tourism industry (Onder, 2018) to authenticate user reviews, facilitate fund transfers across borders and eliminate third party intermediaries to improve the overall experience for travelers.

SUPPLY CHAIN MANAGEMENT

With the advent of globalization, companies world over are becoming more and more geographically dispersed and are entering into partnerships with vendors from around the world.

One common pitfall (Hassanzadeh, Jafarian and Amiri, 2013; Li, 2013) of a supply chain is the bullwhip effect where the demand gets amplified as it travels back from the customer to all the partners in the supply chain. Numerous mathematical models and smoothing algorithms have been developed in an effort to reduce this demand amplification along the supply chain.

The Brundtland Report of 1987 defines sustainable development as "development that meets the needs of the present without compromising the ability of future generations to meet their own needs" (UN, 2018). The emphasis of this report titled "Our Common Future" was that development should not be at the expense of the future. It encourages countries and companies to examine the environmental, economical and sociological impact of developmental efforts and to take necessary steps to minimize or neutralize the negative effects. Though this report came out in 1987, recent years have seen renewed focus on sustainability and a huge part of this is recycling, reuse and remanufacturing of products. In order for companies to be able to recover raw materials or parts from their spent products, customers have to send the parts back to the factories. Hence, there is growing emphasis on reverse logistics which focuses on getting these spent products back to the company for reuse, and recovery. This further exacerbates the complexity of supply chain management.

An important element (Holweg, Disney, Holmstrom, and Smaros, 2005) of effective supply chain management is collaboration among supply chain partners. Collaboration comes in different hues but the underlying purpose remains the same - improving the overall supply chain through improved inventory control (Holweg et al, 2005). Some of the benefits of collaboration include increased sales and profit margins (Ireland & Crum, 2005) through improved forecasts (Bryne and Heavey, 2006) and lowering the bullwhip effect (Trapero, Kourentzes and Fildes, 2012). In the supply chain context, collaboration takes the form of information sharing and exchange. Researchers (Barrat, 2004; Ramayah and Omar, 2010) have shown that there can be improvements to the tune of 50 percent through such information exchange. In order to capitalize on the significant benefits afforded by information sharing, there has been a proliferation of information systems that purport to facilitate such exchange and companies tend to implement these systems with the aim of harnessing technology to make improvements to their market share and profit margins (Ho, Wang, Pauleen and Ting, 2011).

Centralized Enterprise Systems

As technology advanced, production systems have been infused with tools purporting to make the operations more efficient and effective. This all began with material requirements planning and later the more all-encompassing enterprise resource planning. All this is predicated on the cost of transaction, a concept pioneered by Ronald Coase (1937). Coase believed that ideally individuals should be interacting with one another instead of through intermediaries such as the firm. As an example, consider a scenario where a craftsman could directly sell his/her wares to the consumer without having to go through middlemen. Here, the buyer and seller are entities that are transacting between themselves. As the scale increases, due to the transaction costs, it makes economic sense to build a centralized system that would help lower the transaction costs. This was the push towards vertical integration with more and more operations brought in-house either physically or through inter-connected systems. Numerous models (Cannella, 2014) have been proposed that purport to connect supply chain partners through real-time sharing of information to facilitate improve inventory control. Figure 4 shows the interconnectedness of a centralized system.

However, with numerous vendors for these technologies, interoperability between tools have imposed significant challenges. With the advent of globalization, traditional supply chains have become more

Figure 4. Information exchange between supply chain partners

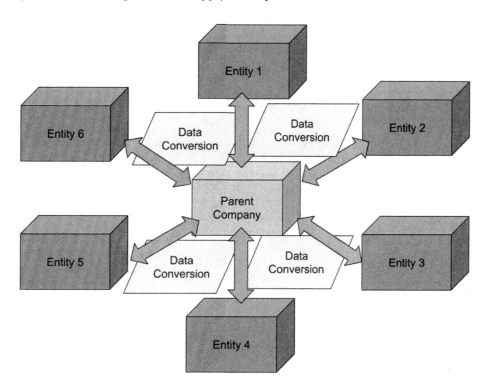

diversified and dispersed thus compounding the already complex network of tools loosely tied together through middleware and third party solutions. Moreover, companies are beginning to realize that their market responsiveness improves with a horizontally integrated organization instead of a vertically integrated one. Hence, there is a push towards decentralization. An article in the Harvard Business Review (Lyall, Mercier & Gstettner, 2018) in fact sounded the death knell for traditional supply chain management with the advent of digital technologies and professed that the supply chain would be replaced by a "self-regulating utility" (Lyall et al, 2018) that functions seamlessly to manage demand without human intervention.

Decentralized Autonomous Systems Through Blockchains

In a complex supply chain, data from the various constituents need to be harnessed and processed to ascertain the overall health of the system which in turn provides venues for improvement and optimization. Transparency, and incorruptibility are some of the affordances of the robust and decentralized blockchain technology that can be leveraged for data management in a supply chain (Casey and Wong, 2017). One of the challenges in a distributed system is the danger of a few recalcitrant or malicious entities on the network going rogue. This in computing literature is known as the Byzantine failure (Gramoli, 2017). Blockchain is considered to be a Byzantine-tolerant system in that it requires more than 51% of the entities on the network to arrive at a consensus to go rogue instead of the network being taken hostage by a few intractable or wayward entities.

Figure 5. Blockchain infrastructure for supply chain

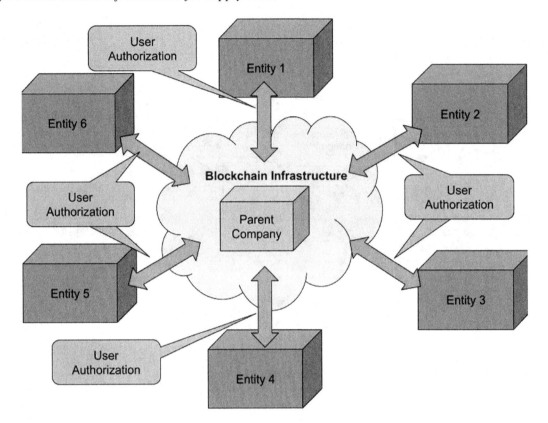

Blockchain has potential in two broad areas in supply chain management viz. storing static information pertaining to the characteristics of the supply chain and for maintaining a record of transactions between partners in the supply chain. The motivation for using blockchain technology in supply chain is due to the following affordances provided by blockchain:

1. **Value Creation**: Value may be created through cost reduction, innovation and incorporating the voice of the consumer.
    a. **Cost Reduction:** Christian Catelini of MIT (Church, 2015) suggests that the two main venues of cost reduction via blockchain is through the elimination of cost of verification of the data and the users and the cost of running a network that supports this distributed system.
    b. **Innovation**: A cohesive system built on the edifice of blockchains can bring to fore the strengths of partners on the supply chain which can be then leveraged to develop new products or services through improved cooperation and collaboration.
    c. **Voice of Consumer:** In order for companies to be responsive to market changes and customer demand, it is imperatives to track the voice of the consumer. In today's digital age, there is a shift in the value as perceived by the consumer from a traditional tangible value to a more experiential value where the emphasis is on experience rather than the actual product itself. Moreover, more and more consumers are opting for the service model where the product is

provided as a service instead of being owned by the consumer. This has resulted in a growing importance to experiential economics and consumption economics (Moore, 2014). In this milieu, it becomes essential for companies to build systems that facilitate consumers to play an active role in creating value for themselves.

2. **System Optimization:** A system as complex as modern-day supply chain can be optimized through a holistic view of the entire system. A blockchain system that brings all partners in a supply chain under a single umbrella can help analyze system characteristics that can be fine-tuned for optimal performance while identifying inefficiencies, discovering redundancies, and exploiting competencies.

Figure 6 shows the benefits of the blockchain infrastructure for an efficient supply chain. The blockchain infrastructure integrates data from different sources into a unified system that facilitates sharing and transparency while ensuring data fidelity through authorized access and change logs. The data transparency and integration can be leveraged to effect cost reductions and process and design improvements.

Figure 6. Affordances of blockchain in supply chain

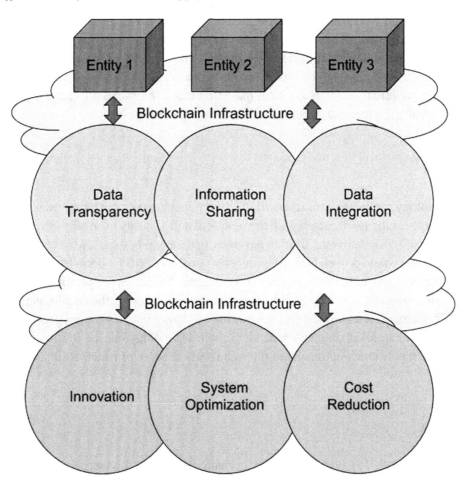

FUTURE DIRECTIONS AND CHALLENGES

In today's age of IoT and Big Data, it becomes imperative to harness the data to gain valuable insights into the behavior of the system and its stakeholders which in turn can lead to continuous improvements to boost efficiency, productivity and satisfaction. Blockchain technology provides a mechanism to improve access to copious amounts of data in a safe and secure manner for researchers and practitioners to employ data analytical tools in an effort to decipher vital clues about system parameters. However, blockchain technology is still in its nascent stages (Carson et al, 2018) and there is considerable research that needs to be done in order to determine standards for universal adoption. In the interim, companies can immediately reap short-term benefits through cost reduction while models for organization-wide transformation are developed through innovative research. In order to maximize the potential of blockchain technology, there needs to be common standards and appropriate government oversight (Batsaikhan, 2017) in the form of regulations without which there is the danger of the market developing a plethora of ad hoc solutions that lack portability, scalability and interoperability. Moreover, since the technology is still in its infancy at least in realms other than cryptocurrency, there needs to be technological solutions that facilitate an easy and seamless implementation of blockchain technology at reasonable costs. Another important consideration is the willingness among competitors to share data across the blockchain network in order to maximize the returns from the system. This is a proverbial insurmountable challenge that necessitates significant shift in mindset and support of regulatory edifice. Hence, all the requirements for a blockchain system discussed earlier in the chapter are in fact its challenges. Thus, it is imperative for adoptions to reach a critical mass that makes blockchain technology economically viable, technologically feasible and organizationally invaluable asset.

CONCLUSION

Blockchain technology can be the proverbial wind in the organization's sail as it wades through murky waters of information exchange and deals with the squalls of data security in an effort to ride the veritable tempest that information age economy is set to engender in the coming years. However, companies with complex supply chains would do well to thoroughly ascertain their needs for data storage and information exchange with the objective of building a cohesive system that facilitates cooperation and collaboration for improved value creation. It is also important to have a firm grasp of the requirements, challenges and pitfalls of blockchain technology before embarking upon its implementation. Thus, with informed decision-making and careful implementation, blockchain technology can be leveraged for enhanced value creation and supply chain optimization through its affordances of immutability, traceability, and transparency.

REFERENCES

Ahmed, S., & Broek, N. (2017). Food Supply: Blockchain could boost food security. *Nature, 550*(7674), 43. doi:10.1038/550043e PMID:28980633

Alabi, K. (2017). Digital blockchain networks appear to be following Metcalfe's Law. *Electronic Commerce Research and Applications*, *24*, 23–29. doi:10.1016/j.elerap.2017.06.003

Anonymous. (2015, October 31). The trust machine - the promise of the blockchain. *The Economist*.

Anonymous. (2017). Blockchain Technology Innovations. *IIE Annual Conference Proceedings*, *49-54*.

Banerjee, L., Lee, J., & Choo, K.-K. R. (2018). A blockchain future for internet of things security: A position paper. *Digital Communications and Networks*, *4*(3), 149–160. doi:10.1016/j.dcan.2017.10.006

Barrat, M. (2004). Understanding the meaning of collaboration in the supply chain. *Supply Chain Management*, *9*(1), 30–42. doi:10.1108/13598540410517566

Batsaikhan, U. (2017). *Cryptoeconomics - the opportunities and challenges of blockchain.* IDEAS Working Paper Series from RePEc, St. Loius.

Beck, R. (2018). Beyond Bitcoin: The Rise of Blockchain World. *Computer*, *51*(2), 54–58. doi:10.1109/MC.2018.1451660

Biktimirov, M., Domashev, R., Cherkashin, A., & Shcherbakov, V. (2017). Blockchain Technology: Universal Structure and Requirements. *Automatic Documentation and Mathematical Linguistics*, *51*(6), 235–238. doi:10.3103/S0005105517060036

Byrne, P. J., & Heavey, C. (2006). The impact of information sharing and forecasting in capacitated industrial supply chains: A case study. *International Journal of Production Economics*, *103*(1), 420–437. doi:10.1016/j.ijpe.2005.10.007

Cannella, S. (2014). Order-up-to policies in information exchange supply chains. *Applied Mathematical Modelling*, *38*(23), 5553–5561. doi:10.1016/j.apm.2014.04.029

Carlozo, L. (2017). What is blockchain? *Journal of Accountancy*, *224*(1), 29.

Carson, B., Romanelli, G., Walsh, P., & Zhumaev, A. (2018). Blockchain beyond the hype: What is the strategic business value? McKinsey & Company.

Casey, M. J., & Wong, P. (2017, March). Global supply chains are about to get better, thanks to blockchain. *Harvard Business Review*, 13.

Chen, R. (2018). A traceability chain algorithm for artificial neural networks using T–S fuzzy cognitive maps in blockchain. *Future Generation Computer Systems*, *80*, 198–210. doi:10.1016/j.future.2017.09.077

Chen, Y. (2018). Blockchain tokens and the potential democratization of entrepreneurship and innovation. *Business Horizons*, *61*(4), 567–575. doi:10.1016/j.bushor.2018.03.006

Church, Z. (2017). Blockchain, explained. *MIT Digital Blog*. Retrieved from http://ide.mit.edu/news-blog/blog/blockchain-explained

Coase, R. H. (1937). The nature of the firm. *Economica*, *4*(16), 386–405. doi:10.1111/j.1468-0335.1937.tb00002.x

Cocco, L., Pinna, A., & Marchesi, M. (2017). Banking on Blockchain: Costs Savings Thanks to the Blockchain Technology. *Future Internet*, *9*(3).

Conn, J. (2016). Could blockchain help cure health IT's security woes? *Modern Healthcare*, *46*(45).

Conte de Leon, D., Stalick, A. Q., Jillepalli, A. A., Haney, M. A., & Sheldon, F. T. (2017). Blockchain: Properties and misconceptions. *Asia Pacific Journal of Innovation and Entrepreneurship*, *11*(3), 286–300. doi:10.1108/APJIE-12-2017-034

Crosby, M., Nachiappan Pattanayak, P., Verma, S., & Kalyanaraman, V. (2016). Blockchain technology: Beyond bitcoin. *Appl Innov Rev*, *2*, 6–19.

Deethman, S. (2016). *Bitcoin could consume as much electricity as Denmark by 2020*. Retrieved from http://motherboard.vice.com/read/bitcoin-could-consume-as-much-electricity-as-denmark-by-2020 on September 20, 2018

Dinh, T. T. A., Liu, R., Zhang, M., Chen, G., Ooi, B. C., & Wang, J. (2018). Untangling blockchain: A data processing view of blockchain. *IEEE Transactions on Knowledge and Data Engineering*, *30*(7), 1366–1385. doi:10.1109/TKDE.2017.2781227

Efanov, D., & Roschin, P. (2018). The All-Pervasiveness of the Blockchain Technology. *Procedia Computer Science*, *123*, 116–121. doi:10.1016/j.procs.2018.01.019

Extance, A. (2017). Could Bitcoin technology help science? *Nature*, *552*(7685), 301–302. doi:10.1038/d41586-017-08589-4 PMID:29293234

Giancaspro, M. (2017). Is a "smart contract" really a smart idea? Insights from a legal perspective. *Computer Law & Security Review*.

Gramoli, V. (2017). From blockchain consensus back to Byzantine consensus. *Future Generation Computer Systems*.

Gurkaynak, G., Yilmaz, I., Yesilaltay, B., & Bengi, B. (2018). Intellectual property law and practice in the blockchain realm. *Computer Law & Security Review*, *34*(4), 847–862. doi:10.1016/j.clsr.2018.05.027

Hassanzadeh, A., Jafarian, A., & Amiri, M. (2013). Modeling and analysis of the causes of bullwhip effect in centralized and decentralized supply chain using response surface method. *Applied Mathematical Modelling*, *38*(9-10), 2353–2365. doi:10.1016/j.apm.2013.10.051

Hawlitschek, N., Notheisen, B., & Teubner, T. (2018). The limits of trust-free systems: A literature review on blockchain technology and trust in the sharing economy. *Electronic Commerce Research and Applications*, *29*, 50–63. doi:10.1016/j.elerap.2018.03.005

Henry, R., Herzberg, A., & Kate, A. (2018). Blockchain Access Privacy: Challenges and Directions. *Security & Privacy, IEEE*, *16*(4), 38–45. doi:10.1109/MSP.2018.3111245

Ho, S. C., Wang, W. Y. C., Pauleen, D. J., & Ting, P. H. (2011). Perspectives on the performance of supply chain systems: The effects of attitude and assimilation. *International Journal of Information Technology & Decision Making*, *10*(4), 635–658. doi:10.1142/S021962201100449X

Holweg, M., Disney, S. M., Holmstrom, J., & Smaros, J. (2005). Supply chain collaboration: Making sense of the strategy continuum. *European Management Journal*, *23*(3), 170–181. doi:10.1016/j.emj.2005.02.008

Huckle, B., Bhattacharya, R., White, M., & Beloff, N. (2016). Internet of Things, Blockchain and Shared Economy Applications. *Procedia Computer Science*, *98*(C), 461–466. doi:10.1016/j.procs.2016.09.074

Ireland, R. & Crum, C. (2005). *Supply Chain Collaboration*. J Ross Publishing.

Kshetri, N. (2017). Blockchain's roles in strengthening cybersecurity and protecting privacy. *Telecommunications Policy*, *41*(10), 1027–1038. doi:10.1016/j.telpol.2017.09.003

Kshetri, N. (2018). 1 Blockchain's roles in meeting key supply chain management objectives. *International Journal of Information Management*, *39*, 80–89. doi:10.1016/j.ijinfomgt.2017.12.005

Kshetri, N., & Voas, J. (2018). Blockchain in Developing Countries. *IT Professional*, *20*(2), 11–14. doi:10.1109/MITP.2018.021921645

Li, C. (2013). Controlling the bullwhip effect in a supply chain system with constrained information flows. *Applied Mathematical Modelling*, *37*(4), 1897–1909. doi:10.1016/j.apm.2012.04.020

Li, J., & Chen, L. (2017). A survey on the security of blockchain systems. *Future Generation Computer Systems*. doi:10.1016/j.future.2017.08.020

Lyall, A., Mercier, P., & Gstettner, S. (2018). The death of supply chain management. *Harvard Business Review*, (June): 15.

Ma, J., Jiang, M., Gao, H., & Wang, Z. (2018). Blockchain for digital rights management. *Future Generation Computer Systems*, *89*, 746–764. doi:10.1016/j.future.2018.07.029

Moore, G. (2014). The nature of the firm - 75 years later. In *Reinventing the company in the digital age*. Madrid: BBVA.

Mougayar, W. (2016). *The Business Blockchain: Promise, Practice, and Application of the Next Internet Technology*. Wiley.

Nakamoto, S. (2008). *Bitcoin: a peer-to-peer electronic cash system*. Retrieved from www.bitcoin.org

Onder, I., & Treiblmaier, H. (2018). Blockchain and tourism: Three research propositions. *Annals of Tourism Research*, *72*, 180–182. doi:10.1016/j.annals.2018.03.005

Ramayah, T., & Omar, R. (2010). Information exchange and supply chain performance. *International Journal of Information Technology & Decision Making*, *9*(1), 35–52. doi:10.1142/S0219622010003658

Trapero, J. R., Kourentzes, N., & Fildes, R. (2012). Impact of information exchange on supplier forecasting performance. *Omega*, *40*(6), 738–747. doi:10.1016/j.omega.2011.08.009

Turk & Klinc. (2017). Potentials of Blockchain Technology for Construction Management. *Procedia Engineering*, *196*, 638-645.

Turrisi, M., Bruccoleri, M., & Cannella, S. (2013). Impact of reverse logistics on supply chain performance. *International Journal of Physical Distribution & Logistics Management, 43*(7), 564–585. doi:10.1108/IJPDLM-04-2012-0132

UN. (2018). *Report of the World Commission on Environment and Development: Our Common Future.* Retrieved from http://www.un-documents.net/wced-ocf.htm

Underwood, S. (2016). Blockchain beyond bitcoin. *Communications of the ACM, 59*(11), 15–17. doi:10.1145/2994581

Xu, L., Chen, L., Gao, Z., Xu, S., & Shi, W. (2018). Efficient Public Blockchain Client for Lightweight Users. *EAI Endorsed Transactions on Security and Safety, 4*(13), 1–8.

Chapter 3
Perspective and Challenges of Blockchain Technology in the Accountability of Financial Information

Jorge Tarifa-Fernández
https://orcid.org/0000-0002-6031-8526
University of Almería, Spain

María Pilar Casado-Belmonte
University of Almería, Spain

María J. Martínez-Romero
University of Almería, Spain

ABSTRACT

The accounting information system could be improved by blockchain technology, but some potential risk could arise. Thus, it is worth considering such risks. The accounting research and academic literature regarding the impact of this technology on the accounting system are in an initial stage of this emergent field. The purpose of this chapter is to go a step further on this topic and to spur additional research regarding accounting and blockchain technology. The contribution of this study is twofold. On the one hand, it shows the main technologies comprising blockchain and their main consequences understood as sources of improvement. On the other hand, it assesses said effects applied to different processes of the accounting information system. Not only does this work show implications for the accounting profession, but the effects on the primary stakeholders are also brought to light.

DOI: 10.4018/978-1-5225-9257-0.ch003

INTRODUCTION

The development of new technologies has involved a drastic change in the way of conceiving the firm. Specifically, digital technology based on the Internet has entailed a great revolution both in the way that firms are managed and in the way in which they relate with other firms (Woodside et al., 2017). These digital technologies have provided new approaches to achieve higher productivity, higher quality, and lower production costs (Nowinski and Kozma, 2017). Moreover, the amount of information and data generated have supported inter-organizational relationships (Parry et al., 2016).

The maintenance of the abovementioned characteristics lies in a good decision-making process, for which it is imperative to have the highest, possible and available information quality. The information quality, in this context, is determined by its ability to represent a faithful image of transactions, being transparent and truthful, easily accessible and relevant for the purposes to which it is intended. Besides, delays cannot be a concern since information exchange is made in real time (Kavassalis et al., 2018; Lemieux, 2016; Nowinski and Kozma, 2017). Consequently, information poses an extra value that has to be managed.

Digital technologies such as blockchain have generated new opportunities in information treatment, offering several possibilities to solve specific problems. For instance, intangible assets were considered a source of problems since they might have been acknowledged as a double spent (Lemieux, 2016). Nonetheless, blockchain technology has overcome this problem through distributed ledger technology (Woodside et al., 2017). Thus, all transactions are recorded and stored across multiple copies over many computers in a decentralized distribution.

Because of its nature, blockchain technology can provide public and free, albeit anonymous information. Accordingly, blockchain technology has been positioned as the perfect candidate to test transactions publicly between two agents without the need for a third party to intervene (Lemieux, 2016; Swan, 2017). Moreover, due to its hash function, no transaction is modified, that is to say, a different operation is generated to complete the information the previous one describes (Nowinski and Kozma, 2017). This procedure eventually gives the sense of integrated information as all the transactions remain immutable, and anyone can monitor the whole process.

In this way, blockchain technology presents different challenges in the development of accounting process and tasks, and therefore, in the exchange of information and its use for decision-making process. For example, through this technology, there would be no firm with a valid excuse not to be responsible for the integrity of their accounting information. The point here is that everybody could have access to it, knowing that it embodies the faithful image of its activity. Nevertheless, this process needs a time of adaptation where the firm and the users of the information should balance their needs to act accordingly.

This book chapter tries to explore the challenges that blockchain poses into the accounting information system to delimitate and classify their actions and opportunities. This chapter attempts to create a new pathway throughout which provides those configurations that best suit the current situation.

The main contribution of this chapter is twofold. First, the impact of blockchain technology in the accounting circuit is discussed, as well as its potential influence on different stakeholders. Second, this chapter provides an analysis regarding the benefits that blockchain applications have in the accounting information system.

The remainder of the study is structured as follows. In the next session, the chapter briefs a background regarding blockchain technology. After the background, the conceptual framework of the blockchain technology, its technical requirements and its main benefits for businesses are highlighted. Subsequently, the main theories regarding the firm's management are analyzed in order to show the background for the study of the impact of blockchain technology on the accounting information system. Finally, the last section discusses the principal results and describes the main implications of our study.

GETTING DEEPER INTO THE BLOCKCHAIN TECHNOLOGY

What Is Blockchain Technology and How It Works

Technological Perspective

The digital economy has led to the advantage of technological production base when the Internet regarding neo-economy transformations has turned out to be a dominant factor in ensuring modern business development (Vovchenko et al., 2017).

The blockchain is not a new technology, but a combination of proven technologies applied in a new way: private key cryptography, which gives it an identity; peer-to-peer network, which provides it with a recording system.

Zhao et al. (2016) stated that there are three generations of blockchains, where blockchain 1.0 refers to digital currency, blockchain 2.0 to digital finance, and blockchain 3.0 to digital society. Although blockchain technology has existed since around 2009 with the introduction of Bitcoin (Nakamoto, 2009), only in recent years other management applications of blockchain networks have become known (Woodside et al., 2017).

Swan (2017) argued that blockchain could be used as a digital registry to record, transfer, and verify asset ownership and to preserve the integrity and authenticity of sensitive documents or records. Hence, numerous business activities, which involve data exchange and require security can benefit of blockchain technology (Nowinski and Kozma, 2017). The application may include organizations responsible for civil registries of birth and death, passports or merely the financial information flows within a firm (Lemieux, 2016).

The current digital world, still developing, relies on a third entity for the security and privacy of our digital assets (Crosby et al., 2016).

Some Definitions: Common Points

The blockchain is a chain of decentralized-computer-terminal participants that are linked together through a key-access system that enables direct contracting between two parties without employing intermediaries. They are creating a permanent transactional record containing a digital signature, timestamp and relevant information (Letourneau and Whelan, 2017). The generated network empowers a secure transfer of money, assets, and information via the Internet without the need for a third-party intermediary (Levy, 2014, Nowiński and Kozma, 2017; Swan, 2015). The result is a long chain of blocks, comprising records of transactions that are shared among participants parties (Zhao et al., 2016). The blockchain is a distributed transaction database in which different computers (called nodes) cooperate as a system to store sequences of bits that are encrypted as a single unit or block and then chained together (Lemieux, 2016).

According to Jayachandran (2017) and O'Leary (2017), the main characteristics that define blockchain comprise the following: (a) each participant maintains a replica of a shared ledger of digitally signed transactions; (b) there is an immutability of the resulting ledger, with transactions only being appended; (c) each replica is maintained through a syncing process of consensus, and (d) the network is entirely open as to whom can participate, execute the consensus protocol and maintain the shared ledger.

Despite the complexity of the definition, other authors suggest that blockchain is nothing more than a mere data structure with distributed multi-version concurrency control (e.g., Mattila, 2016).

Behind the blockchain technology, two main concepts have to be clarified in order to improve people's trust in its usage: reliability and authenticity. According to Duranti and Rogers (2012), reliability, when related to records, is the trustworthiness of a record as a statement of fact, based on the competence of its author, its completeness and the controls on its creation. Authenticity is about the trustworthiness of a record as a record, that is, the quality of a record about what it purports to be and that it is free from corruption (InterPARES, 2015). Under these circumstances, it is of high importance to determine trust, which implies a reasoned risk assessment. Thus, if the risk is low enough, it is possible to trust the artifact concerned (Yeo, 2013). Likewise, Duranti and Rogers (2012) and Lemieux (2016) establish that the application of trust depends on the computation of four types of knowledge that derives from information about the provenance of records: (a) reputation, which results from an evaluation of the trustee's past actions and conduct; (b) performance, which is the relationship between the trustee's present actions and the conduct required to fulfill his or her current responsibilities; (c) competence, which consists of having the knowledge, skills, talents and traits needed to be able to perform a task to any given standard; and (d) confidence, which is an assurance of expectation of action and conduct the truster has in the trustee.

Technical Aspects of Its Functionality

Thus, blockchain uses cryptographic signatures and public keys chain-linked to form an unforgeable record of transactions such as digital cash or any ledger record for that matter (Levy, 2014). It is made up of an electronic chain of hashes of digital signatures. These are a form of asymmetric cryptography for demonstrating the authenticity of a digital message or document (Lemieux, 2016). Consequently, a valid digital signature gives a recipient reason to believe that a known sender created the message, that the sender cannot deny having sent the message and that the message remains unaltered throughout the transit (Lemieux, 2016). Each party completes a transaction by digitally signing a hash of the previous transaction and the public key of the next owner and adding these to the end of the hash chain (Nakamoto, 2009). In doing so, the receiving party can verify the signatures to verify the chain of ownership.

Although the problem of authentication is solved, this process has to be combined with a means of approving transactions and permissions. This is achieved partly due to the distributed network where validators reach a consensus that they witnessed the same thing at the same time. This process is made using scientific verification.

Transactions are blocked and described by a unique hash, a nonce and by a hash from the previous block. Thus, an attempt to forge a block involves the need to reproduce preceding blocks (Nowiński and Kozma, 2017).

Transactions are broadcast out to a distributed network of nodes to agree and approve the order of the operations, which avoids parties transferring an asset twice (Nakamoto, 2009). Therefore, when a computer finds the proof, it broadcasts the block to all nodes, and nodes accept the block only if all transactions in it are valid. According to Nakamoto (2009), this process ultimately establishes a single, but distributed, agreed history for each transaction and creates a way for the receiver of an asset to know that the previous owners did not sign any earlier transaction or double spend. In this sense, blockchain technology provides an alternative mechanism for authenticating assets used in the transaction (Nowinski and Kozma, 2017).

Benefits – Classification

Blockchain technology is increasingly seen as a solution to recordkeeping problems where there is a need for the trustworthy public ledgers, such as ledger of financial transactions (Lemieux, 2016; Szabo, 2005), or public registration systems (Wild et al., 2015).

The blockchain can validate documents and another set of data. It acts as a decentralized proof, which cannot be erased or modified by anyone (e.g., competitors, third parties or governments). It offers to keep records with some assurance about inviolability and longevity that was not possible before (Findlay, 2015). In this sense, centralized databases provide an attractive target for hackers, whereas it is possible that centralized storage records protected by cryptographic signatures on blockchains might dramatically improve network cybersecurity (Swan, 2017).

This technology allows the peer-to-peer transaction, enabling two parts to communicate directly with confidence that the information contained in their respective ledgers accurately represents their chronological dealings (Letourneau and Whelan, 2017).

The blockchain technology contributes to the financial security of the modernization operation of business processes (Vovchenko et al., 2017)

The technology involves a complete verification of participants, which contribute to reducing the risk of the system functioning as it provides transparency of mechanisms and technologies (Vovchenko et al., 2017). In this sense, those transactions carried out by applying blockchain are ensured as they cannot be canceled at any level.

Decentralization cuts the costs of record keeping and verification, hence increased transparency and shorter closing time of the deal process (Nowiński and Kozma, 2017).

Blockchain technology has improved the transaction speed and financial flows transparency (Vovchenko et al., 2017). For instance, money can be transferred immediately in real-time from one continent to another, at meager costs, and in a matter of seconds, instead of waiting days or weeks and paying high commissions (Swan, 2017).

Moreover, blockchain can be a source of a reputation for the parties involved in the transactions (Nowiński and Kozma, 2017). In addition to that, decentralized transactions may reduce intermediary costs, but if no bound by a standardized architecture, they also could enable the dark side of illicit commerce to proliferate (Letourneau and Whelan, 2017).

Letourneau and Whelan (2017) state that blockchain can function very efficiently if the marketplace fulfills two main characteristics: there is a discrete number of transactions comprising the blocks in the chain, and the transaction participants have previous background working together so that they trust each other to join the transaction chain.

Some benefits of blockchain come from their database nature. Thus, it offers data security, transparency and integrity, anti-tampering and anti-forgery, high efficiency and low cost (Zhu and Zhou, 2016). In this vein, blockchain technology, through its decentralized system, allows to keep documents and other sets of data unaltered, that is to say, they cannot be erased or modified by anyone. This fact is what distinguishes using the blockchain from other forms of data timestamping and authentication. It offers a means for society to keep their records with some assurance about inviolability and longevity that was not possible before (Findlay, 2015).

The use and implementation of blockchain technology have risen several benefits for users and firms. Despite these clear benefits, blockchain technology shows some constraints that limit their effect, at least, in the short-term. Among them, Letourneau and Whelan (2017) highlight the real demonstration of blockchain's scalability, the interoperability with existing systems, storage capacity or cybersecurity. However, there is one restriction that deserves special attention, the standardization of the iteration of the blockchain. Numerous firms are currently working on different iterations of blockchain technology, and only one of them will prevail as the dominant (Letourneau and Whelan, 2017). This situation means that the rest are deemed to failure, dragging firms into troubles such as incompatibilities or sunk costs.

Nowiński and Kozma (2017) determine three main ways of creating value through blockchain. Thus, the first is via building transaction-related trust through authenticating assets, which are subjects of the transaction. The second is using decreasing cost because of eliminating intermediaries and operations. The last one is improving operational efficiency (e.g., shortening settlement times).

The ability to use new technologies to create technologies to create new innovative business models may be a vital source of competitive advantage (Chesbrough, 2010; Baden-Fuller and Haefliger, 2013).

Swan (2017) highlights the importance of exploring the new frontier enabled by digital ledgers while managing an environment that simultaneously invites new kinds of scams and wrongdoings. According to Teece (2010), technology changes often lead to changes in the business model and, therefore, in the way we understand them.

All this raise an urgent need for records professionals to gain an understanding of the implications of relying on this technology for the long-term management and preservation of trusted digital records (Lemieux, 2016).

Consequences of the Technologies Included in the Blockchain

Decentralization

- Security: each node verifies the integrity and legitimacy of each block, independently of any trusted third party (De Filipi, 2016). The network will most likely reject any attempt at tampering with the consensus statement as an invalid transaction (De Filipi, 2016).
- Transparency: it provides a higher degree of control to end-users of the information. The transaction history (current and past status) is available to the public, so it is easy to be verified by anyone (De Filipi, 2016). According to De Filipi (2016), although the content of communications can be encrypted so that it can only be accessed by people to whom it was addressed, the metadata related to these communications needs to be visible to a majority of network's nodes. In order to partially avoid this problem, blockchain can use a pseudonymous, that is, an identifier as a way to disguise the real identity. Ensuring full privacy would require the generation of a new account before performing a new transaction, which becomes impractical for users. Therefore, most of them usually reuse their account without noticing that they are publicly disclosing valuable personal information (De Filipi, 2016).

Table 1. Consequences of technologies comprising Blockchain

Technological Issue	How It Works	Consequence/s	Justification
Decentralization	Copies of the ledger are distributed over many nodes. Every node is an administrator of the blockchain. It protects them from getting hacked or lost	Security, Transparency, Autonomy	Not controlled by any single entity and has no point of failure
Unique hash	The transaction is made up of information of a block, paired with the previous block	Authentication, Security	No one can alter one transaction already forged
Key-access system	Public and private keys (a long, randomly-generated string of numbers). It acts as a password	Approval	The combination of these two keys provides secure control of ownership
Cryptographic signature	It does not reveal the link between an individual signature and an individual's public key	Anonymity	The transaction is made without disclosing the source, destination or another characteristic from the transaction that potentially may identify the users
Self-auditing	The blockchain checks in with itself. The network reconciles every transaction that happens in ten minutes intervals.	Integrity, Incorruptibility, Availability	The information is up-to-date almost in real time, and it is available at any time
Time-stamping	It registers the data and the location of the assets at each transaction	Identifiability, Traceability	Each transaction can be located uniquely and unequivocally

Source: Own elaboration

- Autonomy: it can significantly affect the existing power dynamics among firms and condition their interorganizational behavior. This is possible because all the parts involved are exclusively governed by the code/protocol of the technology, avoiding those practices that modify, or even change, the technical rules without the permission of the network. Therefore, anyone is free to participate and implement a different set of features onto the blocks.

Hash

The hash function takes any input and turns into a cryptographic output. This allows making a "proof of work" (Crosby et al., 2016), which favors the verification process.

- Authentication: there is no chance of fraudulent data or transaction. Only when the information required is correct the link is made. Thus, it works as a check of the information. Every pair of blocks is created based on the validated information. In this sense, users can completely trust the information included in the blocks.
- Security: no one can alter the transactions already forged. The particular combination of blocks protects the chains from being hacked. Thus, once the information is validated and the chain created, it is not possible to be modified.

Key-Access System

The use of public and private key generated a personalized password generate for each transaction.

- Approval: the personalized combination of keys makes each party be able to recognize the other/s. It allows direct contracting between parties. Therefore, it assures that the parties are dealing with whom they intended (Letourneau and Whelan, 2017). With this, uncertainty is widely reduced, and safety is spread.

Cryptography

It encompasses the art of building schemes which allow secret data exchange over insecure channels (Mukhopadhyay, 2017). Thus, it aims to find the proper methods to secure and authenticate messages.

- Anonymity: it pretends to maintain the essential characteristic of the blockchain, the independent construction of transactions. Thus, because of the privacy-drawbacks associated with it, cryptography allows the generation of blocks without revealing the link between an individual signature and an individual's public key (De Filipi, 2016). In the end, people keep their transactions private while allowing for the public network to verify the validity of said transactions.

Self-Auditing

The blockchain checks in with itself. The network reconciles every transaction that happens in ten minutes interval.

- Integrity: establishing periodical maintenance it can check if the information remains the same along time and/or if it is altered at any point.
- Incorruptibility: because of said verification process, a "surveillance effect" is produced that allows to guarantee the stability of the information, protecting it permanently from any damage.
- Availability: because this function is executed in short time intervals, it also guarantees the availability, that is, prove that the information is permanently there. It can detect any minor change and make the due correction if necessary, to maintain the stability.

Time-Stamping

It registers the data and the location of the assets at each transaction. Therefore, it acts as a unique identifier (Heber and Groll, 2017).

- Identifiability: it provides a digital proof-of-existence at any moment. It makes any transaction individually located in time and space (Aste et al., 2017). This allows quick identification of any information contented in every transaction generated.
- Traceability: having precise control over when an operation has occurred (e.g., time and hour) verifies the existence of a particular data. This allows chronologically trace the sequence of transactions as well as those relationships created among different blocks (e.g., a modification of an existing block).

THEORETICAL FRAMEWORK

Shareholder Theory

The blockchain technology is thought to have a potential disrupt in businesses and in the way in which firms interact with the environment. Consequently, the firms' relationships with a different group of interests highlight the need for analyzing the impact of blockchain under the Stakeholders theory.

The application of this theory is widely accepted, having been employed in different business research fields ranging from management and corporate social responsibility to finance and accounting. However, some authors argue that Stakeholders theory is formed by an amalgamation of eclectic approaches (Gilbert and Rasche, 2008; Miles, 2017) and that its theoretical concepts remain vague (Crane and Ruebottom, 2011, Fassin, 2009; Stoney and Winstanley, 2001).

In this vein, the study of Miles (2017) provides new insights into the definition of stakeholder. Miles' classification, which is based on a bounded review of 593 definitions, establishes four types of stakeholders: influencer, claimant, collaborator, and recipient. Therefore, influencers are thought to be able to exert influence in the operations and have a strategy to do so. Likewise, claimants are regarded as those who have a right or claim on a firm, but they are not able to exert power to assure the payment of the claim. Collaborators are considered those who cooperate with the firm but without an active interest to influence in the organization. Finally, groups or individuals who are a passive recipient of the firms' impact are classified as recipient stakeholders.

Accordingly, different stakeholders demand clear information regarding the firm depending on their level of influence, power or interest over the firm. In a sense, the information circuit represents a critical element of the relationship with stakeholders. Therefore, the blockchain technology could imply a paradigm shift in the way the firm interacts with stakeholders, providing high levels of information transparency and integrity, as well as reducing information bias (Müller-Bloch and King, 2018). By a blockchain information circuit, the firm may appease the concerns of the different stakeholder.

Agency Theory

One of the potential advantages of blockchain in businesses is the reduction of uncertainty, insecurity, and ambiguity in the information system (Beck et al., 2017). In this vein, the well-known information asymmetries would be reduced with the implementation of a blockchain system. Thus, the concerns stated by the agency theory (Jensen and Meckling, 1976) would be relieved. According to agency theory, when ownership and management are separated, the principal (owner) and agent (manager) could have diverging goals or different attitudes to risk. Because principals need to supervise agents, they implement mechanisms such as designing optimal contracts and establishing trust and control systems.

By contrast, under a blockchain system, there is a premise of a transparent information circuit, being this information accessible to both principals and agents. In such a way, the blockchain offers guarantees and eludes agency problems due to the reduction of asymmetric information (Treiblmaier, 2018).

While the analysis of the blockchain implications from the principal-agent relationship angle is under-researched, some changes are expected such as the harmonization of conflicting goals as well as the alignment of conflicting interest with technology blockchain (Treiblmaier, 2018). What's more, it could be a way to prevent managers from opportunistic actions that constitute another classic concern of agency theory (Wall and Greiling, 2011).

Stewardship Theory

The Stewardship theory is considered as an alternative or complement of the Agency theory (Keay, 2017). While Agency theory posits a conflict between aims between ownership and manager, the Stewardship theory is based on the aim convergence between principal and agent (Van Slyke, 2006). In this vein, the director or manager is regarded as a steward in the firm and will act driven by altruism aims (Vilanova, 2007). Thus, cooperation and collaboration are the cornerstones of the Stewardship theory, due to the assumption that agents will act in the best way of the firms' interests and this will lead to opt for organizational aims rather than self-serving benefits. The core elements of this theory are trust and the fact that agents can be trusted (Kluvers and Tippett, 2011).

The implement of blockchain technology under the Stewardship theory can ease one of the main drawbacks of this theory. The fact that "principals" have to invest too much time engaging management in solving problems, aligning decision-making and exchanging information, has been subjected to criticism (Van Slyke, 2006). A technology blockchain could provide a faster information circuit achieving more transparency and autonomy in the information regarding the organizational aims.

What's more, the managers' desire for achievement (Davis et al., 1997) and the chance of having challenging work could encourage them to support a blockchain system to gain recognition.

Transaction Cost Economy

Blockchain can be considered as a general technology initially created as a solution to problems in the design of digital money (Davidson et al., 2016). This fact makes possible include within the ambit of the economics of information. Under this perspective, blockchain can act as a new institutional technology that makes possible new types of contracts and organizations.

According to Transaction Cost Economics (TCE), firms can perform better if they appropriately adjust their governance mechanisms to underlying transactions (Williamson, 1979). In this sense, blockchain technology is an alternative governance institution. Therefore, economizing on transaction cost leads to an efficient institutional structure of economic organization and governance (Davidson et al., 2016).

As a technology, blockchain becomes a mechanism to control opportunism by eliminating the need for trust using crypto-enforced execution of agreed contracts through consensus and transparency. Therefore, it reduces opportunism as it generates flawless transactions entirely reliable. If blockchains can eliminate opportunism, then they will outcompete traditional organizational hierarchies and relational contracts. This is possible thank to the radical public transparency provided together with crypto-consensus mechanisms, executed automatically. In the end, blockchain creates a particular class of economic system: complete contracts. Thereby, in an environment with no transaction costs, all contract would be complete, and all economic transactions would be market transactions.

THE IMPACT OF BLOCKCHAIN TECHNOLOGY ON THE ACCOUNTING SYSTEM AND ITS IMPLICATIONS WITH STAKEHOLDERS

Accounting is thought to be an information system as both IASB and FASB reported in the former conceptual frameworks (FASB, 1978; IASC, 1989). Basically, the accounting information system (AIS) can be defined as a way to grab information, record and transform it into useful information so as to help to make decisions by users interested in accounting information (AI), being the result of a balance between the possibilities of the system and the demand of users (Christensen, 2010).

Thus, AI aims to report specific financial information (financial reporting) to stakeholders and thus decrease the asymmetry information between the different users. According to the conceptual framework of the IASB (2018), the purpose of AI is to offer useful information regarding an entity to current and potential investors, lenders and other creditors to help them make decisions. In such a way, the AI could be analyzed according to its function in the decision-making process, by the role of decision-influencing information and the role of decision-facilitating information (Demski and Feltham, 1976). Concerning the decision-facilitating function, the AI is regarded as a direct input in the decision-making process and is thought to perform knowledge and prospects. By contrast, the decision-influencing role of AI is thought to affect and influence the actions of management in the decision-making process (Wall and Greiling, 2011).

Subsequently, the importance of the AIS is evident due to the aforementioned functions of the AI or financial reporting. A description of AIS is shown in Figure 1 that provides a diagram of the phases of the AIS, which the internal and external relationships as well as the main stakeholders involved in the process.

The first part of the diagram shows the stage in which AIS has to capture the economic facts and external events. The role of the AIS is to recognize the economic event and register the information, being the invoice or receipt the document that provides the fact that the transaction has occurred. This part includes the relationship with suppliers and customers through the purchase of inventories and fixed assets as well as the sale of products and the rendering of services.

In the internal part of the process, the AIS uses the double-entry method with the accrual basis and in such a way, it satisfies the clean surplus relationship, which implies that any error in current accounting numbers should be balanced by errors in future expected information (Christensen, 2010; Feltham and Ohlson, 1995). The AIS records and stores information through an internal process to produce relevant figures, that is, AI aimed to management to help decision-making. Additionally, a part of the AI regarding the financial situation of the firm is presented according to accounting standards by the financial statements. Afterward, AI by financial statements has to be verified by auditors in order to be reliable information and satisfy the need for verification for an independent professional.

In the final part of the diagram, the external users of the accounting information will use this information to make decisions such us providing resources to the firm. What's more, the Government may be interested in AI in order to collect income taxes and other stakeholders would be affected by this AI.

In this vein, the AI represents a core element of the decision-making process, and therefore, the efficient circuit of information in the AIS is relevant to the vast majority of stakeholders that are eager to seek essential information. So, the impact of the technological advance on AIS is worth taking into consideration and especially, the blockchain technology. Even though a consensus exists regarding its disruptive potential (Woodside et al., 2017), there is an under-explored field that tries to discuss the possible paradigm shift in accounting if blockchain technology would be implemented.

In this section, the possible impact of blockchain on the AIS is going to be explained following the viewpoint of the diagram in figure 1. Accordingly, the potential influence in the different part of the AIS process is analyzed under the Stakeholder theory, Agency theory, Transaction cost economy, and Stewardship theory.

Figure 1. Accounting Information System (AIS)
Source: Own elaboration

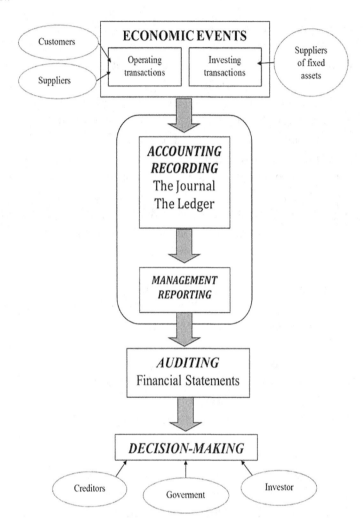

Economic Events and Accounting Recording

In the first stage of the AIS, the operating and investment external activities are the inputs in the system, being relevant information needed to be processed and stored. The business deals with the purchase of productive factors, such as capital investment and labor, which are incorporated in the productive process in order to get outputs. Suppliers and customers are the main stakeholders in this stage, and the invoice or receipt is the document that provides the fact that the transaction has occurred.

In the accounting recording, the AIS is based on a match in the Ledger under the double-entry method and accrual basis. The double-entry method enables to avoid mistakes through the record in the debit and credit part of each entry in the Journal book. In such a way, the invoice offers a control tool for both parties and the information input to register a transaction.

Blockchain technology could improve the role of the traditional invoice in several ways. First of all, the decentralized and distributed ledger would enable that each node holds the transaction history and the network of all nodes may show the correct transaction track. In this vein, some authors (Dai and Vasarhelyi, 2017) points out a triple-entry method, with a third party to validate the transaction. In this case, the third party would be the blockchain.

Additionally, recording transactions on a blockchain system would provide visibility into transactions between parties. For instance, after any external transaction with a signed contract (purchase of inventories or sale of product), each transaction would be identified with an ID number in a node and all purchase order, the payment would have the same ID. In such a way, the blockchain-based ledger may show the entire string of related transactions (Taylor, 2017).

What's more, it would allow all parties to a transaction to have real-time updated information, and if any party change information, the other would have immediate access to up-to-date information. Moreover, using smart contracts, firms can ensure the requirements of the accomplishment of accounting standards or predetermined business rules. This is possible if and only if the smart contracts are based on accounting standards (Dai and Vasarhelyi, 2017)

The use of blockchain technology not only eases the evidentiary force of the invoice but also provides information regarding the supplier selection process (Kouhizadeh and Sarkis, 2018). In such a way, the process of selection vendor/customer is more transparent, reliable and neutral. Consequently, all parties in the transaction get high levels of trust in the other party.

Additionally, the blockchain AIS would be faster and more efficient because it is a real-time process. Therefore, the relevance of the information will be increased. By contrast, the risk of cyber-attacks exists because the information is decentralized. However, blockchain AIS could be based on private nodes to restrict access to the parties to the transactions (Andersen, 2016).

Management Reporting

Once the information is processed and recorded in the accounting recording stage, the management function uses the information in order to make strategic decisions, acting as a decision-influencing role. In such a way, the AI provides internal measures of performance or fixed and variable costs, based on managerial accounting, which are used by managers to achieve the strategic organizational goals. Thus, the goal congruence between management aims and organizational goals is considered a premise (Antle and Demski, 1988; Christensen, 2010; Horngren et al., 2003). Besides, the AI in this stage acts as a control mechanism for the management actions results and the organizational aims.

In particular, the control purpose of AI could be analyzed under the agency theory (Jensen and Meckling, 1976), in which the principal (owners or investors) could have different aims from the agent (manager). The moral hazard exists if the manager wants to act in a different way from owners and to avoid this undesired action, owners could introduce incentive actions based on performance measures. In this manner, AI plays a fundamental role, being considered the information that brings the manager's action to light. Therefore, AI becomes a way of the management commitment with ownership.

Moreover, the actions of management could be studied according to the Stewardship theory. Under this theory, managers act as stewards and maximize their utility as they reach organizational rather than self-serving goals (Davis et al., 1997). Thus, there is an alignment between managers and owners' goals, and managers would pursue self-actualization, a chance to grow as well as a challenging work (Davis et al., 1997) rather than own economic interests. In that way, managers may be tempted to position their organization by focusing on technology trends (Woodside, 2017).

Table 2. Effects of blockchain technologies by accounting information processes

Technological Issue	Consequence/s	Accounting Process Identification	Effects
Decentralization	Security	Accounting recording	Certainty in the accomplishment of the transaction
	Transparency	Economic Events, Management reporting, Auditing, Decision-making	Improvement in the vendor/customer selection in the supply chain
			Alignment of the organizational goal and management actions
			A more harmonious network between manager and owners
	Autonomy	Accounting recording, Auditing	Automatization of some transactions
			Verification of the accounting rules applied
Unique hash	Authentication	Auditing, Decision-making	Alleviation mistakes
			Reliability in the information
	Security	Accounting recording, Management reporting	Deterrent against concealing or altering transactions
Key-access system	Approval	Economic events, Accounting recording, Auditing	Confirmation of both parties that the transaction has occurred
Cryptographic signature	Anonymity	Decision-making	Security in the privacy of information
Self-auditing	Integrity	Auditing, Decision-making	Evidence that the information has not been altered
	Incorruptibility	Accounting recording, Auditing	Impossibility to alter the information
	Availability	Accounting recording, Auditing	Reduction of missing data
Time-stamping	Identifiability	Economic events, accounting recording, Auditing	Avoiding mistakes/ Trails of the transaction
	Traceability	Auditing, Management reporting	Control of the management's actions
			Detection of any need through the process

Source: Own elaboration

The arguments mentioned above highlight the importance of an appropriate design of AIS as a way to give visibility of the mission, vision and organizational goals to managers. Thus, it becomes necessary for firms to link the technology with the AIS. In such a way, the blockchain technology could provide more transparent AIS because it would provide transparency and authentication of the information. So, it becomes an incentive for the manager to select the desired action (Christensen, 2010) because the information is more precise. In addition to that, blockchain AIS would align both interests, from ownership and management. Therefore, the moral dilemma of agency theory would decrease.

Despite this advantage, managers could pursue the application of trendy technologies due to the eagerness of reputation (Stout, 2003) whereas the shift does not assure the effectiveness.

In a nutshell, the blockchain could help to link the actions of the manager with the overall strategy of the firm. Thus, this interaction with organizational aspects of the firm fosters the capability of the firm to act to threats and challenges in the environment. Additionally, the impact of blockchain on AIS is the accuracy of information regarding economic events and strategic goals that could reduce the asymmetry information between owners and managers.

Auditing Process

The provision of audited financial statements is historically regarded as a cost-effective response to agency theory (Carey et al., 2000; DeAngelo, 1981; Watts and Zimmerman 1976). Moreover, the requirement of the mandatory standards of an external verification makes external auditing plays a key role in the AIS. Auditing thereupon provides a flexible framework for explaining the reliability of the AI.

In this vein, auditors have to tackle difficulties due to the overtones of their task. They should aim to protect investors, engage in the business and above all, get and keep clients. However, the role of the auditor is sometimes in question on account of the fraud cases, and it is accepted the existence of an audit expectation gap, suggesting that society does not meet expectations regarding the role of the auditor in fraud cases (Hassink et al., 2010). Regardless of this conception, audited financial statements are thought to provide greater trust and transparency to the AIS, being the Auditing process in charge of giving the "truth stamp" to the financial statements.

It is said that blockchain is "a game changer" in accounting (Anderson, 2016) and some commentators argue that the auditing process is going to change drastically (Borthick and Pennington, 2017). However, this is far from being true. The fact that transactions are recorded in blockchain software, as a hash string, implies an immutable trail because any entry is distributed and cryptographically sealed. In such a way, the hash string becomes the digital fingerprint (Deloitte, 2016). So, the main advantage is the integrity and incorruptibility that the blockchain provides to the ledger since it gives evidence that the original transaction has not been altered. So, concealing is impossible, and the verification of the transaction could be done by the own network immediately. In such a way, it would be real-time auditing and the role of the auditor would be access to the permissioned network. What's more, this blockchain would allow organizations to synchronize audit trails between different parties in a supply chain. Notwithstanding, it still exists a need to verify the original transaction and establish the appropriate controls that surround the transaction (O'Leary, 2017).

Even though blockchain could wholly automate the auditing process, it seems far-fetched that this system could be implemented for all transactions, in particular, those more complex. Therefore, auditing process should focus on the riskiest transactions of the firm in order to provide AI in the decision-facilitating role.

The implementation of blockchain not only facilitates the external verification of any transaction but also allows the auditing process to enhance the key transactions, such as the estimates of assets and liabilities, among other items. In this vein, the possibility of access to the track of any transactions enables the immediate and easy review. So, the main impact on the auditing process is because it will streamline the business workflow.

It is worth noting that the technological changes represent both threats and opportunities to the auditing process. The assurance on the blockchain would not be part of the auditor or will be difficult to ascertain the reliability on the blockchain. So, new control rules are needed to avoid the mistrust in the system.

Decision-Making Process

The final process of the AIS is the decision-making process, being the audited financial statements the output of the circuit system. In this stage, the role of the information is decision-facilitating, and it depends on the different stakeholders the way in which the blockchain may impact on the decision-making process. Although the main characteristics are relevance and reliability, the AI is available later than other sources of information, and it could become less reliable.

Shareholders

The present and potential shareholders are one of the significant groups of interest involving AIS. They provide funding to the firm, so their interest in the AI is twofold. Firstly, they are going to be interested in the performance and risk of the firms' investments due to valuation purposes. In a Value-based Management Approach (VBMA), the firm aims to create value for shareholder and the value is estimated based on realized AI, namely cash-flows (Peasnell, 1982). Secondly, the AI is considered a control mechanism required to evaluate the correct actions of the manager (Holmstrom, 1979) and to assess if the management has used the entity's resources efficiently.

The demand for information is partly due to frictions between the firm and the market. In this vein, a broad research field exists that try to analyze the relationship between AI and market values. From the seminal papers of Ball and Brown (1969) and Beaver, Kettler, and Scholes (1970), there is still a concern about the usefulness of AI and its ability to help investors and users make decisions (Boz et al., 2015).

In order to achieve the usefulness of AI, the accounting standards state that the AI should be relevant and reliable (IASB, 2018) in order to be useful in the decision-making process. Thus, relevance and reliability are the cornerstones of the AI basis. Being said that, the application of blockchain in AIS would affect the way in which the information is conceived and the moment when the information is available. Currently, there is a delay between the moment the information is published and the moment the AIS generates the financial statements partly due to the approval by auditors.

The blockchain provides a real-time accounting and self-auditing process, so the access to information would be in a shorter time (Dai and Vasarhelyi, 2017). In such a way, the relevance of the information may be increased as well as the reliability partly due to the blockchain incorruptibility consequence. Moreover, blockchain assures that the information is transparent, secure and authentic. In such a way, the information will be reliable to make decisions for investors interested in assessing the risk of a firm in the extent to which AI can show all the hazards to the firm regarding the economic and financial situation.

By contrast, there is a risk that information would be accessible for competitors and subsequently, the immediate information could lessen the competitive advantage of the firm showing quickly relevant information. Accordingly, blockchain technology could make investors reluctant to its implementation in the AIS.

Financial Institutions

The financial reporting is also aimed to assure creditors. The access to credit is a key activity in the firm, and the role of AIS in this is vital. Moreover, the AI aims to provide information regarding the risks of the firm and especially the default risk to alleviate the asymmetry of information between the parties involved. In this vein, the accounting information should be transparent and get a high level of integrity.

The theoretical background has taught that due to the asymmetry of information, there are two alternatives ways to access credit (Wang et al., 2018). One way is the use of an external credit rating agency in order to give additional signals in the AIS (Bolton et al., 2012). Another way is pledging collateral security (Berger et al., 2011). Since there is a group of firms, where neither of these alternatives are possible; the blockchain system provides a new channel of information.

In this vein, Wang et al. (2018) establish a theoretical framework where small and medium firms will have more opportunities to access a bank loan. Notably, the problems small firms face regarding credit access (Steijvers and Voordeckers, 2009) will be mitigated by blockchain technology.

Consequently, the implementation of blockchain would allow both lenders and borrowers to access information more transparent and in a shorter period. In such a way, financial firms such as Banco Bilbao Vizcaya Argentaria, S.A., Mizuho Financial Group and Prudential Financial, between others, have invested in blockchain technology to include this system in their business (del Castillo, 2018). Moreover, the fact that information is incorruptible provides reliability to the system and a reduction of uncertainty (Wang et al., 2018) as well as a more efficient system.

Government and Tax Institutions

Government institutions and especially tax agencies have been historically interested in the demand for AI due to tax computation (Tan and Low, 2017). These institutions are users of AI since taxes are based on financial reporting, namely income numbers. In the AIS the financial reporting is the basis for tax collection. Once the AIS provides the AI regarding the income, the following step is to determine the income tax throughout the financial statements, namely income statement.

The implementation of blockchain could provoke many opportunities for tax collection. The blockchain technology enables real-time accounting under the premise of immutable, secure and trustful information. In this vein, the taxation process could be more efficient and secure as well as more straightforward by reducing mistakes. What's more, a potential advantage is that blockchain technology could help to add value between businesses and governments (PwC, 2018). For instance, the study of Hyvärinen et al. (2017) proposed a system based on blockchain technology in order to reduce tax fraud and increase transparency. Although they focus on the Danish context, they propose a discussion about how the model could be generalized.

Furthermore, Government acting as a supervisor could provide information regarding the default risks of other firms and in such a way could enable the decision-facilitating function by lenders (Wang et al., 2017).

DISCUSSION AND CONCLUSION

The problem of information asymmetry in the AIS makes it relevant to consider the application of blockchain technology to provide a more transparent and efficient system (Treiblmaier, 2018). Although the theoretical foundations of the blockchain application in the AIS remain under-explored, it is necessary taking into account the impact of this technology on the information circuit, considering not only the potential benefits but also the risks or drawbacks.

One of the significant strengths of blockchain is in the first part or stage of the AIS, where the relationships with suppliers and customers could be considerably improved with the application of this technology. First, it implies a more secure network for transactions among different parties without a central authority (Dai and Vasarhelyi, 2017) and therefore, all transactions could be verified immediately through the network. An additional advantage arises by reducing the administrative workflow because many transactions could be automated. In such a way, the transactions could achieve a high level of both autonomy and reliability. Since all entries are distributed and cryptographically sealed, the scenario in which someone could destroy or alter the original information seems far-fetched. Second, all parties involved in the transaction can synchronize the trails in their supply chain, and in this way, the selection process of vendor/supplier could be improved by making the information circuit more transparent (Saberi et al., 2018; Treiblmaier, 2018).

Regarding the management reporting, the blockchain influence in this stage is relevant. On the one hand, blockchain allows a more harmonious network between the principal and the agent in the sense that it provides a quick circuit between both parties, where the organizational goals will be clearer for agents (Van and Slyke, 2006). Thus, information asymmetry and opportunistic behaviors might be discouraged due to the information transparency in this process. On the other hand, according to the Stewardship theory, the agent may be prone to implement technological trends in order to gain intrinsic satisfaction (Davis et al., 1997).

In the auditing process, it is said that blockchain would reshape the audit methodologies and thus, retraining staff would be required in a new network where new data sources emerge as a new way of evidence (Borthick and Pennington, 2017; Debreceny et al., 2017; Yoon et al., 2015). The auditors' role might change because blockchain AIS should provide a self-auditing process in real time. The identifiability provides a digital proof of the existence of transactions at any moment, being a quick identification of any information. Although the auditors' workflow could be reduced, there will be needed other tasks, such as valuation's reviews of assets, liabilities that are internal transactions not included in the blockchain AIS. Therefore, the blockchain seems to cause a reorientation in the tasks of the auditor rather than an alleviation of them. In such a way, blockchain AIS becomes a challenge for the auditing process in order to give an exhaustive opinion of the more complex activities and riskiest areas of the firm.

The advantage as mentioned above is, in turn, a potential risk due to the information's visibility. The AI becomes more transparent and available for all stakeholders. In particular, ownership or shareholders could be reluctant to show information and reveal information regarding the competitive advantage. Despite this fact, a blockchain AIS makes the information intrinsically reliable and verifiable, and in such a way, the AI fulfills the decision-facilitating role of the financial reporting. Besides, it would imply that investors could overcome their resilience to AI.

Accordingly, the transparency and authentication consequences of blockchain technology would foster access to credit to small and medium firms (Wang et al., 2018). It implies a new way of screening corporate information due to the reduction of information asymmetry. Furthermore, one of the potential impacts could be in the tax computation, where the blockchain implementation could provide immediate information flow to government institutions. In such a way, the tax collection would be faster and simpler, reducing reporting needs. Additionally, a blockchain system could serve as a deterrent to missed tax payments or unpaid payments.

However, the application of this technology faces new challenges to which accounting setters should try to respond. Firstly, some concerns are addressed based on the cyber attacks. The network could attract criminal and facilitate the access to non-permissioned participants. Secondly, there is a threat of information visibility, in which stakeholders would be reluctant to show strategic data so as not to give information regarding the competitive advantage of the firm to competitors. Thus, knowledge in the cyber-security should be improved. Thirdly, the implementation of blockchain technology implies a great deal of training by accountants and especially auditors. Auditing activity is said to be reshaped, and the role of the auditor seems to focus on exceptions and data regarding the most risky areas in the firm. Finally, the abovementioned challenges imply cost associated with the network that is worth noting to take into consideration.

REFERENCES

Andersen, N. (2016). *Blockchain Technology A game-changer in accounting?* Deloitte.

Antle, R., & Demski, J. (1989). Revenue recognition. *Contemporary Accounting Research*, *5*(2), 423–451. doi:10.1111/j.1911-3846.1989.tb00713.x

Aste, T., Tasca, P., & Di Matteo, T. (2017). Blockchain technologies: The foreseeable impact on society and industry. *Computer*, *50*(9), 18–28. doi:10.1109/MC.2017.3571064

Baden-Fuller, C., & Haefliger, S. (2013). Business models and technological innovation. *Long Range Planning*, *46*(6), 419–426. doi:10.1016/j.lrp.2013.08.023

Ball, R., & Brown, P. (1969). Portfolio theory and accounting. *Journal of Accounting Research*, *7*(2), 300–323. doi:10.2307/2489972

Beaver, W., Kettler, P., & Scholes, M. (1970). The association between market determined and accounting determined risk measures. *The Accounting Review*, *45*(4), 654–682.

Beck, R., Avital, M., Rossi, M., & Thatcher, J. B. (2017). Blockchain technology in business and information systems research. *Business & Information Systems Engineering*, *59*(6), 381–384. doi:10.100712599-017-0505-1

Berger, A. N., Frame, W. S., & Ioannidou, V. (2011). Tests of ex-ante versus ex-post theories of collateral using private and public information. *Journal of Financial Economics*, *100*(1), 85–97. doi:10.1016/j.jfineco.2010.10.014

Bolton, P., Freixas, X., & Shapiro, J. (2012). The credit ratings game. *The Journal of Finance*, *67*(1), 85–111. doi:10.1111/j.1540-6261.2011.01708.x

Borthick, A. F., & Pennington, R. R. (2017). When Data Become Ubiquitous, What Becomes of Accounting and Assurance? *Journal of Information Systems*, *31*(3), 1–4. doi:10.2308/isys-10554

Boz, G., Menéndez-Plans, C., & Orgaz-Guerrero, N. (2015). The Systematic-Risk Determinants of the European Accommodation and Food Services Industry in the Period 2003-2011. *Cornell Hospitality Quarterly*, *56*(1), 41–57. doi:10.1177/1938965514559047

Carey, P., Simnett, R., & Tanewski, G. (2000). Voluntary demand for internal and external auditing by family businesses. *Auditing*, *19*(Supplement), 36–51. doi:10.2308/aud.2000.19.supplement.37

Chesbrough, H. (2010). Business model innovation: Opportunities and barriers. *Long Range Planning*, *43*(2-3), 354–363. doi:10.1016/j.lrp.2009.07.010

Christensen, J. (2010). *Conceptual frameworks of accounting from an information perspective.* Academic Press.

Crane, A., & Ruebottom, T. (2011). Stakeholder theory and social identity: Rethinking stakeholder identification. *Journal of Business Ethics, 102*(S1), 77–87. doi:10.100710551-011-1191-4

Crosby, M., Pattanayak, P., & Verma, S. (2016). Applied Innovation Review. *Applied Innovation Review,* (2).

Dai, J., & Vasarhelyi, M. A. (2017). Toward blockchain-based accounting and assurance. *Journal of Information Systems, 31*(3), 5–21. doi:10.2308/isys-51804

Davis, J. H., Schoorman, F. D., & Donaldson, R. (1997). Toward a stewardship theory of management. *Academy of Management Review, 22*(1), 20–47. doi:10.5465/amr.1997.9707180258

DeAngelo, L. E. (1981). Auditor size and audit quality. *Journal of Accounting and Economics, 3*(3), 183–199. doi:10.1016/0165-4101(81)90002-1

Debreceny, R., Rahman, A., & Wang, T. (2017). Corporate network centrality score: Methodologies and informativenes. *Journal of Information Systems, 31*(3), 23–43. doi:10.2308/isys-51797

Del Castillo, M. (2018). *Big Blockchain: The 50 Largest Public Companies Exploring Blockchain.* Retrieved from https://www.forbes.com/sites/michaeldelcastillo/2018/07/03/big-blockchain-the-50-largest-public-companies-exploring-blockchain/#11f70c6d2b5b

Demski, J. S., & Feltham, G. A. (1976). *Cost determination: a conceptual approach. Iowa.* Ames, IA: State University Press.

Duranti, L., & Rogers, C. (2012). Trust in digital records: An increasingly cloudy legal area. *Computer Law & Security Review, 28*(5), 522–531. doi:10.1016/j.clsr.2012.07.009

FASB. (1978). *Concepts Statement No. 1: Objectives of Financial Reporting by Business Enterprises.* Financial Accounting Standards Board.

Fassin, Y. (2009). The stakeholder model refined. *Journal of Business Ethics, 84*(1), 113–135. doi:10.100710551-008-9677-4

Feltham, G., & Ohlson, J. (1995). Valuation and clean surplus accounting for operating and financial activities. *Contemporary Accounting Research, 11*(2), 689–731. doi:10.1111/j.1911-3846.1995.tb00462.x

Findlay, C. (2015). Decentralised and inviolate: the blockchain and its uses for digital archives. *Record-keeping Roundtable.* Available at https://rkroundtable.org/2015/01/23/decentralised-and-inviolate-the-blockchain-and-its-uses-for-digital-archives/

Gilbert, D. U., & Rasche, A. (2008). Opportunities and problems of standardized ethics initiatives: A stakeholder theory perspective. *Journal of Business Ethics, 82*(3), 755–773. doi:10.100710551-007-9591-1

Hassink, H., Meuwissen, R., & Bollen, L. (2010). Fraud detection, redress, and reporting by auditors. *Managerial Auditing Journal, 25*(9), 861–881. doi:10.1108/02686901011080044

Heber, D., & Groll, M. (2017, August). Towards a digital twin: How the blockchain can foster E/E-traceability in consideration of model-based systems engineering. In *DS 87-3 Proceedings of the 21st International Conference on Engineering Design (ICED 17) Vol 3: Product, Services and Systems Design, Vancouver, Canada, 21-25.08. 2017* (pp. 321-330). Academic Press.

Hölmstrom, B. (1979). Moral hazard and observability. *The Bell Journal of Economics, 10*(1), 74–91. doi:10.2307/3003320

Horngren, C., Foster, G., & Datar, S. (2003). *Cost Accounting: A Managerial Emphasis*. Prentice-Hall.

Hyvärinen, H., Risius, M., & Friis, G. (2017). A Blockchain-Based Approach Towards Overcoming Financial Fraud in Public Sector Services. *Business & Information Systems Engineering, 59*(6), 441–456. doi:10.100712599-017-0502-4

IASB. (2018). *Conceptual Framework for Financial Reporting*. IASB.

IASC. (1989). *Framework for the Preparation and Presentation of Financial Statements*. Published by the International Accounting Standards Committee Board (IASC Board) in July 1989 and adopted by the International Accounting standards Board (IASB) in April 2001. Currently available in the annual volume of IFRS published by the IASB.

Inter PARES. (2015). *Terminology database*. Available at: http://arstweb.clayton.edu/interlex/

Jayachandran, P. (2017). The difference between public and private blockchain. *IBM Blockchain Blog*. Retrieved from https://www.ibm.com/blogs/blockchain/2017/05/the-difference-between-public-and-private-blockchain/

Jensen, M. C., & Meckling, W. H. (1976). Theory of the firm: Managerial behavior, agency costs and ownership structure. *Journal of Financial Economics, 3*(4), 305–360. doi:10.1016/0304-405X(76)90026-X

Kavassalis, P., Stieber, H., Breymann, W., Saxton, K., & Gross, F. J. (2018). An innovative RegTech approach to financial risk monitoring and supervisory reporting. *The Journal of Risk Finance, 19*(1), 39–55. doi:10.1108/JRF-07-2017-0111

Keay, A. (2017). Stewardship theory: Is board accountability necessary? *International Journal of Law and Management, 59*(6), 1292–1314. doi:10.1108/IJLMA-11-2016-0118

Kluvers, R., & Tippett, J. (2011). An exploration of stewardship theory in a not-for-profit organisation. *Accounting Forum, 35*(4), 275–284. doi:10.1016/j.accfor.2011.04.002

Lemieux, V. L. (2016). Trusting records: Is Blockchain technology the answer? *Records Management Journal, 26*(2), 110–139. doi:10.1108/RMJ-12-2015-0042

Letourneau, K. B., & Whelan, S. T. (2017). Blockchain: Staying Ahead of Tomorrow. *The Journal of Equipment Lease Financing (Online), 35*(2), 1–6.

Levy, J. (2014). I love the Blockchain, just not bitcoin. *CoinDesk*. Available at: www.coindesk. com/love-blockchain-just-bitcoin/

Mattila, J. (2016). *The blockchain phenomenon–the disruptive potential of distributed consensus architectures (No. 38)*. The Research Institute of the Finnish Economy.

Miles, S. (2017). Stakeholder Theory Classification: A Theoretical and Empirical Evaluation of Definitions. *Journal of Business Ethics, 142*(3), 437–459. doi:10.100710551-015-2741-y

Mukhopadhyay, D. (2017). Cryptography: Advanced Encryption Standard (AES). Encyclopedia of Computer Science and Technology, 279.

Müller-Bloch, C., & King, J. L. (2018). Governance in the Blockchain Economy: A Framework and Research Agenda. *Journal of the Association for Information Systems, 19*, 2–36.

Nakamoto, S. (2009). *Bitcoin: A Peer-to-Peer Electronic Cash System*. Available at: https://bitcoin.org/bitcoin.pdf

Nowiński, W., & Kozma, M. (2017). How Can Blockchain Technology Disrupt the Existing Business Models? *Entrepreneurial Business and Economics Review, 5*(3), 173–188. doi:10.15678/EBER.2017.050309

O'Leary, D. E. (2017). Configuring blockchain architectures for transaction information in blockchain consortiums: The case of accounting and supply chain systems. *Intelligent Systems in Accounting, Finance & Management, 24*(4), 138–147. doi:10.1002/isaf.1417

Ovenden, J. (2017). Will blockchain render accountants irrelevant? *The Innovation Enterprise*. Retrieved from http://www.iicpa.com/articles/Will%20Blockchain%20Render%20Accountants%20Irrelevant.pdf

Parry, G. C., Brax, S. A., Maull, R. S., & Ng, I. C. L. (2016). Operationalising IoT for reverse supply: The development of use-visibility measures. *Supply Chain Management, 21*(2), 228–244. doi:10.1108/SCM-10-2015-0386

Peasnell, K. V. (1982). Some formal connections between economic values and yields and accounting numbers. *Journal of Business Finance & Accounting, 9*(3), 361–381. doi:10.1111/j.1468-5957.1982.tb01001.x

PwC. (2018). *How blockchain technology could improve the tax system*. Retrieved from https://www.pwc.co.uk/issues/futuretax/how-blockchain-technology-could-improve-tax-system.html

Saberi, S., Kouhizadeh, M., Sarkis, J., & Shen, L. (2018). Blockchain technology and its relationships to sustainable supply chain management. *International Journal of Production Research*, 1–19.

Steijvers, T., & Voordeckers, W. (2009). Collateral and credit rationing: A review of recent empirical studies as a guide for future research. *Journal of Economic Surveys, 23*(5), 924–946. doi:10.1111/j.1467-6419.2009.00587.x

Stoney, C., & Winstanley, D. (2001). Stakeholding: Confusion or Utopia? Mapping the conceptual terrain. *Journal of Management Studies, 38*(5), 603–626. doi:10.1111/1467-6486.00251

Stout, L. (2003). On the proper motives of corporate directors (or why you don't want to invite homo economicus to join your board). *Delaware Journal of Corporate Law, 28*(1).

Swan, M. (2015). *Blockchain: Blueprint for a new economy*. O'Reilly Media, Inc.

Swan, M. (2017). Anticipating the Economic Benefits of Blockchain. *Technology Innovation Management Review*, 7(10), 6–13. doi:10.22215/timreview/1109

Szabo, N. (2005). *Secure Property Titles with Owner Authority*. Available at: http://szabo.best.vwh.net/securetitle.html

Tan, B. S., & Low, K. Y. (2017). Bitcoin – Its Economics for Financial Reporting. *Australian Accounting Review*, 27(2), 220–227. doi:10.1111/auar.12167

Tapscott, A., & Tapscott, D. (2017). How blockchain is changing finance. *Harvard Business Review*, 1.

Taylor, B. (2018). Triple-Entry Accounting And Blockchain: A Common Misconception. *Forbes*. Available at: https://www.forbes.com/sites/forbesfinancecouncil/2017/11/28/triple-entry-accounting-and-blockchain-a-common-misconception/#47b1820c190f

Teece, D. J. (2010). Business models, business strategy and innovation. *Long Range Planning*, 43(2-3), 172–194. doi:10.1016/j.lrp.2009.07.003

Treiblmaier, H. (2018). The impact of the blockchain on the supply chain: A theory-based research framework and a call for action. *Supply Chain Management*, 23(6), 545–559. doi:10.1108/SCM-01-2018-0029

Van Slyke, M. (2006). Agents or stewards: Using theory to understand the government nonprofit social service contracting relationship. *Journal of Public Administration: Research and Theory*, 17(2), 157–187. doi:10.1093/jopart/mul012

Vilanova, L. (2007). Neither Shareholder nor Stakeholder Management: What Happens When Firms are Run for their Short-term Salient Stakeholder? *European Management Journal*, 25(2), 146–162. doi:10.1016/j.emj.2007.01.002

Vovchenko, N. G., Andreeva, A. V., Orobinskiy, A. S., & Filippov, Y. M. (2017). Competitive Advantages of Financial Transactions on the Basis of the Blockchain Technology in Digital Economy. *European Research Studies*, XX(3), 193–212.

Wall, F., & Greiling, D. (2011). Accounting information for managerial decision-making in shareholder management versus stakeholder management. *Review of Managerial Science*, 5(2-3), 91–135. doi:10.100711846-011-0063-8

Wang, R., Lin, Z., & Luo, H. (2018). Blockchain, bank credit and SME financing. *Quality & Quantity*, 1–14.

Watts, R., & Zimmerman, J. (1976). *Positive accounting theory*. Englewood Cliffs, NJ: Prentice Hall.

Wild, J., Arnold, M., & Stafford, P. (2015). Technology: banks seek the key to blockchain. *Financial Times*. Available at: http://on.ft.com/1NiyWWs

Woodside, J. M., Augustine, F. K. Jr., & Giberson, W. (2017). Blockchain technology adoption status and strategies. *Journal of International Technology and Information Management*, 26(2), 65–93.

Yeo, G. (2013). Trust and context in cyberspace. *Architectural Record*, *34*(2), 214–234. doi:10.1080/2 3257962.2013.825207

Yoon, K., Hoogduin, L., & Zhang, L. (2015). Big Data as complementary audit evidence. *Accounting Horizons*, *29*(2), 431–438. doi:10.2308/acch-51076

Zhao, J. L., Fan, S., & Yan, J. (2016). Overview of business innovations and research opportunities in blockchain and introduction to the special issue. *Financial Innovation*, *2*(1), 28. doi:10.118640854-016-0049-2

Zhu, H., & Zhou, Z. Z. (2016). Analysis and outlook of applications of blockchain technology to equity crowdfunding in China. *Financial Innovation*, *2*(1), 29. doi:10.118640854-016-0044-7

Chapter 4
A Brief Analysis of Blockchain Algorithms and Its Challenges

Rajalakshmi Krishnamurthi
Jaypee Institute of Information Technology, India

Tuhina Shree
Jaypee Institute of Information Technology, India

ABSTRACT

Blockchain is the world's most trusted service. It serves as a ledger that allows transaction to take place in a decentralized manner. There are so many applications based on blockchain technology, including those covering numerous fields like financial services, non-financial services, internet of things (IoT), and so on. Blockchain combines a distributed database and decentralized ledger without the need of verification by central authority. This chapter surveys the different consensus algorithms, blockchain challenges, and their scope. There are still many challenges of this technology, such as scalability and security problems, waiting to be overcome. The consensus algorithms of blockchain are proof of work (POW), proof of stake (POS), ripple protocol consensus algorithm (RPCA), delegated proof of stake (dPOS), stellar consensus protocol (SCP), and proof of importance (POI). This chapter discusses the core concept of blockchain and some mining techniques, consensus problems, and consensus algorithms and comparison algorithms on the basis of performance.

INTRODUCTION

Blockchain is one of the most important services. It is a database which contains information about all the transaction ever executed in the past and works on bitcoin protocol. It combines a distributed database and decentralized ledger and there is no need of verification by a central authority. In blockchain, the completed blocks are recorded and added to the blockchain in chronological order so that market participants can keep track of digital currency transaction without central record keeping. Each time the block is completed, the new block is generated and completed blocks goes into the blockchain as a permanent database. Each block contains a hash of the previous block. The blockchain has all the information about user address and their balances from the genesis block to the most recent block. The

DOI: 10.4018/978-1-5225-9257-0.ch004

first block is called as genesis block in blockchain. The blockchain was designed so that the transactions cannot be deleted. The blocks are added using cryptography so that data can be distributed but not copied. The continuous growth of blockchain can be considered as a problem to some, such as creating issue of storage and synchronization. Blockchain works on bitcoin protocol. *So now what is bitcoin?*

Bitcoin is digital currency released as open source software (Singh, 2016) and was first invented by a researcher 'Nakamoto' in 2008. It is a digital token that can be stored in a digital wallet and is designed to work as a currency. It is often called as a cryptocurrency because encryption techniques are used to secure transactions and controls the creation of additional units. It is a decentralized cryptocurrency produced by all the participating nodes in the system at a defined rate. The chain of bitcoin created over period and linked to each other called block chain. Bitcoin, which gave birth to the concept of blockchain and Ethereum. Ethereum, is an open source, public, blockchain based distributed computing platform and operating system featuring smart contract functioning. Through blockchain, bitcoin is solved the double-spending problem which is the risk, particularly when digital currency is exchanged, that a person could concurrently send a single unit of currency to 2 different sources. So, the bitcoin become unique because it solved the double-spending problem through blockchain.

The main objective of this work is overview and compares different consensus algorithms. There are so many algorithms which are currently using for blockchain technology. So, for the comparison, we have taken some commonly used algorithms like Proof of Work (POW), Proof of Stack (POS), Proof of Importance (POI), delegated Proof of Stake (dPOS), Practical byzantine fault tolerance and Ripple Transaction Protocol. Then we will compare those algorithms based on properties of blockchain and how they are fit for the blockchain technology. This work focuses on steps of the algorithm, scalability and method of algorithm and security risks present within the algorithm. We will discuss about consensus problem which includes The Byzantine Generals Problem, Byzantine Fault Tolerance (BFT) and Delegated Byzantine Fault Tolerance (dBFT).

Key contributions of this chapter are:

- First understand the core concept of blockchain.
- Secondly analyze the architecture of blockchain and some mining techniques.
- Then discuss about consensus problems and consensus algorithms including steps of algorithm and scalability of algorithm.
- Then analyze and compare the algorithms on the basis of performance and security risk present in algorithm.
- Finally conclude with limitations of blockchain.

THEORETICAL BACKGROUND

In this section, our focus is on core concept of blockchain, architecture of blockchain and some mining techniques used in blockchain.

Core Concept of Blockchain

Satoshi Nakamoto gave birth to blockchain technology. He is the inventor of the cryptocurrency Bitcoin which is published in 2008. The core concept of this technology is that it is a public, shared and tamperproof ledger that allows people to share information in a trustworthy ledger, where any sorts of immaterial information of value can be stored. The blockchain technology is efficient, can increase transparency. It reduces risks when less assets are tied up during transactions and reduce expenditure. The main idea of the blockchain technology is that it is accessible for everyone but cannot be controlled by any user alone. The participants together enhance and continue the blockchain by complying strict rules and general agreement that means the participants agree on how the chain will be updated. This agreement is called 'The consensus mechanism' (Laura, 2017).

In this technology, a peer-to-peer network is used. In peer to peer network, every node is equally privileged. Nodes can come and go as they placed in the network. Through mining, new blocks can be added by specialized nodes, that nodes are known as miners. In this currency transaction technology, multiple miners supervise that everything is in order and that the person who wants to make transaction actually has the money to spend and verify the transaction. If the transaction is valid, the miners confirm the change. Hereafter the only completed blocks are added to the chain and become blockchain. It is added in the chronological order with all the information. An identifying code has assigned to every transaction known as Hash value, which contains all the original information of the transaction. The hash value of the transaction is bundled together in a block, are combined in a system called as 'The Merkle Tree' (Laura, 2017) shows in Figure 1. The header of a new block contains this combined hash value additional with some more information such as the hash value of previous block and a timestamp. The timestamp proves that the data existed at the time being.

Figure 1. The Merkle Tree

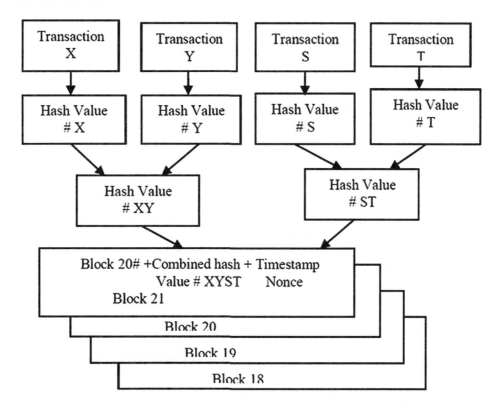

Architecture of Blockchain

A blockchain consist of sequence of blocks. A blockchain database is distributed, shared, fault tolerance and append only database that maintains the record in blocks (Salman et al., 2016). Blocks cannot be deleted or altered though it is accessible by all blockchain users. Blockchain database consist sequence of blocks. Each block has a hash value of its previous block and contains several verified transactions. Also, each block includes a timestamp and a random number (nonce) for cryptographic operations. Timestamp indicates creation of time of block. A block has only one parent block. The first block in the blockchain is known as genesis block which has no parent block and its hash value is entirely zeros. Figure 2 shows the architecture of blockchain (Zheng, 2017).

- **Block**: A block consists of the block header and block body (Zheng, 2017). The block header includes: -
  - **Blockversion:** It indicates which set of block validation rules to follow.
  - **Merkle Tree Root Hash:** The hash value of all the transactions in block.

Figure 2. Architecture of Blockchain

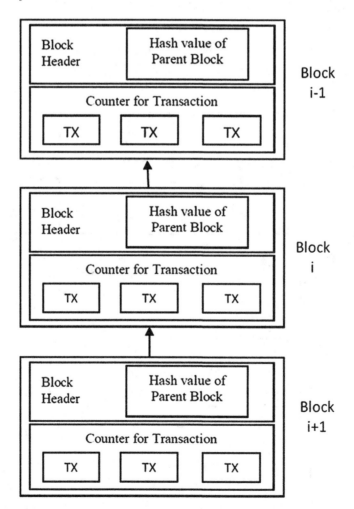

- ◦ **Timestamp:** Current time as seconds in universal time.
- ◦ **nBits:** It is a target threshold of a valid block hash.
- ◦ **Nonce:** It is a 4-byte field, which starts with 0 and increases for every hash calculation.
- ◦ **Parent Block Hash:** 256-bit hash value that point to previous block.

The block body is composed of a transaction counter and transaction. Figure 3 depicts the basic structure of a block. The maximum number of transactions that a block can contain depends on the block size and the size of each transaction. Blockchain uses an asymmetric cryptography mechanism to validate the authentication of transaction.

- **Digital Signature**: Each user of the blockchain owns a pair of private key and public key. Private Key is used to sign the transaction and that shall be kept in confidentiality. There are 2 phases: - signing phase and verification phase. Figure 4 depicts the block network, block, databases and transactions. e.g.: For instance, a user John wants to send another user Max a message.
  - ◦ In the signing phase John encrypts his data with his private key and sends Max the encrypted result and original data.
  - ◦ In verification phase, Max validates the value with John's public key. In this way Max could easily check if the data has been tampered or not.

Mining Techniques

Mining is the process of creating blocks, that blocks will be permanently attached to the database of the blockchain. In some of the blockchain applications, the miners who creates the first valid block for blockchain is rewarded, like in bitcoin. This reward is given by the system and is generally in term of money for financial applications (Salman, 2016). Mining is one of the critical concepts in the blockchain technology. It allows nodes to create blocks which will be validated by others as well (Kaushik, 2017). If the new block is valid, it will be attached to the database. Nodes that try to create the new blocks are called "mining nodes". The mining nodes race to validate the transactions and create a new block as fast as they can to win the reward.

Figure 3. Basic structure of a block

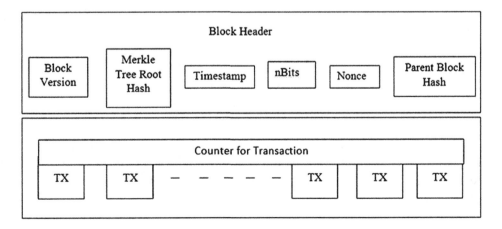

Figure 4. Blockchain network, database, blocks and transaction

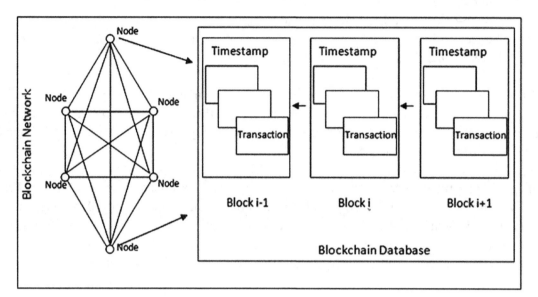

There are so many approaches exist to decide which miner wins as follows:

- **Proof of Work (POW)**: POW is the mining technique used in Bitcoin and is currently used by many other blockchain technologies. In this technique, mining nodes need to solve the hard-mathematical puzzle. Once the nodes validate the transaction and solves the puzzle, the block is added to the blockchain network. Other mining nodes validate the block to make sure the submitted block is not false. Once all the miners agree that the block is legit, that block will be added to the blockchain and submitter mining node is rewarded. The agreement here is based on a majority consensus. Thus, it is difficult to fake unless the attackers compromise more than 50 percent of mining nodes.

- **Proof of Stake (POS):** Unlike POW, in POS mining nodes are not required to solve a computational mathematical puzzle. In this miner or next block creator is chosen in a random way. Here if the nodes wealth or stake is high that node has the chance being chosen to create the new block. In other words, more money a node has, higher its chance to mine the block. POS does not reward the miner in native version, but extended versions of POS awards and punish the miners based on their performance. In this method selection is totally based on richest account, this may result that a single account is handling all the creations. Hence it is unfair to all other miners and may lead to unfair distribution or even centralization. Thus, a randomized node selection and a coin age-based selection process have been proposed. In coin age-based method, the users that have unspent coins and not created any block from past 30 days are considered for mining.

- **Proof of Space:** Proof of space is similar to proof of work except that the puzzle requires a lot of space. In this technique, the mining needs need to have a high storage capability instead of having a high computational capability. Several theoretical and practical implementations of POSPACE have been released however the challenge is high requirement of memory space.

- **Proof of Importance:** This mining technique calculates the significance of an individual node based on the transaction amount and the balance of that node. It assigns a priority with a hash calculation to more significant nodes. Then the node with the highest priority is chosen for the next block creation.
- **Measure of Trust:** This is another way to perform mining. It uses the dynamic trust measurements and selects the node with the highest trust level as the block initiator. The trust worthiness is based on the node's behaviors; therefore, good behaving nodes that follow the protocols are rewarded. The trustworthiness is approximated by the history of good and bad actions that the node has taken so far. If specific node plans to increase its trustworthiness for several interactions in order to attack the network later. The MoT approach could be subject to malicious attacks.
- **Minimum Block Hash:** In this approach, a miner is chosen randomly and not based on its resources. The system selects the miners based on a generated minimum has value across the entire network. The next miner thus is selected randomly and the probability of selecting the same miner is low. This approach was implemented on a modified Bitcoin network and it was shown to offer energy saving for mining.

THE CONSENSUS PROBLEM

The Byzantine Generals Problem

The Byzantine Generals Problem (BGP) is a problem related to communication failure like how can a node ("general") in a system be certain that the information they are receiving are valid (Bach, 2018). This problem includes an imaginary general who makes a decision to attack or retreat and try to communicate with lieutenants. They are traitors including General. Traitors cannot be relied upon the communicate order. They may alter message in attempt to follow the process. Here the generals are known as processes. Source process is the General who initiate the order and the orders that send to the other processes are messages. Here faulty processes represented by traitor generals and lieutenants and correct processes are represented by loyal generals and lieutenants. This is BGP which is applicable to every distributed network. It is more complex in bitcoin network as there is no true "general" or server. All participant nodes need to agree upon every message that is transmitted to the nodes. If the group of nodes is corrupt or the message which they transmit is corrupt, then the network should not be affected by it and should resist this 'attack'. The network should entirely agree upon every message transmitted in the network. This agreement is called consensus.

Byzantine Fault Tolerance

A Byzantine Fault is a faulty operation/algorithm that occurs in a distributed system. These faults can be classified as Omission failure and Execution failure. A failure of not being present is called Omission failure such as failing to respond to a request or not receiving a request. A failure due to sending incorrect or inconsistent data, responding to a request incorrectly is known as Execution fault. Byzantine fault tolerance can guarantee the safety and liveliness of a system given that no more than [(n-1)/3] replicas are faulty over the systems lifetime (Bach, 2018). When n is the total number of replicas within a system. So Byzantine Fault Tolerance can handle up to 33% of faulty nodes. Up to 3f+1 replica to reduce to 2f+1 required replica in order to provide safety and liveliness in a system where f is total number of faulty replicas contained within the system (Bach, 2018).

Delegated Byzantine Fault Tolerance (dBFT)

Delegated Byzantine Fault Tolerance (dBFT) is a variant of standard BFT. There is a simple analogy to explain how dBFT works. There is a country called Neo. Every citizen in this country has right to vote to select the leader known as delegate. The delegate makes laws for the country. If the citizen not agreed with how a delegate voted on a law, then they can vote for different delegate next time. Citizen tells the delegate what makes them happiest. Delegates must follow and keep track of the demand of the citizen and document it on the ledger. A speaker is randomly assigned from the group of delegates when it is time to pass a law. Then speaker process the law. Speaker calculates how the law affects on the Happiness Number of countries in the speaker's proposed law. Then speaker hands out the proposed law to the delegates. Then delegates decide if the speaker's calculation matches to their own calculation, they confer with other delegates to verify the calculated Happiness Number is valid. If 66% of the delegates agree that the calculation is valid then law passes and is finalized. If less than 66% of delegates are agreed, then the new speaker is randomly selected for the process. Likewise, in blockchain, delegates represent Bookkeeping nodes. Bookkeeping nodes verify each transaction. Citizen represent ordinary node which does not take part in validation. So, in the blockchain, if 66% of the Bookkeeper agrees that the transaction is valid then it is permanently attached to the blockchain.

THE CONSENSUS ALGORITHM

There are currently over 1500 active crypto currencies. Here is some high-profile consensus algorithm as follows:

Proof of Work (PoW)

Proof of Work algorithm is most widely used algorithm. This algorithm is used by crypto currencies such as bitcoin and ethereum, each one with its own differences (Sankar, 2017). PoW algorithm is used to confirm transaction and produce new block in the blockchain. Using Proof of Work, miners compete against each other to complete the transaction on the network and get rewarded. In this algorithm, main work is to solve the mathematical puzzle. Now what is mathematical puzzle? It is an issue that requires a lot of computational power to solve. Miners solve the puzzle then confirm the transaction and form the new block.

When other nodes confirm that the transaction is valid then only block is added to the chain permanently. The problem should not be too complex to solve, if it is like that, block generation takes a lot of time. But in other scenario if problem is too easy, it is prone to DOS attack and spam. The solution needs to be easily checked by other nodes otherwise not all nodes are capable of analyzing that calculation is correct. Thus, it will have to trust other nodes and it violates the one of the important features of blockchain - transparency. Complexity of puzzle is depending on the number of users, the current power and the network load. The hash value of each block contains the previous block's hash value which increases the security. The genesis block is an exception as it has no parent block, so its hash value is completely zeros (Mingxiao, 2017).

Bitcoin is the foundation of this kind of consensus. The puzzle called as Hashcash. The Proof of Work algorithm allows changing the complexity of a puzzle based on the total power of the network. The average time of the formation of any block is approx 10 minutes. The main disadvantages of this algorithm are huge expenditure, uselessness of computations and 51 percent attack (Tosh, 2017). Figure 5 depicts the working of the proof of work algorithm.

Proof of Stake (PoS)

Proof of Stake has been mentioned in the first bitcoin project, but it was not used in bitcoin because of its robustness and other reasons (Mingxiao, 2017). It is different from Proof of Work algorithm in which hashing algorithm is used to validate the transaction. Proof of Stake is most commonly used as the replacement of PoW in PeerCoin. Traditionally in this algorithm, selection of miners was based on the account balance i.e higher the balance in account, higher the chance to become the miner. So, the richest person has probability to become permanent miner as it has high balance in his account and that leads to be unfair to other persons. So, this process leads to the centralization that is why several other processes of selection has been devised. In peer coin crypto currencies, proof of Stake combines the randomization with the concept of "coin age". The formula is proofhash< coin age *target (Mingxiao, 2017). Coins that have been unspent for at least 30 days, being competing for the next block. To signing the next block, the older and largest set of coins have greater possibility. Then once the Stake of coin has been selected to sign a block, they must start with zero 'coin age' and then wait at least 30 more days before signing another block. So, this process secures the network and produce new coin without much computational power. Proof of Stake is more efficient than Proof of Work which mainly relies on energy use (Chalaemwongwan, 2018).

Figure 5. Working of proof of work (PoW) algorithm

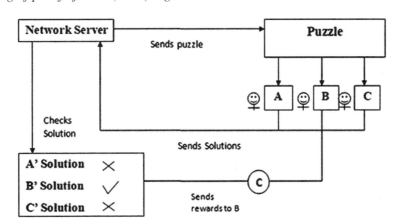

Delegated Proof of Stake

Satoshi Nakamoto hoped that all the participants can use the CPU to mine in initial design stage. So, the hashing power could match the nodes and each node has the opportunity to participate in blockchain. Then finally, the machines that are specially designed for mining are invented. In a delegated proof of stake (dPOS) system, stakeholders vote to elect any number of witnesses to generate blocks (Bach, 2018). During each maintenance interval, the roster of witnesses is shuffled. Each witness has a turn to produce a block at the fixed schedule of 1 block per n number of seconds. Witnesses are rewarded for each block produced. The witness may be voted out in future election when they fail to produce a block after being elected. The N number of witnesses creates new blocks as assigned and then need to ensure some fixed online time. BitShare is an example of dPoS system. The blockchain using DPoS is more efficient and power saving than PoS and PoW.

Proof of Importance

POI uses a method that clusters through transaction graph analysis, utilizing the transaction quantities and the balances of individual nodes as indicators, determining the importance of each node and designating the priority using hash computations to more significant nodes (Tasatanattakool, 2018; Chalaemwongwan, 2018). Proof of Importance was first introduced by NEM. PoI uses a mechanism that determines which network participants (nodes) are eligible to add a block to the blockchain and it is a process that is known as "harvesting" by NEM. Nodes are able to collect the transaction fees in exchange for harvesting a block. Those accounts who has higher importance score will have a higher probability of being chosen to harvest a new block. Proof of importance uses an underlying cryptocurrency called XEM. Each account has a XEM balance within the NEM network. The balance is split into two parts: vested and unvested. When an account receives XEM, the new XEM is added to this account's unvested balance. An account's unvested balance of one tenth is moved into the vested part every 1440 blocks (Bach, 2018). In addition, when an account sends XEM, XEM is taken from both vested and unvested balances in order to retain the same vested and unvested ratio. An account must hold at least 10,000 vested XEM to be eligible for an "importance calculation".

Practical Byzantine Fault Tolerance

Byzantine fault tolerance can be a good method to solve the transmission errors in distributed systems (Wang, 2019). But previously Byzantine system requires exponential operations. In 1999, the PBFT system was proposed and the algorithm complexity was reduced to a polynomial level, this improved efficiency (Mingxiao, 2017).

Ripple Transaction Protocol

Ripple is based around the XRP ledger which is a shared public ledger, that was a consensus process that allows for payments, exchanges and remittance in a distributed process. Ripple payment protocol was first developed in 2004 by Ryan Fugger. The ripple transaction protocol (RTP) was developing by OpenCoin based on Ryan Fugger's concept. The Ripple transaction Protocol enables the direct transfer of money between two parties. Ripple enables security, is fast. It was structure of distributed public ledger of the kind that utilizes consensus procedures which permit payments, exchanges and remittances.

COMPARATIVE ANALYSIS OF ALGORITHMS

Different consensus algorithms of blockchain have different strengths and drawbacks. Table 1 shows comparative analysis of these algorithms for some essential properties of blockchain.

1. **Energy Saving:** In Proof of Work, mining nodes need to solve the mathematical puzzle continuously which leads to consume high computational power. Therefore, the amount of energy is immense (Ogiela, 2018). But in PoS and DPoS, miners work decreases as the search place is produced to be restricted. Regarding PBFT and Ripple, there is no mining in terms of consensus Strategy. Therefore, it saves energy.
2. **Data Model:** A data model is a transaction that focuses on assets. All systems require specific configurations, with several organizations being able to spin up a network to exchange assets with each other (Dinh, 2018). These organizations are known as ledger owners. Ripple issue their own token assests and provide their ledger as a method of exchange.
3. **Application:** Some ledger support running general, user-defined computations. Ethereum and its derivatives, namely Hyperchain, Quorum, Monax, Parity and Definitely let users write arbitrary business logic executed on top of the ledger (Chalaemwongwan, 2018).
4. **D.Examples: -**Bitcoin and ethereum uses Proof of Work algorithm. Peercoin only focus on Proof of Stake in other hand ripple which has account- based data model uses Ripple Transaction Protocol.

Table 1. Comparative analysis of blockchain algorithms for a set of blockchain properties

Parameters/ Algorithms	PoW	PoS	PoI	DPOS	PBFT	Ripple
Developer	Markus Jakobsson and Ari juels	Peercoin	NEM	Danial Larimer	Castro and liskov	Jed McCaleb and Chris larsen
Year	1999	-	2015	2014	1999	2012
Node identity	Public	Public	Public, Private	Public	Private	Public
Computational Power	High	Comparative low	low	low	low	low
Energy Efficiency	No	Partial	yes	Partial	Yes	yes
Data model	Transaction -based	Account - based	Transaction- Based, Account- Based	Transaction- based, Account- Based	Key- value	Account- based
Language	C++, Golang, Solidity, LLL	Michaleson	Java	No scripting	GoLang, java	Java, Go, c++
Applications	Crypto-currency, General application	Michaleson Application	Blockchain Platform	Decentralized Exchange	General Application	Digital Assets, payment
Examples	Bitcoin, Litecoin, Ethereum, ZCash	Peercoin, Tezos, Tendermint	XEM	Bitshares	Hyperledger	Ripple

IMPLEMENTATION

In the implementation section we have taken blockchain structure somewhat similar to the actual blockchain which is used by bitcoin. This implementation section shows the basic structure of blockchain in which we need to create wallet for account holders and make transaction between them. These successful transactions are needed to be verify and then group together to create blocks. This shows that the blocks are nothing but transactions data which is made by users. These blocks are added to the blockchain after verification. Stages of execution of bitcoin-like Blockchain are as follows:

Hash Function and Mining

In actual scenario, Bitcoin uses two rounds of SHA256 hash function. In this example, we will use one SHA256 hash function (Ishan, 2018). Hash function will change a string of arbitrary length into a fixed-length string of 64 hexadecimal characters. Now the process of mining is, when given an arbitrary string x, then find a nonce such that hash(x+nonce) produces a hash string with the number of leading ones. In our example here, we'll "mine" a nonce so that the hash of our message ("hello bitcoin") when concatenated with our nonce will have at least 2 leading ones. Figure 6 depicts the snippet of finding nonce.

After this we are defining two functions: one to hash a string and one to mine a nonce for a given string. Figure 7 showing that the number of iterations required for a difficulty of 3 is much larger than for a difficulty of 1.

Creating a Wallet and Doing Transaction

In bitcoin a wallet is a private and public key pair. The public key is used to receive transactions and the private key is used to spend money. Wallet is more complicated in real scenario. It is a set of multiple private/ public key pairs and an address is not directly the public key. This ensures better privacy and security in Bitcoin.

Figure 6. Finding nonce and return a string

```
In [5]: import hashlib
        import random
        import string
        import json
        import binascii
        import numpy as np

        import logging

In [6]: def sha256(message):
            return hashlib.sha256(message.encode('ascii')).hexdigest()

In [7]: message = 'hello bitcoin'
        for nonce in range(1000):
            digest = sha256(message + str(nonce))
            if digest.startswith('11'):
                print('Found nonce = %d' % nonce)
                break
        print(sha256(message + str(nonce)))

        Found nonce = 32
        112c38d2fdb6ddaf32f371a390307ccc779cd92443b42c4b5c58fa548f63ed83
```

Figure 7. Showing number of iterations required for difficulty of 3

```
In [8]: def dumb_hash(message):
            """
            Returns an hexadecimal hash
            """
            return sha256(message)

        def mine(message, difficulty=1):
            """
            Given an input string, will return a nonce such that
            hash(string + nonce) starts with 'difficulty' ones

            Returns: (nonce, niters)
                nonce: The found nonce
                niters: The number of iterations required to find the nonce
            """
            assert difficulty >= 1, "Difficulty of 0 is not possible"
            i = 0
            prefix = '1' * difficulty
            while True:
                nonce = str(i)
                digest = dumb_hash(message + nonce)
                if digest.startswith(prefix):
                    return nonce, i
                i += 1

In [9]: nonce, niters = mine('42', difficulty=1)
        print('Took %d iterations' % niters)

        nonce, niters = mine('42', difficulty=3)
        print('Took %d iterations' % niters)

        Took 23 iterations
        Took 2272 iterations
```

In our example, we are using single key-pair and use the public key as the address. After creating the Wallet, we will then transfer money from one account to another.

Figure 8 is showing the wallet's balance.

Putting Transactions in Block

When we will create wallet and do some transaction between them, we need to group the transactions into the block. Then miners need to mine the block. Mining a block generally consist of two parts: Verifying the transactions in the block and Finding a nonce such that the block's hash starts with a number of 0. Mining generates money by the convention that the first transaction in a block is a Genesis block which does not have parent hash value. Transaction that gives 25 coins to whatever addresses the miner chose.

Figure 8. Code snippet of showing balance of wallet

```
def compute_balance(wallet_address, transactions):
    """
    Given an address and a list of transactions, computes the wallet balance of the address
    """
    balance = 0
    for t in transactions:
        # Subtract all the money that the address sent out
        for txin in t.inputs:
            if txin.parent_output.recipient == wallet_address:
                balance -= txin.parent_output.amount
        # Add all the money received by the address
        for txout in t.outputs:
            if txout.recipient == wallet_address:
                balance += txout.amount
    return balance

print("Alice  has %.02f dumbcoins" % compute_balance(alice.address, transactions))
print("Bob    has %.02f dumbcoins" % compute_balance(bob.address, transactions))
print("Walter has %.02f dumbcoins" % compute_balance(walter.address, transactions))

Alice  has 15.00 dumbcoins
Bob    has 1.00 dumbcoins
Walter has 8.00 dumbcoins
```

The miner can add transactions to redirect the fees from the transactions in the block to whatever address it chooses. Figure 9 shows creating blocks such that first block is genesis block, second is block1 and third is block2 so on. Figure 10 shows that verification of blocks in terms of true false.

CONCLUSION

Blockchain with its key characteristics, has shown its potential to reshaping traditional industry. In this paper, we first introduce what is blockchain and bitcoin and how bitcoin gave birth to blockchain. Then the core concept and architecture of blockchain is explained. We have mentioned some mining techniques used by blockchain. Mining technique plays essential role in Blockchain. Then discuss consensus algorithm of blockchain regarding theoretical aspect of algorithm and its advantages and disadvantages.

Figure 9. Code snippet of putting transaction in block

```
alice = Wallet()
bob = Wallet()
walter = Wallet()

genesis_block = GenesisBlock(miner_address=alice.address)
print("genesis_block : " + genesis_block.hash + " with fee=" + str(genesis_block.fee()))

t1 = genesis_block.transactions[0]
t2 = Transaction(
    alice,
    [TransactionInput(t1, 0)],
    [TransactionOutput(bob.address, 5.0), TransactionOutput(alice.address, 15.0), TransactionOutput(walter.address, 5.0)]
)
t3 = Transaction(
    walter,
    [TransactionInput(t2, 2)],
    [TransactionOutput(bob.address, 5.0)])

t4 = Transaction(
    bob,
    [TransactionInput(t2, 0), TransactionInput(t3, 0)],
    [TransactionOutput(walter.address, 8.0), TransactionOutput(bob.address, 1.0)]
)

block1 = Block([t2], ancestor=genesis_block, miner_address=walter.address)
print("block1        : " + block1.hash + " with fee=" + str(block1.fee()))

block2 = Block([t3, t4], ancestor=block1, miner_address=walter.address)
print("block2        : " + block2.hash + " with fee=" + str(block2.fee()))

genesis_block : 1162dce8ffec3acf13ce61109f121922eee8cceeea4784aa9d90dc6ec0e0fa92 with fee=0
block1        : 112c9894c0ebf0e33709d73e5d294a0b39f63034e0827f2c95d8c490e79bf50d with fee=0.0
block2        : 11e37778d7935029bd94d3aa188a8a6cc540a35227415abef8b8cd1d7bc2c81a with fee=1.0
```

Figure 10. Verification

```
block2 = Block([t3, t4], ancestor=block1, miner_address=walter.address)
print("block2        : " + block2.hash + " with fee=" + str(block2.fee()))

genesis_block : 1162dce8ffec3acf13ce61109f121922eee8cceeea4784aa9d90dc6ec0e0fa92 with fee=0
block1        : 112c9894c0ebf0e33709d73e5d294a0b39f63034e0827f2c95d8c490e79bf50d with fee=0.0
block2        : 11e37778d7935029bd94d3aa188a8a6cc540a35227415abef8b8cd1d7bc2c81a with fee=1.0

In [20]: verify_block(block1, genesis_block)
         verify_block(block2, genesis_block)

Out[20]: True
```

We analyzed and compare those algorithms on the basis of some essential properties of blockchain. In this paper, we focused on public blockchain which is used by bitcoin and the widely used algorithms like Proof of Work and Prof of Stake. Proof of Work still has some limitations such that 50% attack, huge expenditure and uselessness of computational power in other hand Proof of Stake is more energy efficient as it uses less computational power. There are so many algorithms proposed but still blockchain has some limitations.

FUTURE RESEARCH DIRECTION

Blockchain is chain of blocks which contains the information of transactions. In this paper we have discussed about some mining techniques and architecture of blockchain. We have also discussed use for algorithms and its limitations. Nowadays Blockchain is growing faster but it still has many limitations such as redundancy, complexity, energy and resource consumption, security flaws etc. One of the limitations of blockchain is storage issue. The future research direction would be solution for storage issue of blockchain. What will happen if blockchain is combined with cloud technology? How it will affect the storage and security issue of blockchain.

REFERENCES

Bach, L. M., Mihaljevic, B., & Zagar, M. (2018). Comparative analysis of blockchain consensus algorithms. *41st International Convention on Information and Communication Technology, Electronics and Microelectronics (MIPRO)*, 1545-1550. 10.23919/MIPRO.2018.8400278

Chalaemwongwan, N., & Kurutach, W. (2018). State of the art and challenges facing consensus protocols on blockchain. *International Conference on Information Networking (ICOIN)*, 957-962. 10.1109/ICOIN.2018.8343266

Dinh, T. T. A., Liu, R., Zhang, M., Chen, G., Ooi, B. C., & Wang, J. (2018). Untangling Blockchain: A Data Processing View of Blockchain Systems. *IEEE Transactions on Knowledge and Data Engineering*, *30*(7), 1366–1385. doi:10.1109/TKDE.2017.2781227

Ishan, P. B., & Rai, G. (2018). Analysis of Cryptographic Hash in Blockchain for Bitcoin Mining Process. *International Conference on Advances in Computing and Communication Engineering (ICACCE)*, 105-110. 10.1109/ICACCE.2018.8441688

Jutila, L. (2017). *The blockchain technology and its applications in the financial sector*. Available at: https://aaltodoc.aalto.fi/bitstream/handle/123456789/27209/bachelor_Jutila_Laura_2017.pdf;jsessionid=EB73ECF52889104CB772C6FA3B968EF7?sequence=1

Kaushik, A., Choudhary, A., Ektare, C., Thomas, D., & Akram, S. (2017). Blockchain — Literature survey. *2nd IEEE International Conference on Recent Trends in Electronics, Information & Communication Technology (RTEICT)*, 2145-2148.

Mingxiao, D., Xiaofeng, M., Zhe, Z., Xiangwei, W., & Qijun, C. (2017). A review on consensus algorithm of blockchain. *IEEE International Conference on Systems, Man, and Cybernetics (SMC)*, 2567-2572. 10.1109/SMC.2017.8123011

Ogiela, M. R., & Majcher, M. (2018). Security of Distributed Ledger Solutions Based on Blockchain Technologies. *IEEE 32nd International Conference on Advanced Information Networking and Applications (AINA),* 1089-1095. 10.1109/AINA.2018.00156

Salman, T., Zolanvari, M., Erbad, A., Jain, R., & Samaka, M. (2016). Security Services Using Blockchains: A State-of-the-Art Survey. *IEEE Communications Surveys and Tutorials.*

Sankar, L. S., Sindhu, M., & Sethumadhavan, M. (2017). Survey of consensus protocols on blockchain applications. *4th International Conference on Advanced Computing and Communication Systems (ICACCS)*, 1-5. 10.1109/ICACCS.2017.8014672

Singh, S., & Singh, N. (2016*).* Blockchain: Future of financial and cyber security. *2nd International Conference on Contemporary Computing and Informatics (IC3I)*, 463-467. 10.1109/IC3I.2016.7918009

Tasatanattakool, P., & Techapanupreeda, C. (2018). Blockchain: Challenges and applications. *International Conference on Information Networking (ICOIN)*, 473-475.

Tosh, D. K., Shetty, S., Liang, X., Kamhoua, C., & Njilla, L. (2017). Consensus protocols for blockchain-based data provenance: Challenges and opportunities. *IEEE 8th Annual Ubiquitous Computing, Electronics and Mobile Communication Conference (UEMCON)*, 469-474.

Wang, Y., Cai, S., Lin, C., Chen, Z., Wang, T., Gao, Z., & Zhou, C. (2019). Study of Blockchains's Consensus Mechanism Based on Credit. *IEEE Access: Practical Innovations, Open Solutions*, 7, 10224–10231. doi:10.1109/ACCESS.2019.2891065

Yuan, Y., & Wang, F. (2018). Blockchain and Cryptocurrencies: Model, Techniques, and Applications. *IEEE Transactions on Systems, Man, and Cybernetics. Systems*, 48(9), 1421–1428. doi:10.1109/TSMC.2018.2854904

Zheng, Z., Xie, S., Dai, H., Chen, X., & Wang, H. (2017). An Overview of Blockchain Technology: Architecture, Consensus, and Future Trends. *IEEE International Congress on Big Data (BigData Congress)*, 557-564.

KEY TERMS AND DEFINITIONS

Bitcoin: Is a cryptocurrency based on blockchain technology that enables it to function as a medium of exchange without involving the intermediary, such as a bank.

Decentralized Ledger: Is ledgers or system of records for business economic activities and interest that are dispersed instead of reliant on and housed within one third-party system, such as a financial institution.

Double Spending Problem: Which is the risk, particularly when digital currency is exchanged, that a person could concurrently send a single unit to two different sources.

Ethereum: Is an open source, public, blockchain-based distributed computing platform and operating system featuring smart contract functioning.

Hash Function: It takes a set of digital data and delivers a numeric piece of data with a fixed range. If you deliver a same exact data to a hash function, it will deliver the same exact numeric piece of data every time. If the data input varies even by one variable, the hash function output will change.

Nounce: Is a number chosen at random used once for a specific purpose and then discarded.

Peer-to-Peer Network: Is a computer network based on nodes (e.g., computers that are maintaining the network worldwide). It is a decentralized network where nodes share information with each other without anyone controlling the network.

Chapter 5

Blockchain Technology:
A Review of the Contemporary Disruptive Business Applications

Tarek Taha Kandil
Helwan University, UAE

Shereen Nassar
Heriot-Watt University, UK

Mohamed Taysir
Drakon Tech Solutions, Egypt

ABSTRACT

Blockchain technology starts to reconfigure all aspects of society to make it clear and beneficial for the legal system. The chapter introduces "The Blockchain Revolution" in categories 1.0, 2.0, and 3.0; in the form of analyzing the use of the technology that is being applied in new innovative business models, Blockchain 1.0 starts with the creation of the first blockchain and the introduction of the technology in the "Bitcoin Whitepaper," the crypto-currency model, via Bitcoin's application in services related to cash, payments, and transfers. Blockchain 2.0 starts with the indication that using smart contracts on blockchains will be available via the development of syntax (i.e., "solidity" that would enable developers to create solutions with blockchain technology at the backend). The chapter explores the feature of the new disruptive business models-based blockchain technology as a new approach in delivering business products and services. In the chapter, the authors explore the new technologies raised in different fields of business.

INTRODUCTION

Many scholars use "disruptive innovation" broadly to refer to any situation in which an industry is shaken up due to a dramatic competition and process whereby smaller companies (entrants) using fewer resources, empowered by internet technology via clouds and artificial intelligence, are able to challenge previous incumbents stumble. There is no choice for the blockchain incumbents, but not to lose ground against new entrants and to find their way to disruptive FINTECH (Christidis and Devetsikiotis,2016).

DOI: 10.4018/978-1-5225-9257-0.ch005

On the other hand, the smaller disruptive companies confront the dilemma of gaining the support of the disrupted incumbent companies. Christensen (2006) asserted that the blockchain incumbents' products and services are disrupted by the entrants' innovations and yet are reluctant to relinquish the incumbents' advantage (Christidis and Devetsikiotis, 2016). Such changes in the business environment and the associated drivers for competition considering both the disrupted incumbents and the disruptive entrants open the door for business scholars and practitioners to revisit the IT business models in the disruptive FINTECH contest to understand how companies can create, deliver and capture business values (Mendling et al., 2018)

This new digital disruption revolution started in 2009 with a new fringe economy on the internet using cryptography, creating a crypto-currency as an alternative coin called "Bitcoin" issued by automated consensus among blocked networked users (Dijkstra, 2017). Bitcoin is a digital cash protocol that is transacted through peer-to-peer (P2P) file sharing system via the Internet in a tasteless system (Swan, 2015; Tayeb, 2018). It uses a disruptive public ledger called blockchain (Swan, 2015). Melanie Swan, Founder of the Institute for Blockchain Studies (IBS), reveals that blockchain is essentially a public ledger with potential as a worldwide, decentralized record for the registration, inventory, and transfer of all assets—not just finances, but property and intangible assets such as votes, software, health data, and ideas." (Swan, 2015) p.2. As the world is being disrupted by technological innovation, people are rapidly embracing the Internet of Things (Christidis and Devetsikiotis,2016) gadgets in their day-to-day lives (Mendling et al., 2018)

Disruptive technology of blockchain is made possible because the new entrants use the disruptive technology to create two types of markets (Christidis and Devetsikiotis,2016):

1. **Low-End Footholds (Of Less-Demanding Customers) Market:** Where incumbents pay less attention comparing most profitable and demanding customers market, that provides a great opportunity for the new entrants to focus on satisfying those low-end market with a "disrupted" product and services (Zook and Blankenship, 2018). For example; In 2009, 'Uber Cab' which started as Tech Company by Travis Kalanick and Garrett Camp, released the Uber Cap application to torn consumers of big taxi companies with some requests into their potential consumer's pool, and crowd-sourced taxi drivers who are not owned by Uber (Singhal, Dhameja and Panda, 2018). In considering the disruptive Uber mobile-application-based transportation network, the Uber business model has applied by other taxi companies to leverage the trend globally in 55 countries (200+ cities) (Singhal et al., 2018).

2. **New-Market Footholds Of Non-Consumers:** The new entrants use blockchain disruptive technology to create a new-market foothold where customers are none existed since they use such technology to turn non-consumers into consumers (Christidis and Devetsikiotis, 2016)

Blockchain technology reconfigures all aspects of society and its applications which are associated with economic, political, humanitarian, and legal system. According to Swan (2015), the blockchain and potential blockchain revolution are broken down into three categories: Blockchain 1.0, 2.0, and 3.0. Blockchain 1.0 is all about the crypto-currency, the deployment of cryptography in application related to cash, payments and exchange (Swan, 2015), Blockchain 2.0 is about the benefit of the smart contracts, the entire slate of economic, trading market, and financial technology (FINTECH) industry application using blockchain that are more extensive than normal cash transactions (Swan, 2015). Blockchain 3.0 covers blockchain governance and trusted application beyond currency, finance, and trading markets (Arruñada and Garicano, 2018; Azar and Raouf, 2017)

Although, data safety becomes the prime concern for everyone, many countries all over the world establish the start-ups mechanisms that examine how blockchain technology could change the way services and industries manage governmental transaction data and contracts to discover the best practices of such digitized business model and its implementation challenges in the long-term (Arruñada and Garicano, 2018; Beck and Müller-Bloch, 2017; Christidis and Devetsikiotis, 2016)

An economic framework for identifying blockchain-based solutions to challenges are not only the new engine of disruptive growth in digital commerce, carriers and contracts (Li, Greenwood and Kassem, 2018), but for all transforming assets activities. The transforming assets activities are ranging from equipment, shipping containers, and warranties to healthcare records and data related to supply chains, greater collaboration and more accuracy with less risk to shareholders (Crosby et al., 2016). As the world is being disrupted by technological innovation, people are rapidly embracing the Internet of Things (Christidis and Devetsikiotis) gadgets in their day-to-day lives. Ross, (2015) asserted that John Chambers, former CEO of Cisco who forecast that "at least 40% o {f all businesses will die in the next 10 years… if they don't figure out how to change their entire company to accommodate new technologies". In addition, governments should analyze the digital technology and digitization from macro perspective and examine the general implications for guiding management practice (Singhal et al., 2018; Tayeb, 2018). They also should analyze the current logic of business models, education, skills and desired competencies in the new job market, the value chain be impacted, legal considerations and ethics in the context of digital transformation (Zalan, 2018).

Statement of Aims

The present chapter explores the feature of the new disruptive business models based-blockchain technology as a new disruptive technology in delivering business products and services. The chapter introduces "The Blockchain Revolution" in categories, 1.0, 2.0 and 3.0; in the form of analyzing the use of the technology that are being applied in new, innovative and disruptive business models. In the present chapter, the authors explore the new technologies raised in different blockchain application in business field of businesslike; FINTECH, real estates based smart contracts, banking, insurance industry, healthcare and wellbeing, etc.

Chapter Structure

In this chapter, the three tiers of the Blockchain Revolution are discussed including Blockchain 1.0, 2.0 and 3.0. The chapter will follow the following structure:

Part One: In this part, the authors cover the basic definitions and concepts of Bitcoin and blockchain technology in the form of currency and payments as the core blockchain 1.0 category.
Part Two: Blockchain 2.0 the use of smart contracts.

Part Three: Blockchain 3.0, which focuses on blockchain based apps develop by independent developers. The authors discuss new concepts of the applications of blockchain that have been deployed; in the greater context of the wide-scale deployment of blockchain technology.

Part Four: discusses challenges that the Blockchain will face and their interactions in developing new business topography and on (re)shaping markets and the associated service context.

BACKGROUND: THE FUNDAMENTALS OF BLOCKCHAIN

Before delving in the fundamentals of Blockchain, it's important to briefly look at the history of Blockchain.

To grasp to mechanisms of Blockchain, let's discuss "Yap Island" a small south pacific isle. The island had a unique form of currency, "Rai Stones" or "Micronesian Money"; these disc-like stones would weigh up to 700kgs each and reach diameters of 4 meters or more; making these stones hard to move or retain so they depended on the decoupling of possession and ownership of the discs. To transfer the ownership of the discs, the process had to be done through "Public Declaration" between the parties and the community making the transaction public knowledge and immutable to double spending through transparency. Seems similar to blockchain. The question would then be why hasn't this technology emerged since then? The answer is simple, File Storage and Record keeping of every Transaction; these two factors play an important factor in keeping the system decentralized. In the times of Yap Island, the population was low, and the economic system wasn't as complex as today's, so keep the entire spending of Rai Stones public knowledge was easy, but for a country like the USA not so much. But today data storage is no longer an issue and the "Bitcoin Whitepaper" introduced "Block Chain" Technology later to be changed to the widely used term "Blockchain" as a solution to the maintenance of the ledger in a decentralized manner with it falling under political or economic instabilities.

It is worthy to note that this idea of a digital currency is as old as the Internet itself research in existence show the early attempts started as early as in the 1980s early 90s, but with no success on how to govern the ledgers without the need for a central entity like a Central Bank to maintain the records and solve to problem of double spending. The ingenuity of "Bitcoin" was in its ability to solve these two problems. Firstly, it is decentralized; secondly, it relayed on cryptography to solve the problem of double spending. Blockchain is a genius mixes and matches of new tech with existing tech; i.e. Distributed Ledgers, IPFS (Inter Planetary File Sharing System), Cryptography.

Topics that are related to the history of Blockchain:

1. David Chaum and DigiCash
2. E-gold.
3. Byzantine Generals Problem.
4. Bitcoin Whitepaper.
5. Ethereum Whitepaper.
6. Hyperledger & the Linux Foundation.

What Is Blockchain?

Blockchain is a "Distributed Data Storage System", it is similar to a cloud-based network but instead of having multiple select nodes that act as one big server owned by "One Entity"; the network is spread out on top of "Independent Nodes" that hold the data and add to the computational power of the overall network; the network is not owned neither is it maintained by its creators. Most Blockchain projects are open-source projects that allow independent people to alter and update the code to create variations of a blockchain through "Hard" or "Soft" Forks.

A Blockchain consists of a chain of blocks; each block contains verified transactions and identified by a unique "Hash Number" or "Hash". The "Chain" side lies in the addition of the "Hash" of any block in the one following it, so that when the new block is created it would contain the "Hash" of the previous block in addition to the new verified transactions before being hashed. The process is repeated endlessly (Arruñada and Garicano, 2018; Beck and Müller-Bloch, 2017; Singhal et al., 2018; Tayeb, 2018).

What Are the Types of Blockchains?

There are different types of Blockchains; their use simply depends on the needs of the client and the attributes that are to be linked to the built solution.

1. **Public Blockchains Vs. Permissioned/ Private Blockchains:** Referrers to who can write/add info to a block.
   a. **Public Blockchains:** Everyone.
   b. **Permissioned/Private Blockchains:** Some participants.
2. **Open/Closed Blockchains:** Referrers to who can read the data.
   a. **Open Blockchains:** Everyone.
   b. **Closed Blockchains:** Some Participants.

How Does Blockchain Work (Briefly)?

When a network/blockchain is created there are some defined parameters the creators publicize in their "Whitepaper" that shows the details of different aspects including governance, technical knowledge, proof of concept, etc.

Figure 1 is a diagram of the life cycle of a transaction on a blockchain.

1. A sends a request to the network notifying them of his transaction between him and B.
2. The "Validators/Miners/Nodes" validate the transaction.
3. The transaction is added to the Block.
4. When the Block is completed, holds max (N) of transactions.
5. The Blocked is hashed.
6. A New Block is added with the hash of the previous block as the first data entry in the new block, automatically.

Based on any Whitepaper of any blockchain, any block contains a predefined number (N) entity of verified transactions.

Comparing with other digitized technology, Figure 2 shows significant advantages offered by Blockchain technology (Beck and Müller-Bloch, 2017; Dijkstra, 2017).

Figure 1. Blockchain technology the new internet
Source: https://blockgeeks.com/guides/what-is-blockchain-technology

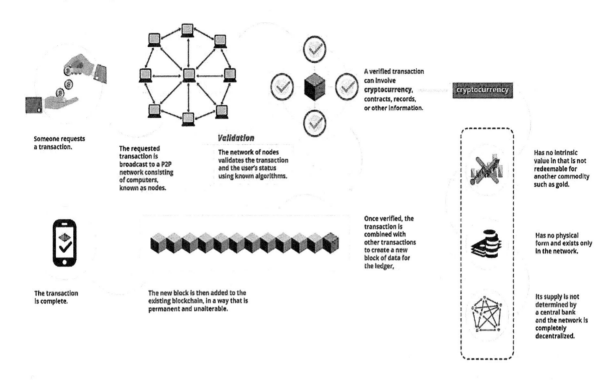

1. **Distributed Networks (Swan, 2015):** Usage of a distributed ledger technology opens up new options for secure collaboration creating trustworthy network between competitors.

2. **Programmable (Lee, 2017):** All the blocks created by verified transactions are individually encrypted.

3. **Anonymous and Secured (Veuger, 2018):** The identity of the verified transactions in the blocks created by individuals is either pseudonymous or anonymous. But it is worthy to note that this specific attribute is NOT a given, but it depends on the type of blockchain used.

4. **Time- Stamped and Immutable (Singhal et al., 2018):** The time frame of the transactions made by the individual in each block is stamped and recorded.

5. **Consensus (Atzori, 2015; Barabási, 2016, Hacker, 2017):** Each record and transaction made in the network has been verified and agreed in the block

Such a technology has developed by IT developers into three categories:

Blockchain 1.0: The Disruptive Technology Stack and Protocol, "Bitcoin"

Crypto-currency offers a welcomed alternative, particularly for those living in nations wrecked by high inflation like Zimbabwe, Venezuela, or Argentina. While more and more people enter the crypto-currency sphere, constraints are becoming opportunities for this new tech to be the solution of many of the people's problem. (Bentov, Gabizon and Mizrahi, 2016, Casey and Vigna, 2018):

Figure 2. Blockchain technology offers significant advantages
Source: [online] https://home.kpmg/xx/en/home

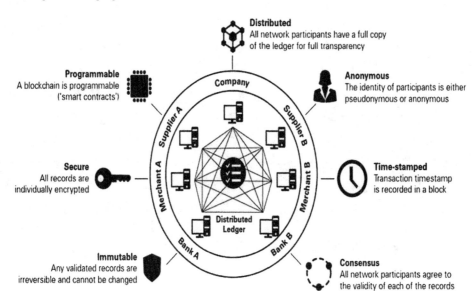

Firstly, Bitcoin transaction fees have expanded dramatically with the expansion of the network enabling blockchain utility as a means of exchange (Swan, 2015).

Secondly, the increasing number of voices in the crypto-currency space support the conclusion that blockchain simply do not scale (Bentov et al., 2016, Casey and Vigna, 2018)This conclusion can be reached by holding a comparison between centralized versus decentralized systems using an example from nature (see Figure 3 which shows grasses versus trees) (Swan, 2015; Tayeb, 2018)

Figure 3 depicts the structures formed by units of decentralized networks which simply do not reach the size of units of centralized networks (Mendling et al., 2018). This is not a reflection of the superiority of one model rather; each is suited to unique contexts. Changing climatic patterns can turn a forest into savanna, or desert into grassland (Zook and Blankenship, 2018).

In light of these circumstances, it becomes necessary to consider how blockchain can be utilized to address the grievances being felt worldwide as a result of the political and economic status quo (Mendling et al., 2018; Ølnes, Ubacht and Janssen, 2017; Swan, 2015).

Bitcoin as a Community-Based Cryptocurrency

According to a number of authors there are two essential considerations when adopting Bitcoin: (Zook and Blankenship, 2018):

1.   To achieve the adoption of the fiat currency system.
2.   To structure the distribution of the fiat currency system.

"Bitcoin, crypto currencies and Fiat currencies all have a common element; THEY ARE ALL WORTHLESS."

Figure 3. Comparison of centralized vs. decentralized systems in nature
Source: adapted by author

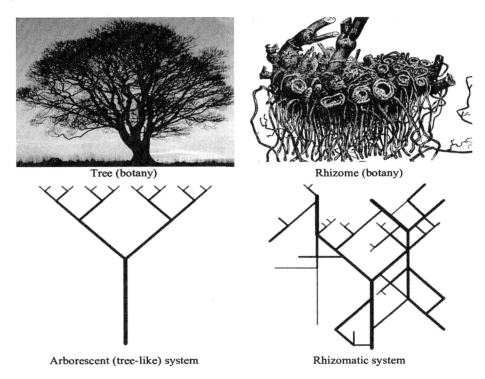

Some would argue the validity of the previous statement, but in the simplest notion they all incur value placed on them due the societies, acceptance of the systems governing them; giving way to their value to be assigned and then transferred between members of the community.

A currency will only have value if people use it and assign value to it. There is currently a competition between, established crypto-currencies, Banks and governments. This means any currency seeking to enter the market at this point in time needs a unique strategy to create a real competitive advantage and provide something that is lacking in the market as a whole. (Young, 2018; Zalan, 2018)

This leads to a discussion on the distribution of the currency. The success of a currency depends on the ability to distribute it to an enormous number of users. Distribution of a currency should consider both qualities as well as quantity dimensions. This is an essential issue that must be considered when seeking to build a crypto-currency social movement (Schmitt et al., 2015)

The birth of a number of crypto-currencies has made a principle increasingly clear- that an economy can be understood as a network and that Metcalfe's law for the valuation of networks application very much to currency networks (Tayeb, 2018; Zalan, 2018).

Metcalfe's law states that the value of a network is proportional to the square of the number of connected nodes in a network. In the case of currency, each user of the currency becomes a node in the network (Barabási, 2016).

From Bitcoin's inception, it has been clear that the success of a crypto-currency is propelled by a number of idealists promoting stability and development, while volatility is largely caused by those whose main interest in the currency is to make money (Zook and Blankenship, 2018). This means that,

Figure 4. An illustration of Metcalfe's law

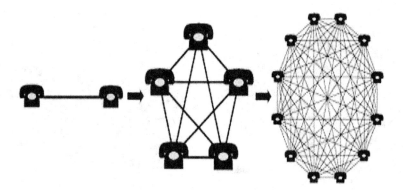

counter-intuitively, the best course for a currency is to seek out core supporters who are minimally interested in profit (Cong and He, 2018; Crosby et al., 2016)

Core supporters have to bear the most risk, and risk tolerance increases in proportion to how much the supporters identify with the ideals underlying the project. In the case of Bitcoin, development was driven largely by anarchists and libertarians, who believed in the power of the technology to bring about positive social change (Bentov et al., 2016)

While speculators and investors induced considerable volatility, they also play an essential role in the development of the infrastructure by attracting developers who then help build the infrastructure necessary for wider adoption. It is not, however, in the best interest of a currency to build on a basis of profit seeking investors. To survive the turbulent growth cycle of an emerging crypto-currency requires individuals who will under no circumstances give up on the project (Barabási, 2016; Beck et al., 2016).

Bitcoin did a spectacular job of addressing the concerns of a small subset of highly ideologically oriented individuals, and this group subsequently became the basis for wider adoption (Ølnes et al., 2017). The question is; can this technology (or a variation of it) be used to address the concerns of the global community in the same way that Bitcoin addressed concerns for the anarchist and libertarian communities. To answer this question, any analysis should consider which values are served (Mendling et al., 2018; Ølnes et al., 2017; Schmitt et al., 2015). In the case of the libertarian/anarchist community they are:

- The ability to circumvent unjust laws
- Freedom from theft via monetary expansion
- Self-determination (Zook and Blankenship, 2018)
- Protection from surveillance (Bentov et al., 2016)

BLOCKCHAIN 2.0: THE DEVELOPMENT OF SYNTAX ALLOWING FOR THE USE OF SMART CONTRACTS

Blockchain 2.0 creates a big tier in the development of blockchain disruptive technology. Such phase is still under development since there are many different understandings and standard classifications that are still emerging. Blockchain 2.0 signifies the development of "Decentralized Applications" that go beyond digital currency. Some of Blockchain 2.0 disruptive products are broadly referred to the

Bitcoin 2.0, Crypto 2.0, smart contracts, smart property (Arruñada and Garicano, 2018),(decentralized application), DAOs (decentralized autonomous organizations), and DACs (decentralized autonomous corporation) (Atzei, Bartoletti and Cimoli, 2017).

Whereas Blockchain 1.0 is referred to the decentralization of currencies and payments, Blockchain 2.0 is concerned with the decentralization of trading markets and transformation of assets beyond currency (Singhal et al., 2018). Unlike Bitcoin which can be considered a G1 or 1st generation blockchain unlike Ethereum and Hyper ledger that are considered to be G2 or 2nd generation blockchains; the difference lies in the G2 blockchains' ability to employ code and programmable smart contracts to build applications. Essentially allowing anyone to build his or her own "Bitcoin like app" but have it run on Ethereum. For that reason the Ethereum blockchain has expanded to over 1 terabyte, leading to the possibility of a decrease in the number of nodes due to the hardware requirements of operating a node (Swan, 2015). Ethereum is considered as the most open-ended and well-recognized decentralized software platform that empowers distributed application and smart contracts to be developed and work without fraud, downtime, interference or control from third party (Xu et al., 2016). Besides, Ethereum is a blockchain that employs a programming language, Solidity, to enable developers to build and publish distributed applications on Blockchain. (Atzei et al., 2017).

Smart Contracts

Smart contract is defined by Nick Szabo back to 1995 as "a computerized transaction protocol that executes the terms of a contract''. Smart property was the catalyst for the emergence of blockchain-based smart contracts (Karamitsos, Papadaki and Al Barghuthi, 2018; Preston et al., 2018). A smart contract addresses contractual terms programmatically using special algorithms in a way that allows a contract to automatically execute once the entered data matches the identified terms(English, Auer and Domingue, 2016). Smart contracts allow parties to sell realities, documents, money, exchange shares or any proprietary. The key feature of smart contracts is the absence of the intermediary services or brokers at the point of signing deals or performing transactions (English et al., 2016).

Smart contracts are stored as a onetime written code in the distributed register. Blockchain transactions have more extensive instructions embedded into the simple form of buy/sell currency transaction. Smart contracts are contracts that use Bitcoin to form agreements between two or more than two parties to perform a transaction to do or not to do something in exchange of something else via blockchain technology (Zook and Blankenship, 2018)

Trust is an important factor in the traditional form of contract agreement, so that all parties must trust each other that obligations will be met. On the other hand, trust is not up to the parties or a prerequisite for smart contracts. Smart contracts are automatically defined and executed by the codes that build trust in the system. The following are the key features that make smart contracts more distinct (Preston et al., 2018; Reheul, Van Caneghem and Verbruggen, 2014).

1. **Autonomy**, after launching and running a smart contract, the contract initiator might not need to be part of any further contact (Swan, 2015).
2. **Self-sufficient,** smart contracts should have the ability to collect money, understand and fulfill transactions, distribute resources e.g. raising funds by providing services and spending them on needed resources (Mendling et al., 2018).

3. **Decentralized,** in smart contracts there is no centralized server. The autonomy concept is built in the smart contract technology. This is described as decentralized service that is distributed and self-executed across network nodes (Zook and Blankenship, 2018).

Vending machine is a good example of a smart contract that acts astronomically when a person deposits money and, then, makes a selection, the item is released. A vending machine which works based on certain algorithm follows the same instructions set every time in every case (Wang et al., 2018).

Smart contracts and the cryptographically activated assets systems have raised a concern related to whether a new body of regulations is needed to distinguish between technically code-based contracts and the flexible lawfully compulsory human based contracts. Furthermore, smart contract impacts the notion of a social contract within society not only contract law. Therefore, for smart contracts it could be an array of legal frameworks as well as an array of currencies (Cong and He, 2018).

Smart Contract Technology: From simple Application to More Complex

Smart contracts allow common agreement problems to be released in a way that minimizes the need for trust that makes things more convenient by taking human judgment out of the analytic equation, thus allowing complete automation. A transaction can be created that remains on blockchain and goes uninitiated until certain future event or certain time triggers the transaction (English et al., 2016). Although, smart contracts running on blockchains have great potential in the financial domain, it is constrained by the cost and the lengthy transaction time; but this is currently being addressed by multiple Blockchains or the, G3, 3rd generation blockchains.

Smart contracts can be varied from simple ease of use to even more complexed utility in various verified transactions, reaching from simple structured financial agreements as a digital value exchange to complex structures such as distributed autonomies society as seen in figure 5 (Dolwick, 2009, Governatori et al., 2018).

Benefits and Limitations of Smart Contracts

The main benefits of smart contracts are related to a number of factors including elimination of unethical or biased behavior in signing transactions, data security through the use of decentralized register (data cannot be cyber attacked or lost), elimination of human errors and time saving due to automation (Ølnes et al., 2017).

There are limitations to the use of the smart contracts, with regards to different elements. The first limitation focuses on the inability to amend the smart contract after being published, acting as a hinder if there is a mistake in the code or if corrections to some of the key elements of the contract need to be revised. In addition, the lack of widely used circumstances to show whether smart contracts can meet the requirements of the stakeholders considering the immutability of blockchain i.e. any error in entering requirements' data cannot be corrected which constitutes a major source of risk (Karamitsos et al., 2018; Mendling et al., 2018; Preston et al., 2018). This requires a new blockchain language that can improve verification of stakeholders' requirements through enhancing the ability to capture valid requirements by offering constructs matching the conception of stakeholders (Huang & Chiang, 2017). Communication failure or other types of social conflicts need a mechanism to deal with this emerging

Figure 5. Smart contract technology from simple application to more complex
Source: https://blockchainhub.net/blog/infographics/smart-contracts-simple-complex/

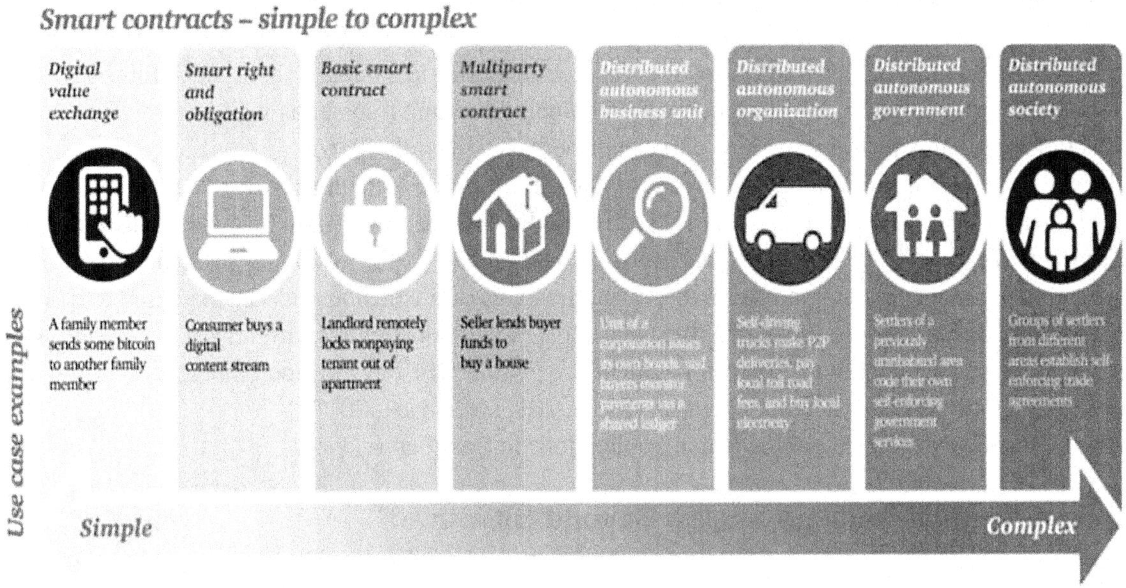

Smart contracts – simple to complex

| Digital value exchange | Smart right and obligation | Basic smart contract | Multiparty smart contract | Distributed autonomous business unit | Distributed autonomous organization | Distributed autonomous government | Distributed autonomous society |

Use case examples

| A family member sends some bitcoin to another family member | Consumer buys a digital content stream | Landlord remotely locks nonpaying tenant out of apartment | Seller lends buyer funds to buy a house | Use of a corporation issues its own bonds and buyers moving payments tax a shared ledger | Self-driving trucks made P2P deliveries, pay local toll road fees, and buy local electricity | Settlers of a previously uninhabited area code their own self-enforcing government services | Groups of settlers from different areas establish self-enforcing trade agreements |

Simple   Complex

tech i.e. lawyers with experience in IT might be needed to inform the future design of smart contracts to address the social as well as legal context (Sundaram et al., 2007).

BLOCKCHAIN 3.0: APPLICATIONS IN CURRENCY AND BUSINESS MARKETS

This stage started with the first incorporation of Bitcoin in a widely accepted setting as well as the publishing of the 1st decentralized app published on the Ethereum Blockchain. This classification is based on the ability to have a basic layer of tech with customizable solutions being created on top of that layer by members of the general public and not "Mass Adaptation".

Blockchain 3.0 is expected to be the most challenging phase to pass; with Government and private Sectors adaptation being the start of Blockchain 4.0, due to a couple of reasons:

1. The lack of Standards or Best Practices.
2. The wide spread misunderstanding concerning the technology itself and its uses, i.e. Bitcoin is Blockchain, is a statement that anyone in the blockchain sphere has heard more often than not.
3. The Disruptive nature of the technology that is still being explored to its fullest potential.
4. The need for legal frameworks that better serve the stakeholders in the industry in lieu of the ambiguous landscape that exists today. It is notable to look at progressive countries like Malta and Cyprus that introduced new Bills to help protect users and investors alike.

BLOCKCHAIN CASE USES

Blockchain Application in Financial Services

Blockchain technology can be implemented to disrupt the traditional banking ecosystem through allowing banks to perform financial transactions directly including fund transfer as well as foreign exchange transactions without a broker or a third-party intermediary (Burrell, 2016).

PayPal as an example of innovative payments market solution, is moving slowly towards Bitcoin aiming at larger scope of adoption (Sundaram et al., 2007). PayPal became a more formal payment industry, collecting and validating detailed personal information about its customers. It has been known for being at the top of financial service innovation, however, the focus of the business has been altered to be more corporate focused hence missing out on the chance to be the market leader with regard to Bitcoin. After announcing a partnerships with Bitcoin payment processors (Bit Pay) in September, 2014; PayPal is slowly moving towards full Bitcoin adoption (Swan, 2015; Yermack, 2017).

Figure 6 shows examples of blockchain applications in financial services.

Applications for Social-Financing Beyond Bitcoin

The expansion of the user base can be multiplied by means of a social financing model, whereby users must get recommendations from others in order to increase their likelihood of receiving financing (Atzori, 2015; Swan, 2015; Yermack, 2017). When a user invites someone to the network, the new user's actions will affect the reputation of the user who invites them (Crosby et al., 2016). This also ensures that users will select the highest quality members of their analog social networks to invite. This reputa-

Figure 6. Blockchain 3.0 application in business finance models

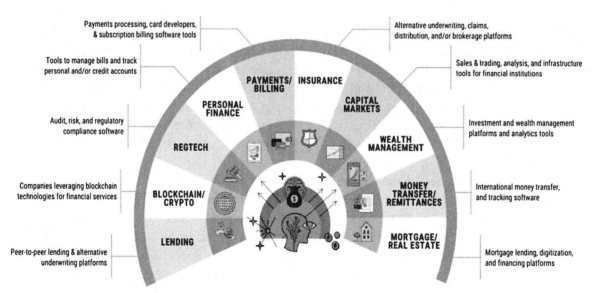

tion system could theoretically be applied to any application that has a rating function, for example, eBay, Air BnB, file sharing services, etc. (Dijkstra, 2017; Ølnes et al., 2017). A social trusted financial system can serve three main purposes:

1. To attract more users to the network by means of a sort of referral system whereby users must convince their family, friends, and neighbors to register in order to secure financing (Cong and He, 2018).
2. To incentivize honest behavior in contracts through both peer pressure and the promise of rewards (Li et al., 2018).
3. To filter out unethical funding behaviors and make application islands of trusted community, and to eventually link these to form larger ventures (Yermack, 2017).

Applications for Project Backers

People who need to invest their saving money are invited by those who have investment experience and seeking financing and agree to support someone's project are called "project backers" (Kuppuswamy and Bayus, 2018). A project backer ties their reputation to a project. If the project is successful, their reputation increases. If the project is not profitable, their reputation goes down. Projects are ranked in the application based on an aggregate of the reputation of the backers and the user issuing the project (Agrawal, Catalini, & Goldfarb, 2014). Many studies highlighted the backing successful projects (Swan, 2015). There are three rewards for backing successful projects:

1. **Credit:** Backing a successful project is an indicator that a backer is part of an honest, hardworking, and successful community, so it results in an increase in reputation. This increases the likelihood that the backer will receive financing if they wish to request it (Swan, 2015).
2. **Block Reward:** With a higher reputation, the user will be able to claim more of the block reward, becoming a recipient of the currency distribution (Wang et al., 2018; Zalan, 2018).
3. **Money:** Backers, along with investors, will receive a small percentage of profits, proportional to their reputation (Reheul et al., 2014; Saarikko, Westergren and Blomquist, 2017).

Applications for Super-Backers and Collateral

A super-backer is essentially an ambassador for the platform who has reached a high level of trust, and who uses his knowledge of a community to help people gain financing (Swan, 2015). A system for pledge of collateral is integrated into the application, so new users entering the network can show goodwill via "crowd collateral." In the case of negligence or theft, part or all of the initial investment can be returned to the investors by the superior collecting on the collateral pledge. Supervisors also play an essential role in helping people who are unable to read register and use the platform. The supervisors allow the leveraging of informal, unwritten legal systems in use in many of the target communities. For the extra effort put in, super-backers receive a bigger share of profits than ordinary baker's (Kuppuswamy and Bayus, 2018).

Crowd-Funding Application, Initial or Security Coin/Token Offerings, ICOs/STOs

The Crowd-funding is another prime example of a financial services with blockchain-based decentralized models (Booth, 2015) . The idea is that peer-to-peer financial funding models can supplant the need for traditional venture capital funding for startups. Blockchain-based crowd-funding platforms create their own digital currencies and selling "crypto-graphic shares" to early backers (Booth, 2015). Swan, (2015) asserted that "Investors in a crowd-funding campaign receive tokens that represent shares of the startup they support. Some of the leading crypto-currency included a crowd-funding platforms include Swarm, an incubator of digital currency–focused startups that raised $1 million in its own crowd-funding, completed in July, 2014 (Swan, 2015). Holding the company's own crypto-currency, Swarm coin, gives investors rights to the dividends from the startups in the incubator's portfolio. Swarm has five projects comprising its first class of funded application: Manna, a developer of smart personal drone networks; Coins pace, an operator of a decentralized crypto-currency workplace; Swarm-ops, a decentralized organizational management software platform; Judo baby, a decentralized gaming platform; and DDP, a decentralized dance-party entertainment concept (Swan, 2015).

Expert in the Crowd-funding field argues over its legality that there is currently no legal way to do crowd-funding whereby a person actually owns shares in the underlying company and there might be chances for security law violation by crowd-funding. Crowd-funding platforms like Swarm, Koinify, and Ethereum sell non-share items, such as early access to software (Swan, 2015). in general, the marketing seems still to be about selling shares. The outcome is that some investors in crypto-currency projects might not get much more than early access to open source software in a decentralized yet a legal way (Veuger, 2018; Wang et al., 2018). More effective balances and checks is needed to crowd-fund Blockchain based projects under a decentralized legal way (Young, 2018; Zalan, 2018).

Extrapolating on the crowd-funding case use that signified the rise of blockchain and the noted recent surge in the prices of crypto-currencies; was actually misinformation and ignorance. People started investing in startup companies via ICOs, Initial Coin Offerings, these offerings are unregulated by any entity as a result scammer started using these ICOs to steal millions of dollars off of people. Today regulations are still being discussed on how to regulate these activities. Another aspect to ICOs is the Classification the Tokens, but this is not related to the underlying technology, Blockchain. Tokens of Crypto currencies exist in a blockchain by choice not as a default.

Smart Property Application

Blockchain can be employed for any form of asset including registry, inventory, exchange and trading that offers the opportunity of using multiple classes of application functionality across all types of businesses involved in currency and financial market transactions (Swan, 2015). According to Swan (2015), blockchain-encoded property is a smart property which can be managed and transacted using "smart contracts". Smart property uses blockchain-based models for all property transactions as a means for controlling ownership and access of an asset using smart contracts (Ølnes et al., 2017; Singhal et al., 2018; Sundaram et al., 2007; Swan, 2015)

In physical-world there are physical and intangible assets or properties. The former includes homes, cars, bicycles, computers, etc. and the latter combines assets such as stock shares, reservations, or

Figure 7. Smart property
Source: samer_hassan/law-is-code-blockchain-as-a-regulatory-technology

copyrights (e.g., e-books, music, illustrations, and digital fine art). Blockchain can be used to regulate the ownership of an asset that is registered as a digital asset. Every transaction is stored in the form of a block in the chain secured by a private key. A buyer is essentially buying a private key that will be used as a proof of ownership (Ølnes et al., 2017; Preston et al., 2018; Reheul et al., 2014). The owner of digital asset can sell it through transferring the private key to another party.

Government and authority parties control the ownership and the access to an asset that could be "smart matter" with blockchain embedded technology (Ølnes et al., 2017; Preston et al., 2018; Reheul et al., 2014; Salman and Razzaq, 2018) The concept of having assets to be considered as "Smart" is another example of blockchain smart property that is associated with physical assets for secure access of an asset. For example, blockchain technology can be embedded in a physical property (e.g. doors of a car or a house) and the access is controlled by digital records on the blockchain using the private keys as evidence of ownership. Smartphones can unlock based on confirming a user's digital identity encoded in the blockchain. The door of a physical property e.g. homes or cars can be "Smart" allowing secure access in a real time supported by embedding technology (e.g. software code, QR codes, sensor, Wi-Fi access, i-Beacons, NFC tags, etc.). Therefore, when a user who seeks access to a property has his software or hardware that matches the one of the property, the blockchain smart contract will send a token access to the physical property to open the door (Karamitsos et al., 2018).

With Blockchain, there is a new way regulate and enforce someone's copy rights via the use of smart contracts to allow for new ways to enable publish and sell their work digitally while preserving their legal rights without the need to worry about legal enforceability of contracts via the use of smart contracts.

BUSINESS CHALLENGES

The noted challenges related to the business model is that there are still many worthwhile revenue-generating products and services to provide a new business model in the new blockchain economy than the point of decentralized peer-to-peer models. By improving blockchain technology's infrastructure, scholars can understand blockchain principles, with many opportunities and other potential value-added (Christidis and Devetsikiotis, 2016; Crosby et al., 2016; Dijkstra, 2017; Xu et al., 2016). In the following part, the authors attempt to link the new blockchain 4.0 with the potential disruptive business models in terms of Governance, Decentralized Audits, Flags and Arbitration.

The contemporary issues in these challenges are:

Security and Governance

Collusion Attacks

One of the important concerns of this chapter is how to prevent the system from being tricked. The obvious attack vector is to create a number of puppet accounts and to run fraudulent transactions; that is, contracts that are not actually taking place. In this way reputation can be artificially increased. Accounts involved in suspicious contracts (for example, contracts involving large numbers of low reputation accounts) will have their reputation automatically and provisionally set to 0 (Arruñada and Garicano, 2018; Beck and Müller-Bloch, 2017; Christidis and Devetsikiotis, 2016; Crosby et al., 2016; Dijkstra, 2017; Xu et al., 2016). The main problem with this defense is that it will often flag innocent users as well (Atzori, 2015) .

Hacking a system requires extensive research and trial and error. There are a limited number of people with the ability and access to the resources necessary to hack a crypto-currency exchange or platform. It is logical that those who are capable of doing so are going to focus their attention on the most lucrative potential targets.

This is one advantage of a decentralized wallet system. If funds are stored locally on user devices and the average funds held by users are low, it makes the network, and most importantly the servers of applications running on the network, unattractive targets (Li et al., 2018).

Decentralized Audits

This can be worked around by means of a decentralized audit, whereby a user with sufficient reputation and identity verification who also has a provable degree of disconnection from the audited can independently verify the authenticity of projects by means of a personal visit, interview, and documentation of the authenticity of the project. Both the auditor and audit can be rewarded for a successful audit with an increase in reputation. It also has the beneficial side effect of increasing connections and trust between members of the network. The managers of the platform can initially decide the outcome of these audits, but as the network grows a governance structure must be phased in. For example, the auditor would have to be application roved by a minimum number of high reputation users, who communicate with both the auditor and the user requesting the audit (Atzori, 2015).

Flags and Arbitration

Behavior that goes against the terms and conditions of the blockchain may be flagged. If a group of five high reputation arbiters confirms that the behavior was a valid violation, the violator will receive a decrease in reputation and the user who reported the violation will receive an increase. If the flag turns out to be invalid, the user who reported the violation will receive a decrease in reputation. Arbitration can also be settled by selecting users, where their decision making clout is a reflection of their reputation (Beck and Müller-Bloch, 2017).

Blockchain Is Transforming Enterprise Business Models

A prime area for blockchain as a new model of business is related to the introduction of crypto-currencies to the traditional financial and banking services like cross-border transfers. In blockchain, peer to peer payment network allows direct financial transactions and funds across the involved parties without the need for a trusted intermediary or a third-party(Christensen, Raynor and McDonald, 2015; Christidis and Devetsikiotis, 2016). The following are simple situations where Blockchain tech can be deployed (Beck and Müller-Bloch, 2017):

- Pay as you go or Subscription Model: Pay only for services which are used.
- Customer experience model: Provide the customer with an experience they've never had before (Cong and He, 2018).
- On-demand model: Provide customer service on demand and with superior speed.
- Marketplace model: Provide a platform for buyer and seller interact with each other directly
- Free model: Provide the typical services to users free and sell their behavior data to different businesses
- Crowd-sourcing model: Receive money for engaging crowd for common goal, innovation, problem solving (Cong and He, 2018).
- Bundling model: Selling similar products or services together.
- Gamification model: Use of game-like feature to simplify the User interaction experience.
- Bloch chain new platform business model: how blockchain technology can replace inefficient back-office systems or create new business models (Azar and Raouf, 2017; Dogru, Mody and Leonardi, 2018).

Blockchain and Its Application in Smart Property Finance

Disruptive FINTECH in property world developed some important competencies such as dynamic skills and capabilities, strategic alliances, customer engagement's mechanism and governance and level trust for public and private acceptance (Veuger, 2018). The disruption changes in different fields, education, healthcare, retailing and transportation markets have their impacts on the technology of the property investment and its new comer's investors consequently. In order to know, what the impacts of blockchain on the property world are, the authors need to address how disruptive FINTECH work in property world (Mendling et al., 2018).

Blockchain Technology has met the expectations of stakeholders across various industries to make record keeping more efficient. The development of blockchain was behind the decentralized digital currency, crypto-currency (bitcoin) as verification technology (Li et al., 2018; Ølnes et al., 2017) Blockchain allows actors in a system called nodes or miners to distribute data structure through moving coins/token from one peer to another (digital assets: TenX, OMG, Red Pulse) using a Peer to Peer (P2P) network. By using public key and digital signature, all owners of the digital assets and the transactions will be recorded on a ledger (Li et al., 2018; Singhal et al., 2018). Every transaction in the network is validated by the nodes through employing different consensus protocols such as Proof of Work, Proof of stake, etc. Blockchain is a general technology term, but each Blockchain implements a consensus protocol that governs the blockchain see figure (4). Each blockchain has its own protocol and, therefore each protocol has a different coin/token based on the application used on the protocol (Yermack, 2017).

This is an open system of blockchain, there is another blockchain system called closed blockchain where the security was controlled by consortium consensus mode. In such blockchain system, transactions do not have economic incentives to exchange digital assets as there is no need for a crypto-currency or token because of the governed security consortium (Azar and Raouf, 2017; Dogru et al., 2018).

Blockchain Technology in Real Estate Investment Validation

Is the real estate sector, investment validation and valuation are going though changes due to the introduction of new business models driven by disruptive technologies that real estate market can use to organize and manage the sector. (Veuger, 2018). Blockchain technology has emerged as a disruptive technology to support authentication and trusted information transactions for businesses, governments and society and can present the next step in e-government enhancement (Ølnes et al., 2017).

The real estate market stakeholders (like notaries, brokers, property owners, developers, notaries and the land registry) use blockchain as distributed real estate database in order to maintain a growing list of recorded properties and real estate services and items which plays an important role in hardening against manipulation and counterfeiting. Blockchain innovation, therefore, a profound, irreversible, anticipatable tilting of real estate ecosystem (Dijkstra, 2017). Most Blockchain technology literature have focused on the architectural and the technology application levels in the first place, addressing blockchain technology

Figure 8. Blockchain technology, protocol, and cryptocurrency/token
Source: Adapted from (Arruñada and Garicano, 2018; Beck and Müller-Bloch, 2017; Christidis and Devetsikiotis, 2016; Crosby et al., 2016; Dijkstra, 2017; Xu et al., 2016)

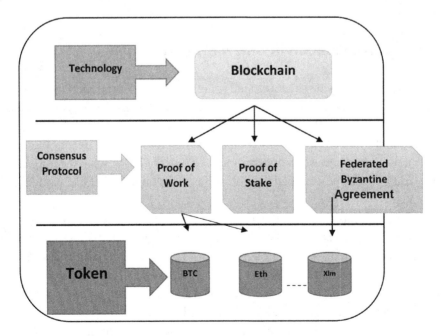

benefits and challenges and redesign opportunities for better use of information exchange in the private domain. Ølnes et al., (2017) revealed that hardly any study has addressed and explored in a systematic manner the blockchain business, government or social models.

The International Monetary Fund (IMF) also contributes to main requirements of disruptive FINTECH to the changes in financial and thus real estate system in April 2017. It summarized the main viability determinants of competitive development of blockchain FINTECH in financial and real estate investment development as follows (Veuger, 2018):

- Strategizing (long term and large external focus);
- Transforming leadership style (connecting leadership);
- Flexibility of work design (flexible organization) (Kaplan and Haenlein, 2016); and
- Useful modelling and application (flexible IT usages).

Disruptive FINTECH in real estate world developed some important competencies such as dynamic skills and capabilities, strategic alliances, customer engagement mechanisms and governance and level trust for public and private acceptance (Veuger, 2018). The disruption changes in different fields, education, healthcare, retailing and transportation markets have their impacts on the technology of the real estate investment and in turn on its new investors. In order to know, what are the impacts of blockchain on real estate world? Figure 5 depicts how disruptive FINTECH works in real estate world (Atzori, 2015; Preston et al., 2018).

CONCLUSION

As the world is being disrupted by new innovations; people are rapidly embracing the Internet of Things (Christidis and Devetsikiotis, 2016) gadgets in their day-to-day lives. However, Personal data and cybersecurity have become the prime concern for business, customers and governments alike. In such cases 'Blockchain Technology' offers a convenient and virtual solution for connected devices (Swan, 2015).

Blockchain technology has become the new engine of enterprise growth in digital economy via Internet to conduct digital commerce and share personal data and life events. This new digital disruption revolution of blockchain, in its first category, uses cryptography to create a crypto-currency, as an alternative issued and controlled by code and the ledger is open and transparent with no central entity to regulate it. Numerous new accounts application eared on forums predicting the doom of the bitcoin main chain (Young, 2018). Blockchain contributes to the business environment; not only new digital currencies but also the use of smart contracts to automate processes and enhance the security of asset and portfolio management. Assets ranging from equipment, shipping containers, and warranties to healthcare records and data related to supply chains can now be shared, exchanged, or transferred via blockchain networks more efficiently, and with greater collaboration and less risk to shareholders, than is practical using traditional centralized approaches. In the Blockchain Revolution tiers 1.0, 2.0 and 3.0 (Swan, 2015), the crypto-currencies and smart contract technologies have contributed to social community core values including (Alketbi, Nasir and Talib, 2018; Atzori, 2015; Casey and Vigna, 2018; Dijkstra, 2017; Huang and Chiang, 2017; Kaplan and Haenlein, 2016; Karamitsos et al., 2018):

- Justice and Fairness
- Transparency and honesty (Swan, 2015)
- Accountability
- Helping those in need
- Trading in real assets
- Avoiding speculation (Karamitsos et al., 2018; Veuger, 2018)
- Prohibition of interest
- Profit/Risk sharing (Cong and He, 2018)
- Minimizing harm to living creatures, i.e. social and environmental consciousness
- Maximizing Wellbeing, i.e. optimal wealth distribution and employment opportunities (Li et al., 2018; Veuger, 2018).

There are vast array of applications or problems that can be solved using Blockchain based technology, spanning from Financial (remittance to investment banking to non-financial applications like Notary services (Ali et al., 2016). But for now, there is still much research needed to come up with best practices and standards for the industry.

Companies in the industry will need to conduct thorough SWOT analysis and create a real add-value to the community. By doing that companies will be able to address the new emerging threats to their eco-system from various stakeholders in society:

- Ignorance from the general public.
- Increasing fears by traditional businesses from the disruptive capabilities of such a technology.
- The implementation of restrictive legal frameworks to try to control the industry and monitor it.
- The emergence of scammers that will utilize the technology to steal money.
- The low barrier to entrants in the sector; increases the number of companies that will likely fail due to the fact that they have no business plan nor have they got any experience or the network to make their platform succeed.

Blockchain technology can replace the old system that required "Conveyers of Trust" (Third Parties) to limit the number of hidden costs in any transaction. It could also be used to shift fees for low reputation addresses, thereby further increasing the cost of a spam attack (Burrell 2016; Ali et al. 2016).

REFERENCES

Ali, M., Nelson, J. C., Shea, R., & Freedman, M. J. (2016). Blockstack: A Global Naming and Storage System Secured by Blockchains. *USENIX Annual Technical Conference*, 181-194.

Alketbi, A., Nasir, Q., & Talib, M. A. (2018). Blockchain for government services—Use cases, security benefits and challenges. In *Learning and Technology Conference (L&T), 2018 15th* (pp. 112-119). IEEE. 10.1109/LT.2018.8368494

Arruñada & Garicano. (2018). *Blockchain: The birth of decentralized governance*. Academic Press.

Atzei, N., Bartoletti, M., & Cimoli, T. (2017). A survey of attacks on ethereum smart contracts (sok). In Principles of Security and Trust (pp. 164-186). Springer.

Atzori, M. (2015). *Blockchain technology and decentralized governance: Is the state still necessary?* Academic Press.

Azar & Raouf. (2017). Sustainability issues in the GCC. In *Sustainability in the Gulf* (pp. 27–30). Routledge.

Barabási, A.-L. (2016). *Network science.* Cambridge University Press.

Beck & Müller-Bloch. (2017). *Blockchain as radical innovation: a framework for engaging with distributed ledgers as incumbent organization.* Academic Press.

Beck, R., Czepluch, J. S., Lollike, N., & Malone, S. (2016). Blockchain-the Gateway to Trust-Free Cryptographic Transactions. ECIS.

Bentov, I., Gabizon, A., & Mizrahi, A. (2016). Cryptocurrencies without proof of work. In *International Conference on Financial Cryptography and Data Security* (pp. 142-157). Springer. 10.1007/978-3-662-53357-4_10

Booth, P. (2015). Crowdfunding: A Spimatic application of digital fandom. *New Media & Society, 17*(2), 149–166. doi:10.1177/1461444814558907

Burrell, J. (2016). How the machine 'thinks': Understanding opacity in machine learning algorithms. *Big Data & Society, 3*(1). doi:10.1177/2053951715622512

Casey & Vigna. (2018). In blockchain we trust. *MIT Technology Review.*

Christensen, C. M., Raynor, M. E., & McDonald, R. (2015). What is disruptive innovation. *Harvard Business Review, 93,* 44–53. PMID:17183796

Christidis, K., & Devetsikiotis, M. (2016). Blockchains and smart contracts for the internet of things. *IEEE Access: Practical Innovations, Open Solutions, 4,* 2292–2303. doi:10.1109/ACCESS.2016.2566339

Cong, L. W., & He, Z. (2018). *Blockchain disruption and smart contracts.* National Bureau of Economic Research. doi:10.3386/w24399

Crosby, M., Pattanayak, P., Verma, S., & Kalyanaraman, V. (2016). Blockchain technology: Beyond bitcoin. *Applied Innovation, 2,* 6–10.

Dijkstra, M. (2017). *Blockchain: Towards disruption in the real estate sector. In An Exploration on the Impact of Blockchain Technology in the Real Estate Management Process.* Delft: University of Delft.

Dogru, Mody, & Leonardi. (2018). *Blockchain Technology & its Implications for the Hospitality Industry.* Academic Press.

Dolwick, J. S. (2009). 'The social' and beyond: Introducing actor-network theory. *Journal of Maritime Archaeology, 4,* 21-49.

English, M., Auer, S., & Domingue, J. (2016). Block chain technologies & the semantic web: a framework for symbiotic development. In J. Lehmann, H. Thakkar, L. Halilaj, & R. Asmat (Eds.), Computer Science Conference for University of Bonn Students (pp. 47–61). Academic Press.

Governatori, G., Idelberger, F., Milosevic, Z., Riveret, R., Sartor, G., & Xu, X. (2018). On legal contracts, imperative and declarative smart contracts, and blockchain systems. *Artificial Intelligence and Law*, *26*(4), 377–409. doi:10.100710506-018-9223-3

Hacker, P. (2017). *Corporate Governance for Complex Cryptocurrencies? A Framework for Stability and Decision Making in Blockchain-Based Monetary Systems*. Academic Press.

Huang & Chiang. (2017). *RegTech Evolution: The TrustChain*. Academic Press.

Jun, M. (2018). Blockchain government-a next form of infrastructure for the twenty-first century. *Journal of Open Innovation: Technology, Market, and Complexity*, *4*(1), 7. doi:10.118640852-018-0086-3

Kaplan, A. M., & Haenlein, M. (2016). Higher education and the digital revolution: About MOOCs, SPOCs, social media, and the Cookie Monster. *Business Horizons*, *59*(4), 441–450. doi:10.1016/j.bushor.2016.03.008

Karamitsos, I., Papadaki, M., & Al Barghuthi, N. B. (2018). Design of the Blockchain Smart Contract: A Use Case for Real Estate. *Journal of Information Security*, *9*(03), 177–190. doi:10.4236/jis.2018.93013

Kuppuswamy, V., & Bayus, B. L. (2018). Crowdfunding creative ideas: The dynamics of project backers. In The Economics of Crowdfunding (pp. 151-182). Springer.

Lee, I. (2017). Big data: Dimensions, evolution, impacts, and challenges. *Business Horizons*, *60*(3), 293–303. doi:10.1016/j.bushor.2017.01.004

Li, J., Greenwood, D., & Kassem, M. (2018). *Blockchain in the built environment: analysing current applications and developing an emergent framework*. Diamond Congress Ltd.

Mendling, J., Weber, I., Aalst, W. V. D., Brocke, J. V., Cabanillas, C., Daniel, F., ... Dustdar, S. (2018). Blockchains for business process management-challenges and opportunities. *ACM Transactions on Management Information Systems*, *9*(1), 4. doi:10.1145/3183367

Ølnes, S., Ubacht, J., & Janssen, M. (2017). *Blockchain in government: Benefits and implications of distributed ledger technology for information sharing*. Elsevier.

Preston, J. D., Preston, D. A., Vance, T. M., Simpson, B. C., Madakson, P. A., & Rieger, W. R. (2018). *Systems and methods for using smart contracts to control the trade, supply, manufacture, and distribution of commodities*. US Patent App. 15/675,697.

Reheul, A.-M., Van Caneghem, T., & Verbruggen, S. (2014). Financial reporting lags in the non-profit sector: An empirical analysis. *Voluntas*, *25*(2), 352–377. doi:10.100711266-012-9344-3

Saarikko, T., Westergren, U. H., & Blomquist, T. (2017). The Internet of Things: Are you ready for what's coming? *Business Horizons*, *60*(5), 667–676. doi:10.1016/j.bushor.2017.05.010

Salman, A., & Razzaq, M. G. A. (2018). Bitcoin and the World of Digital Currencies. In *Financial Management from an Emerging Market Perspective*. InTech. doi:10.5772/intechopen.71294

Schmitt, A. J., Sun, S. A., Snyder, L. V., & Shen, Z.-J. M. (2015). Centralization versus decentralization: Risk pooling, risk diversification, and supply chain disruptions. *Omega*, *52*, 201–212. doi:10.1016/j. omega.2014.06.002

Singhal, B., Dhameja, G., & Panda, P. S. 2018. Blockchain Application Development. In Beginning Blockchain (pp. 267-317). Springer. doi:10.1007/978-1-4842-3444-0_5

Sundaram, S., Schwarz, A., Jones, E., & Chin, W. W. (2007). Technology use on the front line: How information technology enhances individual performance. *Journal of the Academy of Marketing Science*, *35*(1), 101–112. doi:10.100711747-006-0010-4

Swan, M. (2015). *Blockchain: Blueprint for a new economy*. O'Reilly Media, Inc.

Tayeb, S. (2018). *Blockchain Technology: Between High Hopes and Challenging Implications*. Academic Press.

Veuger, J. (2018). Trust in a viable real estate economy with disruption and blockchain. *Facilities*, *36*(1/2), 103–120. doi:10.1108/F-11-2017-0106

Vovchenko, N., Andreeva, A., Orobinskiy, A., & Filippov, Y. (2017). Competitive Advantages of Financial Transactions on the Basis of the Blockchain Technology in Digital Economy. *European Research Studies*, *20*, 193.

Wang, P., Liu, X., Chen, J., Zhan, Y., & Jin, Z. (2018). QoS-aware service composition using blockchain-based smart contracts. In *Proceedings of the 40th International Conference on Software Engineering: Companion Proceeedings* (pp. 296-297). ACM. 10.1145/3183440.3194978

Xu, X., Pautasso, C., Zhu, L., Gramoli, V., Ponomarev, A., Tran, A. B., & Chen, S. (2016). The blockchain as a software connector. In *2016 13th Working IEEE/IFIP Conference on Software Architecture (WICSA)* (pp. 182-191). IEEE. 10.1109/WICSA.2016.21

Yermack, D. (2017). Corporate governance and blockchains. *Review of Finance*, *21*, 7–31.

Young, S. (2018). Changing Governance Models by Applying Blockchain Computing. *Catholic University Journal of Law and Technology*, *26*, 4.

Zalan, T. (2018). Born global on blockchain. *Review of International Business and Strategy*, *28*(1), 19–34. doi:10.1108/RIBS-08-2017-0069

Zook, M. A., & Blankenship, J. (2018). New spaces of disruption? The failures of Bitcoin and the rhetorical power of algorithmic governance. *Geoforum*, *96*, 248–255. doi:10.1016/j.geoforum.2018.08.023

Chapter 6
Blockchain Technology in Solar Energy

Erginbay Uğurlu
Istanbul Aydın University, Turkey

Yusuf Muratoğlu
Hitit University, Turkey

ABSTRACT

Two of the important topics concerning scientists and governments are blockchain and climate change. After the paper of Satoshi Nakamoto, blockchains became a global phenomenon. After its usage for cryptocurrencies, blockchain is starting to be used for digital protocols and smart contracts. Blockchain technology is used in many sectors, such as banking, finance, car leasing, entertainment, energy, etc. Climate change leads to global warming, which means the long-term warming of the planet. Therefore, governments have made an effort to decrease global warming or keep it stable. One of the mitigation ways of global warming is to use renewable energy. Solar energy is one of the most used types of renewable energy sources, and also blockchain technology is widely used in this sector. In this chapter, the authors investigate the use of blockchain technology in the solar energy sector.

INTRODUCTION

Blockchain provides peer-to-peer transaction platforms that use decentralized storage to record all transaction data. Blockchain applications are used in different industries. These industries are digital securities trading industry, digital identity industry, proof of ownership industry, peer-to-peer transactions industry, network infrastructure industry, etc. Based on their stage of development Blockchain applications can be divided into three broad categories namely: "Blockchain 1.0", "Blockchain 2.0", "Blockchain 3.0". The first category comprises cryptocurrencies, the second category represents a digital protocol, and the last category is the stage where the smart contract concept is developed.

Solar energy is one of the renewable energy sources which is essential for sustainable human life and fight against climate change. Solar energy is widely used green energy type which can intelligently integrate the actions of all connected users thus they can both produce and consume electricity using

DOI: 10.4018/978-1-5225-9257-0.ch006

smart-grid technologies. The users, which both produce and consume electricity are called as a "pro-sumers" Smart-Grid system has some advantages such as improve the robustness of grid, self-healing capability of grid and internality of the grid. Also, a smart-grid system has some characteristics such as; reliability, security, efficiency, deployment and integration of distributed resources, generation demand response and demand-side resources, advanced electricity storage and peak-shaving technologies, etc. Because the countries mitigate environmental degradation; they start to use Smart Grid.

Smart grid systems have different technologies, but mostly centralized technologies have been used in the sector. Blockchain is better than non-decentralized technologies owing to transparent transactions and no single user controls. Compared with traditional methods; using decentralized technology, the distance between generation sites and load centers are decreasing. Moreover decentralized public ledger is a barrier of vulnerabilities of a central store of data. For the solar energy prosumers; it provides a safe and easy way to exchange their energy production.

One of the Blockchain project in smart grid is provided by Belgian Enervalis company and Dutch Eemnes Energie company. Also, there are some projects in UK and USA which use Blockchain technology. For example, LO3 Energy, a young New York company, is working in the Brooklyn Microgrid project. In UK Centrica company aim to make a local energy market using Blockchain technology,

The contributions of the chapter to the book are providing knowledge of Blockchain technology and Blockchain usage in solar energy production. We do not aim to provide information about the logic of the blockchain but aim to focus on blockchain in solar energy production. The first section is an introduction, in the second section fundamentals of smart grid and solar energy are discussed generally. In the third section, the chapter will be focused on blockchain applications in solar energy production smart-grid systems. In the last section of the chapter, the chapter will be summarized.

SMART GRID IN SOLAR ENERGY

Solar Energy

Solar energy is one of the types of renewable energy sources. Non-renewable energy sources are finite, dependent, the emitter of greenhouse gasses and more expensive than renewable energy sources because of these reasons renewable energy is essential for sustainable human life. In recent years renewable power capacity of the world has been increased, and the most used renewable energies are solar PV, wind power and hydropower. According to the International Renewable Energy Agency, IRENA (2018) the costs of renewable energy have declined therefore the capacity of the renewables has been increased, by 2017. Cumulative global investment in the sector totaled USD 2.9 trillion since 2004.

Perez and Perez (2009) present the planetary energy reserves for both renewables and non-renewables. Figure 1 presents the known reserves; in the figure yearly potential energy is given for renewables because they are not finite, known reserves are given for the fossil and nuclear resources because they are finite.

It can be understood from Figure 1, the difference of the potential of solar energy from other renewable and non-renewable sources' potential is very high.

Solar energy is generated from the sun. The sun emits light and heat in the form of electromagnetic radiation; this radiation is captured and turn into energy. Thus it is called solar energy. One of the challenges of the solar energy is its density; solar energy density is influenced by location, season and some other factors. Also after the sunlight has reached the earth's atmosphere, effects resulting from weather,

Figure 1. Comparing finite and renewable planetary energy reserves (Terawatt years)
Source: Perez and Perez (2009)[1]

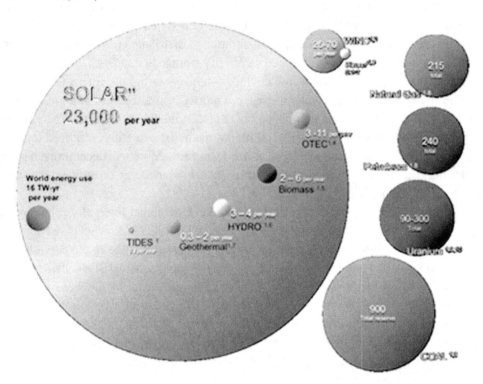

and photon absorption by water vapor, ozone, and other atmospheric constituents reduce the solar energy density (Neville, 1995). In addition to all these, to capture the radiation, electromagnetic waves must be converted to useful heat or electricity by using a material that can absorb the energy of a photon by placing an electron into a higher energy level thus this process cannot do efficient and cost-effective devices (Mackay, 2015).

According to Tabak (2009), solar energy use was started as "passive solar." Passive solar means that a suite of technologies that use the Sun's energy directly, usually for heating and cooling. Ancient Indian and Greek homes are the example of passive solar technologies. In these civilizations, homes were built to absorb the maximum amount of sunlight during the coldest days. In the 1990s, growing attention of passive solar then today it is widely common in new building designs mostly the Netherlands and Germany.

As is stated above the sunlight is captured, and solar energy is converted to electricity or heat, these process made by thermal method or photovoltaic method. The thermal method is concentrating solar power by mirrors or another type of reflectors to produce high temperature to generate water vapour or other liquids with high pressure to rotate turbines to generate electricity (Wasfi,2011). Photovoltaic (PV) technology converts sunlight into electricity without first converting it into heat. This method electrical current is generated as photons from sunlight. In PV technology solar cells have the backbone of the system. They have to have high performance, low-cost concentrators, which only work well in direct sunlight. To ensure these conditions different kinds of cells are used. According to Inganas and Sundstrom (2016), silicon photovoltaic cells, hybrid organic/inorganic solar cells and solid-state organic solar cells are developed in current technology.

Based on their system configuration PV systems can be divided into three categories: stand-alone PV system, grid-connected PV system, and hybrid PV system. The basic PV system principles and elements remain the same (Jäger et al., 2014). Xiarchos and Vick (2011) give information about PV grids. The authors state that: Although most household devices use AC electricity, PV systems produce DC power. Therefore, the output of the PV is converted to AC with an inverter. PV applications are divided into two categories: on-grid systems and off-grid systems. On-grid PV systems are connected to the utility grid; off-grid PV systems are not connected to the utility grid. A grid-tied electrical system is a semi-autonomous electrical generation system which links to the local electrical grid. Sometimes excess electricity may be generated; in this case, it feeds the excess electricity back into the grid. On-grid systems solar system connected to the electrical grid directly thus there is no need to battery storage. Therefore, a grid-tied system costs less than an off-grid system.

Smart Grid in Solar Energy

Electrical grid refers to the interconnected transmission system. The power grid is a platform that realizes energy conversion and power transmission; because of the countries mitigate the environmental degradation, they start to use Smart Grid and try to develop it related with their national conditions (Sun et al., 2011). "A Smart Grid is an electricity network that can intelligently integrate the actions of all users connected to it - generators, consumers and those that do both—in order to efficiently deliver sustainable, economic and secure electricity supplies" (Vijayapriya and Kothari,2011). Sun et al. (2011) define Smart Grid is an inevitable trend of the power grid. Also, they state that features of smart grids, which had not been in traditional grids, are information, automation, and interoperation. Smart Grid system includes generation, transmission, and distribution.

Not only governments/countries but also many well-known companies try to develop smart grid systems such as IBM Smart Grid Maturity Model, the DOE Smart Grid Development Evaluation System, the EPRI Smart Grid Construction Assessment Indicators, and the EU Smart Grid Assessment Benefits Systems. Smart grids turned energy consumers to energy producers. The new paradigm came in to use in the energy sector: prosumers. The role of the users is transformed from passive users to active players by using smart grids. Smart grid users "not only consume the energy; they also produce and supply the energy back to the grid. This type of energy user is known as a prosumer" (Rathnayaka et al., 2012). Mainly Microgrids or Smart Microgrids are used for energy consumers, producers, and prosumers at a small scale and are able to manage themselves.

Gomez-Sanz (2014) discuss the elements that make power grid to smart grid such as sensor and metering network, network nodes with computation capabilities, switches or actuators. Smart grid setup can be changed and have to capability of plug-in or plug out new devices. Also, these elements should provide answers to how such capabilities could be incorporated coherently. Moreover, El-Hawary (2014) gives eleven issues concerned to develop a smart grid and its elements that are below:

1. Aging and underinvested infrastructure.
2. Overstressed system equipment.
3. To reduce CO_2 emissions and increase energy efficiency.
4. Increasing distance between generation sites and load centers.

5. Combination of power generation in the world. Central power plants and large numbers of small, decentralized generation in the market.
6. Intermittent and fluctuating energy availability of renewable energy sources.
7. Additional and new consumption models
8. Increasing cost and regulatory pressures.
9. Utility unbundling increased energy trading.
10. Consumers need transparent consumption and pricing.
11. Regulatory necessities are pushing for more competitive and lower energy prices.
12. There is a need for securing supply and meeting the increase in energy needs.
13. Utilities need to adopt information and communication technologies to handle new operational scenarios and challenges while maintaining profitability and retaining the ability to invest in infrastructure
14. Efficient and reliable transmission and distribution of electricity are fundamental to maintaining functioning economies and societies.
15. Sustainability.

In addition, El-Hawary (2014) refers to attributes and impediments of a smart grid. Attributes are efficiency, accommodation, motivation, opportunism, focusing quality, resiliency and being green. Impediments are negative perceptions of the engagement of stakeholders, increasing security risk, high initial costs, fear of obsolesce and privacy.

Due to its continuous availability, solar power is most used renewable energy sources in smart grids. In the solar power sector, smart grid technology provides a new energy value chain, facility to reduce CO_2 emission. Also, it is needed to streamline the distributed solar power generation; smart grids help to feed electricity into the grid by using rooftop arrays (Swaminathan and Umashankar,2012). Consumer interest is growing in the solar power system and rooftop solar PV in line with the developing technology of smart grid technologies.

BLOCKCHAIN TECHNOLOGY IN SOLAR ENERGY

Blockchain Technology in Renewable Energy Sector

Although there are intermediate companies and regulatory institutions in energy sector blockchain technology makes transactions in the energy sector decentralized. Therefore blockchain technology has disruptive effects on the energy sector. Renewable energy (RE) prosumers sell their excess energy easier than before, using blockchain technology.

Hagström and Dahlquist (2017) present criteria to help to understand whether blockchain should be used or not in the energy sector. The criteria are named as Greenspan's blockchain criteria. Table 1 shows the reasons to use or not to use blockchain according to Greenspan's criteria.

Montemayor and Boersma (2018) provide information about companies involved in blockchain and energy in their report. The key statistics of the companies used in the report are: %64 of them are from the European continent, the top countries are the Netherlands, Germany and the USA, around %50 of

Table 1. Greenspan's criteria on the energy sector

Criteria	Why Blockchain?	Why Not Blockchain?
Shared database, decentralized	Several actors in the energy sector.	No necessary in-house.
Multiple writers	All actors are active in their part of the chain.	May not be affected by others' transactions.
Absent of trust	Companies not trusting companies, users not trusting users	User to the company has high trust.
No central governance	If wanting more transparency, more actors with equal power	Big actors want to keep power. Regulations decide
Transactions dependent on each other	Proving that you have what you are selling	If there is trust, there is no need for proof

Source: Hagström and Dahlquist (2017), p. 53

the projects use Ehtereum, and nearly %74 of the companies started/founded in 2016 or 2017. They divide the companies into five categories based on their field, that are peer-to-peer companies, utility-scale companies, cryptocurrency companies, platform companies, electric vehicles (EV) companies, and other companies. Table 2 to 7 show started/founded year and country of the companies and their blockchain technology.

Peer-to-peer companies mainly focus on blockchain applications such as P2P energy trading or decentralized energy projects. They are summarized in Table 2.

Utility-scale companies aim to use blockchain and other tools to provide energy or transform energy infrastructure. A few companies are specialized about this aim that are below in Table 3.

Cryptocurrency companies share their energy using a blockchain technology or generate tokens which represent cash value. Table 4 summarizes the information of these companies.

Platform companies aim to develop a common open source network based on Blockchain or develop the sharing network for the energy industry, etc. (See Table 5).

Another category is EV companies in Table 6. They use blockchain technology for the payment system for parking or charging etc. of the vehicles.

The rest of the companies are categorized in other that are shown in Table 7.

Blockchain Technology in Solar Energy Sector

Whereas there is no consensus of definition of Blockchain, theories and researches are developing about it, and the application in the energy field has just begun and has great potential. Using blockchain in energy sector gives many advantages to both producers and consumers.

Blockchain has five characteristics such as decentralization, openness, automatic execution contract, traceability, anonymity (see: Figure 2) and four key technologies such as a consensus mechanism, encryption algorithms, the smart contract, and distributed data storage (Wu & Tran,2008). Further information about these characteristics and key technologies is given in the following sections.

In a centralized network; central nodes control the network, and if removed, the network fails. In a decentralized network, each nodes contributes to the control of the network. A distributed network

Table 2. Peer-to-peer companies

Company	Country	Year	Blockchain
Power Ledger	Australia	2016	Ethereum
Divvi	Australia	2017	Ethereum
Too much.energy	Belgium	2017	N/A
Energo Labs	China	2016	Qtum
Ponton	Germany	2001	Tendermint
Conjule	Germany	2017	N/A
Oursolargrid	Germany	2016	Ethereum
WePower	Gibraltar	2017	Ethereum
Greeneum	Israel	2016	Ethereum
OneUp	Netherlands	2014	N/A
Energy21 & Stedin	Netherlands	2013	Quasar
ToBlockchain	Netherlands	2009	N/A
PowerPeers	Netherlands	2016	N/A
Energy Bazaar	Netherlands	2017	Ethereum
Solar Bankers	Singapore	2011	Skyledger
SunContract	Slovenia	2016	Ethereum
Pylon Network	Spain	2017	Own
Verv by Green Running LTD	UK	2015	Ethereum
Dajie	UK	2017	N/A
BP/Shell/Statoil	UK	2017	N/A
LO3 Energy	US	2016	Own
Grid+	US	2017	Ethereum
Volt Markets	US	2016	Ethereum
OmegaGrid	US	2017	N/A

Table 3. Utility-scale companies

Company	Country	Year	Blockchain
Electron	UK	2015	Ethereum/ IPFS
Drift	US	2011	Ethereum
TenneT/IBM/Vandebron/Sonnen	Netherlands	A pilot project in 2017	Hyperledger
Fortum	Finland	2016	N/A
CGI & Eneco	Netherlands	2017	Tendermint

Table 4. Cryptocurrency companies

Company	Country	Year	Blockchain
Spectral Energy	Netherlands	2017	MultiChain
EcoCoin	Netherlands	2016	Hyperledger
ElectriCChain/SolarChange/SolarCoin	Andorra	2016	Multichain efforts:
NRG Coin	Belgium	2015	Ethereum
Veridium	Hong Kong	2017	Ethereum
ImpactPPA	US	2017	Ethereum
Energi Token/Energi Mine	UK	2017	Ethereum
Farad	UAE	2017	Ethereum

Table 5. Platform companies

Company	Country	Year	Blockchain
Grid Singularity	Austria	2016	Own
BTL Group	Canada & UK	2015	Own (Interbit)
Energy Blockchain Labs	China	2016	Hyperledger
DAISEE	France	2016	Ethereum
Slock.it	Germany	2015	Ethereum
StromDAO	Germany	2017	Fury Network
DAO IPCI	Russia	2016	Own
Alastria	Spain	2017	Own
Energy Web Foundation	Switzerland	2017	Ethereum
Prosume	Switzerland	2016	Own
EnLedger	US	2016	Own

Table 6. EV companies

Company	Country	Year	Blockchain
Oxygen Initiative	US	2014	Ethereum
Share&Charge	Germany	2016	Ethereum
Car eWallet	Germany	2017	Hyperledger
Everty	Australia	2016	Ethereum

the computers or nodes are full nodes; therefore, control is distributed equally throughout the network (Figure 3).

Transactions are verified by the nodes in the network with consensus among them. For the consensus, different blockchain protocols use different consensus algorithms such as Proof of work, Proof of stake, Practical Byzantine Fault Tolerance. Figure 4 shows the process of the transaction which is written below:

Table 7. Other

Company	Country	Year	Blockchain
CarbonX	Canada	2017	Ethereum
M-PAYG	Denmark	2013	N/A
Guardtime	Estonia	2007	N/A
Freeelio	Germany	2016	Tobalaba
Solar DAO	Israel	2017	Ethereum
Clearwatts	Netherlands	2017	BigchainDB (Ocean
WaveX	Saudi Arabia	2016	ArabianChain
BCDC (BlockChain Development Company)	Scotland	2017	Ethereum
The Sun Exchange	South Africa	2015	N/A
Bankymoon	South Africa	2014	N/A
Poseidon	Switzerland	2017	Stellar.org
MyBit	Switzerland	2017	Ethereum
4New	UK	2017	N/A
DNVGL/Deloitte	UK	2017 (1864)	Own

Figure 2. The characteristics of blockchain
Source: Wu & Tran (2018), p. 5

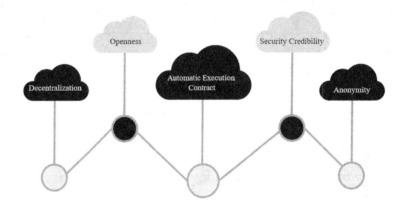

Figure 3. Different Network Structures
Source Hagström & Dahlquist (2017) p.10

1. A transaction is suggested.
2. Transaction sent.
3. Transaction is verified
4. The transaction is put into a block, and it is added to the blockchain.
5. The transaction is completed.

Blockchain technology has been widely used in solar energy all over the world. In Austria Wien Energie and Grid Singularity companies, in Germany Innogy, Oursolargrid and Freeelio companies company, in the UK Electron company, in USA LO3 Energy company, in Australia Power Ledger company, in the Netherlands PowerPeers company, in Singapore Solar Bankers company, in Andorra ElectriCChain company, in South Africa The Sun Exchange company, in Denmark M-Payg company, in Saudi Arabia WaveX company and in Israel Solar DAO company (Montemayor and Boersma, 2018, Basden and Cottrell, 2017) use blockchain in the solar energy sector. However, the companies mentioned here are not all companies in the sector, they are more than mentioned here.

"Compared to the existing power grids, the Energy Internet involves a wider variety of energy forms and broader participants, and it changes the interactive mode of information to build a new type of energy supply system with multi-energy complementary and highly integrated energy and information" (Ming& Jun, 2017). In blockchain technology trading can be done without a central actor; in traditional energy systems, transaction among consumers, producers, banks take many days, but in the blockchain technology, there are no intermediate controlling transactions. Furthermore, these developments change billing, charging, validating and the trading process of the solar energy market. By these developments, financial and operational transaction cost is decreasing

Notwithstanding so many companies aim to use the blockchain technology in solar energy, one of the first operational examples in Europe was obtained from the Dutch Government in Eemnes in 2018 (altenergymag, 2018). The project is carried out from Belgian tech provider Enervalis and Dutch energy provider Eemnes Energie under the consultancy of Bax & Company.

Enervalis were founded in 2013. It builds the artificial intelligence (AI) SmartPowerSuite® software as a service (SAAS) of the future energy systems. SmartPowerSuite® is used in energy monitoring, forecasting of availability and usage, data visualization of all systems, heating and ventilation control, flexibility control and energy trading. The core element of SmartPowerSuite® is 'Internet of Energy.'

Figure 4. The process of a transaction on blockchain
Source: https://www.pwc.com/gx/en/industries/assets/pwc-blockchain-opportunity-for-energy-producers-and-consumers.pdf

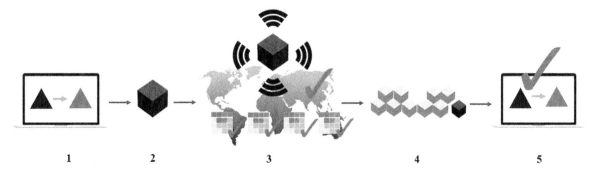

Internet of Energy (IoE) design resilience, redundancy, security, and low barrier enablement also uses the bidirectional flow of energy and information within the smart grid (Jaradat et al., 2015).

Enervalis currently focuses on three market segments: Smart Electric vehicle (EV) charging, Smart buildings, and Smart Micro-grids. They have operations in Belgium, Netherlands, Spain, and USA. Figure 5 shows the proposed solutions of Enervalis.

The key technologies of the blockchain are consensus mechanism, encryption algorithms, the smart contract, and distributed data storage. Likewise, a microgrid is described as decentralized energy resources (DER) and energy storage systems (ESS) which are operated in coordination (Goranovic et al., 2017). The decentralized structure of blockchain looks like as if designed for microgrids. Any house, which is equipped with a PV system, a heat pump, a hot water storage system and multiple sensors, have to estimate its optimal use of different systems. Weather forecasts and machine learning driven energy consumption predictions are used for this estimation. This process can be applied to an environment which is consisted of different buildings. The process aims to optimize the total energy consumption for the environment. Although it is aimed to optimize the total energy consumption of the environment, sometimes group or subgroup of prosumers can lead to an overall better solution. To get this solution, information of individuals must be transferred within the group as resilient and tamper-secure. Therefore the use of blockchain is suggested to provide this transfer. Figure 6 compares the transformation of traditional processes and processes in a blockchain-based system.

Although the purpose of the chapter is not to explain the blockchain technology but aims to explain the use of blockchain technology in the solar energy sector, we will briefly discuss foundational principles of the technology to understand its usage in the sector. At first, blockchain can be divided into three categories based on access permissions and alteration capabilities. If anyone is able to access the blockchain, it is called as public blockchain. If specific groups control blockchain it is consortium blockchain; at last, if one individual owns it, it is private blockchain. Furthermore, blockchain can be classified according to architectures, their development purpose, governance and protocol rules of the system operations (Andoni et al. 2019). The authors define these classifications; regarding architectures, public permissionless ledgers, and private permissioned ledgers, regarding the development purpose, general purpose and specific purpose, regarding classification, open-source or closed-source.

Moreover, there is a hybrid approach for these classifications, which use a combination of each classification's categories. In addition blockchain technologies have different consensus algorithms. The

Figure 5. The proposed solution of Enervalis
Source: https://tbb.innoenergy.com/wp-content/uploads/2015/11/Enervalis.pdf

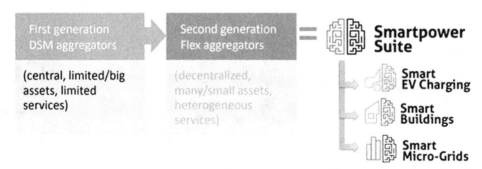

Figure 6. Compare of transformation of traditional processes and blockchain processes
Source: https://www.pwc.com/gx/en/industries/assets/pwcblockchain-opportunity-for-energy-producers-and-consumers.pdf

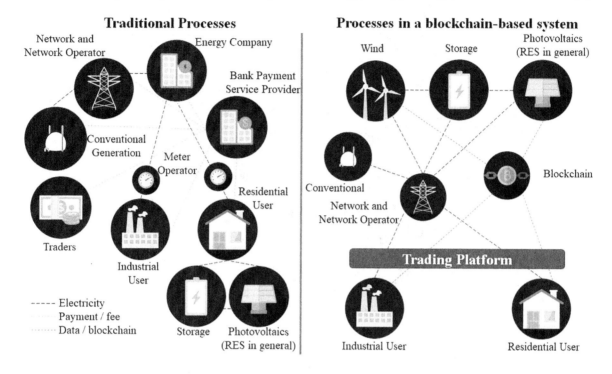

algorithms determine the performance of blockchain technology such as scalability, transaction speed, transaction finality, security and spending of resources such as electricity. The algorithms are Proof of Work (PoW), Proof of Stake (PoS), Practical Byzantine Fault Tolerance (PBFT), Proof of Elapsed Time (PoET), Proof of Burn (PoB), Byzantine Fault Tolerance (BFT), Proof of Activity (PoAc), Proof of Capacity (PoC), Proof of Authority (PoAu), Federated Byzantine Agreement (FBA), Delegated Proof of Stake (DPoS) and Round Robin-based (RR). According to the study on 140 blockchain initiatives in the energy sector mostly used algorithms are PoW, BFT, PoAu and PBFT with the percentage of %55, %15%13 and %8 respectively. Figure 7 presents the percentage of the Blockchain use cases in the energy sector according to consensus algorithm used.

Konashevych (2018) analyzes the features of the selected blockchain projects. The selected projects are Ethereum, NXT, Maidsafe, Colored coins, Ripple, Omni Layer (Mastercoin), Counterparty, Dash, Zerocoin. The author states that there are seven common properties in these projects: self-organized, self-governed, crypto rules, open ledger, public peer-to-peer computer network, distributed cooperation with no intermediaries and open source code. These properties were used to distinguish the projects in the paper. The process of blockchain technology in microgrid consists of some task. In the first step smart controllers are authenticated which have their own "wallet"/"address" in the blockchain, in the second step information of produced and consumed energy are stored in the wallet therefore wallet shows the current stock of energy and allows a participant to make peer-to-peer transaction, in the last step users make deals to buy-sell electricity directly with each other. In this process transaction between participants

Figure 7. Percentage of the blockchain use cases

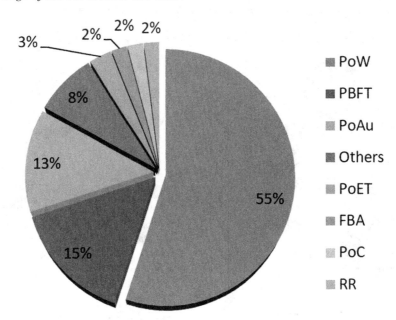

*For a more accurate representation see the electronic version.

of the microgrid is done by "smart contracts." Also, there is no need for manual and centralized managing and intermediaries. West and Parker (2017) define smart contracts as a "concept are not intrinsically linked to the blockchain. 'Smart contract' is often used interchangeably with a broad range of terms, from 'smart legal contract' to 'digital contract' to 'smart contract code.' Generally, the definitions include some type of automated, self-executing transaction." In the blockchain technology, smart contracts are stored and digitally executed between two or more parties. Smart contracts are implemented automatically by defined parameters, such as an event or price. For example in Share&Charge, smart contracts sources will be published on GitHub after completing ongoing security audits. In Table 8 selected projects are presented by Blockchain, blockchain type, consensus mechanism, open source.

According to Goranovic et al. (2017), two innovative blockchain projects in the solar energy sector have done by Key2 Energy and LO3 Energy. In the Key2Energy uses blockchain to transactions and smart contracts. The project is for multi-apartment houses provide self-generated PV energy. The members of the project can be divided into two groups; one aims to maximize revenue other aims to minimize cost. To get this aims one agent is a solar energy producer, and other is a consumer. Other projects are leaded by LO3 Energy; the company developed TransActive Grid platform and Brooklyn Microgrid project. In the platform blockchain is used to create microgrid intelligence system, in the Brooklyn Microgrid, P2P blockchain is used to generate renewable energy for the local market where the produced solar energy surplus can be sold. Another project is ElectriCCChain which is launched in 2016 from the consortium "Chain of Things" (Nehaï and Guerard, 2017 and Meinel et al., 2018) launched the project. The project approach aims to link a combination of several blockchains and to send the real-time usage data to a blockchain. In the process of ElectricChain, the transaction between two agents are done by blockchain. Figure 8 presents a transaction between two persons that are "A" and "B." "A," produced 8 kWh, consumed 5 kWh and still has 3 kWh; "B" needs 4 KWh (Nehaï and Guerard, 2017).

Table 8. Technical comparison

Projects	Blockchain	Blockchain Type	Consensus Mechanism	Open Source
PWR.Company TransActiveGrid TheSunExchange	Ethereum	/	PoW	/
PowerLedger	EcoChain Ethereum	Public Private	PoW PoS	X
BrooklynMicrogrid	Ethereum	Public	PoW	/
Share&Charge	Ethereum	Public	PoS	X
NRGcoin	various	Public Private	various	X
GrünStromJeton	Ethereum	Public Private	PoA	X
SolarCoin	Litecoin	Public	PoW	/
Bankymoon	Bitcoin	Public	PoW	/
GridSingularity	Ethereum EWF	Public	PoW PoA	X
Electron	Ethereum	/	PoW	X

Notes: / and x denotes no information available and attribute applies respectively.
Source: Goranovic et al. (2017), p. 657

Figure 8. Process of an energy transaction
Source: Meinel et al. (2018), p. 77

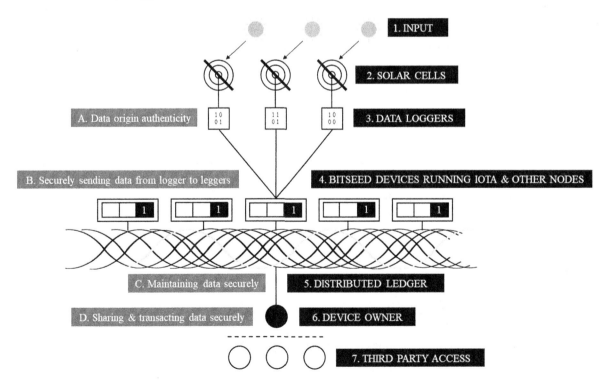

The flow of the process occurs in two levels which are microgrid level and miners level. In the microgrid level, there are six steps; then in the miners level, there are two steps. The steps are defined below Nehaï and Guerard (2017):

Microgrid level:

1. "A" wants to send 3 kWh to "B."
2. The microgrid checks whether it is possible to perform a transaction, based on the electrical routing and the power line support.
3. Once the routing is validated, the microgrid allows to "A" to transmit the amount of energy to "B," concerning the capacity of the lines to support the transaction.
4. The microgrid demands the 1 kWh left for "B" to the T&D network for meeting conditions of the transaction.
5. The network provides the remaining 1 kWh to the microgrid.
6. Finally, the microgrid sends to "B" the 1 kWh.

Miners level:

1. A transaction wanted to be carried out between two persons of the same microgrid according to the rules of the smart contract (A and B), "A" wants to send 3 kWh to "B."
2. The transaction between "A" and "B" is stored in a block with other transactions, and ready to be verified by miners. If the proof-of-stake (PoS) is verified, the block is validated and then stacked on the oldest chain.

Transactive Grid project has set the goal of conjunction with blockchain and IoT technology. In Brooklyn Microgrid project the first trial was completed and in the first-ever energy transaction recorded in blockchains worldwide (Andoni et al., 2019). The trial includes five prosumers and five neighboring consumers. Prosumers traded their surplus electricity, which is registered in the blockchain, between neighbors by smart contracts. Figure 9 shows the transaction process of Transactive Grid (Meinel et al. 2018).

In this section, several blockchain projects in the solar energy sector are reviewed, and their process is introduced. The section shows that blockchain technology is an innovative technology for the energy sector. Although in the sector there are small-scale projects the number of companies is growing and spreading to the world. As a new technology, it must prove its speed and security — also, some distinctions among the projects concerning the blockchain, blockchain type, consensus mechanism, etc. Users of the technology have to choose some different types of the blockchain, but there is no consensus on types.

CONCLUSION

Blockchain technology first used in Bitcoin and cryptocurrency then blockchain starts to use in many sectors. Moreover, it has disruptive and revolutionary effects on the sectors. In this chapter, we provide information blockchain technology in the solar energy sector. The scope of the chapter is to discuss the

Figure 9. Transactive grid transaction local energy with neighbors
Source: Meinel et al. (2018), p. 78

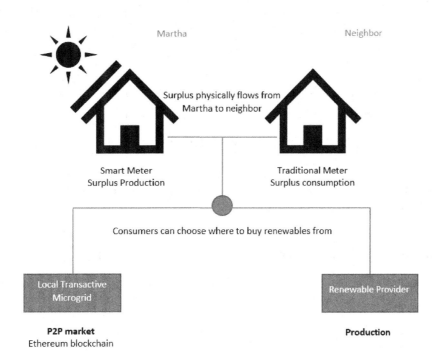

logic of blockchain, the logic of smart girds, and blockchain process in energy production and energy providers that uses blockchain to manage renewable energy grids.

The results show that blockchain promotes environmental and economic benefits for smart grid users. Also, it helps to share energy between users. The contribution of this work is to provide an overview of the fundamentals of blockchain technologies in renewable energy and solar energy. Moreover, we present major projects in the solar energy sector which use blockchain technology.

REFERENCES

Altenergymag. (2018). Retrieved from https://www.altenergymag.com/news/2018/01/15/bax--company-co-develop-first-large-scale-peer-to-peer-energy-market-in-nl/27712/

Andoni, M., Robu, V., Flynn, D., Abram, S., Geach, D., Jenkins, D., ... Peacock, A. (2019). Blockchain technology in the energy sector: A systematic review of challenges and opportunities. *Renewable & Sustainable Energy Reviews*, *100*, 143–174. doi:10.1016/j.rser.2018.10.014

Basden, J., & Cottrell, M. (2017). How utilities are using blockchain to modernize the grid. *Harvard Business Review*.

Cohn, A., West, T., & Parker, C. (2017). Smart After All: Blockchain, Smart Contracts, Parametric Insurance, and Smart Energy Grids. *Georgetown Law Technology Review*, *1*(2), 273–304.

El-Hawary, M. E. (2014). The smart grid—State-of-the-art and future trends. *Electric Power Components and Systems, 42*(3-4), 239–250. doi:10.1080/15325008.2013.868558

Gomez-Sanz, J. J., Garcia-Rodriguez, S., Cuartero-Soler, N., & Hernandez-Callejo, L. (2014). Reviewing microgrids from a multi-agent systems perspective. *Energies, 7*(5), 3355–3382. doi:10.3390/en7053355

Goranović, A., Meisel, M., Fotiadis, L., Wilker, S., Treytl, A., & Sauter, T. (2017). Blockchain applications in microgrids an overview of current projects and concepts. In *Industrial Electronics Society, IECON 2017-43rd Annual Conference of the IEEE* (pp. 6153-6158). IEEE. 10.1109/IECON.2017.8217069

Hagström, L., & Dahlquist, O. (2017). *Scaling blockchain for the energy sector*. Uppsala: University of Uppsala.

Inganäs, O., & Sundström, V. (2016). Solar energy for electricity and fuels. *Ambio, 45*(1), 15–23. doi:10.100713280-015-0729-6 PMID:26667056

IRENA. (2018). *Renewable Energy Policies in a Time of Transition*. Retrieved from https://www.irena.org/publications/2018/Apr/Renewable-energy-policies-in-a-time-of-transition

Jäger, K. D., Isabella, O., Smets, A. H., van Swaaij, R. A., & Zeman, M. (2016). *Solar Energy: Fundamentals, Technology and Systems*. UIT Cambridge.

Jaradat, M., Jarrah, M., Bousselham, A., Jararweh, Y., & Al-Ayyoub, M. (2015). The internet of energy: Smart sensor networks and big data management for smart grid. *Procedia Computer Science, 56*, 592–597. doi:10.1016/j.procs.2015.07.250

Konashevych, O. I. (2016). Advantages and current issues of Blockchain use in Microgrids. *Electronic Modelling, 38*(2), 94–103.

Mackay, M. E. (2015). *Solar energy: An introduction*. OUP UK. doi:10.1093/acprof:oso/9780199652105.001.0001

Meinel, C., Gayvoronskaya, T., & Schnjakin, M. (2018). Blockchain: Hype or Innovation. *Hasso-Plattner-Institute, Prof.-Dr.-Helmert-Straffe*, 2-3.

Montemayor, L., & Boersma, T. (2018). *Comprehensive Guide to Companies involved in Blockchain& Energy Blockchain Business*. Retrieved from https://ipci.io/wp-content/uploads/2017/12/Energy-Blockchain-Report.compressed.pdf

Nehaï, Z., & Guerard, G. (2017). Integration of the Blockchain in a smart grid model. In *The 14th International Conference of Young Scientists on Energy Issues (CYSENI)* (pp. 127-134). Academic Press.

Neville, R. C. (1995). *Solar energy conversion: the solar cell*. Elsevier.

Perez, R., & Perez, M. (2009). A fundamental look at energy reserves for the planet. *IEA SHC Solar Update*. Retrieved from http://www.asrc.cestm.albany.edu/perez/Kit/pdf/a-fundamental-lookat%20the-planetary-energy-reserves.pdf

Rathnayaka, A. J. D., Potdar, V. M., & Kuruppu, S. J. (2012). Design of smart grid prosumer communities via online social networking communities. *International Journal for Infonomics, 5*(1/2), 544–556. doi:10.20533/iji.1742.4712.2012.0062

Sun, Q., Ge, X., Liu, L., Xu, X., Zhang, Y., Niu, R., & Zeng, Y. (2011). Review of smart grid comprehensive assessment systems. *Energy Procedia*, *12*, 219–229. doi:10.1016/j.egypro.2011.10.031

Swaminathan, G., & Umashankar, S. (2012, November). Influence of Solar Power in Smart Grids. *Energetica India Magazine*, 52-53.

Tabak, J. (2009). *Solar and geothermal energy*. Infobase Publishing.

Vijayapriya, T., & Kothari, D. P. (2011). Smart grid: An overview. *Smart Grid and Renewable Energy*, *2*(04), 305–311. doi:10.4236gre.2011.24035

Wasfi, M. (2011, February). Solar Energy and Photovoltaic Systems. *Cyber Journals: Journal of Selected Areas in Renewable and Sustainable Energy*, *1*(2), 1–8.

Xiarchos, I. M., & Vick, B. (2011). *Solar energy use in US agriculture: Overview and policy issues*. US Department of Agriculture, Office of the Chief Economist, Office of Energy Policy and New Uses.

ADDITIONAL READING

Andoni, M., Robu, V., Flynn, D., Abram, S., Geach, D., Jenkins, D., ... Peacock, A. (2019). Blockchain technology in the energy sector: A systematic review of challenges and opportunities. *Renewable & Sustainable Energy Reviews*, *100*, 143–174. doi:10.1016/j.rser.2018.10.014

Brilliantova, V., & Thurner, T. W. (2018). Blockchain and the future of energy. *Technology in Society*. doi:10.1016/j.techsoc.2018.11.001

Marke, A. (Ed.). (2018). *Transforming Climate Finance and Green Investment with Blockchains* (1st ed.). London: Elsevier.

Mengelkamp, E., Notheisen, B., Beer, C., Dauer, D., & Weinhardt, C. (2018). A blockchain-based smart grid: Towards sustainable local energy markets. *Computer Science-Research and Development*, *33*(1-2), 207–214. doi:10.100700450-017-0360-9

Singhal, B., Dhameja, G., & Panda, P. S. (2018). Introduction to Blockchain. In *Beginning Blockchain* (pp. 1–29). Berkeley, CA: Apress. doi:10.1007/978-1-4842-3444-0_1

Singhal, B., Dhameja, G., & Panda, P. S. (2018). *Beginning Blockchain: A Beginner's Guide to Building Blockchain Solutions*. Apress. doi:10.1007/978-1-4842-3444-0

Tyagi, H., Agarwal, A. K., Chakraborty, P. R., & Powar, S. (Eds.). (2018). *Applications of Solar Energy*. Springer Singapore. doi:10.1007/978-981-10-7206-2

Van Rijmenam, M., & Ryan, P. (2018). *Blockchain: Transforming Your Business and Our World*. Routledge. doi:10.4324/9780429457715

KEY TERMS AND DEFINITIONS

Blockchain: Essentially a distributed database of records or public ledger of all transactions or digital events that have been executed and shared among participating parties. Each transaction in the public ledger is verified by consensus of a majority of the participants in the system.

Cryptocurrency: A type of digital currency that uses cryptography for security and anti-counterfeiting measures.

Microgrid: A group of interconnected loads and distributed energy resources within clearly defined electrical boundaries that acts as a single controllable entity with respect to the grid.

Renewable Energy: An energy produced from sources that do not deplete or can be replenished within a human's life time, any naturally occurring, theoretically inexhaustible source of energy.

Smart Contracts: A set of promises, specified in digital form, including protocols within which the parties perform on these promises.

Smart Grid: An electricity network that can intelligently integrate the actions of all users connected to it—generators, consumers, and those that do both—in order to efficiently deliver sustainable, economic, and secure electricity supplies.

Solar Energy: Any type of energy generated by the sun. Solar energy is created by nuclear fusion that takes place in the sun.

ENDNOTE

[1] OTEC = Ocean thermal energy conversion. Numbers on the right exponents show the source of the data in the paper: 1. S. Heckeroth, Renewables.com, adapted from Christopher Swan (1986): Sun Cell, Sierra Club Press 2. C. Archer & M. Jacobson, Evaluation of Global Wind Power -- Stanford University, Stanford, CA 3. World Energy Council 4. G. Nihous, An Order-of-Magnitude Estimate of Ocean Thermal Energy Conversion (OTEC) Resources, Journal of Energy Resources Technology -- December 2005 -- Volume 127, Issue 4, pp. 328-333 5. R. Whittaker (1975): The Biosphere and Man -- in Primary Productivity of the Biosphere. Springer-Verlag, 305-328. ISBN 0-3870-7083-4. 6. Environmental Resources Group, LLC http://www.erg.com.np/hydropower_global.php 7. MIT/ INEL The Future of Geothermal Energy-- Impact of Enhanced Geothermal Systems [EGS] on the U.S. in the 21st Century http://www1.eere.energy.gov/geothermal/egs_technology.html -- based on estimated energy recoverable economically in the next 50 years. Ultimate high depth potential would be much higher. 8. BP Statistical Review of World Energy 2007 9. http://www.wise-uranium. org/stk.html?src=stkd03e 10. R. Price, J.R. Blaise (2002): Nuclear fuel resources: Enough to last? NEA updates, NEA News 2002 – No. 20.2 11. Solar energy received by emerged continents only, assuming 65% losses by atmosphere and clouds.

Chapter 7

Paradise Found?
The Disruption and Diversification of Funding in Higher Education

Edward Lehner

https://orcid.org/0000-0001-6487-5410
Bronx Community College, USA

John R. Ziegler
Bronx Community College, USA

ABSTRACT

This chapter conceptualizes a process for cryptocurrency to diversify traditional methods of higher education funding in the United States. Cryptocurrency funding augments traditional revenue streams and shifts the discussion of education costs from expenses to a more robust conversation about innovative avenues to wealth generation as a potential solution to fund the mission of American higher education. This chapter acknowledges the central concerns of higher education funding as it explores these arguments as legacy discourses rooted in career preparation, accessibility and affordability, and arguments about the need for a broad-based education vs. more technical skills training. Further, an alternative model to current higher education funding models is presented, and if deployed, this asset class could help to serve education needs by funding research, students, and the academy through an illustrated conceptual framework for funding.

INTRODUCTION

If higher education is not already amid what may be legitimately characterized as a funding crisis (The Pew Charitable Trusts, 2015), then it inevitably will be (Barr & McClellan, 2018; Roger & Baum, 2017). In response, this conceptual chapter presents a framework whereby cryptocurrency can serve as a wealth-generation model to open a new avenue in the vital, complex discussion around higher education funding. The existing conversation tends to pit investment in students, viewed as human capital, against the expenses of education, a discourse that is historically entwined with discussions about the

DOI: 10.4018/978-1-5225-9257-0.ch007

workforce and corporate needs to recruit technically skilled workers (Alexander & Kim, 2017; Barr, 2004; Chan, 2017). In contrast, this chapter maintains that funding for higher education must be approached as a longstanding and ongoing issue not merely of human capital but also of access to higher education as a human right. The authors elucidate this position in five sections: (1) higher education as a human right and its alignment with career outcomes; (2) careerism, technological disruption, and a call for new funding models; (3) cryptocurrency as wealth generator and enacting disruption of higher education funding; (4) coin farming, revenue stream, how it works, and an example model; and (5) conclusion, limitations, and future research.

HIGHER EDUCATION AS A HUMAN RIGHT AND ITS ALIGNMENT WITH CAREER OUTCOMES

Viewing higher education as a human right does not mean that it cannot simultaneously benefit the nation and the individual. While Keller (2006), for instance, who examined an international sample of countries, concluded that lower levels of education should be financially prioritized, she also avowed, "College enrollment rates and expenditures thereon are important to political rights" (p. 32). Further, McMahon and Oketch (2013), examining citizens of the United Kingdom, quantified higher education's effects on individuals' life opportunities, arguing that higher education is a type of inalienable right and therefore must be accessible and affordable if industry is to access a pool of qualified and well-trained applicants. Similarly, McMahon (2009) maintained that a generous higher education funding policy directly correlates with the public good and a modern human capital approach, an approach through which he argued for considering and valuing not only the market but also the nonmarket benefits of higher education. McMahon (2009) reminded us that higher education confers advantages beyond the economic, which can affect the welfare of households and communities, including of future generations.

Existing scholarship that examines human capital theory and its relationship to the economic growth of the nation state notes that in the U.S., citizens' well-being, as well as the well-being of the nation state itself, is highly interconnected with the state's investment in human capital (Clemes, Hu, & Li, 2016; McMahon, 2009; Neher, Patterson, Duffield, & Harvey, 2017). However, Jemielniak and Greenwood (2015) highlighted a growing neoliberal cast to social and economic policy related to higher education, policy which tends to underfund important projects for development of human capital in disadvantaged classes. For example, The Pew Charitable Trusts (2015) observed that since the Great Recession, federal funding for higher education continues to decline, placing a growing financial burden on the states and ultimately, on individual students and families. Leachman, Masterson, and Wallace (2016) reported that these increasing burdens and the concomitant decline in funding are now fixtures of the reality facing higher education leadership, and the almost certain persistence of these conditions is underscored by the fact that after nearly a decade of economic growth, educational funding has yet to reach even pre-recession levels.

Since the end of World War II, higher education in the U.S. has greatly expanded and democratized a social institution that had previously centered primarily on providing opportunities for society's elite. By the early 1950s, as Thelin (2011) wrote, higher education had rapidly expanded due to a unique combination of veteran enrollment, expanded federal funding, and unprecedented philanthropic support. Further, Hutcheson and Kidder (2011) highlighted how U.S. nationalism, combined with concerns over the Cold War, precipitated historic levels of university funding for math, science, and technological research. Even during what Gumport (1997) dubbed the "golden era" of higher education (1945-1970), funding was mostly drawn from the federal government in the form of tax dollars and grants or from large charitable foundations. From these heights, American funding of higher education has, as Selingo (2013) described, fallen to near record lows, with the brunt of costs now borne by students.

Currently, the American government's policies would seem to abdicate the responsibility to provide greater access to higher education for students, making the results of increasing calls to create options for free higher education appear doubtful. In contrast to the individual and communal benefits that McMahon (2009) described, the ongoing public disinvestment in higher education that so damagingly influences current funding practices preserves socioeconomic hierarchies that intersect with hierarchies of race and gender (Harackiewicz & Priniski, 2018). McMahon observed that the fact that public funding has not kept pace with rising costs places a greater economic burden on families, causing greater reliance on student loans and decreased participation by the underserved, namely lower-income and minority students (Emdin & Lehner, 2006; Lehner, 2007; Lehner, Thomas, Shaddai, & Heren, 2017). While arguably itself an inflation, the increased requirement of college degrees for a wide swath of employment opportunities is unlikely to reverse itself, much as the decline in government funding presents no signs of ending (Barr & McClellan, 2018; The Pew Charitable Trusts, 2015).

In the U.S., the contention that free or heavily loan-subsidized education automatically strengthens the nation state is a complicated proposition, one that several scholars are currently interrogating. For instance, Bowen and Qian (2017), building in part on the work of Winters (2013a, b), questioned the conventional wisdom in higher education circles that increased funding improves the state's economic growth. They also contested that free education straightforwardly develops human capital and that these educational opportunities are solely responsible for an individual's expanded economic opportunities. However, as Winters (2013a, b) and Bowen and Qian (2017) acknowledged, education is still commonly accepted to be the most effective route to economic success. Additionally, even if education offers only a partial solution to economic advancement, we must consider both its less readily measurable benefits and our obligation to employ all available tools for a more equitable society.

Often, however, even when students have access to higher education, a misalignment exists between educational funding patterns and what employers require, leading to the ongoing problem of positions for highly skilled workers remaining unfilled. For instance, Herman and Stefanescu (2017) demonstrated that traditional higher education has little influence on the career outcomes of engineering students, a field with abundant corporate and entrepreneurial opportunities, primarily because the course of study precluded broader training on available careers and how the students could deploy their education. Relatedly, Chan (2016) extensively studied the disjunction between students' understandings of the purposes of higher education and the job market's needs for highly trained technology workers competing in an expansive world economy. Chan (2016) noted profound differences between preparing students to enter the workforce, as seen, for example in The National Task Force's Report (2012), and a need to educate students to be good citizens (Lagemann & Lewis, 2012). These disjunctions create problems for both individuals and businesses. Diosdado (2017) detailed the difficulties that companies face when unable to readily meet employment needs, including loss of revenue or growth due to vacant positions. Diosdado (2017) noted that beyond possibly losing market competitiveness, companies with such vacancies also overwork and put a disproportionate strain on the employees that they do have, thereby risking the departure of their most loyal and talented employees. Even a detailed study such as the examination by McMahon and Oketch (2013) of the quantitative effects of education on the individual in the U.K. labor force does not, or could not, if applied to the U.S., account for the complex interplay between industry's employment needs and the individual's educational track toward employment or the counternarratives presented by Diosdado (2017) and Herman and Stefanescu (2017). In both its curricula and funding allocation patterns, U.S. higher education reflects the ongoing and problematic split, as explained by Chan (2016), between a broader education preparing the student for life and a more technical education centered on career preparation.

CAREERISM, TECHNOLOGICAL DISRUPTION, AND A CALL FOR NEW FUNDING MODELS

As noted, historically, a great concern regarding higher education funding is its reliance on tax dollars and expansive student debt (Christensen & Eyring, 2011; Dolvin, 2012; Selingo, 2013). In light of an ongoing and worsening student loan crisis, persistent funding cuts, and other economic pressures, it is time to seek new approaches to the complexities of financing higher education for U.S. citizens. Christensen, Horn, Caldera, and Soares (2011) argued that college and university education will be greatly transformed by technological disruption, potentially bringing about a more affordable type of education to most Americans. According to their work, the nearly threefold escalation in fewer than 20 years of the average price of college tuition not only signals an unsustainable cost trajectory but also indicates that the academy is ripe for technological disruption.

Following this report, Christensen and Eyring (2011) made the case that higher education will face significant change due to technological innovation, reshaping what is currently called the university. Lederman (2017) and Hess (2017) noted that Christensen has repeatedly contended that colleges and universities will face technological disruption to such a great degree that many will face bankruptcy and closure. Admittedly, Lederman (2017) also noted that Christensen's predictions that half of traditional colleges or universities would meet this fate in under two decades, primarily due to online education, will not come to pass despite an increase in closings. However, half of American higher education does not have to disappear for serious problems to be facing it from neoliberal austerity and challenges from other types of education providers. Whatever the exact timeframe and extent of disruption, the claims by Christensen et al. (2011) and Christensen and Eyring (2011) remain compellingly relevant: that higher education will be disrupted primarily because its business model has become outdated, it is unable to effectively meet its students' needs, and its collective leadership is not sufficiently prepared for the changes that colleges and universities will face. The arguments of Christensen et al. (2011) and Christensen and Eyring (2011) are not far afield from assertions by Greenwood and Levin (2005) that, with a growing separation between academic research and government policy and a practice of promoting faculty members who engage in arcane forms of research devoid of the political and social capital to actually influence change in their respective domains, higher education fails also to meet the needs of the communities that it supposedly serves.

Now, the fact that higher education seems to be misaligned with the needs of its students and society more broadly does not represent a new observation. Giroux, Giroux, and White (2018) maintained that the very notion of truth within a university is bound up with funding factors, and that narratives presented as truth can be manipulated to best secure that funding (in this case, as they described, the truth about abuse in the Penn State athletics department was manipulated to preserve the funding and revenue streams brought in by the football program). Another influence on the production of truth within the academy is that academic researchers can often end up on arcane issues removed from the changing world around them. While such work can be very valuable, it is also worth considering whether the perspective thereby engendered influences, for example, the way that Keller (2006), McMahon and Oketch (2013), and an entire cohort of modern educational funding researchers rarely tackle the seemingly obvious and consequential issue of actual funding. Specifically, a good deal of educational funding scholarship centers on how to stretch fewer federal and state dollars into a substantive educational experience. Meanwhile, calls and proposals for improving that experience, much less for free and universal higher education, will unquestionably be met with the question of how to afford such proposals.

A Call for New Funding Models

In light of the work above, this chapter centers on a disruptive call for higher education funding that could be decoupled from traditional financial markets. For example, Keller (2006) and McMahon and Oketch (2013) teased out the strain of utopianism that runs through calls for free higher education, an outlook that sharply contrasts the neoliberal higher educational reforms that have swept the country (Jemielniak & Greenwood, 2015). Utopianism in educational funding research, while of course laudable, is more effective when paired with practical explanation of how such policies could be enacted. Utopianism alone loses axiological worth when public good is determined by neoliberal capitalism and risks, particularly in the humanities and social sciences, an overly reductive picture of the complexities of the lived world. Such an approach avoids responsibility for enacting advocated policies and for concretely mitigating the disenfranchisement of those whom its proposals are meant to aid. Educators must engage with the political and ontological structures and realities governing these changes. Otherwise, calls for free educational opportunities have little chance of implementation in the face of neoliberal austerity, technological disruption, and a misalignment between the academy and community needs.

Surveying the neoliberal policy changes that are affecting higher education, the authors present one practical response. Influenced by Kincheloe, McLaren, Steinberg, and Monzó, (2017), the authors developed a funding mechanism to fund meaningful education projects by engaging the opportunities in the cryptocurrency financial markets. This work, similarly to Lehner, Hunzeker, and Ziegler (2017), is designed to engage state and national policymakers, community stakeholders, and higher education providers by providing them with an alternative perspective that centers on higher education wealth generation rather than the zero-sum policies reflected in the current realpolitik of education funding.

Admittedly, the goals of this chapter are far-reaching, perhaps employing the authors' own form of utopianism. Nonetheless, this work purposefully sets out to provide models, both conceptual and financial, that have the power to enact change. Specifically, the model presents a proven strategy to generate U.S. dollars (USD) that can be used for the specific purposes of higher education. In discussing this model, the authors deploy critical theory, cryptocurrency frameworks for wealth generation, analysis of the financial markets, and open source tools in a strategy to challenge the status quo of the current student debt and tax dollar-funded higher education system.

CRYPTOCURRENCY AS WEALTH-GENERATOR: ENACTING DISRUPTION ON HIGHER EDUCATION FUNDING

A subsection of the educational funding literature, including the extensive work of Barr (1993, 2001, 2003, 2004, 2017), has proposed an alternative to the type of utopianism described above. This body of work consists primarily of practical models centered on student participation and detailed student loan repayment policies. Barr's body of work specifically, and this body of literature generally, is situated in the legacy discourse of cost sharing and underestimates the degree to which governmental funding for higher education is dramatically shifting and being disrupted (Christensen et al., 2011; Selingo, 2013). Additionally, Barr (2017) combined cost sharing with the principles of regulated competition in a way that resembles the ardent call to allot public education resources through competition. Barr (2017) described this process, writing that

consumer tastes are diverse and degrees increasingly diverse. Thus, it can be argued that students are mostly well-informed, so consumer sovereignty is more useful for post-compulsory education than for earlier education. Though that argument is generally robust, it frequently does not apply to students from poorer backgrounds. (p. 4)

Barr's (2017) proposal is neoliberal in the ways in which it employs business terminology to describe the public's educational resources and students' approach to them. Shore (2008) described neoliberalism's attempt to privatize public goods, and Barr's proposals fall clearly within this realm. Neoliberal higher education policies tend to stress austerity, budget cuts, and for-profit higher education models, the latter currently enjoying a renaissance of governmental favor in the U.S. Neoliberal policies are nonpublic and profit-seeking by their very definition. The notion of free education stands at odds with the neoliberal practice of commodifying public resources.

In terms of higher education institutes, many academic researchers, particularly policy advocates, have written about this systemic problem. However, the question must be asked: What incentives are there to radically critique the current higher education funding model? Although contradictory to the suppositions of this work, there seems to be too few reasons for the tenured faculty to seriously address the grave concerns of higher education funding (Christensen et al., 2011; Christensen & Eyring, 2011; Greenwood & Levin, 2005). Lehner and Finley (2016) contended, for instance, that university researchers often follow a careerist path, focusing on publishing in high-ranking academic journals and collecting funding from traditional sources, practices that contribute little to the longer-term mission of higher education but that are encouraged by the corporatization of academia and its emphasis on easily quantifiable results.

Going Beyond Cost-Sharing and Privatization Models

This cryptocurrency funding model will not redress the complicated arguments and valid assertions around the benefits of cost-sharing or, for that matter, the disadvantages of this practice in higher education. Great importance inheres in the conversations, debates, and scholarly literature centered around the purposes of higher education and its relationship to a knowledge-driven and democratic society (Keller, 2006). The authors' model adds to the conversation new forms of wealth generation for higher education, the proceeds of which can be deployed consistent with the mission of the beneficiary institution and without reliance on the currently predominant external sources of funding (Lehner et al., 2017). The model is framed from the perspective of catalytic authenticity (Lincoln & Guba, 1989) combined with the principles of technological distribution (Christensen et al., 2011). It configures open source tools to be employed as technological disruptors. The model has been tested. Its methodologies have used cryptocurrencies and investment strategies to generate new capital, in USD, to be used for the purposes of higher education.

Lehner et al. (2017) described how a group of educational researchers and Wall Street bankers developed a cryptocurrency fund that generated more than a 400% return, despite a volatile market. This initial model was created to serve as an alternative funding mechanism for scientific research since its returns, and initial capital allocation, were not tied to traditional governmental or industrial sources. In this first cryptocurrency funding model, Lehner et al. (2017) focused on funding basic scientific research, critiquing current science funding models, and explaining the potential function of a cryptocurrency fund as a portfolio diversifier. This chapter extends beyond Lehner et al. and contends that a similar strategy may be deployed to: (a) fund higher education costs across the academy to benefit American college students; (b) alleviate some of the need for traditional governmental assistance and other forms of subsidy; and (c) reduce inequity by reducing higher education's dependency on local, state, and federal revenues.

Cryptocurrencies are purely digital assets, as Burniske and Tatar (2018) explained. These cryptographic assets are unique in that they based on cryptography and cannot be duplicated or infinitely inflated, as fiat currency can. Blau (2017) argued that cryptocurrencies' function in storing value makes them an asset class, one created by Bitcoin (BTC), or more precisely, the open source code in which it was written. Burniske and White (2017) saw this as uniquely immutable because of its characteristics. Cryptocurrencies, including BTC, can be leveraged against other asset classes, providing beneficial financial diversification for higher education. This research demonstrates how cryptocurrencies' wealth-generation potential can change the dynamics of higher educational funding, potentially shifting the emphasis from away from tax dollars, student contributions, and student debt. Although developed and deployed unrelatedly, the work aligns with some of the initial work enacted by Eyal Herzog and Galia Benartzi (2017) that would later become the Bancor protocol. Benartzi, inspired by the work of Lietaer and Dunne (2013), framed cryptocurrency as a third wave of money that should be user generated and easily available and accessible to the everyone. More precisely, and aligned with this chapter, Benartzi and Lietaer understand money, and more particularly the access to it, as a human right. Lietaer and Dunne underscored that if people need monetary capital to meet their daily needs, said capital simply should be created without the oversight of any authority. Lietaer and Dunne's notion of creating currency, or at least developing a means of value transfer, is seemingly fully aligned with the origins of the cypher-punk roots of BTC, but also seems to be imbued with the premise that centralized authorities are unable to effectively plan for the robust economic needs of its citizens.

This chapter outlines a proven approach to actively managed cryptocurrencies yielding both compound interest and coin appreciation. This fund was developed by a group of academics and bankers who used USD to purchase enough of the selected coins to set up the initial investment positions. The pooled cryptocurrencies were then invested to earn lucrative dividends, using an active investment strategy enacted primarily with open-source tools, such as Linux's Ubuntu, PuTTy, and Unix. This fund is predicated on cryptocurrency valuation modeling, combining traditional valuation models with the data derived from an expansive Google Cloud Project. Over a one-year period, this strategy yielded exponential returns, well above 400%.

Wealth Generation vs. Endowment Growth

From a less technical perspective, this fund's strategy coheres with Reiss's (2017) notion of dividend reinvestment. Reiss detailed that one way to generate wealth is by investing into dividend producing assets and reinvesting these dividends into the same strategy. Reiss's work, combined with the valuation metrics and Google Cloud Project data, informed the coin selection that later populated this fund. Coins that use the proof-of-stake (PoS) algorithm were chosen because PoS moves beyond BTC's straightforward proof-of-work (PoW) model, which rewards only mining that requires expensive computer hardware and a disproportionate amount of electricity. As it relates to the consensus algorithms, PoS provides an important alternative to PoW for blockchain projects that is both more energy efficient and provides incentives to all holders to fully support the network. Although PoW coins could be used to fund science, the nature of that consensus mechanism is predicated only on computing power and not a 'stake' in the network. Even though PoW mining rewards could be used to fund education, the dividend reinvestment principle is not applicable in these systems and, consequently, would result in a lack of incentive to hold the coins for educational purposes.

Predicated on Lehner et al. (2017), this chapter explains the process of this innovative deployment of staking coins. In terms of valuation, once processed through valuation metrics, the portfolio ultimately consisted solely of coins that returned high-yield dividends. Staking cryptocurrencies are backed by the complexity of cryptography while simultaneously earning dividends. Although cryptocurrencies are prone to volatile price extremes, a staking coin's dividend features can offset extreme price fluctuations. The open-source tools allowed the fund to generate dividends by hosting what are known as network full nodes, resulting in the fund receiving a portion of the block reward.

COIN FARMING REVENUE MODEL

At the heart of this model, illustrated in three figures, rests the fact that certain cryptocurrencies can be invested to yield dividends for higher education. This chapter maps out a conceptual process, based on Lehner et al. (2017), that potentially yields a strategic framework for creating a cryptocurrency farm for higher education wealth generation. In particular, although not all the technical aspects are fully described herein, open source tools are front and center in the deployment of coin farming, since both the implementation of the protocol and any future improvements on the code are distributed to the community. Additionally, in terms of enacting a farming model, this framework required the development of our own code base to monitor dividend growth, interface with various virtual private servers, and deploy new master nodes.

Figure 1 details the revenue model and how a farming model generates new cryptocurrency. While Lehner et al. (2017) provided two examples of cryptocurrencies (Dash and PIVX) to deploy in this fashion, this type of framework can be utilized with more than 50 different cryptocurrencies, all generating substantial dividends. The investor (represented by the box in Figure 1) can be either an individual investor or, more likely, an institutional investor, such as a college of university, which it is hoped to adopt this model. The revenue model shown in Figure 1 illustrates the process of sweeping earned dividends from the nodes, either to add a node or to spend the collective dividends. For example, with some PoS coins, only 1,000 coins are required to run a full node. As the node accrues coins, the dividends can be saved to start a new node or spent by the institution. In terms of dividend growth, the authors describe the details related to how quickly a new node can be generated (see Figure 1). What is important to the discussion of the proposed framework is the degree of dynamic interaction between generating new coin and sweeping new coin into new nodes, an interaction captured in the section of Figure 1 that represents

Figure 1. The revenue model and how a farming model generates new cryptocurrency

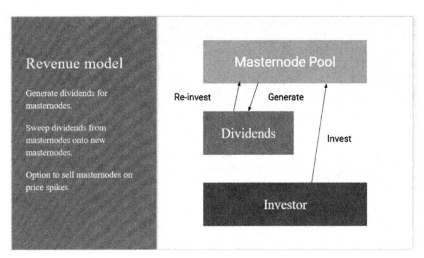

the reciprocal relationship between the coin farm and the dividends. The dynamic interaction between the generation of new coin and the creation of new nodes constitutes a type of compound interest.

The power of this conceptual model lies in that if several institutions collaborate, running their own coin farms, the value of each coin could grow exponentially. While such collaboration obviously would require a radical rethinking of business-as-usual, the exponential dividend coin growth that it generated could be reinvested into the farm, providing the dividends in the manner illustrated above. Additionally, an institution could dedicate its dividends, or portions thereof, to student scholarships, faculty funding, or other areas of funding consistent with its vision. Beyond simply benefitting one institution, newly generated coin and/or new nodes could be shared. This sharing of nodes, paradoxically, increases the power of the network and could simultaneously address educational disparities. As will be covered in the discussion portion of this chapter, for example, the Council for Aid to Education (2018) recently released its annual endowment report, noting that already highly supported schools, such as Stanford and Harvard, continue to receive the largest amount of USD contributions. Although this type of news is commonplace, the notion of an institution sharing its dividends in USD remains unheard of, primarily because fiat currency has already achieved its network effect. However, staking coins introduce the promising possibility for a wealthy institution to share its nodes, thus increasing its own value. Now, in a Bear market, such as the one in 2018-2019, a network's value will not always increase in terms of fiat. Nonetheless, the dividends continue to grow, and the model is robust. The notion that cryptocurrency grows in value when it is shared derives from network-effect principles, including Metcalfe's (2013) and Reed's (2001) laws. Although network effect is not the focus of this work, the authors propose additional research to further elucidate how this phenomenon occurs and how it can benefit higher education.

Figure 2 outlines the process of acquiring coins, setting up nodes using open source tools, and writing scripts for reporting to monitor progress for each respective node or farm of nodes. For example, the first step (see Figure 2) focuses on the coin-acquisition process, which involves metrics for cryptocurrency coin value. Although the specifics of coin valuation lie beyond the scope of this conceptual chapter, valuation is a critical part of this process. Therefore, the authors will call for more research on valuation methods in the conclusion. Step one also includes the garnering of funds and assumes that institutional

Figure 2. The process of acquiring coins

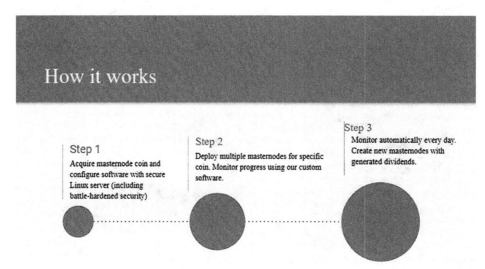

investors are acquainted with procuring cryptocurrencies. Traditional ways of garnering cryptocurrencies are expensive. More detailed research, which will be called for in the conclusion, should investigate this process to better serve the needs of institutions.

Conceptually, Figure 2 depicts the process from start to finish, in a broad framing of an intricate process that will be detailed in ongoing research. It is illustrative of the process, including noting the need for wrapper scripts or another type of automated reporting. The automated reporting is not simply for an institutional investor that may be running its own nodes, but, depending on the way that it is coded, could also report out several institutions, creating an accountability measure to ensure that those who committed to running nodes are in fact doing so. This idea of group accountability may vastly increase the value of the network. It needs more research, as well as deeper and more nuanced framings of Metcalfe's (2013) and Reed's (2001) laws. Peterson (2018), for instance, has postulated that BTC's value adheres to the social network laws touched on above. However, deeper investigation is required to apply them to the staking coin ecosphere.

Figure 3 illustrates in finer detail what is presented in Figures 1 and 2. In doing so, it focuses specifically on the operation of a coin farm solely dedicated to one cryptocurrency. Figure 3 depicts only one deployment of a specific staking coin that provides compound interest, and under the example model illustrated to the far left, the figure outlines a farm with only five nodes. The model shows how the nodes' collective dividends, as shown in the middle section of Figure 3, can be used to start a new node. Lastly, the earned dividends, shown to the right, can be allocated according to institutional needs. While this model is conceptual, similar frameworks have been prototyped and tested by researchers in conjunction with software engineers and bankers, resulting in significant appreciation in USD. As a prototype, however, it should be viewed as a portfolio diversifier and requires additional testing.

New nodes can be generated very quickly (see Figure 4). The dividend management process can be detailed using the following mathematical model. For clarity, the model makes very conservative investment assumptions and assumes linear coin generation amounts. The model uses the following variables, with initial values noted parenthetically.

Figure 3. Finer detail

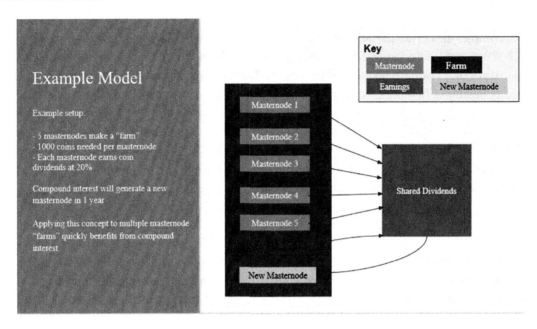

Figure 4. Total number of nodes (N) and days to create a node (Q) over time in days (T)

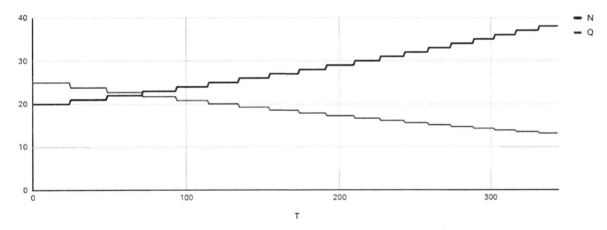

N = total number of nodes (starts at 20 nodes)

E = average number of coins generated per node per day (fixed: 10)

M = coin collateral required to run a node (fixed: 5000)

Q = days to create a new node from generated coins on existing nodes, literally M/(E * N) in this formula
    (starts at 25 days)

As time passes in days (T), the days to create a new node (Q) decreases. The number of nodes (N) increases. If the number of initial nodes is large enough, these nodes will begin to generate a new node in fewer than 25 days. New nodes are added to the initial node pool to generate more coins. The larger that N is, the fewer days it requires to generate a new node. As time passes, new nodes grow exponentially as a result of compounding coin dividends.

CONCLUSION, LIMITATIONS AND FUTURE RESEARCH

While the complexities of understanding and evaluating PoS cryptocurrencies and their relationship to a network effect may seem foreboding to the uninitiated, adopting the kind of model explained above can reduce difficulties of participation in the market. This will open a new way to both gain and reconceptualize educational funding. From small-scale interventions, including individual scholarships or flexible funding to help higher education more quickly adjust to the needs of the labor market without abandoning the core mission of liberal education, to large-scale solutions like the potential for multiple institutions to collaborate on investment, forays into the sphere of cryptocurrency hold promise for improving the position of the academy in an age of neoliberal austerity.

In terms of additional research, this chapter primarily surveyed the problems inherent in higher education funding and proposed an alternative model. In future research directions, the intricacies of the open source technical stack need to be more fully described and delineated. Sweeping dividends into new nodes, for example, is a robust technical deployment that, if employed without proper development, could result in the loss of coins. As cryptocurrencies are increasingly used to fund higher education, the details of the open source work flow, as noted above, need to be more fully fleshed out.

There are, of course, concerns that arise, primarily about volatility and, relatedly, emerging regulation, itself currently a somewhat unpredictable process. However, neoliberal capitalism is extremely adept at absorbing the transgressive into the mainstream and repurposing it for its own ends (witness, for a recent example, Chrysler's use of a sermon by Martin Luther King, Jr. whose complete texts criticizes consumerism, including automobiles specifically, to sell trucks in a 2018 Super Bowl commercial). While the problematic nature of this mainstreaming is a discussion for another time, its consistent success suggests that whatever the downside of government and corporate banking increasing involvement in cryptocurrency trading, it may bring added stability to the market over the long term.

This work underscores how staking coins are potentially lucrative ways to provide funding for higher education. The success of the coin farm prototype model is promising and invites further research and development in the areas enumerated above to illustrate more clearly the strategy's long-term feasibility and applications. As this research is done, colleges and universities, as well as development offices and endowment officials, would do well to become better acquainted with the wealth-generation properties of cryptocurrencies. More research on coin valuation, procurement methods, collaborative coin farming, and the network effect are all required and may further address current and potential concerns and obstacles for funding higher education with cryptocurrency. So, too, studies of the results of specific implementations of the proposals contained in this chapter can continue to advance innovation in this area, which may facilitate further disruption.

CODA: A NOTE ON BEAR MARKETS AND THIS WORK

Since December 2017, when BTC hit its all-time high, the cryptocurrency market capitalization began slowly, but assuredly, to move substantially lower and, eventually, transition into a full bear market. At the time of writing this coda, in early February 2019, this model, even though BTC is well below $3500, can still be applied. The underpinning frameworks in this model – game theory, open-source software, dividend reinvestment, network infrastructure deployment – although not altogether unscathed, are not fully reliant on BTC's price or market capitalization. Moreover, in more completely aligning with Lietaer and Dunne's (2013) work, this type of model can create an alternative decentralized currency even if the staking coin is only trading on one exchange as the blocks are produced. Or, for that matter, even if the coin did not have a BTC pairing and was not redeemable for any fiat, the model could still be deployed, caveats acknowledged. As a call for more scholarship, the authors reiterate that more research into the ways that decentralized currencies, and moreover decentralized networks, are deployed into the world.

REFERENCES

Alexander, N. A., & Kim, H. (2017). Adequacy by any other name: A comparative look at educational spending in the United States and the Republic of Korea. *Journal of Education Finance*, *43*(1), 65–83.

Barr, M. J., & McClellan, G. S. (2018). *Budgets and financial management in higher education*. Somerset, NJ: John Wiley & Sons.

Barr, N. (1993). Alternative funding resources for higher education. *Economic Journal (London)*, *103*(418), 718–728. doi:10.2307/2234544

Barr, N. (2001). Funding higher education: Policies for access and quality. *House of Commons Education and Skills Committee, Post-16 student support. Session, 2*, 24.

Barr, N. (2003). Financing higher education: Comparing the options. London School of Economics and Political Sciences, 10.

Barr, N. (2004). Higher education funding. *Oxford Review of Economic Policy*, *20*(2), 264–283. doi:10.1093/oxrep/grh015

Barr, N. (2017). Funding post-compulsory education. In G. Johnes, J. Johnes, T. Agasisti, & L. López-Torres (Eds.), Handbook on the Economics of Education. Academic Press. doi:10.4337/9781785369070.00021

Blau, B. M. (2017, October). Price dynamics and speculative trading in Bitcoin. *Research in International Business and Finance*, *43*, 493–499. doi:10.1016/j.ribaf.2017.05.010

Bowen, W. M., & Qian, H. (2017). State spending for higher education: Does it improve economic performance? *Regional Science Policy & Practice*, *9*(1), 7–23. doi:10.1111/rsp3.12086

Burniske, C., & Tatar, J. (2018). *Cryptoassets: The innovative investor's guide to bitcoin and beyond*. New York, NY: McGraw-Hill.

Burniske, C., & White, A. (2017). *Bitcoin: Ringing the bell for a new asset class* (White paper). Ark Invest. Retrieved from https://research.Ark-invest.com/hubfs/1_Download_Files_ARK-Invest/White_Papers/Bitcoin-Ringing-The-Bell-For-A-New-Asset-Class. pdf

Chan, R. Y. (2016). Understanding the purpose of higher education: An analysis of the economic and social benefits for completing a college degree. *Journal of Education Policy, Planning and Administration*, *6*(5), 1–40.

Chan, R. Y. (2017). The future of accessibility in higher education: Making college skills and degrees more accessible. In H. C. Alphin Jr, J. Lavine, & R. Y. Chan (Eds.), *Disability and Equity in Higher Education Accessibility* (pp. 1–45). Hershey, PA: IGI Global. doi:10.4018/978-1-5225-2665-0.ch001

Christensen, C. M., & Eyring, H. J. (2011). *The innovative university: Changing the DNA of higher education from the inside out.* Somerset, NJ: John Wiley & Sons.

Christensen, C. M., Horn, M. B., Caldera, L., & Soares, L. (2011). *Disrupting college: How disruptive innovation can deliver quality and affordability to postsecondary education.* Washington, DC: Center for American Progress. Retrieved from https://files.eric.ed.gov/fulltext/ED535182.pdf

Clemes, M. D., Hu, B., & Li, X. (2016). Services and economic growth in China: An empirical analysis. *Journal of the Asia Pacific Economy, 21*(4), 612–627. doi:10.1080/13547860.2016.1190492

Council for Aid to Education. (2018) *Colleges and universities raised $43.60 billion in 2017.* Retrieved from https://cae.org/images/uploads/pdf/VSE-2017-Press-Release.pdf

Diosdado, B. (2017, June 22). The price of vacancy: The cost of unfilled technology jobs [blog post]. Forbes Community Voice. Retrieved from https://www.forbes.com/sites/forbestechcouncil/2017/06/22/the-price-of-vacancy-the-cost-of-unfilled-technology-jobs/#5849a6c85747

Dolvin, S. D. (2012, November 28). Student loan debt [blog post]. Butler University. Retrieved from https://digitalcommons.butler.edu/jmdallchapters/49/

Emdin, C., & Lehner, E. (2006, March). Situating cogenerative dialogue in a cosmopolitan ethic. *Forum Qualitative Sozialforschung/Forum: Qualitative Social Research, 7*(2).

Giroux, H., Giroux, S. S., & White. (2018). *Sport and the neoliberal university: Profit, politics, and pedagogy.* New Brunswick, NJ: Rutgers University Press.

Greenwood, D. J., & Levin, M. (2005). Reform of the social sciences and of universities through action research. The Sage handbook of qualitative research, 3, 43-64.

Gumport, P. J. (1997). In search of strategic perspective: A tool for mapping the market in postsecondary education. *Change: The Magazine of Higher Learning, 29*(6), 23–38. doi:10.1080/00091389709602344

Harackiewicz, J. M., & Priniski, S. J. (2018). Improving student outcomes in higher education: The science of targeted intervention. *Annual Review of Psychology, 69*(1), 409–435. doi:10.1146/annurev-psych-122216-011725 PMID:28934586

Herman, E., & Stefanescu, D. (2017). Can higher education stimulate entrepreneurial intentions among engineering and business students? *Educational Studies, 43*(3), 312–327. doi:10.1080/03055698.2016.1277134

Herzog, E., & Benartzi, G. (2017). *Bancor protocol-white paper.* Retrieved from: https://website-bancor.storage.googleapis.com/2018/04/01ba8253-bancor_protocol_whitepaper_en.pdf

Hess, A. (2017). Harvard Business School professor: Half of American colleges will be bankrupt in 10 to 15 years. *CNBC.* Retrieved from https://www.cnbc.com/2017/11/15/hbs-professor-half-of-us-colleges-will-be-bankrupt-in-10-to-15-years.html

Hutcheson, P. A., & Kidder, R. D. (2011). In the national interest: The college and university in the United States in the post-World War II era. In *Higher education: Handbook of theory and research* (pp. 221–264). Springer. doi:10.1007/978-94-007-0702-3_6

Jemielniak, D., & Greenwood, D. J. (2015). Wake up or perish: Neo-liberalism, the social sciences, and salvaging the public university. *Cultural Studies? Critical Methodologies*, *15*(1), 72–82. doi:10.1177/1532708613516430

Keller, K. R. (2006). Investment in primary, secondary, and higher education and the effects on economic growth. *Contemporary Economic Policy*, *24*(1), 18–34. doi:10.1093/cep/byj012

Kincheloe, J. L., McLaren, P., Steinberg, S. R., & Monzó, L. D. (2017). *Critical pedagogy and qualitative research: Advancing the Bricolage*. Thousand Oaks, CA: Sage.

Lagemann, E. C., & Lewis, H. (2012). Renewing the civic mission of American higher education. In E. C. Lagemann & H. Lewis (Eds.), *What is college for? The public purpose of higher education* (pp. 9–45). New York, NY: Teachers College Press.

Leachman, M., Masterson, K., & Wallace, M. (2016). *After nearly a decade, school investments still way down in some states*. Washington, DC: Center on Budget and Policy Priorities.

Lederman, D. (2017, April 28). Clay Christensen, doubling down. *Inside Higher Ed*. Retrieved from https://www.insidehighered.com/digital-learning/article/2017/04/28/clay-christensen-sticks-predictions-massive-college-closures

Lehner, E. (2007). Describing students of the African Diaspora: Understanding micro and meso level science learning as gateways to standards based discourse. *Cultural Studies of Science Education*, *2*(2), 441–473. doi:10.100711422-007-9062-0

Lehner, E., & Finley, K. (2016). *Should the New England education research organization start a journal in the age of audit culture? Reflections on academic publishing, metrics, and the new academy*. CUNY Academic Work. Retrieved from https://academicworks.cuny.edu/cgi/viewcontent.cgi?article=1017&context=bx_pubs

Lehner, E., Hunzeker, D., & Ziegler, J. R. (2017). Funding science with science: Cryptocurrency and independent academic research funding. *Ledger*, *2*, 65–76. doi:10.5195/LEDGER.2017.108

Lehner, E., Thomas, K., Shaddai, J., & Hernen, T. (2017). Measuring the effectiveness of critical literacy as an instructional method. *Journal of College Literacy and Learning*, *43*(1), 26–53.

Lietaer, B. A., & Dunne, J. (2013). *Rethinking money: How new currencies turn scarcity into prosperity*. Oakland, CA: Berrett-Koehler Publishers.

Lincoln, Y. S., & Guba, E. (1985). *Naturalistic inquiry*. Beverly Hills, CA: Sage. doi:10.1016/0147-1767(85)90062-8

McMahon, W. W. (2009). *Higher learning, greater good: The private and social benefits of higher education*. Baltimore, MD: JHU Press.

McMahon, W. W. (2015). Financing education for the public good: A new strategy. *Journal of Education Finance, 40*(4), 414–437.

McMahon, W. W., & Oketch, M. (2013). Education's effects on individual life chances and development: An overview. *British Journal of Educational Studies, 61*(1), 79–107. doi:10.1080/00071005.2012.756170

Metcalfe, B. (2013). Metcalfe's law after 40 years of ethernet. *Computer, 46*(12), 26–31. doi:10.1109/MC.2013.374

Neher, C., Patterson, D., Duffield, J. W., & Harvey, A. (2017). Budgeting for the future: The long-term impacts of short-term thinking in Alabama K-12 education funding. *Journal of Education Finance, 42*(4), 448–470.

Peterson, T. (2018). Metcalfe's Law as a model for Bitcoin's value. *Alternative Investment Analyst Review, 7*(2), 9–18. doi:10.2139srn.3078248

Reed, D. P. (2001). The law of the pack. *Harvard Business Review, 79*(2), 23. PMID:11213694

Reiss, D. (2017, January 12). What you should know about dividend reinvestment plans. *U.S. News & World Report.* Retrieved from https://money.usnews.com/investing/articles/2017-01-12/what-you-should-know-about-dividend-reinvestment-plans

Roger, J., & Baum, R. C. (2017). Student loans: This economic bubble will wreak havoc when it bursts. *Fortune.* Retrieved from http://fortune.com/2017/07/10/higher-education-student-loans-economic-bubble-federal//

Selingo, J. J. (2013). *College (un)bound: The future of higher education and what it means for students.* Boston, MA: Houghton Mifflin Harcourt.

Shore, C. (2008). Audit culture and illiberal governance: Universities and the politics of accountability. *Anthropological Theory, 8*(3), 278–298. doi:10.1177/1463499608093815

The National Task Force. (2012). A crucible moment: College learning and democracy's future. Washington, DC: Association of American Colleges and Universities (AAC&U).

The Pew Charitable Trusts. (2015, June 11). *Federal and state funding of higher education: A changing landscape.* Retrieved from http://www.pewtrusts.org/en/research-and-analysis/issue-briefs/2015/06/federal-and-state-funding-of-higher-education

Thelin, J. R. (2011). *A history of American higher education.* Baltimore, MD: JHU Press.

Winters, J. V. (2013a). Human capital externalities and employment differences across metropolitan areas of the USA. *Journal of Economic Geography, 13*(5), 799–822. doi:10.1093/jeg/lbs046

Winters, J. V. (2013b, December). *STEM graduates, human capital externalities, wages in the US.* IZA Discussion Paper No. 7830. Retrieved from http://ftp.iza.org/dp7830.pdf

Chapter 8
A Call for Second-Generation Cryptocurrency Valuation Metrics

Edward Lehner
 https://orcid.org/0000-0001-6487-5410
Bronx Community College, USA

John R. Ziegler
Bronx Community College, USA

Louis Carter
 https://orcid.org/0000-0002-9773-8217
Best Practice Institute, USA

ABSTRACT

This chapter builds on the body of work that has depicted cryptocurrency as a model for science and higher education funding. To that end, this work examines the degree to which one or more cryptocurrencies would need to be adopted and achieve a network effect prior to implementation of such a funding model. Empirical data from three different cryptocurrencies were examined. The current work deploys generalized autoregressive conditional heteroskedasticity (GARCH) to analyze stochastic volatility. This work contends that the examined coins are likely overdistributed and too volatile, thereby limiting the wealth generation possibilities for funding science or higher education. Additionally, based on the GARCH analysis, this work highlights that cryptocurrency pricing metrics and valuation models, to this point, may be insufficiently complex to persuade institutional investors to seriously allocate capital to this ecosphere.

DOI: 10.4018/978-1-5225-9257-0.ch008

INTRODUCTION

The phenomenon of the underfunding of science research specifically, and of higher education more broadly, is a significant and pressing issue whose complexities require innovative approaches to begin to ameliorate the persistent diminishment of financial resources. Although science research and higher education funding are, admittedly, separate and fund specific fields with distinct practices and obstacles, this work investigates how an enacted two-sided network effect, in which additional users create additional value, could provide alternative portfolio diversification to fund both areas. By continuing previous work on portfolio modeling using cryptocurrency (Lehner, Hunzeker & Ziegler, 2017) and the conceptual framing of cryptocurrency-based funding (Lehner & Ziegler, Ch. 7, this volume), this work further examines the importance of an enacted two-sided market effect as it relates to the type of cryptocurrencies to effectively augment science research and higher education funding. More specifically, we employ cryptocurrency data to examine the degree to which three different currencies have achieved a network effect and whether these currencies could serve as viable academic funding streams.

We elucidate this position in seven distinct sections: 1) science research and higher education funding as a human right and subsequent alignment with budgetary realities; 2) cryptocurrency as wealth generator, enacting disruption of science research and higher education funding; 3) examination of cryptocurrency volatility and pricing metrics; 4) specific examination of Bitcoin, Dash, and PIVX; 5) and limitations, directions for future research, and conclusions.

RECLAIMING SCIENCE RESEARCH AND HIGHER EDUCATION AS PUBLIC GOODS AND HUMAN RIGHTS

Worldwide, the funding of science research and higher education is closely intertwined with politics, an interrelationship that produces undesirable influences that might be mitigated by alternative funding sources. Lehner et al. (2017) argued that in the U.S., for instance, scientific research currently models a version of private equity investment, as various stakeholders compete for the intellectual property that government- and corporate-sponsored research produces. Consequently, researchers must always consider how best to position external stakeholders as they pursue work internally. The results of their research are likely to be published in the walled gardens of commercially controlled academic journals (Lehner & Finley, 2016), all while under the constant threat of diminished funding and other resources. This work centers on alternative funding; however, its fundamental underpinnings also closely align with the argument that science and higher education are fundamental human rights and that the primary purpose of both is to benefit the public.

University funding for scientific research is tied to a host of implicit and often underexplored corporate factors in complicated ways. Chomsky (2011) noted that scientific researchers find themselves at a troubling impasse, with austerity measures and conservative politics at one end of the spectrum and the need to advance scientific inquiry for societal benefit on the other.

To again take the U.S. as an example of wider trends, Aud et al. (2010) noted, in their report for the National Center for Education Statistics, that federal funding for higher education is declining, despite a growing number of student loans. In addition, the Pew Trusts (2015) underscored that federal funding for higher education has consistently declined during a decade of economic growth. Echoing the complex negotiations inherent in the funding of science, U.S. higher education, as reported by the Pew Trusts

(2015), may be approaching an unprecedented crisis that may lead to college and university closings (Barr & McClellan, 2018; Christensen et al., 2011; Christensen & Eyring, 2011). Noting the paradox of diminished federal funding while nearly every other sector of the economy has flourished, Birkhead (2016) emphasized that this precipitous underfunding has led to more state responsibility for higher education and more student debt. Hillman (2014), building on two decades of scholarly literature on student loan defaults (Aud et al., 2010; Christman, 2000; Dillon and Carey, 2009; Dynarski, 1994; Gladieux, 1995; Gladieux & Perna, 2005), highlighted that as students bear more of these costs, their debt responsibilities become overwhelming, leading to mass levels of student loan defaults. The probability of massive student loan defaults, as Roger and Baum (2017) keenly noted, is an underresearched issue that will likely have damaging effects not only within higher education but throughout the American economy.

In contrast to the language and epistemology of consumer capitalism—as Barr (2017), for example, uses in discussing educational costs—framing the funding of science and higher education as human rights advances pertinent concerns that are not immediately mediated or constrained by either a profit motive or the budgetary limitations imposed by the dominant paradigm of fiscal austerity. For instance, in science research, Luke et al. (2018) contended that a government should consistently fund basic science research because it collectively provides value to both the nation-state and the individual (pp. 77-78). Parallel to this argument, McMahon (2009, p. 6) contended that a supportive higher education policy substantially contributes to the public good by affording both career opportunities that may not otherwise be available to students and societal benefits to the community at large.

However, communitarian arguments centered on beneficence (National Institutes of Health, 1979; Emdin & Lehner, 2006) have found increasingly less support from the political and ideological power factions. For example, in the U.S., since the election of President Donald Trump in 2016, the National Institutes of Health has been repeatedly slated for dramatic budgetary cuts. The Centers for Disease Control and Prevention, the Food and Drug Administration, and the Environmental Protection Agency, among others, face similar proposed reductions. Yet, it remains paradoxical to frame these cuts as austerity measures, since at the time of writing the U.S. economy is experiencing a full 8-year bull market. Nonetheless, significant scientific research funding has been consistently positioned for cuts primarily because of ideological differences between the Trump administration and the long-tail, theoretically bipartisan value of scientific research. The notion that a single administration can fundamentally reframe the mission, ideological underpinnings, and logic frameworks of decades of scientific research has many within the research community greatly disturbed (Hempel, 2018). Indeed, the underfunding of science is often contextualized within a broader rise in authoritarian populism (Peters, 2018), combining the neoliberal agenda of privatizing public goods (Greenwood & Levin, 2011) with political messaging aimed at the average American citizen (Kazin, 2016; Mead, 2017). For example, cancer research, an American medical concern that one would expect to cross political lines, may be underfunded predicated on the administration's framing of cancer research not as a societal good but as putative governmental waste. Political allegiances aside, should not an agency such as the National Institutes of Health, which is tasked with biomedical and public health research, be shielded from extensive budgetary cuts, since its mission is so closely tied to the welfare of the citizens that the government supposedly exists to serve?

As discussed in Lehner et al. (2017), the funding of science research should ultimately supersede epistemological, ideological, and political differences. As Lehner and Ziegler (Ch. 7) noted, higher education funding should similarly be viewed as a societal good exempt from austerity measures and funded differently than the traditional annual budget. Extending these rights to the individual may of course be both a cause and effect of benefit to the public good. For example, Gittleson and Usher (2017) argued that education should be extended to all people living in the U.S., primarily for the benefit of the nation-state, although the individual would also significantly benefit, an argument that can be extended to any number of international contexts. Building on the framework of Gittleson and Usher, Gilchrist (2018) contended that higher education embodies catalytic attributes that fundamentally advance the individual and the nation-state simultaneously; yet, austerity proposals abound, often framed as common-sense populism, even though such measures are frequently actual impediments to economic growth. For example, Rickman and Wang (2018) explained how extreme cuts to education funding tend to be based on the underlying ideological principles informing state administrations in the U.S., as demonstrated by two midwestern state governments, interrogating the populist notion that austerity measures help to stimulate the economy. Providing an in-depth quantitative analysis of the economic impact of austerity funding, the authors concluded that "rather than experiencing stimulative growth effects from reductions . . . [states,] if anything, experienced negative economic multiplier effects from reduced state and local government spending" (Rickman & Wang, 2018, pp. 53-54), observations that are again suggestive for a wide range of contexts beyond the example of the United States.

Finally, as informed by the long tradition of *Bildung* (Levin & Greenwood, 2011), this work envisions catalytic change (Emdin, 2010; Lehner, 2007; Lincoln & Guba, 1989; Roth, 2010; Tobin, 2010) through the deployment of cryptocurrency as an agent to disrupt and eventually reconfigure conceptualizations of science and higher education funding. To reiterate, science research and higher education funding must be positioned as fundamental rights, primarily because when properly oriented, both greatly advance the concerns of the individual and society. Levin and Greenwood (2011) underscored how universities and the social sciences could be revitalized by deploying, as a fundamental mission, the principles of community beneficence, growth, and self-cultivation. Situating their work in a critique of the neoliberal university, which mirrors corporate structures, Greenwood (2008) called for university researchers to engage in their work in responsible and socially meaningful ways, noting that "academic professional organizations ostracize activist scholars through a combination of self-policing censorship and the imposition of intellectual frameworks inimical to activist scholarship" (p. 319). In the tradition of activist scholarship, building on the ideal of *Bildung*, we formulate that the research act is a lifelong process that is meant to both influence and initiate social change.

CRYPTOCURRENCY AS WEALTH GENERATOR: ENACTING DISRUPTION OF SCIENCE AND HIGHER EDUCATION FUNDING

By repositioning scientific research and higher education as public goods, more members of the public may become involved, by taking advantage of the potential for cryptocurrencies to produce a network effect. There is little reason to believe that the current march toward ever-increasing budget cuts, direct and indirect corporate influence, and the entrenchment of neoliberal austerity as orthodoxy has an end in sight. Countering these trends is vital if we are to increase the ability of educators and researchers to determine the direction of their own work by reducing the extent to which they are beholden to external stakeholders and move toward universalizing the social and individual benefits of scientific research and higher education. Therefore, any alternative mechanisms for funding must be considered. Cryptocurrency offers one such mechanism that may be enhanced by a network effect.

Cryptocurrencies form a class of entirely digital assets based in cryptography and are viewed as a store of value (Burniske & White, 2017; Burniske &Tatar, 2017; Lehner et al., 2017; Lehner & Ziegler, Ch. 7), akin to commodities and precious medals. Having evolved from the open-source code in which Bitcoin (BTC) was written, cryptocurrencies, including BTC, constitute a "unique asset class—meeting the bar of investability, and differing substantially from other assets in terms of its politico-economic profile, price independence, and risk-reward characteristics. . . [and are] subject to the strong network effects of users and developers" (Burniske & White, p. 24). These characteristics make cryptocurrencies strong candidates for financial diversification (Lehner et al., 2017) with potential to generate wealth; they also have the potential to emerge as a mitigator of ongoing disinvestment in college students, citizens, and the public good.

Before discussing the network effect in relationship to cryptocurrencies as a funding source, this work briefly summarizes an approach to managing a cryptocurrency fund that generates returns via compound interest and coin appreciation. This model used cryptocurrency coins that employ the proof-of-stake algorithm (Lehner et al., 2017), which progresses beyond BTC's proof-of-work algorithm. Successful proof-of-work mining depends on costly computer hardware and an outsized amount of electricity. Removing those barriers allows for more flexibility and perhaps even individual or institutional cooperation in generating returns for funding. The model additionally facilitates flexibility and accessibility by using open-source tools, demonstrating Christensen et al.'s (2011) definition of technological disruption. Finally, the dividend features of proof-of-stake coins can offset extreme price fluctuations in the sometimes-volatile cryptocurrency market.

To create the crypto fund, a group of academics and bankers purchased an initial group of high-yield coins selected according to valuation metrics developed by members of the group and Google Cloud Project data. Then, open-source tools including Linux's Ubuntu, PuTTy, and Unix were employed as part of an investment strategy that involved hosting network full nodes, which entitled the fund to a portion of each block reward. By reinvesting the dividends earned, a practice influenced by Reiss (2017), the model fund generated returns of more than 400% over 12 months. Researchers or educators using this strategy could apportion returns as needed to both reinvestment and funding, potentially reducing reliance on student debt, grants from government and industry, and local and national budgets. This shift in funding could help to reclaim for the public good the advantages, economic and otherwise, derived from scientific research and higher education.

CRYPTOCURRENCY STOCHASTIC VOLATILITY MODELING

Having framed this work in the tradition of *Bildung*, noting that society is the essential beneficiary of science and higher education funding, this paper methodologically centers on cryptocurrency stochastic volatility modeling, a modeling approach that treats price volatility as a random variable in order to increase the accuracy of predictions. To this point, the cryptocurrency asset class lacks full-fledged valuation methods. Current metrics need to be examined and reframed in order to assemble a coherent methodological framework. To this end, we review, in the next section, the relevant cryptocurrency volatility metrics. In reviewing this literature, we examine and deploy generalized autoregressive conditional heteroskedasticity (GARCH) modeling as a way to understand what types of coins may fund science and education. By deploying GARCH, a well-known econometrics tool, we are able to model the statistical volatility within a time series underscoring standard returns from the examined asset. Additionally, GARCH affords the opportunity to forecast the type of wealth generation that may be created over a period of time.

METHOD

Below, using GARCH, we examine PIVX, Dash, and BTC to elucidate the volatility of cryptocurrency markets (Byun et al., 2015). Engle and Bollerslev (1986) detailed how GARCH modeling underscores the way financial markets change, highlighting price volatility during turbulent periods and reverting to price stability during times of market stability. GARCH and other stochastic volatility models have been used in conjunction with the Black Scholes options model to afford a more robust pricing framework (Bollerslev et al., 1988). Moreover, by employing a stochastic volatility model, developed to redress some of the methodological complexities and shortcomings of the Black-Sholes (Andersen & Bollerslev, 2018), this chapter examines the propensity for the examined crypto assets to continue to generate wealth. GARCH's statistical modeling is predicated on financial time-series data, underscoring how heteroskedasticity depicts patterns of irregularity and variation in a financial model. Specifically, a GARCH analysis of the above-mentioned coins will provide insight into whether these cryptocurrencies have wealth generating possibilities.

Cryptocurrency researchers have widely used GARCH to model price fluctuation in the asset class. Dyhrberg (2016), Gronwald (2014), and Katsiampa (2017), as primary examples, all deployed GARCH to frame BTC's, and to a lesser degree, ALTcoins' volatility metrics to determine whether the assets were overbought or oversold. However, Dyhrberg (2016), Gronwald (2014), and Katsiampa (2017), representing the most highly cited authors who employed GARCH specific to cryptocurrency, used this measure while generally overlooking the nuances of this asset class. Chu et al. (2017), for example, recently argued that GARCH and other related models are the best tools for modeling volatility in the largest and most popular cryptocurrencies.

By bringing forward the work of Chu et al. (2017), Dyhrberg (2016), Gronwald (2014), and Katsiampa (2017), this work deploys GARCH to analyze three different coins and to retrospectively examine the models to determine if the coins could provide a starting point for a fund to support science or education. Below, using GARCH, we analyze the historical returns and detail these data in five different charts to illustrate the wealth generating possibilities. The first two charts denote the specific coin's historical market cap and returns through late July 2018. The third chart illuminates the univariate GARCH coefficients, including mu, omega, alpha 1, and beta 1, noting the confidence of the model's fit to studied coins. Chart four uses GARCH to fit a conditional sigma. Lastly, chart five forecasts conditional SD with 95% confidence within a 20-day window.

THE RESULTS

PIVX

See Figures 1-4 and Table 1.

Figure 1. PIVX pricing over a 16 month time horizon

Figure 2. PIVX daily returns over a 16 month time horizon

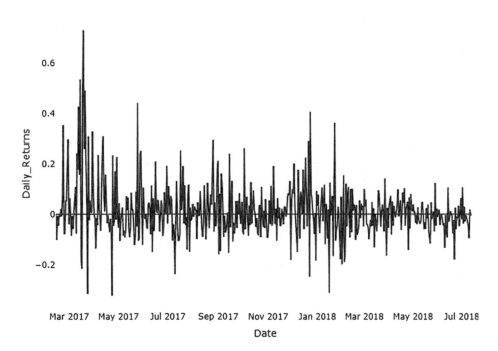

Figure 3. Fitted conditional sigma

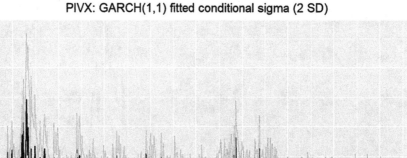

Figure 4. PIVX Forecast for conditional SD

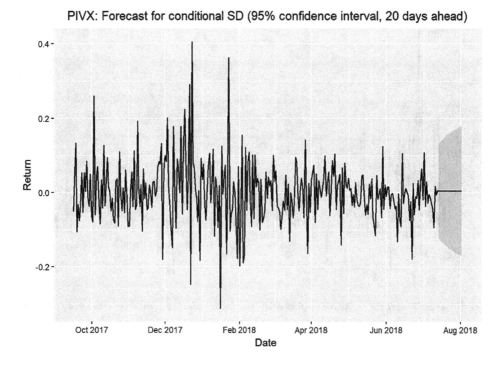

Table 1. PIVX coefficients: GARCH (1,1)

	Estimate	Std. Error	t Value	Pr(>|t|)
Mu	0.0042	0.0039	1.0695	0.2848
omega	0.0004	0.0005	0.8649	0.3871
alpha1	0.1199	0.0636	1.8859	0.0593
beta1	0.8461	0.0984	8.5997	0.0000

DASH

See Figures 5-8 and Table 2.

BTC

See Figures 9-12 and Table 3.

THE DISCUSSION OF RESULTS

Above, we used GARCH to analyze the volatility of PIVX, Dash, and BTC. For each of the examined coins, respectively, the first two charts highlight historical market cap and daily returns. In this discussion, we turn our attention to the third, fourth and fifth charts, named, respectively, 1) *Coefficients- GARCH (1,1)*, 2) GARCH (1,1) fitted conditional sigma, and 3) Forecast for conditional SD. These three charts

Figure 5. Dash pricing over a 16 month time horizon

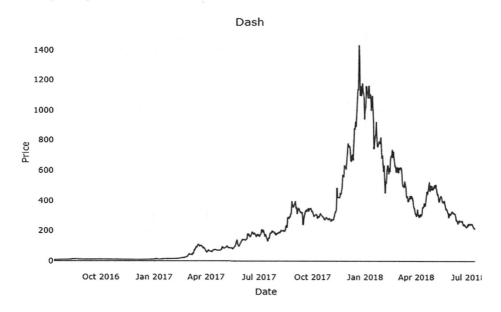

Figure 6. Dash returns over a 16 month time horizon

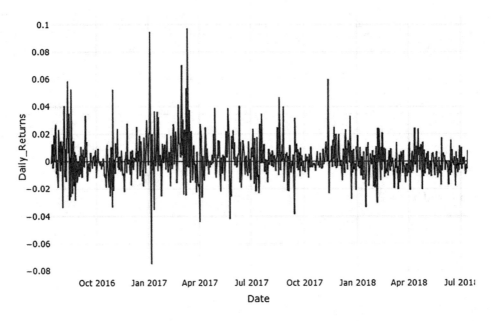

Figure 7. Dash fitted conditional sigma

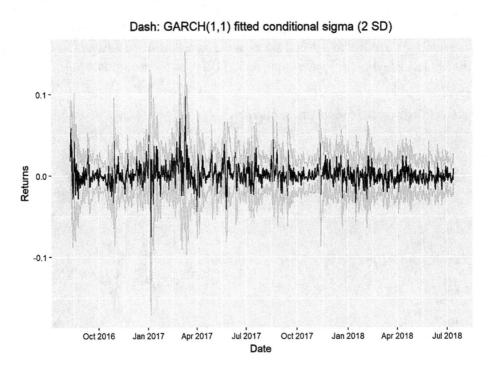

Figure 8. Dash forecast for conditional SD

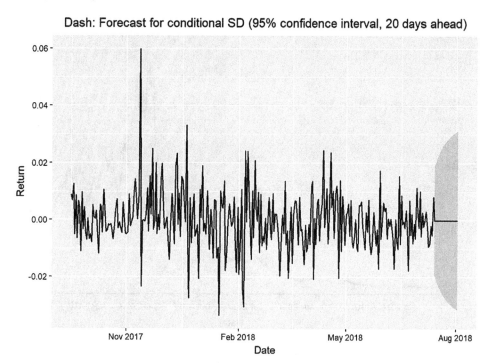

Table 2. Dash coefficients: GARCH (1,1)

	Estimate	**Std. Error**	**t Value**	**Pr(>|t|)**
Mu	-0.0001	0.0005	-0.1822	0.8554
Omega	0.0000	0.0000	3.5344	0.0004
alpha1	0.2552	0.0561	4.5481	0.0000
beta1	0.6819	0.0556	12.2739	0.0000

highlight that these three coins will experience only extreme volatility. That is, PIVX, Dash, and BTC, at the time of the analysis, seem to exhibit only aspects of extreme price swings. The assets do not seem to embody, based on the GARCH analysis, any of the wealth generating possibilities that all three of these currencies exhibited in 2017.

The volatility of these assets is illustrated in the above analysis. However, in the fifth chart, the forecast for conditional SD only predicts with 95% confidence that PIVX, Dash, and BTC will experience only volatility. In other words, there may be possibilities to generate alpha—alpha underscoring the profits derived from the trade—by shorting the assets; however, the wealth generating possibilities seemed to be exhausted, or at least temporarily stalled, at the time of analysis.

These findings, in context, greatly differ from the initial studies of Dyhrberg (2016), who posited that BTC "showed several similarities to gold and the dollar indicating hedging capabilities and advan-

Figure 9. BTC pricing over a 16 month time horizon

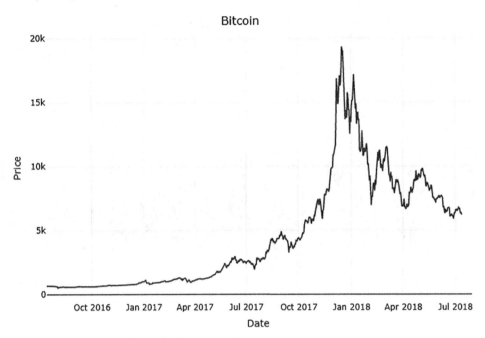

Figure 10. BTC Returns of a twenty-month time horizon

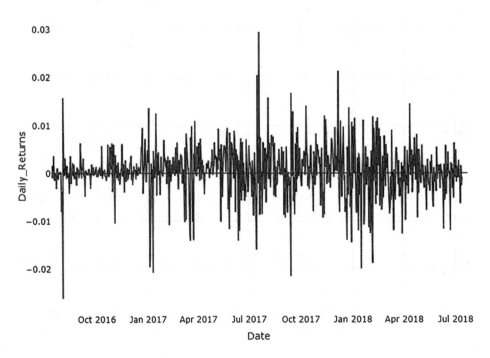

Figure 11. BTC GARCH

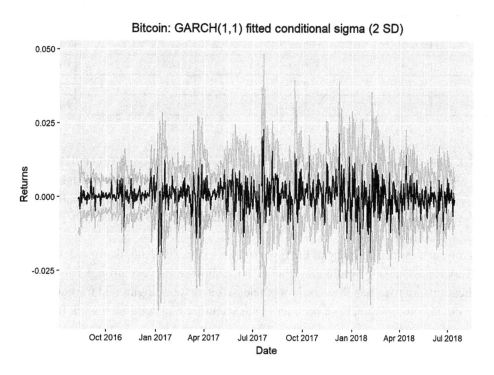

Figure 12. BTC conditional SD

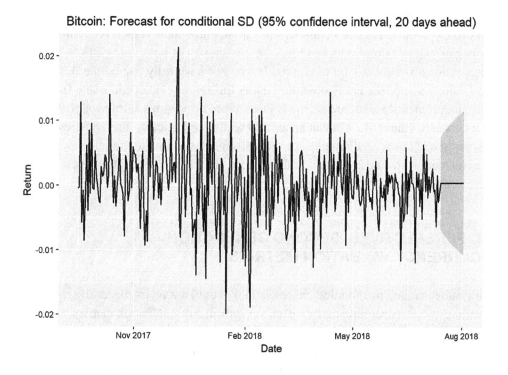

Table 3. BTC coefficients: GARCH (1,1)

	Estimate	Std. Error	t Value	Pr(>ltl)
Mu	0.0004	0.0002	2.8439	0.0045
omega	0.0000	0.0000	3.1357	0.0017
alpha1	0.2145	0.0366	5.8632	0.0000
beta1	0.7691	0.0342	22.5001	0.0000

tages" (p. 85). Underscored in charts GARCH (1,1) and Forecast for conditional SD, BTC does have a mu, omega, alpha 1 and beta 1 under .05, but this still is not likely predictive enough for the asset class to be any type of mitigating hedge against either gold or the U.S. dollar. Moreover, the results indicate, much like the work of Walther, Klein, and Thu (2018), that PIVX, Dash, and BTC may only continue to experience volatility.

More plainly, and mirroring many of the reports from early 2018, the likelihood that cryptocurrency markets will continue to create wealth may not be, in the short-term, very strong. This contention, by the time of publication, is altogether obvious. Nonetheless, the methodologies and frameworks employed to derive such conclusions, to date, have been less than scientific and continued work in this area remains important.

LIMITATIONS AND FUTURE RESEARCH, AND CONCLUSIONS

As indicated in the results, both Dash and BTC cohere with and standardly fit into a GARCH analysis, yet neither is likely to fund science or higher education, since their respective returns are extremely volatile. Moreover, the work above underscores the complexity of purchasing PIVX, Dash, or BTC as part of an institutional portfolio. Chu et al. (2017) may not have fully parsed the differences between volatility and valuation models, likely operating under the assumption, as do many financial modeling tools, that cryptocurrencies' values are narrowly intertwined only with arbitrage opportunities related to profits in fiat currency. Chu et al., while nuanced and with a sophisticated literature review and relevant conclusions, suggested that a need remains for more stringent, systematic literature and methodological reviews. In agreement with Chu et al., and building upon Baur et al. (2018), this research calls for more detailed valuation metrics in cryptocurrency.

THE EMIC PERSPECTIVES: SECOND GENERATION CRYPTOCURRENCY VALUATION METRICS

In our call for more detailed methodological research, it would not be intellectually rigorous to overlay a first-generation/second-generation narrative onto cryptocurrency valuation metrics. More specifically, GARCH is likely only a first-generation cryptocurrency model that needs to be nuanced to more fully align with the asset class. With that caveat aside, further research likely should incorporate the work of Hayes (2015, 2017). Extending Pike's (1967) theoretical framework, built upon by numerous qualitative researchers such as Emdin (2006) and Kincheloe and Tobin (2009), the *etic* and *emic* refer, respectively, to outsider and insider observational perspectives. To date, Hayes (2015, 2017) has conceptualized a valuation metric centered on BTC that is more aligned with an emic perspective, nuancing the model and covering new ground. Hayes's models represent some of the more advanced framings of BTC, and more broadly, of the ALTcoin markets. Hayes's postulations tend to reflect an insider's vantage point, if not a completely new imagining of valuation metrics. For instance, citing Yermack's (2013) conception of BTC 'moneyness' and Gertchev (2013), Harwick (2014), and Bergstra's (2014) contention that BTC is a store of value akin to gold, Hayes (2015) proffered a number of valuation formulas, from a metric for BTC mining to a formula for ALTcoin values. In later work, Hayes (2017) accounted for the value inherent in cryptocurrency by parsing out issues that are not applicable and centering on deploying metrics that focused on the cost of mining, the intersection of software and network architecture, the acceptance of cryptocurrency as a means of exchange, and whether a currency was widely available on multiple exchanges. The next modeling for cryptocurrency valuation models likely needs to employ Hayes's (2015, 2017) modeling that is a hybrid of the more traditional time-series modeling, primarily because this type of modeling more thoroughly represents the cryptocurrency markets.

THE ETIC: FIRST-GENERATION CRYPTOCURRENCY VALUATION METRICS

Generally, the first generation of cryptocurrency valuation metrics should be viewed as etic approaches to understanding a new asset class, with traditional economists overlaying industry-standard tools in ways that did not altogether fit. For instance, the etic is perceived in the straightforward deployment of GARCH as a tool to measure volatility and price targets. Specifically, the appropriation and extension of GARCH tends to confine the multivariate valuation metrics needed to understand BTC and alternative coins (ALTcoins) to an overly formulaic account, not fully accounting for the complexity of the ecosphere or the specific modes of thought that tend to drives its currency development and deployment.

MOVING AWAY FROM ETIC MODELS

While GARCH admittedly has many iterations and new models, the deployment of a GARCH-only analysis nevertheless overlooks Greer's (1997) contention that assets within a class share some fundamental characteristics, and some of these characteristics are distinct to cryptocurrencies. Burniske and White (2017), for instance, noted that BTC is unique in that it is not affected by price movements in other asset classes, meaning that, despite volatility within cryptocurrency, there are no price correlations to other asset classes. Burniske and Tartar (2017) extended the initial framework by including in valuation the number of outstanding coins, the velocity of the currency, and the price and quality of the community supporting the currency. Considering both Burniske and White (2017) and Burniske and Tartar (2017), who provided emic perspectives, the initial GARCH cryptocurrency models may be too focused on conditional standard deviation and volatility clustering to provide long-term perspectives on price. GARCH modeling may therefore be more helpful if nuances are made to better reflect the distinctiveness of cryptocurrencies. Although various GARCH analyses arguably represent the more advanced modeling in this area, there are still a number of methodological problems, even in the most sophisticated work, related to using only this type of modeling.

Although a comprehensive scoping of GARCH analysis and cryptocurrency is beyond the scope of this paper, this work underscores that the time has come for full-length methodological reviews to be published on both cryptocurrency volatility and valuation models. As cryptocurrency matures as an asset class, both the scholarly literature and methodological reviews need to advance and broaden their respective scopes. Chu et al. (2017), for example, recently argued that IGARCH and GJRGARCH models are the best tools for modeling the volatility in the largest and most popular cryptocurrencies. Chu et al. (2017) persuasively highlighted the need to nuance metrics and deploy different models in order to more accurately gauge valuation of cryptocurrencies.

ADVANCING THE RESEARCH: NEXT STEPS

In spite of its sophistication and emic perspectives, Hayes's (2015, 2017) work may be insufficient on its own to the task of appraising which cryptocurrency can be deployed for science and higher education funding, since an accurate evaluation must consider not only valuation metrics but also an enacted network effect. Hayes's (2017) work, in particular, is a production framework, rather any type of valuation metric, although this work has been widely cited as the latter (Indera et al., 2017; Parham, 2017). The predictable cost of BTC, and moving forward with insights of Hayes, Balcilar et al. (2017) articulated a model for BTC returns, accounting for volatility, by employing a nonparametric causality-in-quantiles test. Balcilar et al. (2017) underscored the significance of modeling nonlinearity and the need to calculate for complexities of tail behavior related to causal relationships. More precisely, Balcilar et al. (2017) noted that a straightforward conditional distribution is not sufficiently complex to predict BTC's volatility. Balcilar et al. (2017) thereby greatly improved the valuation metrics for cryptocurrency by providing a methodological bridge that conjoined valuation with network effect theory. While Hayes (2017) improved on the various GARCH-only models of analysis, his work should likely be blended with consideration of network effect in order to construct tenable funding mechanisms. As a result, hybrid methodologies must be advanced. Peterson (2018) provided an overview of network models, which was modified by Van Vliet (2018). Collectively, Balcilar et al. (2017), Hayes (2015), and others, may provide the beginnings of new methodological work for cryptocurrency valuation metrics.

RETURNING TO FUNDING SCIENCE AND EDUCATION

In previous work, we described how a group of education researchers and Wall Street bankers developed a fund that generated significant returns, in spite of the market's volatility. Our first model was developed to serve as an alternative funding mechanism for scientific research. As the market has developed, this model, although initially successful, is insufficiently complex to enact now. In our first cryptocurrency model, we focused specifically on funding basic scientific research. We continue to see potential in the vision of ALTcoins to fund science and education, yet it will likely more fully cohere with Lehner and Ziegler (Ch. 7) and not our initial framework.

POSTSCRIPT: A FULL YEAR INTO THE BEAR MARKET

Let us follow the logic of things from the beginning. Or, rather, from the end: modern times. We are, as I am writing these lines, witnessing a complete riot against some class of experts, in domains that are too difficult for us to understand, such as macroeconomic reality, and in which not only the expert is not an expert, but he doesn't know it. (Nassim Nicholas Taleb, 2018, Foreword p. XIII, The Bitcoin Standard)

At time of final editing, in February 2019, Nassim Nicholas Taleb's writing, as cited above, is particularly prescient. More specifically, Taleb posited a particularly salient contrarian framework that today's economic authorities are not altogether the authorities that they think they are. The knowledge claims of a generation of Keynesian authorities are seemingly null and void. When these experts are pressed about climbing inflation, bank-bailouts, and underfunded education, they seemingly can only shrug and print more currency, rather than redressing the complexities of the global economy. Summers (2017) noted that the asset bubbles created by the incessant printing of money from central banks can only go badly.

Yet, economic experts tend to discount Summers's (2017) warnings. And, over the last year of the cryptocurrency Bear Market, traditional financial experts and markets are denouncing cryptocurrency as a bubble, akin to the tech bubble of the late 1990s or the housing bubble of 2007. Nonetheless, such experts are dismissing the innovation that cryptocurrencies represent whether BTC is at 20 K or 1 K. If price is all that matters, the authors could concede that the 'experts' are right. However, even a decade later, the authors would be remiss if we did not fully contemplate the complexities, the disillusionment, and full existential crisis that was the Financial Crisis of 2008. As Taleb noted, in 2008, the financial experts were not, sadly, aware of their nonexpert status.

Having considered Taleb's insight on the 'experts' and contemplated the Financial Crisis of 2008, we return to the notion of wealth generation. More specifically, in order to fully fund education and science, modern society needs to contemplate how to generate wealth to fund such endeavors. Lietaer (2013) posited a type alternative framework currency, noting:

The underlying mechanisms referred to here turn out to be specific features of our money system. Money or lack thereof, is a fundamental component of our lives. It is not, however, just the lack of money that is precipitating present trends or preventing us from addressing current challenges. Rather, it is the limited functionality of our money and monetary system that is a major force behind our present disorders. Many of the problems we face, and the solutions we seek, reside within the architecture of our current monetary system and in our understanding of, and our agreements around, money. (B.A. Lietaer, The Future of Money, pg. 4)

Although this chapter underscored that the examined cryptocurrencies cannot, in their current iteration generate sufficient wealth to overturn existing funding paradigms, the authors emphasize the aspirational merit of Lietear (2013). That is, if governments and funding experts worldwide deem it acceptable to continue to underfund education and science, it may be high time to generate our own currencies for such needs.

REFERENCES

AlterNet. (2011). Retrieved from https://www.alternet.org/story/151921/chomsky%3A_public_educa-tion_under_massive_corp orate_assault_%E2%80%94_what%27s_next

Andersen, T. G., & Bollerslev, T. (2018). *Volatility*. Edward Elgar Publishing Limited.

Aud, S., Hussar, W., Planty, M., Snyder, T., Bianco, K., Fox, M. A., . . . Drake, L. (2010). *The condition of education* (NCES 2010-028). Retrieved from https://eric.ed.gov/?id=ED509940

Balcilar, M., Bouri, E., Gupta, R., & Roubaud, D. (2017). Can volume predict Bitcoin returns and volatil-ity? A quantiles-based approach. *Economic Modelling*, *64*, 74–81. doi:10.1016/j.econmod.2017.03.019

Barr, M. J., & McClellan, G. S. (2018). *Budgets and Financial Management in Higher Education* (3rd ed.). San Francisco: Jossey-Bass.

Barr, N. (2017). Funding post-compulsory education. In G. Johnes, J. Johnes, T. Agasisti, & L. López-Torres (Eds.), *Handbook on the Economics of Education*. Academic Press; doi:10.4337/9781785369070.00021

Baur, D. G., Dimpfl, T., & Kuck, K. (2018). Bitcoin, gold and the US dollar: A replication and exten-sion. *Finance Research Letters*, *25*, 103–110. doi:10.1016/j.frl.2017.10.012

Bergstra, J. A. (2014). *Bitcoin: not a currency-like informational commodity*. Informatics.

Birkhead, N. A. (2016). *State Budgetary Delays in an Era of Party Polarization*. State and Local. doi:10.1177/0160323X16687813

Bollerslev, T., Engle, R. F., & Wooldridge, J. M. (1988). A capital asset pricing model with time-varying covariances. *Journal of Political Economy*, *96*(1), 116–131. doi:10.1086/261527

Burniske, C., & Tatar, J. (2017). *Cryptoassets: The Innovative Investor's Guide to Bitcoin and Beyond*. New York: McGraw Hill Professional.

Burniske, C., & White, A. (2017). *Bitcoin: Ringing the bell for a new asset class*. Retrieved from https://research.ark-invest.com/hubfs/1_Download_Files_ARK-Invest/White_Papers/Bitcoin-Ringing-The-Bell-For-A-New-Asset-Class.pdf

Byun, S. J., Jeon, B. H., Min, B., & Yoon, S.-J. (2015). The role of the variance premium in Jump GARCH option pricing models. *Journal of Banking & Finance*, *59*, 38–56. doi:10.1016/j.jbankfin.2015.05.009

Chomsky N. (2011). *Public Education Under Massive Corporate Assault—What's Next?* Academic Press.

Christensen, C. M., & Eyring, H. J. (2011). *The Innovative University: Changing the DNA of Higher Education from the Inside Out*. San Francisco: Jossey-Bass.

Christensen, C. M., Horn, M. B., Soares, L., & Caldera, L. (2011). *Disrupting college: How disruptive innovation can deliver quality and affordability to postsecondary education*. Retrieved from https://www.americanprogress.org/issues/economy/reports/2011/02/08/9034/disrupting-college/

Christman, D. E. (2000). Multiple realities: Characteristics of loan defaulters at a two-year public institution. *Community College Review*, *27*(4), 16–32. doi:10.1177/009155210002700402

Chu, J., Chan, S., Nadarajah, S., & Osterrieder, J. (2017). GARCH modelling of cryptocurrencies. *J. Risk Financ. Manage.*, *10*(4), 17. doi:10.3390/jrfm10040017

Dillon, E., & Carey, K. (2009). *Drowning in Debt: The Emerging Student Loan Crisis*. Washington, DC: Education Sector.

Dyhrberg, A. H. (2016). Bitcoin, gold and the dollar–A GARCH volatility analysis. *Finance Research Letters*, *16*, 85–92. doi:10.1016/j.frl.2015.10.008

Dynarski, M. (1994). Who defaults on student loans? Findings from the national postsecondary student aid study. *Economics of Education Review*, *13*(1), 55–68. doi:10.1016/0272-7757(94)90023-X

Emdin, C. (2006). Beyond coteaching: Power dynamics, cosmopolitanism and the psychoanalytic dimension. *Forum Qualitative Social Research*, *7*(4). doi:10.17169/fqs-7.4.189

Emdin, C. (2010). *Urban Science Education for the Hip-Hop Generation*. Boston: Sense.

Emdin, C., & Lehner, E. (2006). Situating cogenerative dialogue in a cosmopolitan ethic. *Forum Qualitative Social Research*, *7*(2). doi:10.17169/fqs-7.2.125

Engle, R. F., & Bollerslev, T. (1986). Modelling the persistence of conditional variances. *Econometric Reviews*, *5*(1), 1–50. doi:10.1080/07474938608800095

Gertchev, N. (2013). *The moneyness of bitcoin. Mises Daily*. Auburn: Ludwig von Mises.

Gilchrist, H. (2018). *Higher education as a human right*. Retrieved from https://ssrn.com/abstract=3100852

Gittleson, K., & Usher, B. (2017). Higher education for refugees. *Stanford Soc. Innov. Rev.* Retrieved from https://ssir.org/articles/entry/higher_education_for_refugees

Gladieux, L. (1995). Federal student aid policy: A history and an assessment. In *Financing Postsecondary Education: The Federal Role*. Retrieved from http://www2.ed.gov/offices/OPE/PPI/FinPostSecEd/gladieux.html

Gladieux, L., & Perna, L. (2005). *Borrowers who drop out: A neglected aspect of the college student loan trend*. Retrieved from http://www.highereducation.org/reports/borrowing/index.shtml

Greenwood, D. J. (2008). Theoretical research, applied research, and action research. In C. R. Hale (Ed.), *Engaging Contradictions: Theory, Politics, and Methods of Activist Scholarship* (pp. 319–340). Berkeley, CA: University of California Press.

Greenwood, J. D., & Levin, M. (2011). *Introduction to Action Research* (2nd ed.). Thousand Oaks, CA: Sage.

Greer, R. J. (1997). What is an asset class, anyway? *The Journal of Portfolio.*

Gronwald, M. (2014). *The economics of bitcoins: Market characteristics and price jumps.* Retrieved from https://ideas.repec.org/p/ces/ceswps/_5121.html

Guba, E. G., & Lincoln, Y. S. (1989). *Fourth generation evaluation.* Thousand Oaks, CA: Sage.

Harwick, C. (2014). *Crypto-Currency and the Problem of Intermediation.* Available at SSRN. doi:10.2139srn.2523771

Hayes, A. (2015). *What factors give cryptocurrencies their value: An empirical analysis.* Retrieved from https://papers.ssrn.com/sol3/papers.cfm?abstract_id=2579445

Hayes, A. S. (2017). Cryptocurrency value formation: An empirical study leading to a cost of production model for valuing bitcoin. *Telematics and Informatics, 34*(7), 1308–1321. doi:10.1016/j.tele.2016.05.005

Hillman, N. W. (2014). *College on credit: A multilevel analysis of student loan default* (37th ed.). Rev. High.

Indera, N. I., Yassin, I. M., Zabidi, A., & Rizman, Z. I. (2017). Non-linear autoregressive with exogeneous input (NARX) Bitcoin price prediction model using PSO-optimized parameters and moving average technical indicators. *Rev. Sci. Fondam. Appl., 9*(3S), 791–808. doi:10.4314/jfas.v9i3s.61

Katsiampa, P. (2017). Volatility estimation for Bitcoin: A comparison of GARCH models. *Economics Letters, 158,* 3–6. doi:10.1016/j.econlet.2017.06.023

Kazin, M. (2016). Trump and American populism: Old whine, new bottles. *Foreign Affairs, 95,* 17.

Kincheloe, J. L., & Tobin, K. (2009). The much exaggerated death of positivism. *Cultural Studies of Science Education, 4*(3), 513–528. doi:10.100711422-009-9178-5

Lehner, E. (2007, July 25). level science learning as gateways to standards based discourse. *Cultural Studies of Science Education, 2*(2), 441–473. doi:10.100711422-007-9062-0

Lehner, E., & Finley, K. (2016). *Should the New England Education Research Organization start a journal in the age of audit culture? Reflections on academic publishing, metrics, and the new academy.* Retrieved from https://academicworks.cuny.edu/bx_pubs/15/

Lehner, E., Hunzeker, D., & Ziegler, J. R. (2017). Funding science with science: Cryptocurrency and independent academic research funding. *Ledger, 2.* Retrieved from https://ledger.pitt.edu/ojs/index.php/ledger/article/view/108

Levin, M., & Greenwood, D. J. (2017). *Creating a New Public University and Reviving Democracy.* New York: Berghahn.

Lietaer, B. (2013). *The future of money.* Random House.

Luke, D. A., Sarli, C. C., Suiter, A. M., Carothers, B. J., Combs, T. B., Allen, J. L., ... Evanoff, B. A. (2018). The translational science benefits model: A new framework for assessing the health and societal benefits of clinical and translational sciences. *Clinical and Translational Science, 11*(1), 77–84. doi:10.1111/cts.12495 PMID:28887873

McMahon, W. W. (2009). *Higher Learning, Greater Good: The Private and Social Benefits of Higher Education*. Baltimore, MD: Johns Hopkins University.

Mead, W. R. (2017). The Jacksonian revolt: American populism and the liberal order. *Foreign Affairs, 96*, 2.

Parham, R. (2017). *The predictable cost of Bitcoin*. Retrieved from https://papers.ssrn.com/sol3/papers.cfm?abstract_id=3080586

Peters, M. A. (2018). The end of neoliberal globalisation and the rise of authoritarian populism. *Educational Philosophy and Theory, 50*(4), 323–325. doi:10.1080/00131857.2017.1305720

Pike, K. L. (1967). *Language in Relation to a Unified Theory of the Structure of Human Behavior* (2nd rev. ed.). The Hague, The Netherlands: Mouton. doi:10.1515/9783111657158

Reiss, D. (2017). *What You Should Know About Dividend Reinvestment Plans*. Academic Press.

Rickman, D. S., & Wang, H. (2018). Two tales of two US states: Regional fiscal austerity and economic performance. *Regional Science and Urban Economics, 68*, 46–55. doi:10.1016/j.regsciurbeco.2017.10.008

Roger, J., & Baum, R. C. (2017). Student loans: This economic bubble will wreak havoc when it bursts. Fortune. Retrieved from http://fortune.com/2017/07/10/higher-education-student-loans-economic-bubble-federal//

Roth, W. M. (2010). *Language, learning, context: Talking the talk*. Routledge. doi:10.4324/9780203853177

Summers, R. (2017). *The Everything Bubble: The Endgame for Central Bank Policy*. Random.

Taleb, N. N. (2018). Foreword. In S. Ammous (Ed.), *The Bitcoin Standard: The Decentralized Alternative to Central Banking*. Hoboken, NJ: Wiley.

Tasca, P., Aste, T., Pelizzon, L., & Perony, N. (Eds.), *Banking Beyond Banks and Money. New Economic Windows*. Cham: Springer.

The Belmont Report (1979). Retrieved from https://www.hhs.gov/ohrp/regulations-and-policy/belmont-report/read-the-belmont-report/index.html

The Pew Charitable Trusts. (2015, June 11). *Federal and state funding of higher education: A changing landscape*. Retrieved from http://www.pewtrusts.org/en/research-and-analysis/issue-briefs/2015/06/federal-and-state-funding-of-higher-education

Tobin, K. (2010). Tuning in to others' voices: Beyond the hegemony of mono-logical narratives. value. *Applied Economics Letters, 26*(7), 554–560.

Van Vliet, B. (2018). (Forthcoming). An Alternative Model of Metcalfe's Law for Valuing Bitcoin. *Economics Letters*. doi:10.2139srn.3087398

Walther, T., Klein, T., & Thu, H. P. (2018). Bitcoin is not the new gold: A comparison of volatility, correlation, and portfolio performance. *International Review of Financial Analysis*, *59*, 105–116. doi:10.1016/j.irfa.2018.07.010

Yermack, D. (2015). Is Bitcoin a real currency? An economic appraisal. In Handbook of digital currency. Academic Press. doi:10.1016/B978-0-12-802117-0.00002-3

Chapter 9

Blockchain 2.0:
An Edge Over Technologies

Charu Virmani
Manav Rachna International Institute of Research and Studies, India

Dimple Juneja Gupta
Poornima University, India

Tanu Choudhary
Manav Rachna International Institute of Research and Studies, India

ABSTRACT

Blockchain is a shared and distributed ledger across an open or private processing system that expedites the process of recording transactions and data management in a business network. It empowers the design of decentralized transactions, smart contracts, and intelligent assets that can be managed over internet. It formulates the revolutionary decision-making governance systems with more egalitarian users, and autonomous organizations that can control over internet without any third-party involved. This disruptive technology has tremendous opportunities that open the doors to detract the power from centralized authorities in the sphere of communications, business, and even politics or law. This chapter outlines an introduction to the blockchain technologies and its decentralized architecture, especially from the perspective of challenges and limitations. The objective is to explore the current research topics, benefits, and drawbacks of blockchain. The study explores its potential applications for business and future directions that is all set to transfigure the digital world.

INTRODUCTION

It takes a revolution to challenge the stigmas and stereotypes prevalent in the spectrum of technology and open the window for new methodologies and ways to gush in and take over, to lead the next generation. By the same token, blockchain technology is nothing short of a revolutionary sensation for the digital world today and it would require exponential efforts to realize and utilize the potential to its full capacity.

DOI: 10.4018/978-1-5225-9257-0.ch009

Blockchain was developed to annihilate the need of an efficient and secure system for recording and tracking transaction volumes. A blockchain is a decentralized, shared, encrypted-database of records that have been administered and distributed among engaged users (Pilkington, M., 2016). It is a digital decentralize mechanism that helps the participating users to reach a consensus on the existence of a transaction/event eliminating the need of third-party/central authority. Each transaction in the distributed and shared ledger is authenticated by consensus of a majority of the users in the network (Atzori, 2015). The information is irreversible and incorruptible once it is stored in the database (Yli-Huumo et al., 2016). In fact, it is an authenticated record of each, and every transaction ever made. It provides the user's a unique experience to transfer the assets (tangible or intangible) in safe, secure and immutable way, thus eliminating the middleman from the society who plays an important role in the economic and regulatory bodies (Underwood, 2016; Mettler,2016; Peters et al.,2015). This disruptive technology can provide digital currencies, smart contracts, decentralized communications, marketplace, smart property to name a few and to enter in a new epoch focused on decentralize, immutable, secure and transparent governance; and legal systems (Mainelli and Smith, 2015). Financial administrations, democratic institutions and healthcare are the other transforming areas that could impact using blockchain solutions. Financial administrations core elements of verifying and reassigning financial data and resources very closely resemble with the blockchains key transformative impact. Cross-border outflows and trade finance are the significant current pain sockets that can be solved by blockchain-based solutions, which reduce the number of necessary intermediaries and are geographically skeptic (Nguyen, 2016).

Apart from the above-mentioned avenues of opportunity, the blockchain technology has tremendous potential to essentially change the manner in which users prepare their affairs and can create new ventures for software-primarily based businesses. The decentralized aspect of blockchain can re-implement certain attributes of traditional governance, permitting parties to obtain the advantages of formal corporate and autonomous structures, while on the same time keeping the flexibility and scale of informal online groups, with no human intercession (Wright and Filippi, 2015). This section throws light on the basic characteristic of blockchain that makes it a cost-effective and reliable solution for business while also exploring the challenges that still needs to overcome.

The history has observed a drastic shift to simplify the transfer of value and protect trust between buyers and sellers in terms of minted note and banking systems. Internet and mobile technologies have been the important technological revolutions that expedited the process of transactions while minimizing the distance between buyers and sellers. The digital economic scenario today relies heavily on a certain trusted authority. Each transactions take place via third parties — it can be an email service provider to confirm the delivery of mail; certification authority certifying the digital certificate; online social network like Facebook to make users believe that our posts/events have been shared with the ones whom they have given permission like friends/friends of friends or it can be a bank playing a significant role in managing and delivering currency remotely. The facet of trusting third-party remains same for the security and safety of the information/data in the digital world (Reid and Harrigan, 2013; Miers et al., 2013; Decker and Wattenhofer, 2013). This revolutionizing trend of transactions still possesses major concerns that remain intact like inefficiency, expensive, and vulnerability and prevents the business from efficiently exploiting services, thus suffers from the limitations as listed in Figure 1.

The growing complexity of doing business over web have emerged the need of the growth of transaction volumes that will magnify the efficient, secure and reliable transaction system (Wust and Gervais,

Figure 1. Limitations of current transactions current systems

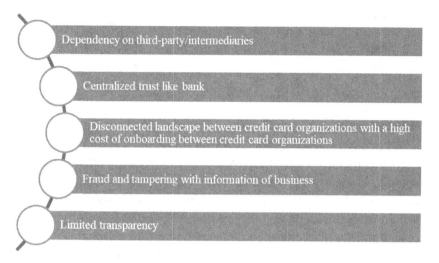

2017; Peck, 2017). Given the high volume and veracity of transactions, it deserves the energies of faster bookkeeping open payment networks to establish trust and ensuring transparency. Blockchain as the technological innovation solution was first used when the Bitcoin crypto currency was introduced. Many relate the two terms, Bitcoin and Blockchain and use it interchangeably; the following discussion will clear the difference among the two.

The Case of Bitcoin

The history of blockchain is very intricately linked to its first application i.e. Bitcoin. Blockchain essentially came to life with the birth of Bitcoin in 2008 trailed by its implementation in 2009. The architecture and principles of the network technology were initially designed for Bitcoin to address the perennial issue of a secure and widely distributed database and it was not until 2010 that Bitcoin's had started to be minted. The innovative network technology is a brainchild of 'Satoshi Nakamoto' but there have been speculations regarding as to if it were a group or an individual. After the publication of his paper "Bitcoin: A Peer-to-Peer Electronic Cash System", in 2008 Nakamoto shared his blockchain code the following year via the internet, releasing the first ever open source Bitcoin client and issuing the original Bitcoins. He was the pioneering figure to explain how the technology works and since then there has been no stopping whatsoever for this magnanimous invention rolled.

Unlike the traditional transaction system where banks play an important role as the central identity for currency, Bitcoin is a distributed electronic currency system that is based on a peer-to-peer public open transaction ledger famously known as Blockchain that maintains the integrity of currency and consequently eliminates the role of middlemen from the transaction process (Decker and Wattenhoffer, 2013).Bitcoins have distributed monetary authority. Bitcoins empowers "dollars" or "euros" as it is "mined" by users/businesses eradicating the centralized entity to monitor, authenticate and approve transactions and manage the transaction volume (Nakamoto, 2008; Yermack, D. 2015). The features of Bitcoin over other current transaction systems are depicted in Figure 2.

Figure 2. Features of Bitcoin

Evolution of Blockchain

As with most inventions, blockchain is also a combination of various theories and techniques especially the encryption methods. Many experts (Paul Bryzek, 2018; Logan Brutsche, 2017) argue that a lot of cryptology and techniques that make blockchain so secure dates back to the 90's and the only new add on that sets it apart is that every transaction over the network is hashed and carefully 'braided' together with each new transaction that takes place. Anyhow, the ever burgeoning innovation has a long life to spend and the technology is here to stay. A possible future that calls for an overhauling of present governance systems worldwide offers a big role for blockchain where an influential country like Dubai has already announced its plans for the first ever blockchain powered government in the world by 2020.

The traditional method of keeping and tracking transaction requires participants to keep their own ledger and records that makes it more expensive as third-party charges fees for providing the services such as credit card organizations. The traditional way of transaction is inefficient due to unavoidable delays in accomplishing agreements and efforts that are required to manage ledgers. Blockchain is secure unlike the traditional approach that focuses on a central system such as bank which can affect the entire business network if compromised due to reasons such as fraud, cyber security attacks, or a rudimentary human mistake/error. The architecture in focus has the ability to distribute the ledger which can be updated from time to time involving each node in the network to function as a publisher and also as a subscriber when a transaction takes place. The data is synchronized as each node can receive or send transactions to other nodes in the network. The technology offers an edge over other mechanisms as it is not only efficient as compare to current transaction systems but also economical as it eradicates plagiarism of efforts and reduces the role of intermediaries. It's also more secure over the traditional approaches as it validates information using consensus models. Thus, blockchain provides less vulnerable, legitimated and verifiable transaction volumes. Figure 3 depicts a graphical representation of the blockchain.

Although, the nodes are the same in both transaction systems, however; the way the transaction record is maintained and updated differentiates the technology from others. In the case of blockchain, the transaction will be shared and available to all the peers in the network. Consensus, provenance and immutability are the major characteristics of blockchain where consensus maintains the validity of all the transactions as all the participating nodes has to agree on one consensus before making a transaction and provenance makes sure that nodes aware about the meta information about the asset and how its proprietorship has changed over stipulated time (Pilkington, 2016; Atzori, 2015).

A transaction once recorded cannot be changed by the node assures immutability; if there is any error then a new transaction will be issued that has the responsibility to undo the effects of errors and thus forming visibility of both the transactions. Thus, the technology has become a buzzword in today's technological market owing to its various features that set it apart from the previous transaction systems as summarized in Figure 4 and are further discussed in upcoming sections.

Figure 3. Graphical representation of the blockchain

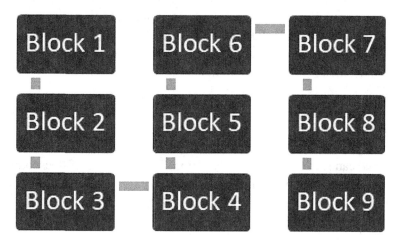

Figure 4. Features of blockchain

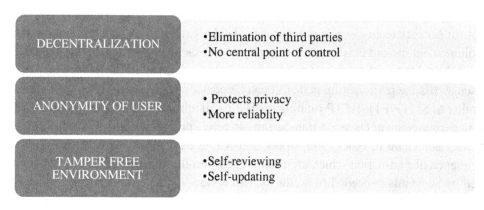

1. **De-Centralization:** Contrary to the centralized transaction systems, Blockchain destroys the functional role of third-parties as it does not require each transaction to be validated via a centralized trusted agency that naturally adds to the cost and performance of central servers. To maintain data consistency in distributed network, consensus algorithms in Blockchain are used. Further, decentralized system,
   a. Allows the users to keep control of their information and transactions thus empowering them.
   b. Is less likely to fail because of its reliance on many separate components.
   c. Offers lower transaction costs and also time is among the many fruits that one reaps out of this system feature because of elimination of third-parties required for validations.
   d. Lacks a central point of control, there is a much better chance of survival against malicious attacks.
2. **Anonymity of User:** Blockchain is verifiable by public and yet anonymous. Keeping the identity of the user as anonymous, every user can interact with the Blockchain via a generated address thereby ensuring the security of transactions which otherwise would be a daunting task.

3. **Tamper Free Environment:** Simply put, the ledger is incorruptible. The network automatically checks and updates itself every few minutes, thus operating as a self-reviewing system that ensures robustness. All the data is linked and verified at every block thus eliminating potential points of failure in the system. The nodes together create a very strong network where every node can be thought of as an operating "administrator" in itself.

It can be approximately categorized under three main types: Public Blockchain, Consortium Blockchain, and Private Blockchain (Lin and Liao, 2017; Buterin, 2015). As clarified with the name itself, in a public blockchain, anyone in the network can participate in the transaction. Each node maintains its own copy of ledger and can review/audit the transaction. The consortium Blockchain authorizes some of the nodes to be open and some kept as private whereas in case of private Blockchain, mainly nodes are private and only few nodes will decide to distribute the ledger among them. The difference among the three types is shown in the Figure 5.

BLOCKCHAIN ARCHITECTURE

The Blockchain network technology is not a routine database, that is, it is not comprised of tables with rows and columns but instead exists as a ledger of past transactions over a decentralized network. It is a peer-to-peer shared ledger that is protected, append-only, very difficult to change and can be updated via consensus across the participating nodes. It can be considered as a layer of network running on Internet as similar to SMTP/FTP/HTTP running on TCP/IP. It eliminates the central identity where nodes participate in exchanging values using transactions and thus provides a potential platform. Blockchain may be viewed as a chain of blocks that stores transaction data. Each block records and affirms the time and sequence of transaction which are then logged into the Blockchain inside a discrete network administered by standards conceded to by the system nodes (Zheng et al., 2017; Reid and Harrigane, 2013; Meirs et al, 2013). It comprises of transactions and its size is variable relying upon the sort and

Figure 5. Feature based comparison of different types of blockchain

Public blockchain	Consortium blockchain	Private blockchain
• open to the public • anybody can participate in transaction • review/audit the transaction • permissionless ledger • Ex- Bitcoin, Litecoin	• Partially decentralized. • The private part is under the control of a group of few individuals while the public part is open for participation to anybody. • Not all data is open to all of its participants. • Selected members can participate in transaction and review/audit transaction • Ex - EWF, r3	• Major part is private and is open only to a consortium or small group of individuals or organizations that have agreed to share the ledger among themselves. • A central entity controls and manages the rights to access or modify the database. • Any one cannot make and review/audit transaction • Ex - Bankchain

structure of the blockchain being used. Except for a genesis block, a reference to the previous block is additionally incorporated into the block. A beginning block is the primary block in the blockchain that was hardcoded since the inception of blockchain. The architecture of a block is likewise dependent on the type and plan of a blockchain, yet by and large there are a couple of credits that are basic to the usefulness of a block. Each block consists of hash, nonce containing timestamp of recent valid transaction, transaction and the hash of the previous block as depicted in the Figure 6.

The blocks can be further categorized into three types as shown in Figure 7 followed by a detailed description of the three.

1. **Genesis Block:** Usually, the first block of a blockchain is called a 'genesis' which is devoid of parent blocks and hence no previous hash. Bitcoin core software is the most common application of genesis block.
2. **Stale Block:** A block that is no longer required by miners to work upon is termed as a Stale block. One important aspect is that almost every miner that is working to solve the hash puzzle would also be working on this block.

Figure 6. Structure of blocks in Blockchain

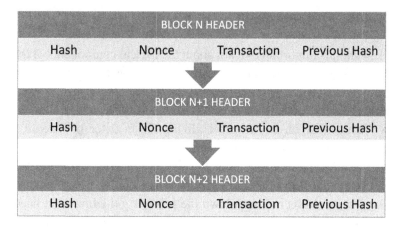

Figure 7. Types of blocks

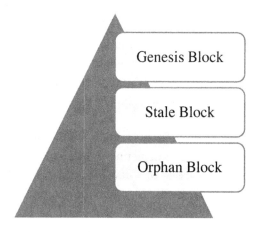

3. **Orphan Block:** Orphan blocks are usually occurred at times when two miners happen to create blocks simultaneously and are also referred as detached blocks. At one time in history these blocks were accepted to be valid but when a longer chain was created without this previously accepted block, they were ultimately rejected.

The other components of a block also include:

- A block number
- Previous Block's hash
- **Nonce:** Basically, a 4-byte field that usually begins with zero and increments for every hash calculation.
- **Timestamp:** The current time as seconds along with the time of creation of the block.
- Hash of the current block

Basically, every block has a block number that is combined with the previous and current hashes which helps the user to determine the order in which the transaction took place. The nonce in the block is used for proof-of-work.

Logical Components of Blockchain

To understand Blockchain, it is important to learn about the logical components of the underlying architecture. The ecosystem comprises of four architectural components as depicted in the Figure 8 below:

- **Node Application:** Every Internet-connected participant needs to install and run an application particular they wish to take an interest in. Utilizing the instance of Bitcoin for instance, every participant must run the Bitcoin wallet application.
- **Shared Ledger:** The shared ledger implies the shared contents and databases accessible to the participants of a particular Blockchain Ecosystem. It is a data structure managed inside the node application. The distributed record logs down the rules or guidelines that need to be followed in each participant involved in the system. It is an immutable record in which the transaction can be recorded once and can be accessed by all the participants on the network. For instance, in a Bitcoin hub application, at that point one need to maintain every one of the principles set down in the ledger and can interact as per the rules of the Bitcoin hub application. Once the node application is running, one can sight the shared ledger for that ecosystem. There is no upper limit to have node application per participant, but it is important to note that regardless the number of the ecosystem of the participant, there is one ledger for each ecosystem. A shared ledger is not only the single source of truth wherein each participant holds a duplicate copy of the ledger via replication, but also only authenticated and authorized participants can view the transactions they are permitted to.
- **Consensus Algorithm:** The "rule of the game" describing how the ecosystem is arrived at an agreement of the distributed ledger and depicting the status of the network is the major concern of the consensus algorithm. Introduction of a new block can only alter the state of the blockchain and thus protects it from tampering. Each ecosystem may adopt a different consensus varied upon

Figure 8. Architectural components of a blockchain

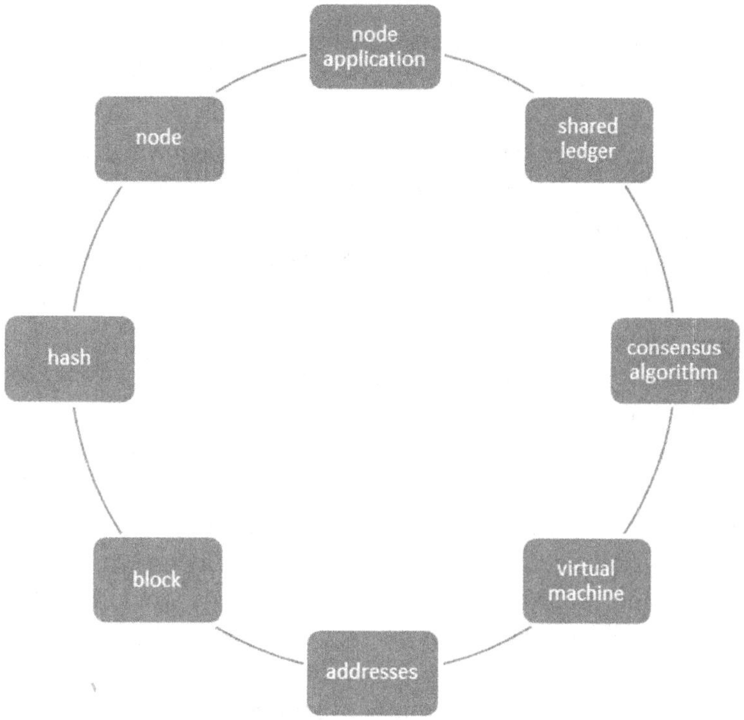

the characteristic of the required ecosystem; the following two broad classifications of consensus exist:

○ *Proof-based, leader-based*, or the Nakamoto consensus: A leader is chosen who professes a final value
○ *Byzantine fault tolerance-based*: Based upon the rounds of votes.

Some of the consensus algorithms are discussed as below:

- **Proof of Work:** The foundation of PoW (proof of work) is based upon the fact that a random node is designated every time to produce a new block. To create a valid block, the consensus algorithm trusts on the proof that sufficient computational resources have been disbursed. Every node of the network calculates a hash value of the block header in PoW. The block header consists of a nonce and miners that would change the nonce frequently to obtain different hash values. The calculated value must be equal to or smaller than a certain given value is one requirement of the consensus. When one node reaches the target value, it would broadcast the block to other nodes and all other nodes must mutually confirm the correctness of the hash value. Other miners would append this new block to their own blockchain, if the block is validated Nodes that calculate the hash values are called miners and the PoW procedure is called mining in Blockchain. In this model, nodes compete with each other in order to be selected in proportion to their computing capacity.

The following equation sums up the Proof of Work requirement in blockchain:

$$H \ (N \parallel P\_hash \parallel Tx \parallel Tx \parallel \ldots Tx) < Target$$

where N is a nonce, P_hash is a hash of the previous block, Tx represents transactions in the block, and Target is the target network difficulty value.

- **Proof of Stake:** A node or user has enough stakes in the system which lays the foundation of this algorithm. For example, the user holds a definite proportion of the network's total value so that any malicious attack would compensate the advantages of performing any kind of an attack on the system (Wood, 2014; King and Nadal, 2012). Thus, increases protection and makes it very expensive to accomplish an attack. A formula is used that searches for the lowest hash value in the combination along with the size of the stake. In comparison to PoW, PoS saves more energy and is much effective. Attacks might arrive as a consequence as the mining cost is estimated around zero. Many block- chains adopt PoW at the beginning stage and gradually move to PoS. For instance, Ethereum is planning to move from Ethash (a kind of PoW) to Casper (a kind of PoS).
- **Practical Byzantine Fault Tolerance:** PBFT (Practical byzantine fault tolerance) is a replication algorithm to tolerate byzantine faults. Since PBFT could handle up to one-third of the malicious byzantine replicas, Hyper ledger Fabric utilizes the PBFT as its consensus algorithm. A new block is determined in a round. According to some rules, a primary would be selected, in each round. And it is also responsible for ordering the transaction (Lamport, 1982). The whole process could be divided into three phases: *pre-prepared, prepared and commit*. In each phase, a node would enter next phase if it has received votes from over two-third of all nodes. Every node is known to the network is a pre-requisite of the PBFT. Like PBFT, Stellar Consensus Protocol (SCP) is also a Byzantine agreement protocol. In PBFT, each node has to query other nodes while SCP gives participants the right to choose which set of other participants to believe. Based on PBFT, Antshares has implemented their dBFT (delegated byzantine fault tolerance). In dBFT, some professional nodes are voted to record the transactions.

Many protocols have been proposed for distributed systems and blockchain like PAXOS, RAFT, and Federated Byzantine Agreement (FBA) based on the implementations done for the same.

- **Delegated Proof of Stake:** PoS is direct democratic while DPOS is representative democratic is the major difference between the two. To generate and validate blocks, stakeholders elect their delegates. The block could be confirmed quickly, with significantly fewer nodes to validate the block ultimately leading to the quick confirmation of transactions. While the parameters of the network such as block size and block intervals could be tuned by delegates. Additionally, the users need not to worry about the dishonest delegates as they could be voted out easily. The DPOS consensus forms the backbone of Bit-shares.
- **Ripple:** Ripple is a consensus algorithm that utilizes collectively-trusted sub-networks within the larger network. In the network, nodes are divided into two types namely server (for participating consensus process) and client (for only transferring funds).

Each server has a Unique Node List (UNL). UNL is important to the server. When determining whether to put a transaction into the ledger, the server would query the nodes in UNL and if the received agreements have reached eighty percent, the transaction would be packed into the ledger. For a node, the decentralized ledger will remain correct as long as the percentage of faulty nodes in UNL is less than twenty percent (Schwartz et al., 2014).

- **Tendermint:** It is a byzantine consensus algorithm. A new block is determined in a round. To broadcast an un-confirmed block in this round, a proposer would be selected. It could be divided into three steps for understanding (see Figure 9).

If the node has received two-third of the commits, it accepts the block. In contrast to PBFT (Practical byzantine fault tolerance), nodes have to lock their coins to become validators and a validator would be punished, once found to be dishonest, (Kwon, 2014).

- **Virtual Machine:** The final logical module is virtual machine which is instigated as part of node application. It is an abstraction of a machine, held inside a machine (real or imaginary) produced by a computer program and activated with instructions embodied in a language. Like Bitcoin, Ethereum is a blockchain ecosystem that implements a virtual machine. The virtual machine resides in the Ethereum node application, called a wallet, and unlike Bitcoin, it is capable of understanding a wider range of instructions making it possible to effectively manage the state of a digital contracts aka smart contracts. To instruct the Ethereum virtual machine in the node application, the instructions take the form of a special programming language to enforce the terms of the contract consuming and releasing a digital token called "ether" as part of the transaction. Mainly because of the cryptographic integrity of information on the Ethereum blockchain, the contract cannot be tampered with.

Figure 9. Byzantine consensus algorithm

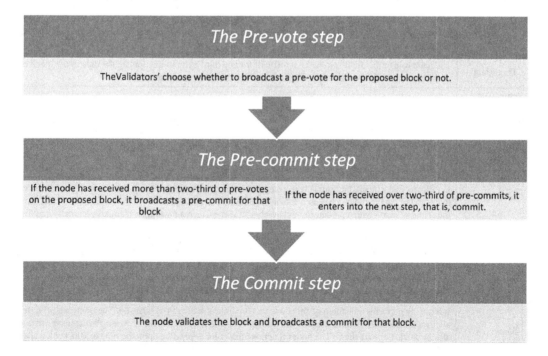

- **Addresses:** Addresses are used to uniquely identify the senders and receivers during a transaction on the distributed ledger system. The address of a block is mostly a public key or a key derived from the public key. The addresses, though unique, can be reused by the very same user. Practically, a user cannot reuse the same address for the purpose of creating a new address for each of his transactions. The address, thus created would be altogether unique. Though, direct identification of users was not thought to be possible earlier, recent researches have pointed out at its possibility. Furthermore, to prevent identification, users are expected to generate new addresses for each one of their transactions which can prevent the linking to a common owner of the proposed transaction.

- **Block:** A block consists of a number of transactions and includes few additional components which are the hash of the previous block, a timestamp, and a nonce. The aim of the block is to facilitate transaction process, that is, the transfer of values from one user to the other. A block usually consists of a *block header* and a *block body*. Block header is used to mainly identify a specific block on the entire Blockchain and it is repeatedly hashed. A block header comprises of six main components delineated in table 1.

The next section throws light on advantages and applications of Blockchain.

Table 1. Components of block header

Sr. No.	Component	Functionality
1.	Version	It is the block version number in block chain that lays down validation rules for the network system to follow.
2	Previous block header hash	In order to identify the parent block, the block header hash is used. This is a double SHA-256 key hash of the previous block's header. The blocks can have only one parent though simultaneously, multiple child blocks can exist. This element is of utmost importance because it is hashed with some other information to get the current hash.
3	Merkle root hash	It is a double SHA-256 hash of the merkle tree of all the existing transactions in the block where a merkle is a binary tree that is known to contain cryptographic hashes on its leaves and each leaf in the tree is a double SHA256 of the transaction data
4	Timestamp	The main role of this field is to make it difficult for any third party to manipulate the data in the block chains or the block thereby also serving as the source of validation in the system
5	Difficulty target	Usually, it deals with the difficulty to find a hash below a specified given target.
6	Nonce	A nonce is pseudo-random number that can be used only once. To fulfill the target of difficulty in blockchain, a nonce is generally used. With every transaction that takes place, the nonce is incremented by one and hence equals to the number of transactions and also, uniquely identifies the transaction.
7	*Hash*	In order to find a block, hashing is being employed. Any random number, i.e. a nonce is chosen and is added to the end of data in the block. Later, the block is hashed using a SHA algorithm for 256 bit keys. If the hash, thus created, starts with a predetermined number of zeroes, then a new block is found eventually and if not the steps have to be repeated again, this time with a different nonce. The hash is considered to be the most expensive part of a Blockchain as it involves looking for a block. The hashing rate primarily showcases the rate of calculating hashes in a second. The rate used to be considerably low in the earlier times of the technology mainly because CPU's were used at that time. Over the years with the introduction of mining pools and ASCI's, it has invariably gone up which has posed increased difficulty. Usually, miners are computing greater than 1,000,000,000,000,000,000 hashes in a second.
8	*Node*	It basically performs a plethora of functions that are linked to the role it takes up. The node can propose and approve transactions. It can even perform mining to secure the Blockchain network. Payments verifications can also be carried out via these. The nodes functions may vary depending upon the type of Blockchain and the task assigned to it

ADVANTAGES

The technology has many feats to its name which make it a compatible choice for wide ranged applications over the traditional databases. Firstly, being a virtual ledger, it eliminates the role of banks/facilitators and allows direct transactions between peers. There is no central server for communication and all the users are at the same level to communicate with each other. Also, the transaction time is reduced. This property also makes the technology much more transparent and secure as any change can be made to the ledger without the approval of all stakeholders. Secondly, it has the ability to enhance real time visibility in the functioning of supply chain that prevents leakages and increases efficiency. The data can't be removed as the data structure of blockchain can be appended only. It can be tampered if more than 50% of the computation power is controlled and all the transactions are rewritten. It uses protected cryptography that makes it immutable and more secure (Tschorsch and Scheuermann, 2016; Noyes, 2016). It is a single point of trust as all the transactions and data can be verified. Figure 10 highlights the advantages of Blockchain to the organization.

APPLICATION OF BLOCKCHAIN

The technology has proved not just to be revolutionary but also foundational in the sense that other applications can be built on it. Bitcoin is just one of the applications of the technology whose use is being tested across diverse sectors (Lee, 2015) (Foroglou and Tsilidou, 2015). Ranging from healthcare, banking, education, agriculture, electricity distribution and land records that can directly benefit, there'd be many a sector that would benefit indirectly with its implementation.

Figure 10. Advantages of blockchain

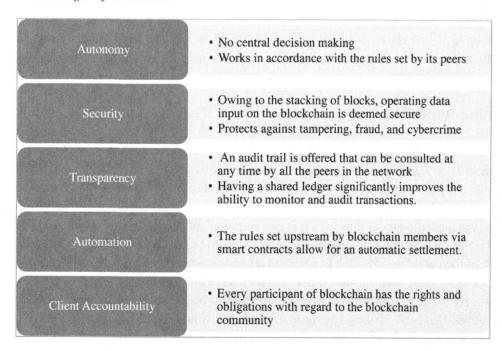

Smart Contracts

A smart contract is namely a contract between two or more parties that can be programmed electronically and are executed automatically with the aid of its underlying Blockchain in response to certain events that are encoded within the contract. Blockchain- powered smart contracts, where every piece of information is recorded can enhance the ease of doing business (Peters et al., 2015) (Buterin, 2014). It will augment the accuracy, efficiency and credibility of contracts while reducing the risks of frauds substantially. The data needed to execute the contract may be situated / stored outside the blockchain. A new type of third party called "oracle" is responsible for pushing this information onto a specific position in the Blockchain at a particular time. The smart contract reads the data and acts accordingly (Kosba et al., 2016). For instance, the case of cancellation of insurance for a train journey, information about the train's arrival time etc. are supplied by oracle.

Insurance

The technology could play a crucial role in health sector by reducing the risks associated with health insurance claims and thus pulling down the frauds! Possessing the ability to provide a public ledger across multiple distrusted parties, Blockchain has the potential to eliminate errors and detect fraudulent activity. A decentralized digital repository can independently verify the authenticity of customers, policies and transactions (or claims) by providing a complete historical record (Akins et al., 2013). As such, insurers would be able to identify duplicate transactions or those involving suspicious parties. Global insurers can use blockchain to cut asset management costs by reducing the hedging fees they pay to protect themselves from currency fluctuations in international transactions.

The recent roll-out of PM-JAY (Pradhan Mantri –Jan Arogya Yojana) aka the Aayushmaan Bharat scheme that is being seen as the biggest health insurance scheme around the world could prove to be a wonderful platform to implement the Blockchain network technology in order to ensure the successful implementation of this well-thought out scheme to reach the remotest people in the villages of India. For the effective and timely treatment of patients in the 1.5 lack health and wellness centers across the country, the network technology can provide the required help in maintaining the records and their updating on a regular basis.

Maintaining Records

Critical citizen information like land records, census data, birth and death records, business licenses, criminal records, intellectual property registry, electoral rolls could all be maintained as Blockchain-powered, tamper-proof public ledgers (Sharples and Domingue, 2015). It could change forever the government record keeping system that would be sure to miss no one and also to not include fraudulent personalities in the national database which is quite a prevalent activity owing to political interests.

Economic inequalities that surface in developing countries like India are mainly due to the tampering in most of the public records such as land and other property related documents. Corruption plays a big role in flaming these incidents to greater heights thus depriving the true owner of his/her very own fundamental rights. If land records were to be maintained on a distributed ledger, it would solve the problem forever. Land and various other property holdings would not be concentrated in the hands of a few influential personalities and would curb the problem of illegal acquisitions.

Government sector schemes and projects that are allotted funds in millions are never transparent about the progress of the work done and amount of fund utilized oe siphoned-off. Having a Blockchain technology that is a self-reviewing and self-updating system could look into the better implementation of such projects and also curb the underlying problem of corruption in all sectors due to its transparent behavior.

Internet of Things

AI and IoT are the technologies that have been taking the world over by a storm, but the security and privacy has been the most heated debate when it comes to Artificial intelligence or IoT. Real time interactions are the key to operating these technologies and Blockchain technology could be missing piece in the god puzzle of technological revolution. In an IoT world, thousands of devices would need to rapidly and seamlessly transact with each other in real time and what better to complement it than Blockchain. At present, a minor failure in an IoT ecosystem exposes a number of connected devices, revealing amounts of highly critical and confidential data (Zhang and Wen, 2015) (Dori et al., 2016). Such security flaws typically revolve around three areas: authentication, connection, and transaction.

By employing the use of blockchain in managing access to data from IoT devices, any attacker would have to bypass an additional layer of security that is underpinned by some of the most robust encryption standards available. In addition to this, as there is an absence of a centralized authority, single-point failure concerns become a distant memory, no matter how populated a particular network is (Kang et al., 2018). Complementing these three together is surely set to prove as a merger of future possibilities that can essentially change the way we talk, travel, eat and perform our routine tasks.

Some of the real-time use cases of Blockchain are depicted in Figure 11 and discussed below.

Figure 11. Use-cases of blockchain

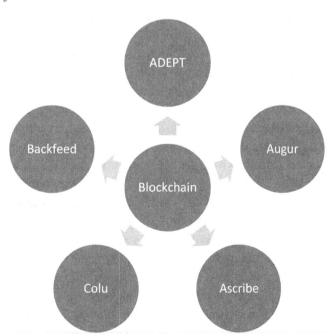

ADEPT

ADEPT (Autonomous Decentralized Peer-to-Peer Telemetry) is a system established in association between IBM Samsung and Ethereum, utilizing components of bitcoin's hidden outline to assemble a distributed network of nodes– a decentralized Internet of Things. The ADEPT lays o give the foundation of the framework, using a blend of proof of-work and proof-of-stake to anchor exchanges to fill in as a scaffold between numerous nodes at truncated cost (Samaniego and Deters, 2016).

Augur

Augur is a future of forecasting, a Prediction Market protocol built on Ethereum Blockchain that owned and operated by the users that use it (Peterson and Krug, 2015). It enables any user to generate a forecast due to its decentralized nature, not at all like wagering trades like Betfair which just permit wagering on inquiries that are selected by the site. The current market price of an offer is then a gauge of the likelihood that occasion will happen. Effectively, numerous scholarly analysts validate that such stages, while fusing parts of betting, do have functional esteem. Possibly the most developed venture in the Ethereum eco system, being bolstered by the network. The most popular use case of augur can be observed as Companies to guide decision making by forecasting vital information such as total product sales and project completion times. It can also be utilized to harness the power of crowds to create a more accurate weather prediction tool for events like hurricane landfalls, heat waves, and daily temperature averages. One of the primary applications will take shape over the time.

Ascribe

With Ascribe user's advanced work will dependably be credited to him. It is easy to copy digital work which makes it hard to demonstrate user's original work that is his unique creation. Similarly as marking a composition helps attribution, crediting your computerized creation demonstrates validness and provenance of your work. It empowers artists to claim their licensed innovation and exchange or pitch it, without hosting to depend on a third party for help with the legalities (Jacobovitz, 2016). The organization is utilizing Bitcoin's distributed blockchain to enable artists to enlist their works. As the proprietors of their protected innovation, they can shield it from theft and misuse, exchange it to other people or offer it safely. Since every one of its records is put away in an openly available database, specialists can ensure their cases of possession on this independent registry. Ascribe isn't only for digital art, photography and outline — it additionally works with physical art like sculptures and establishments. All one has to do to enlist your creation is take an image and transfer it to Ascribe. The organization's innovation traits shortage of advanced works, accordingly giving them authentic esteem, much the same as a stand-out painting or a constrained version photograph print. Utilizing Ascribe's service, artists can disseminate their work on their terms. For instance, a photographer can credit their most recent arrangement to a display on the web, and afterward pitch few each piece to intrigued purchasers. Different duplicates of those photos may exist on the web, however as they aren't represented by the originator, they are modestly imitations. Likewise, an online commercial center can safely offer work that is enlisted with Ascribe to gatherers, who can rest guaranteed that they are the sole proprietors of a bit of art they've acquired. Ascribe's Blockchain-based innovation can follow the voyage of any enrolled record to track its circulation — giving rights holders an approach to demonstrate their possession and a superior shot of arraigning any individual who may have stolen their work. The organization is additionally chipping away at machine learning innovation that can distinguish duplicated take a shot at the Web, regardless of whether it's had its watermarks digitally evacuated. This is a highly budding application, and one can observe nearly for the improvement of cutting-edge joint collaboration.

Colu

The payment landscape had been shifting radically due to the rapid explosion of mobile payment systems. Colu is an Israel-based digital wallet designed for digitizing the responsibility for your goods through the blockchain and thus transforming the way local economies work. It aims to incentivize local users and sellers via its local currency so that every participant in the local economy offered an advantage. The administration gives a simple method to utilize the blockchain innovation, initially implied for Bitcoin exchanges, for a wide variety of things from cars, to art, to show tickets. Residents can own community currencies, which allow the entire community to bootstrap its local economy. This creates an incentive for consumers to buy locally while reinvesting in local businesses they believe in. And a local currency and its circulation can help business owners with reduced fees, increased cash flow, and financial services via the Colu network (Mattila, 2016).

These local currencies are connected globally — the CLN connects the local currencies to a global network. This allows communities to raise capital and provides new local currencies with instant liquidity. The CLN token supports an entire ecosystem of services that will be added over time, including currency exchange, payments, and lending services. These payment solutions have been improvements of an existing ecosystem where it enables decentralized control to experiment with new types of governance, compliance, and new flavors of privacy, providing more prominent comfort and versatility. Blockchain technologies, however, promise to overturn the present state of affairs.

Backfeed

Backfeed is a social operating system that enables massive open source and new cost-effective models to sustenance large scale, effective collaboration. It provides the infrastructure for decentralized cooperation and distribution of value that develops a meritocratic governance system. The proof of value mechanism of Backfeed enables a decentralized network of peers to reach consensus regarding the perceived value of any contribution within the network, and reward it accordingly. The Backfeed protocol drives communities into consensus by empowering aligned individuals, and translates disagreement into a diversity of networks. Backfeed conventions make it feasible for individuals to effectively convey and sustain decentralized applications and associations that depend upon the unconstrained and intentional commitment of hundreds, thousands or millions of people (Allen, 2017).

Backfeed's framework embraces decentralized administration tools, value sharing plans, crowdsourcing systems, and instruments for the synergistic assessment and curation of substance. The Backfeed convention can fuel an assortment of endeavors, including decentralized news coverage, protection, ride-sharing applications and whatever other venture that would profit by the decentralized, backhanded coordination of vast gatherings of people. It would probably empower the bootstrapping of decentralized associations over the blockchain as effectively as one would convey a site today.

WHAT'S STOPPING BLOCKCHAIN?

There is a difference of a fine thread between the use and "misuse" of technology. Gone are the days when the world regarded oil as the epitome of wealth. Today the status is being enjoyed by data and thus they say, "Data is the new oil". Data leakages from technological giants such as Facebook and Google imply what a big menace it could be to keep the data of millions of citizens into safe hands and no matter the scrutiny of security, there are always the loopholes, which drives us home to the point that "Data privacy is a myth" is true after all.

The other big challenge is the dark abyss of blockchain that still needs to be explored and for the time being keeps our knowledge very limited. Regardless of the huge potential of Blockchain, it faces umpteen problems (see Figure 12), which restrict its pan-world usage.

Scalability

The blockchain becomes bulky with the number of transactions increasing by the day. In order to check if the source of the current transaction is unspent or not, each node has to store all transactions for the purpose of validating them on the blockchain. Besides, due to the original restriction of block size and the time interval used to generate a new block, the Bitcoin blockchain can only process nearly seven transactions per second, which cannot meet the requirement of processing millions of transactions in real-time fashion. Due to the small capacity of blocks, numerous small transactions might be delayed because miners prefer transactions with a high transaction fee (Zheng et al., 2016; Herrera-Joancomartí and Pérez-Solà, 2016).

Integration With Legacy Systems

To create a robust and effective Blockchain based system, there'd be a need to either completely overhaul the previously existing system or find a way to integrate it in the existing one which poses much of a challenge because it would completely eliminate the legacy systems plus this would require huge

Figure 12. Challenges to blockchain technology

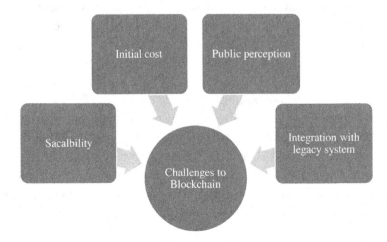

investments in time, funds along with human expertise (Poru et al.,2017). There are many factors at play to achieve such a mega change in countries which include political motivations, selfish mining or probably a government and business nexus.

Initial Costs

Though the adoption of Blockchain technology promises to reap humungous benefits in the long run with regard to its efficiency, incorruptible nature, timeliness so on and so forth, it is quite expensive to put in place initially. The software required to run the technology in organizations has to be developed specifically for that firm and hence is expensive to purchase. Along with that a specialized hardware would also be required to use with the software that adds to the cost many times over. Currently, not much has been done in this field and hence expert guidance would be necessary for company employees which today face a dearth.

Public Perception

A huge number of the population is completely oblivious of the technology's existence and hence unaware of its potential. For the technology to completely take over, a major challenge to be countered with is the public buy-in. Though rapid in its spread across various sectors, the technology is hugely restricted to those who are involved in the technology space and mainly industries that are adopting this technology.

CONCLUSION

The technology today is near synonymous to Bitcoin and the shadowy and heinous associations of Bitcoin with money laundering, black market trade and other illegal activities tend to take over and thus prevent them from exploring further about it. This limited exposure to knowledge regarding the technology could prove to be a big blockade when overhauling of traditional systems would take place and looking at the recent trend in technology, it could prove to be the next big thing providing employment to the youth of countries with a high demographic dividend and exposure to such technologies is a must in order to trek forward in its advance applications.

REFERENCES

Akins, W., Chapman, J. L., & Gordon, J. M. (2013). *A whole new world: Income tax considerations of the bitcoin economy*. Available: https://ssrn.com/abstract=2394738

Allen, D. (2017). *Discovering and developing the blockchain cryptoeconomy*. Academic Press.

Atzori, M. (2015). Blockchain technology and decentralized governance: Is the state still necessary? In *The Layman's Guide to Bitcoin: What it is, How it works, and why it matters. Brutsch.*

Bryzek, P. (2018). *A quick glimpse of Blockchain and its Revolutionary Applications*. Academic Press.

Buterin, V. (2014). *A next-generation smart contract and decentralized application platform* (white paper). Academic Press.

Buterin, V. (2015). *On public and private blockchains.* Available: https://blog.ethereum.org/2015/08/07/on-public-and-private-blockchains/

Decker, C., & Wattenhofer, R. (2013, September). Information propagation in the bitcoin network. In *Peer-to-Peer Computing (P2P), 2013 IEEE Thirteenth International Conference on* (pp. 1-10). IEEE. 10.1109/P2P.2013.6688704

Dorri, A., Kanhere, S. S., & Jurdak, R. (2016). *Blockchain in internet of things: challenges and solutions.* arXiv preprint arXiv:1608.05187

Foroglou, G., & Tsilidou, A-L. (2015). *Further applications of the blockchain.* Academic Press.

Herrera-Joancomartí, J., & Pérez-Solà, C. (2016, September). Privacy in bitcoin transactions: new challenges from blockchain scalability solutions. In *Modeling Decisions for Artificial Intelligence* (pp. 26–44). Cham: Springer. doi:10.1007/978-3-319-45656-0_3

Hyperledger project. (2015). Available: https://www.hyperledger.org/

Jacobovitz, O. (2016). *Blockchain for identity management.* The Lynne and William Frankel Center for Computer Science Department of Computer Science, Ben-Gurion University.

King, S., & Nadal, S. (2012). Ppcoin: Peer-to-peer crypto-currency with proof-of-stake. Self-Published Paper.

Kosba, Miller, Shi, Wen, & Papamanthou. (2016). Hawk: The blockchain model of cryptography and privacy-preserving smart contracts. *Proceedings of IEEE Symposium on Security and Privacy (SP),* 839–858. 10.1109/SP.2016.55

KuoChuen, L. (Ed.). (2015). *Handbook of Digital Currency.* Elsevier. Available: http://EconPapers.repec.org/RePEc:eee:monogr:9780128021170

Kwon, J. (2014). *Tendermint: Consensus without mining.* Retrieved from http://tendermint. com/docs/tendermint v04. pdf

Lamport, L., Shostak, R., & Pease, M. (1982). The byzantine generals problem. *ACM Transactions on Programming Languages and Systems, 4*(3), 382–401. doi:10.1145/357172.357176

Li, Z., Kang, J., Yu, R., Ye, D., Deng, Q., & Zhang, Y. (2018). Consortium blockchain for secure energy trading in industrial internet of things. *IEEE Transactions on Industrial Informatics, 14*(8), 3690–3700.

Lin, I. C., & Liao, T. C. (2017). A Survey of Blockchain Security Issues and Challenges. *International Journal of Network Security, 19*(5), 653–659.

Mainelli, M., & Smith, M. (2015). *Sharing ledgers for sharing economies: an exploration of mutual distributed ledgers (aka blockchain technology).* Academic Press.

Mattila, J. (2016). *The blockchain phenomenon.* Berkeley Roundtable of the International Economy.

Mazieres, D. (2015). *The stellar consensus protocol: A federated model for internet-level consensus.* Stellar Development Foundation.

Merkle, R. C. (1980, April). Protocols for public key cryptosystems. In *Security and Privacy, 1980 IEEE Symposium on* (pp. 122-122). IEEE. 10.1109/SP.1980.10006

Mettler, M. (2016, September). Blockchain technology in healthcare: The revolution starts here. In *e-Health Networking, Applications and Services (Healthcom), 2016 IEEE 18th International Conference on* (pp. 1-3). IEEE.

Miers, I., Garman, C., Green, M., & Rubin, A. D. (2013, May). Zerocoin: Anonymous distributed e-cash from bitcoin. In *Security and Privacy (SP), 2013 IEEE Symposium on* (pp. 397-411). IEEE.

Miguel, C., & Barbara, L. (1999). Practical byzantine fault tolerance. *Proceedings of the Third Symposium on Operating Systems Design and Implementation*, 99, 173–186.

Nakamoto, S. (2008). *Bitcoin: A peer-to-peer electronic cash system.* Academic Press.

Nguyen, Q. K. (2016, November). Blockchain-a financial technology for future sustainable development. In *Green Technology and Sustainable Development (GTSD), International Conference on* (pp. 51-54). IEEE. 10.1109/GTSD.2016.22

Noyes. (2016). *Bitav: Fast anti-malware by distributed blockchain consensus and feedforward scanning.* arXiv preprint arXiv:1601.01405

Peck, M. E. (2017). Blockchain world-Do you need a blockchain? This chart will tell you if the technology can solve your problem. *IEEE Spectrum*, *54*(10), 38–60. doi:10.1109/MSPEC.2017.8048838

Peters, G., Panayi, E., & Chapelle, A. (2015). Trends in crypto-currencies and blockchain technologies: A monetary theory and regulation perspective. *Online (Bergheim)*. doi:10.2139srn.2646618

Peterson, J., & Krug, J. (2015). *Augur: a decentralized, open-source platform for prediction markets.* arXiv preprint arXiv:1501.01042

Pilkington, M. (2016). 11 Blockchain technology: principles and applications. *Research handbook on digital transformations*, 225.

Porru, S., Pinna, A., Marchesi, M., & Tonelli, R. (2017, May). Blockchain-oriented software engineering: challenges and new directions. In *Proceedings of the 39th International Conference on Software Engineering Companion* (pp. 169-171). IEEE Press. 10.1109/ICSE-C.2017.142

Reid, F., & Harrigan, M. (2013). An analysis of anonymity in the bitcoin system. In *Security and privacy in social networks* (pp. 197–223). New York, NY: Springer. doi:10.1007/978-1-4614-4139-7_10

Samaniego, M., & Deters, R. (2016, December). Blockchain as a Service for IoT. In *Internet of Things (iThings) and IEEE Green Computing and Communications (GreenCom) and IEEE Cyber, Physical and Social Computing (CPSCom) and IEEE Smart Data (SmartData), 2016 IEEE International Conference on* (pp. 433-436). IEEE. 10.1109/iThings-GreenCom-CPSCom-SmartData.2016.102

Schwartz, Youngs, & Britto. (2014). *The ripple protocol consensus algorithm.* Ripple Labs Inc White Paper.

Sharples, M., & Domingue, J. (2015). The blockchain and kudos: A distributed system for educational record, reputation and reward. *Proceedings of 11th European Conference on Technology Enhanced Learning (EC-TEL 2015)*, 490–496.

Tschorsch, F., & Scheuermann, B. (2016). Bitcoin and beyond: A technical survey on decentralized digital currencies. *IEEE Communications Surveys and Tutorials*, *18*(3), 2084–2123. doi:10.1109/COMST.2016.2535718

Underwood, S. (2016). Blockchain beyond bitcoin. *Communications of the ACM*, *59*(11), 15–17. doi:10.1145/2994581

Vukoli'c, M. (2015). The quest for scalable blockchain fabric: Proof-of-work vs. bft replication. *International Workshop on Open Problems in Network Security*, 112–125.

Wood, G. (2014). *Ethereum: A secure decentralisedgeneralised transaction ledger*. Ethereum Project Yellow Paper.

Wright, A., & De Filippi, P. (2015). *Decentralized blockchain technology and the rise of lexcryptographia*. Academic Press.

Wust, K., & Gervais, A. (2017). Do you need a Blockchain? *IACR Cryptology ePrint Archive, 2017*, 375.

Yermack, D. (2015). Is Bitcoin a real currency? An economic appraisal. In Handbook of digital currency (pp. 31-43). Academic Press. doi:10.1016/B978-0-12-802117-0.00002-3

Yli-Huumo, J., Ko, D., Choi, S., Park, S., & Smolander, K. (2016). Where is current research on blockchain technology? A systematic review. *PLoS One*, *11*(10), e0163477. doi:10.1371/journal.pone.0163477 PMID:27695049

Zhang, Y., & Wen, J. (2015). An iot electric business model based on the protocol of bitcoin. *Proceedings of 18th International Conference on Intelligence in Next Generation Networks (ICIN)*, 184–191. 10.1109/ICIN.2015.7073830

Zheng, Z., Xie, S., Dai, H., Chen, X., & Wang, H. (2017, June). An overview of blockchain technology: Architecture, consensus, and future trends. In *Big Data (BigData Congress), 2017 IEEE International Congress on* (pp. 557-564). IEEE.

Zheng, Z., Xie, S., Dai, H. N., & Wang, H. (2016). Blockchain challenges and opportunities: A survey. *Work Pap.*

Chapter 10

Scientific Paper Peer–Reviewing System With Blockchain, IPFS, and Smart Contract

Shantanu Kumar Rahut
East West University, Bangladesh

Razwan Ahmed Tanvir
East West University, Bangladesh

Sharfi Rahman
East West University, Bangladesh

Shamim Akhter
https://orcid.org/0000-0003-1408-9133
East West University, Bangladesh

ABSTRACT

In general, peer reviewing is known as an inspection of a work that is completed by one or more qualified people from the same profession and from the relevant field to make the work more error-free, readable, presentable, and adjustable according to the pre-published requirements and also considered as the primary metric for publishing a research paper, accepting research grants, or selecting award nominees. However, many recent publications are pointing to the biasness and mistreatment in the peer-review process. Thus, the scientific community is involved to generate ideas to advance the reviewing process including standardizing procedures and protocols, blind and electronic reviewing, rigorous methods in reviewer selection, rewarding reviewers, providing detailed feedback or checklist to reviewers, etc. In this chapter, the authors propose a decentralized and anonymous scientific peer-reviewing system using blockchain technology. This system will integrate all the above concern issues and eliminate the bias or trust issues interconnected with the peer-reviewing process.

DOI: 10.4018/978-1-5225-9257-0.ch010

INTRODUCTION

In general sense, peer-reviewing is known as an inspection of a work that is completed by one or more qualified people from the same profession and from the relevant field to make the work more error free, readable, presentable and adjustable according to the pre published requirements. Peer-reviewing is considered as the primary metric for publishing a research paper, accepting research grants, or selecting award nominees. However, many recent publications are pointing question to the biasness and abuse in peer-review process including author conflictions, authors from less prestigious institution, awarding women author, negative studies, idea stealing etc. Thus, scientific community is involved to generate ideas to advance the reviewing process (despite abandoning it) including standardizing procedures and protocols, blind and electronic reviewing, rigorous methods in reviewer selection, rewarding reviewers, providing detailed feedback or checklist to reviewers, and etc. In this chapter, we are proposing a decentralized and anonymous scientific peer-reviewing system using Blockchain technology with modified cryptocurrency (as reputation points) method. The system will integrate all the above concern issues, and able to eliminate the bias or trust issues interconnected with peer-reviewing process using decentralized authorities or without intermediaries, but improve reliability, transparency, and streamlining in the entire process. Publishing a research paper takes several steps from start to finish. Peer-reviewing process is one such step where a proposed article or work is evaluated or scrutinized by other experts in the matching subject to ensure quality of research contribution and to increase credibility. Experts play an important role in this process and help to validate a research, evaluate the method, establish the strengths and weaknesses and finally provide a reasonable judgment to publication. However, many recent publications are pointing question towards the biasness and abuse in peer-reviewing process including authors conflicts of interests, authors from less prestigious institution, awarding women author, negative studies, idea stealing etc. As a consequence, peer-reviewing is very successful in many instances however it also has few fail instances. Abandoning peer-reviewing may cause unreliability and less navigability in scientific article publication, and thus scientific community is involved to generate ideas to improve the reviewing process despite abandoning it. In this chapter, we will inspect different peer reviewing processes, applications, technological advancements, and drawbacks or challenges in existing peer reviewing system. Thereafter, we will propose an innovative decentralized and anonymous scientific peer-reviewing system using Blockchain, IPFS, cryptocurrency and smart contact technology.

EXISTING PEER REVIEWING SYSTEM, DRAWBACKS AND CHALLENGES

It is assumed that the first peer- reviewing process was archived in a book named "Ethics of the Physician", written by a Syrian physician, Ishap bin Ali Al Rahwi (CE 854–931). Back then, other physicians used peer-reviewing on a given prescription to the patients to see if they are being treated according to the standards (Spier, 2002) or not. The idea of peer-reviewing was started from here. Later, many media, and literature societies started practicing the peer-reviewing system for their own development and improvement of knowledge. The societies submitted their works to the committee where the committee reviewed papers, accepted or recommended for any changes (kronick, 1990). In 1731, the Royal Society of Edinburgh instigated the peer-review system in Scholarly publication with a bunch of peer-reviewed medical papers. But the publication of articles was decided almost 100 years later after (Shema, 2014). In 1831, William Whewell of royal society of London proposed the *Proceeding of the Royal Society* where the new papers were included. That's where the real peer-reviewing was started (INFOGRAPHIC). At first, the single blind review was adopted, where the reviewer was anonymous, but the author name was known to the reviewer. This process was garbage as the papers were not well reviewed and most of the time the reviewer was biased (Csiszar, 2016). "Editor plus two referees system" became quite popular among the scholars for peer-reviewing. Then "Double-blind" peer-reviewing was adopted to avoid bias (Rowland, 2002). This process is now used to review most of the scientific papers with some updates which will be discussed later.

Currently peer-reviewing is the "most standard" process for any scholarly publication. Researchers are relying on the peer-reviewing process which they found most useful for a better research paper. Almost 90% scientist recommends peer reviewing is effective for the development and improvement in technological areas (Mulligan, Hall & Raphael, 2012). Researchers and Scholars are getting their works reviewed by peers, which is helping them to work further and gives them the room for improvement. The papers which are being accepted is adding values to the scientific inventions and technological advancement. Papers which are being sent back to the author for a correction are getting a second chance to remove their lacking.

As the history says, the peer review started at the medical sectors, still the medical journals use peer reviewing which helps to get more realistic results in different sectors in medical science. Besides journals for Computer science, Biotechnology, Genetics, Physics, Mathematics also use peer reviewing system (omicsonline).

When a scientific paper is submitted for peer -reviewing, it goes through several steps. After finishing the research work, at first, the author submits his paper to journal. Here comes a journal editor, who reviews the paper if it meets the criteria of the journal. Not all the journals follow the same pattern for accepting a paper, some journal may have different criteria than traditional approach. The Editor makes sure of the paper submitted has met all the criteria and it can proceed further. But if the paper does not stand up to the mark of the journal, the editor informs the author that his paper was rejected. In next step, when the paper has passed the test and has met all the requirements of the journal, it is sent to the reviewers, who are eligible to review the paper. The reviewers are also known as the referees. After the paper has reached to the reviewers, they examine the paper thoroughly. They mark every detail and evaluate the papers methodology or proposed models; how much they can contribute or there is any error or corrections in the paper. They also determine the originality of the work. The references are also checked by them. The reviewers write a report on the findings from the submitted paper and give it to the editor.

What editor does is, he checks the reports from the reviewers. If there is no error, the paper gets accepted. But if the reports recommend any major or minor correction in the paper, the editor notifies the author to make changes and then resubmit. After updating the paper as per the recommendation, the paper is again sent to the editor who hands them to the reviewer again. If this time everything is fine by the report of the reviewer, the paper is accepted and published in the journal. The papers also can be rejected if the report is negative from the reviewers.

Not all the journals follow the same pattern for accepting a paper; some journal may have different criteria than traditional approach. Different journal uses different type of peer-reviewing system. There are a few forms of peer-reviewing that are currently being used by the journals. Here are some common types of peer-reviewing systems:

- **Single Blind Peer Review:** Author does not know who will evaluate the paper; the identity of the reviewer is unknown to the author of the paper. On the other hand, reviewer will know the authors identity.
- **Double Blind Peer Review:** In this system, author and reviewer, both sides are not disclosed to each other's identity.
- **Open Peer Review:** There is no hiding in this system. Author and reviewers are well aware of opposite side's identities. When the final paper is published, reviewers comment as well as authors response can be published in this system.
- **Collaborative Peer Review:** Most of the time reviewer's identity is hidden which is disclosed at the time of publication. Authors and reviewers are given a platform where they can discuss about the improvement sides of the paper.
- **Third Party Peer Review:** Before approaching to any journal, author does a review by an independent peer reviewing source. After getting review from there, author submits it to the journal.
- **Cascading Peer Review:** Various journals have target readers. If the submitted paper is not for those particular readers, the paper can be rejected after review. In that case the journal may suggest the author to submit the paper to another journal. Most of the time the journal gets published in the next one.
- **Post Publication Peer Review:** After the paper is published, it is available in a platform where others can read the paper and comment of their perspective and thoughts about the paper.

In the peer-reviewing system, no paper can get through easily without going through a several stages. Those have to go through the heavy guard of the reviewers who have their own field of expertise. These reviews are called as the "Gatekeepers" of science (Hojat, Gonnella & Caelleigh, 2003). They have a vital role on the inventions and research areas. They always keep their guard on when it comes to the paper reviewing, as it can make a huge difference in science and belief. Though peer-reviewing is the most used process among the scientific community, it faces much criticism. Even with so much popularity, the process has many drawbacks. The accusations on the process are like these:

- **Poor Evaluation:** Sometimes the reviewers are not so careful about evaluating the paper with full consciousness. The mistakes are not always found by the reviewers. The reviewer may not even read the paper and the paper gets through the journal. A few times the reviewers overlook the errors and the paper gets published. This type of carelessness can create a mislead idea on the particular topic.
- **Personal Conflict:** In peer reviewing system, there can be a conflict between author and reviewer, as the identity is known. In that case, if the editor sends the paper to the reviewer who has internal conflict with the author, can willingly give bad reviews about the paper submitted. As a result, the paper can be rejected by the journal despite of having quality content.
- **Gender Biasness:** The gender discrimination is a worldwide problem. In every sector, gender biasness exists. The cases are found like when the editor is male; he refers the paper to a male reviewer. Same thing happens when the editor is female (Stoye, 2017). Again, the acceptances of the paper submitted by the female authors are more likely to be accepted than the male authors. But a smaller number of females are invited by the journals to review papers (Lerback & Hanson, 2017).

- **Manipulated Priority:** When a paper is submitted under a particular journal or in any conference, if the author who submitted the paper is related to that situation, the publishers tend to prioritize their paper to be submitted and get published.

- **Conformity Bias:** The reviewer's point of view can be different from the authors. In that case, reviewer can give negative feedback about the paper that has not matched his view to that. This does not mean the submitted paper has misconception. The paper can be disqualified even if the editor does not agree with the concept of the paper. These decisions can put important inventions to danger (Mahoney, 1977).

- **Professional vs. Newbie:** In almost every aspect of life, people tend to prioritize the professionals and who is well recognized to people rather than a newcomer who may have the potential to serve something good. In this peer reviewing system, editors and reviewers try to make the known author's paper published rather than the newcomers. This is known as the "Matthew Effect" in scientific arena (Sharp, 1990), which is a tendency to highlight the high profiled author more than the low profiled ones.

- **Reviewer's Background:** A submitted paper can be reviewed by a number of reviews. Each reviewer has their expertise in their own field. There can be a different number of opinions from the reviewers, which can lead to the rejection of the paper. Even the journals can reject a paper based on the reviewer's feedback. It is not rare that a paper has been reviewed by a professional from another field. It makes a biasness form the reviewer's own expertise field.

- **Journal Policy:** Many journals can have their own hidden policies by which most papers submitted cannot go through. These journals are not often public about their policies. So, it is hard to tell if a journal will be published or not in a particular journal (Hojat et al, 2003).

- **Manuscript Fraud:** It is possible that the author can change some parts of the original paper and submit another paper as a new one. This can happen when the paper is rejected at the first place. Sometimes the reviewers can also steal an idea from the paper and make the idea as his own.

So, despite of being so popular among the science area, the peer-reviewing process has many challenging sides. From all the above problems, we can see that the biasness between author and reviewer gets the most focus. Most of the problems are related to the reviewer's opinion about the author, relation between them, competitiveness, point of view etc. In many cases there are accountability problem, the people in power which are editors and reviewer are doing as they want without being accountable to anyone. Conflict of interest also has a huge impact on this peer-reviewing system. These problems can be misleading for anyone who is related to science. It can take the new scientists to a wrong path. Science has its own risk with the peer-reviewing system. These identified problems should be solved as soon as possible to make sure the science to not go to a wrong direction. For the welfare of the science, a new concept of paper reviewing should be adopted. Thus, in the current peer-reviewing system, a journal holds the control of the whole system of peer-reviewing if the paper should be published or not. If we can have a system that the review system is not centralized; not only one person handles the whole process, but everyone has the ability to justify the process, the biasness in the system can be reduced. Both the editor and reviewer would be accountable for their deeds, also the author. Everything would be transparent so that the others can make sure the right thing has been done. In this platform, everyone would get a chance to participate in the development of the future of science with transparency.

In these recent years, Blockchain technology has emerged which can bring transparency in any system where it is implemented. We will have a detail discussion on Blockchain in next section. This technology can make sure of the proper reviewing of a paper in many extend. If we can make a platform where Blockchain technology is implemented, the distribution of the paper can be safe and secured as it will have node to node encryption system, so there is no possibility to go the paper in wrong hand. Without this, the system has an approval option for all the nodes, so it is not possible for a single human to spread anything wrong. Besides, the Blockchain system is decentralized, so there is no chance for manipulation of the paper in case of any biasness. If the file uploaded is manipulated somehow, the encryption of both ends will not work. So, this Blockchain technology can bring a change when it comes to the transparency of the scientific paper peer-reviewing system.

BLOCKCHAIN AND OTHER REQUIRED TERMINOLOGIES FOR PROPOSED PEER REVIEWING SYSTEM

Blockchain

In general, Blockchain is a digital ledger of transactions that are continuously updated and broadcasted within a distributed network. Every node in this network has an exact copy of that ledger or accounting book. Each and every transaction between the nodes is echoed in that distributed ledger. By storing the same ledger across the network, Blockchain cannot be controlled by any single authority and it has no single point of failure. For every successful transaction, a block is appended to the existing chain of blocks by a secure and strong cryptography and the updated ledger is shared among the distributed network. To ensure every node in the network has identical version of the ledger. Proof of Work (PoW)

Figure 1. Mechanism of blockchain

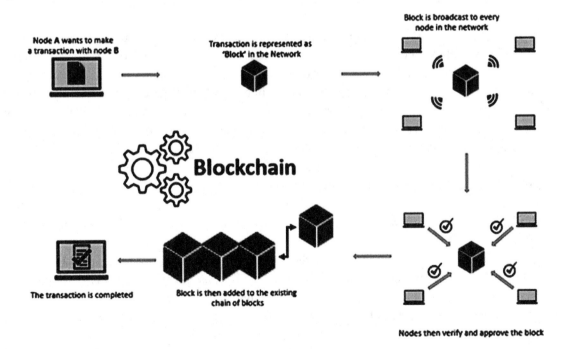

mechanism integrates a system of collective consensus and verification through mining to certify that no conflicting versions of that ledger is emerged. This mechanism also ensures the immutability of the stored data in a block without having a central authority.

The uniqueness in Blockchain technology lies in the distinctive properties of this system. Some of its protocol features are listed below:

- **Replication:** The data on the Blockchain is stored on every node that is a part of the network. So, the ledger is replicated and kept on each computer connected to the network.
- **Immutability of Data:** The blocks are linked with one another, storing the previous node's hash. So, if a node is edited then the hash of that node is also changed. Therefore, the hash stored on the next block will not match with the changed hash of the edited block. Thus, if one node is edited then all the blocks after that will be unverified. By this, the immutability of the data on Blockchain is reserved.
- **Irreversibility of Transactions:** Once a transaction is recorded on Blockchain then there is no way to reverse, hide or alter that transaction. Only a new transaction should be done to retract the effect of that transaction. Say, user A accidentally made a transaction of 5 units to user B. Then there is no way to reverse this transaction unless B makes a transaction of 5 units back to A.
- **Distributed System:** The Blockchain ledger is distributed to all the individual nodes on the network. The ledger is maintained by the users of the network.
- **No Central Authority:** No central authority can govern the network. All the nodes are part of the decision and this is ensured by the consensus among the nodes of the network.
- **No Single Point of Failure:** As the ledger is distributed all over the network, there is no central point of failure in Blockchain. Everyone has the copy of the exact same ledger.
- **Resilient:** Blockchain network utilizes the consensus model to resolve the changing state of the ledger. By a consensus algorithm, the ledger accepted by the network always reflects the exact scenario of transactions. A ledger will be accepted if 51% or more nodes have the exact same ledger. This ensures the resiliency of the network.
- **Anonymity:** Bitcoin – is built on Blockchain technology. Bitcoin only uses public-private keys to identify a user. The user needs not to provide any other information like name, address, age, gender etc. (BLOCKCHAIN COUNCIL). So, in another words, Blockchain technology provides anonymity.

The usage of Blockchain is excitingly increasing nowadays. Various applications have been seen in recent years which rely on Blockchain mechanism. The application domain of the Blockchain Technology (BCT) is vast and expanding. Presently, Blockchain technology is mostly used in the field of Finance, Healthcare (Ekin & Unay, 2018) (Zhang, Walker, White, Schmidt & Lenz, 2017), Gaming, File Transfer (Kiyomoto, Rahman & Basu, 2017), Security, IoT (Chen, Ma, Ye, Zheng, & Zhou, 2018) etc.

Blockchain has shown a new path to the gaming industry. By using crypto-currency the players can transact their unique avatar and all. (CryptoKitties, 2018) is considered the most successful Blockchain based game. The player of the game can make transactions using smart contract on Ethereum Blockchain. There are other games based on Blockchain such as (CryptoCelebrities, 2018), (Etherbots,2018) etc. E-voting system is emerging to provide transparency to the voting system. The inherit properties of Blockchain technology provides transparency to any system. Nowadays the E-voting is gaining attention.

Various models of E-voting based on Blockchain (Hjalmarsson, Hreioarsson, Hamdaqa, & Hjalmtysson, 2018; Kshetri&Voas, 2018) are proposed. Even, government information can be stored in Blockchain because of the immutability, which is very important especially for government information.

CRYPTO-CURRENCY

One of the fields where Blockchain is being currently used is crypto-currency. The "crypto" in the word crypto-currency stands for cryptography which is a technology that keeps information safe from unauthorized access. So, crypto-currency is a cryptographically secured digital exchange. This peer-to-peer digital exchange system requires the distributed verification of transactions as this system has no central authority. In 1983, eCash (Chaum, 1997) was developed by Chaum which is an anonymous electronic money exchange system. But unlike crypto-currencies, the eCash was centralized and controlled by banks. PayPal (Valenta & Rowan, 2015) is also an online Money Transfer System which issued to send and receive money from each other. These systems do not have their own currency. But crypto-currency has its own currency. In 2008-09, Bitcoin (Nakamoto, 2015), the first crypto-currency, was implemented by Satoshi Nakamoto. And after that various crypto-currency systems came into existence like Ethereum (Wood, 2014), Litecoin (Litecoin, 2018), Ripple (Schwartz, Youngs & Britto, 2014), Namecoin (Kalodner, Carlsten, Ellenbogen, Bonneau & Narayanan, 2015) etc. But the functionality of all the crypto-currency systems is somewhat similar. A user of a crypto-currency has a wallet address which is a public key of that user. That public key has a private key. Public and private key are together known as Public-Private Key pair. The private key is used to sign the transactions the user makes. The ownership of a coin is given to the person who has in possession of the private key of the public/private key pair. The user sends money to other users' address which is the payees' public key and signs the transaction using his (sender) private key. Then the transaction needs verification by the miners. These are the steps which need to be performed to exchange currency in any crypto-currency exchange systems. The key pairs are stored in a file named 'wallet.dat' which is the most important file as if any user loses or has the file stolen, and then he will lose the ownership of those coins. Through decentralization, the control of the network is given to the users of the network. So, everyone is responsible for the security of their files. There are different types of crypto-currency at present. Bitcoin, Litecoin, Ether etc. are the most used crypto-currency.

SMART CONTRACTS

American cryptographer Nick Szabo described smart contract in 1996, long before the development of Blockchain. Szabo described a contract as – 'a set of promises agreed to in a "meeting of the minds", is the traditional way to formalize a relationship.' In the article on smart contracts (Szabo, 1996), according to Szabo, smart contracts are set of rules for transferring information that automatically execute, when the conditions of the contracts are met. Back at 1996, this definition did not mean much to that time, because required technologies like distributed ledger were absent at that period. After the appearance of Bitcoin, the first crypto-currency, the distributed ledger was implemented by Blockchain technology and that is how a new era for smart contracts started. Though Bitcoin only allow that the information of the transaction must be in the block. So, still smart contracts were not useful with Bitcoin.

Smart contract can be considered a sophisticated Blockchain network's node that can store procedures to be called under some specific rules. It provides features to eliminate intermediaries from a contract happening between two or more parties. This is a computer or computer program which is used to en-list the terms of the contracts in "if-then" form when two parties agree to the contract's terms, then the encrypted code is securely replicated to the decentralized ledger which ensures the transparency. If the conditions stated in the contracts are met, then the code autonomously executes the transaction. After every execution of a smart contract, the states of that contract are changed. By 'state' here it means the data that smart contract stores in a certain point of time. The autonomous execution and surety of the agreement remove third party interference on the contracts. Smart contract provides services to exchange money, goods or other assets which have some value. So, smart contracts can be applied to make trans-actions on a variety of use cases.

Below a simple visualization of how smart contracts work is depicted.

Smart contract is now being implemented to solve wide range of problems. Healthcare, Finance, Elections, E-commerce, Taxation and many more sectors are using the services of smart contract along with Blockchain. In the health care sector, faster data sharing is important and related to the chance of recovery of any patient. Blockchain is also integrated with IoT (Dey, Jaiswal, Sunderkrishnan & Katre, 2017) to store health data in Blockchain to provide faster medical response. Considering the privacy of medical data, Blockchain and smart contract are helping to provide security for medical data. In finance or in business, the use of smart contract is rapidly increasing. The supplier role automation in the electric-ity supply (Thomas, Long, Burnap, Wu, & Jenkins, 2017) was developed based on the smart contract. In business the trading and the privacy of the users can be ensured by the smart contract (Niya, Shupfer, Bocek, & Stiller, 2018) which make trading reliable and flexible. Blockchain and smart contract have opened a new possibility of developing a transparent E-voting system (Hjalmarsson et al, 2018) and (Kshetri&Voas, 2018). These E-voting systems based on Blockchain and smart contract provides the reduced chances of fraud and increase voter access. Everyday new use cases are designed utilizing the possibilities of smart contract and Blockchain. Various new innovations (Ahram, Sargolzaei, Sargolzaei, Daniels &Amaba, 2017) are a matter of time now which will be implemented by smart contract and Blockchain based systems.

Figure 2. Working mechanism of smart contract

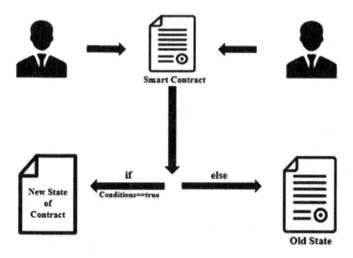

Pros and Cons of Smart Contract

Pros

- **Reliability:** As smart contract works with Blockchain, the data stored in Blockchain cannot be altered or modified. So, alteration of contract's conditions is impossible. So, smart contract provides the reliability.
- **Speed:** Smart contract does not have any personal involvement. Thus, its execution is faster which saves huge amount of time. It eliminates the time delay of the completion of contract objectives which serves faster transaction and contract completion.
- **Low Cost Execution:** Smart contract serves its services with minimal cost as it removes the third-party interference in the contract. The operational cost is thus reduced.
- **Accuracy:** All the conditions of the contract are inspected by the contract program automatically which provides higher accuracy than human inspected contracts.
- **Independence**: Smart contract eliminates the involvement of third party in a contract. The trust issues are handled by programming. So, the integrity is ensured by the contract itself.

Cons

- **Immutability:** Smart contract is inherently immutable that is, no one can alter any part of a contract. So, if the parties want to alter or modify the condition after forming the contract, they must need to create a new separate contract. So, immutability is providing the security, but this may cause problem when parties want to modify the contract.
- **Lack of Knowledge:** General people lack the knowledge of Smart Contract and Blockchain. This throttles the rapid development of application backed by these technologies.

IPFS TECHNOLOGY

Inter Planetary File System or IPFS is a protocol and a network. It has been designed to create a content-addressable, peer-to-peer storing and sharing hypermedia in a distributed file system (Finley, 2016).

IPFS will be used for a user to submit article for reviewing through the system. Some peer-to-peer systems like P2P sharing software (Ratnasamy, Francis, Handley, Karp &Schenker, 2001) use hash of the content to address it. Other technologies such as Git use complex Merkle-Linked Structures (Loeliger & McCullough, 2012). IPFS integrates both the use of complex Merkle-Linked structure with the data-addressability of P2P file sharing systems. The content is distributed over a peer-to-peer network (Tenorio-Fornés, Hassan & Pavón, 2018). So, IPFS is a peer-to-peer distributed file system that seeks to connect all computing devices with the same system of files. In some ways, IPFS is similar to the World Wide Web, but IPFS could be seen as a single BitTorrent swarm, exchanging objects within one Gitrepository. In other words, IPFS provides a high-throughput, content-addressed block storage model, with content-addressed hyperlinks (Allison, 2016). IPFS combines a distributed hash table, an incentivized block exchange, and a self-certifying namespace. IPFS has no single point of failure, and data transit cannot be tampered with (IPFS is the Distributed Web, 2018). Distributed Content Delivery saves bandwidth and prevents DDoS attacks, which HTTP struggles with (Cointelegraph, 2017).The file system can be accessed in a variety of ways, including via FUSE or "File system in User space" (Filesystem in Userspace, 2018) over HTTP (Allison, 2016). A local file can be added to the IPFS file system, making it available to the world. Files are identified by their hashes, so it is cached-friendly. They are distributed using a BitTorrent-based protocol. Any user who downloads the file also serves the file to the other users of the network. IPFS has a name service called IPNS, a global namespace based on PKI, serves to build trust chains, is compatible with other NSes and can map DNS, onion, bit, etc. to IPNS (Ipfs/README.md, 2018).

TECHNICAL CHALLENGES OF BLOCKCHAIN

There are several technical challenges in adapting Blockchain. Many researchers identified different challenges of using a Blockchain technology. These are discussed below:

- **Throughput:** As for now, Bitcoin network can process only seven (7) transactions per second which is very few in compare to other money transferring networks like VISA and Twitter. So, the big scale implementation of Blockchain is a challenge.
- **Latency:** In Bitcoin Blockchain, all the transactions are verified by the miner nodes to ensure that no one can spend one coin more than once which is known as Double-spending. So, to ensure valid transactions Blockchain has to verify all the block added in the Blockchain every time a transaction occurs. This makes latency a great problem for the Blockchain technology.
- **Security:** Current Blockchain is vulnerable to 51% attack. 51% attack is an attack where only one party has the power over the majority of the network's mining hash-rate. Thus, he can manipulate the Blockchain. This issue is one of the big risk factors of a Blockchain based application.
- **Usability:** Nowadays, implementing Blockchain based application is hard because of the complex usage of the Blockchain API. More sophisticated yet easy-to-use technology should be developed to ensure usability of the features of the Blockchain technology.
- **Wasted Resource:** Huge energy is wasted to mine Bitcoin. Proof-of-Work causes this wastage of energy. There are also some alternatives to Proof-of-Work like Proof-of-Stake. Proof-of-Stake is used by the industrial applications to reduce the energy consumption. Proof-of-Work depends on the work done by the miner but on the other hand, Proof-of-Stake depends on the amount of Bitcoin the miner holds. So, different approaches need to be introduced to increase resource utilization by the Blockchain network.
- **Size and Bandwidth:** The size of the Blockchain grows with the usage of the network by its users. As of June 2018, the size of the Bitcoin Blockchain is 173gigabytes which is increasing since the creation of Bitcoin crypto-currency in 2009. If Blockchain is used by the mass people, the Blockchain size would be a problem. So, size of the Blockchain is a challenge which needs to be solved for the usability of the system.
- **Scalability:** The main issue of scalability problem in Blockchain is that every transaction in the network must be verified by the mining nodes (Mitra, 2017). Ethereum does 20 transactions per second and Bitcoin does only 7. So, obviously the scalability of these systems must be improved to compete with the existing transaction speed of money transfer systems. Presently the scalability problem of Blockchain is being addressed to make this technology useful for big scale imple-

mentations. There are several approaches to solve the scalability problem like Bitcoin Lightning Protocol (Hay, 2018), Ethereum Sharding (Jordan, 2018), DPoS Solution by EOS (Arora, 2018).

- **Privacy:** All the transactions in the Blockchain network are broadcasted to public. Transparency in the Blockchain network is ensured by the flow of information to all parties. But public can only see the transactions not the senders' and receivers' identities (Nakamoto, 2008). Around 24% studies of recent researches are on the anonymity issue of the Blockchain network (Yli-Huumo, Ko, Choi, Park, &Smolander, 2016). Centering on the ownership of the Bitcoin (Meiklejohn & Orlandi, 2015), presents a definitional model of anonymity. Again, various researches are based on the evidence that the Bitcoin Blockchain lacks the anonymity of its users (Koshy, Koshy & McDaniel, 2014) (Valenta& Rowan, 2015). To solve this anonymity problem many researchers proposed numerous solutions. Transaction mixing technique is applied to increase anonymity in the network. (Valenta and Rowan, 2015) has modified the Mix Coin protocol to prevent the address mapping of the receivers and senders.

PROPOSED BLOCKCHAIN BASED PEER-REVIEING SYSTEM

Generally, a peer-review process can be divided into three steps. First step is the authors will submit papers in the hope to get it reviewed and published. Second stepis the editorwill distribute the submitted paper to eligible reviewers. Third step is the reviewers will accept and review the submitted paper and send their reviews to the editor, and then editor will forward their reviews to the specific author.

The proposed method integrates all these steps with Blockchain technology and creates a decentralized platform for peer-reviewing process. Our proposed decentralized method of peer-reviewing system is also divided into three (3) different steps and presented in three (3) different sections. Section 1.4.1 includes information on how authors will submit their articles to the system for reviewing, how the system will find eligible reviewers, and how the submitted articles will be distributed among the reviewers with the help of IPFS. Section 1.4.2 includes information on how the reviews will be verified as a good, authentic and valid review. Section 1.4.3 includes information on the idea of crypto-reward system. It also utilizes smart contract for creating transactions. These transactions are used for passing information and selecting eligible reviewers, distribute papers for reviewing and etc. These transactions are affiliated with costs and that needs to be paid through Crypto-Currency. This section will examine all details of these implementations.

ARTICLE DISTRIBUTION

For distributing article through Blockchain for peer-reviewing process, the first step is to submit the article for reviewing through the system. The users of our proposed system can act on three (3) different types of roles-

1. Author
2. Primary Reviewer
3. Secondary Reviewer

If a user submits an article for the peer-reviewing process, he is an author or author node. He is denoted as #Author. If a user reviews an article, he acts as a primary reviewer or primary reviewer node, and denoted as #PR. If a user reviews the review of a primary reviewer, he is a secondary reviewer or secondary reviewer node, and denoted as #SR.

For reviewing each article, the system will find out and enlist Eligible Reviewers or #ER through TAG matching and Ranking Process. First three (3) of the enlisted #ERs who accept the proposal of reviewing an article, will be selected as #PR. After all, three (3) #PRs submit their reviews, there will be a similar enlisting process to enlist #SRs, first two (2) #ER from the list who accepts the proposal of reviewing the reviews given by the #PR on the submitted article will be selected as #SR. More details on TAG matching and Ranking Process will be given later.

Submitting Article: Use of IPFS Technology

Current Blockchain technology supports transfer of large amount of data in a single transaction but is very costly. So, our framework takes the help of IPFS for sharing large amount of data at low cost. The idea is simple. Upload something using IPFS. IPFS then provides a download link. The link is then shared with another user of Blockchain using a single transaction.

So, how does one user can share his file or article or paper through the system with the help of IPFS?

Let's look at the figure 3, #Author wants to submit an article or paper through the system. First, he/she puts the article in his/her directory and then tells the IPFS system that he wants to upload it. Then the IPFS system takes the address of the article and generates a hash that can be shared with anyone on the same network.

This process lacks the security of the submitted article as anyone could read it. But with Blockchain, in our proposed system the security will be assured. For better understanding let's look at the figure 4.

First, he/she puts the article in his/her directory and then tells the IPFS system that he wants to upload it. Then the IPFS system takes the address of the article and generates a hash that will be shared with anyone on the same network. Then the system encrypts the hash with the public key of #PR (who the author wants to share the article with). As it was encrypted with #PR's public key, only #PR could decrypt the hash and collect the submitted article using that decrypted hash as only he has the associated Private Key.

So, this is how #Author will submit his/her article or paper through the proposed system for peer-reviewing process, in a secure manner, with the help of IPFS.

Figure 3. Submitting article through IPFS

Figure 4. Submitting article through IPFS used with Blockchain (i.e. proposed system)

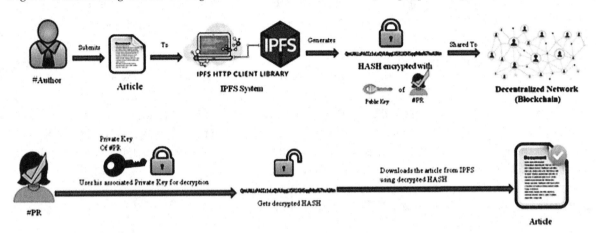

Whom to Ask for Reviewing?

One of the most important parts of a peer-reviewing process is to send or distribute the submitted article to the perfect reviewers. A reviewer must be eligible enough to review that paper and needs to accept the job of reviewing the paper. A reviewer can be assumed eligible if he has sufficient knowledge about the field of study of the submitted article. It is presumable that a PhD holder from social science does not have sufficient knowledge to review an article submitted from the field of Data analysis. To review a paper related to Data analysis a reviewer should have sufficient knowledge regarding the study of Data analysis.

A reviewer can be assumed to be willing to accept the offer of reviewing the article if he explicitly agrees to do so. When asked if a reviewer wants to review a particular paper or not, he must answer "yes" or "no", and if the answer is "yes" it can be safely assumed that the reviewer is willing enough to accept the proposal of reviewing the paper submitted for peer-review. The proposed system solves the issue of selecting eligible reviewers and distributes submitted paper to the peer review process in a decentralized and anonymous manner.

Tag Based Field of Study Matching System: For Finding Eligible Reviewers

TAG is a text-based label attached to the users of the proposed system for the purpose of their identification or to give other information. When a person becomes a user of this system, he/she must provide some information so that it can be ensured that the person is authentic. She/he along with his/her other details must provide the area of research interest (or Field of study). Whenever, one of his papers gets published, she/he will be mentioned the field related to that published paper in his account. Every update in the account or related activity of a user will be treated as a transaction. Every transaction that happens in a decentralized system is kept as a record. During each transaction the system will automatically check the record and select TAGs for each user. From the figure 5 we can see a clear view of how the TAG selection process for a user works. When a user includes his/her field of study or the field of his/her published paper in his/her account, a transaction happens, and that field is saved as that user's TAG. If

Figure 5. TAG selection process

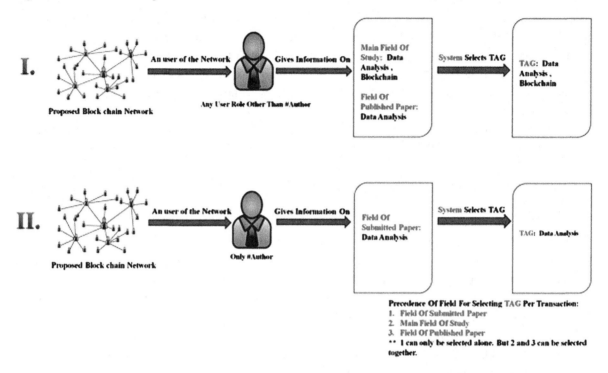

someone submits a paper through the system for reviewing, it is treated as a transaction and the field of that submitted paper is also saved as a TAG for that user. So, the system can select TAG for a particular user from three (3) different sources –

1. **Field of Submitted Paper:** The field of study related to the submitted article by #Author. #Author will give the related field name while submitting the article. (Source #1)
2. **Main Field of Study:** Main area of interest or field of study of a user. A user will give his/her main area of interest or field of study while opening an account on the system. He can always update the information when he/she wants. (Source #2)
3. **Field of Published Paper:** The field of study related to a published paper of a user. If he/she published it elsewhere he/she could just fill in the information in his/her account. If the paper was first submitted and then published in the proposed system, the system will automatically collect the field of the published paper from the previously given TAG while it was in submission phase (Source #1).For example, if a user submits an article or paper on Data Analysis, he/she includes the field of his/her submitted paper. If the article is published on the system, then the previously given field of submitted paper will be automatically collected by the system and it will be saved as the field of published paper. (Source #3)

The TAGs are selected from these three (3) sources while maintaining a special kind of precedence. If (Source #1) is found, then the system won't look for (Source #2) or (Source #3). If (Source #1) is not found, then the system will use (Source #2) and (Source #3) both as sources. The TAGs will be non-repeated and cumulative for each transaction.

So, in this way, a user who's Field of study is Data analysis (Source #2) and has some published works in the field (Source #3) will have TAG of Data analysis. If a user submits a paper related to Data analysis (Source #1) as an author, then he will also have a TAG of Data analysis. These TAGs will be selected, updated, modified and saved at each transaction in every user's block. Every user's account will always accommodate his TAG information so that the system causes the information whenever needed.

Now let us look at the figure 6for a better understanding of how the eligible reviewers are selected for article distribution.

So far, the system has collected or selected some words based on TAGs from three (3) different fields. The TAG represents two (2) things-

1. The related field of a paper that was submitted for peer-review process
2. The field of expertise of a user

If both fields match that means a user's field of expertise matches with the field of the paper which was submitted for review. So, from the figure 6, a user who's Field of study is Data analysis (Source #2) and has some published work in the field (Source #3) will have a TAG of Data analysis. If a user submits a paper related to Data analysis (Source #1) as an author, then he will also have a TAG of Data analysis. The system matches the TAG of the author with the TAGs of other users to find the eligible reviewers for reviewing a paper submitted by the author whose TAG is Data analysis.

When a user acts as #Author node and submits his/her paper for peer-review process through the system, the user must mention the name of the field related to the submitted paper which will be used as the TAG. After he/she submits the paper through his/her machine, a request will be automatically generated. This request can be perceived as a "Hello" message. Every block in the system receives this request, asking them if anyone has the same TAG as the #Author. In each node, a string matching algorithm matches the TAG of the #Author with the TAG of the node. And if the TAG matches, then a reply is generated automatically, that can be perceived as something like "I have the same TAG as you!"

Figure 6. Eligible reviewer selection process

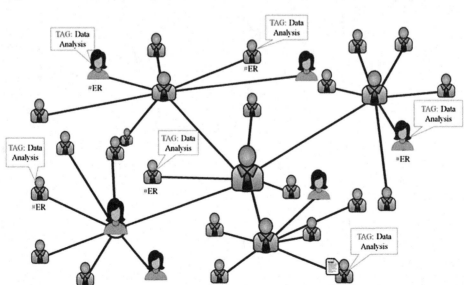

Every block or node that sends reply message to the #Author is enlisted as an eligible reviewer by the system. If there is a situation where no block is sending reply, there can be two (2) possible reasons-

1. There is no available user with same TAG
2. The reply was sent but was somehow lost

To solve this problem the #Author node will continue to send request automatically after an interval, until the node gets at least two (2) replies. The system will only start enlisting users as eligible reviewers only if there are at least three (3) replies.

There is not limitation on the number of users that can be selected as eligible reviewers. Any number of users can be selected as eligible reviewers by the system if the criteria of having the same TAG meet.

Reputation Point Based Ranking System: To Rank the Reviewers

After finding eligible reviewers through TAG matching process, the system will automatically rank those reviewers based on their reputation points and no. of published papers. Reputation points will be automatically generated by the system and given to a user if he/she successfully completes task as a review.

For better understanding of the Ranking procedure, let's take a look at figure 7.

Only the users who were found eligible by the TAG matching process will be enlisted for probable review process as an eligible reviewer. They are denoted as #ER or Eligible Reviewer. The users who

Figure 7. Ranking of eligible reviewers based on rank score

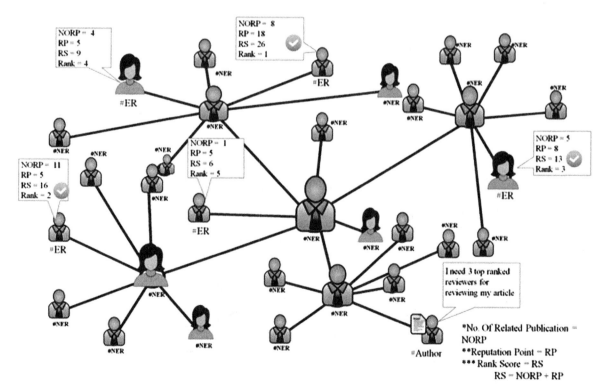

were not enlisted will be denoted as #NER or Not an Eligible Reviewer. After finding all available #ER, the system will try to give them rank through a simple process. Every #ER will get his own Rank Score after every time an enlisting process is completed. This Rank Score will be determined on the basis of two (2) different criteria-

1. No. of related publications
2. Reputation Points

So, Rank Score = No. of related publications + Reputation Points; where No. of related publications indicates the number of published papers of a user on the same field as the submitted article.

No. of published papers will indicate the capability of the user as a researcher and reputation points will indicate the reputation of a reviewer. More will be discussed on Reputation Point (RP) in the next section.

Now, let's look at figure 8. All #ER that has been ranked based on their Rank Scores will be asked by the system if they want to accept the proposal of reviewing the submitted article or paper. An #ER has to explicitly agree to this proposal for becoming a primary reviewer or #PR of that submitted paper. There can be at least two (2) and at most three (3) #PR for reviewing one paper. After the criteria is met, the system will close the process of reviewing and until the review process is completed, selected #PR will not show up in TAG Selection or Reviewer Selection process for other submitted papers. In another word, #PR busy with one review process will not be bothered with new review proposals until the completion of his current job.

Figure 8. Top Three #ER getting selected as #PR after accepting proposal

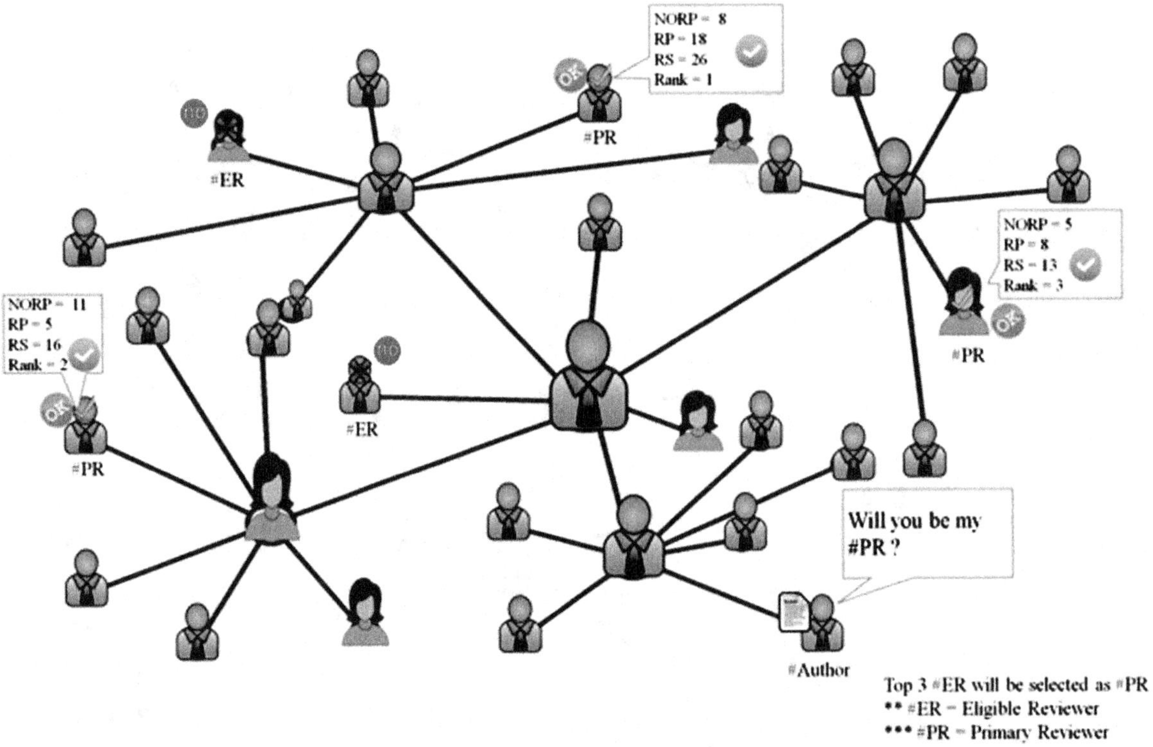

After review process is completed by a #PR, he/she will give one of the below four ratings to that article-

- Accepted (A)
- Major Revision (MAR)
- Minor Revision (MIR)
- Rejected (R)

The submitted paper and the review decision of that paper together will be sent to the secondary reviewer as a part of two-step verification process. More on this process will be discussed in the next section.

If the submitted paper gets any other review decision than Accepted, it will be sent back to the #Author. If "Accepted", then the submitted paper will get published in the system. Here, publishing refers to adding the accepted paper to the Blockchain and becomes a part of an open access and eternal journal.

Transaction Using Smart Contract: Keeping Records

It has been said earlier that every update in the account or related activity of a user will be treated as a transaction. In this case Transaction is an exchange of information and may or may not be recorded for ever and may or may not be added to the Blockchain. The core infrastructure of Blockchain requires transaction to happen between two users in each time. And for one Blockchain based system, all transactions should carry same type of information. This framework utilizes smart contract to create all kinds of transactions.

Submitting an article or requesting reviewers, sending information about user's TAG, accepting review proposal, sending hash of the article to the selected reviewer etc. can be done through transaction. The figures given below could help us to understand more about how the transactions will occur in the system while distributing the article. These transactions should be similar to the nature of smart contracts (Szabo, 1996).

Transaction during TAG matching process could be as shown in Figure 9.

Figure 9. Transaction during TAG matching

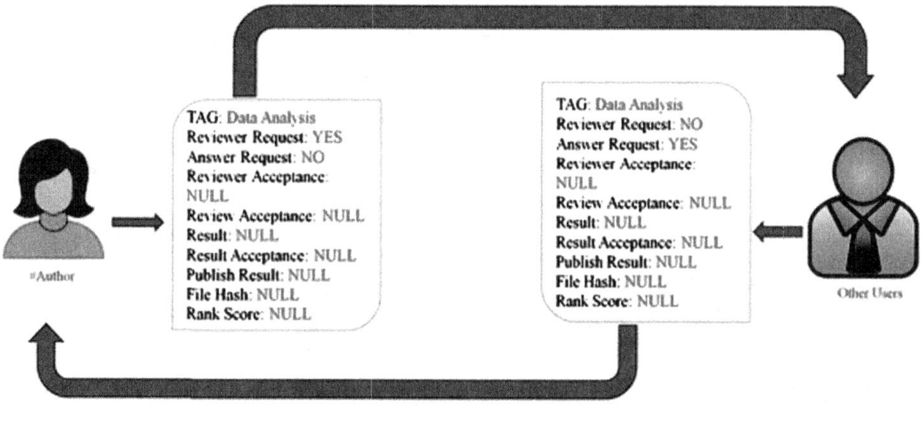

Transaction during reviewer ranking process could be as shown in Figure 10.

Transaction during a #ER accepting review request and becoming a #PR could be as shown in Figure 11. And transaction during #Author sending file hash to #PR could be as shown in Figure 12.

Each transaction happens between two (2) users at a time and is validated by every user on the system other than the two who did the transaction. So, when not reviewing a particular article, a user of the system will act as a potential block validation node by default, for the system of validating the transactions regarding that article. This is how article submitted through the proposed Blockchain based peer-review system will be getting distributed to the most capable reviewers for peer-reviewing process.

ARTICLE REVIEW VERIFICATION SYSTEM

After #PR or primary reviewer gives review of the submitted article, there remains a question whether the review was authentic or not. A #PR could just not review the submitted article and gives "Accepted" rating to it. This could pave a path for what the system tries to avoid, biasness and corruption in peer-

Figure 10. Transaction during eligible reviewer ranking process

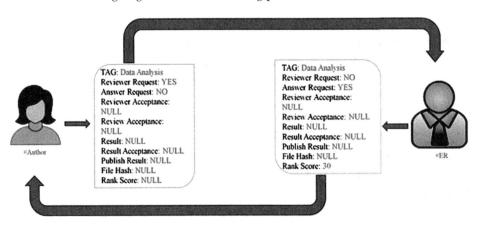

Figure 11. Transaction during an #ER becoming a #PR

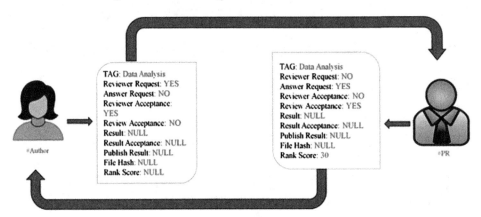

Figure 12. Transaction during #Author sending hash of his article to #PR

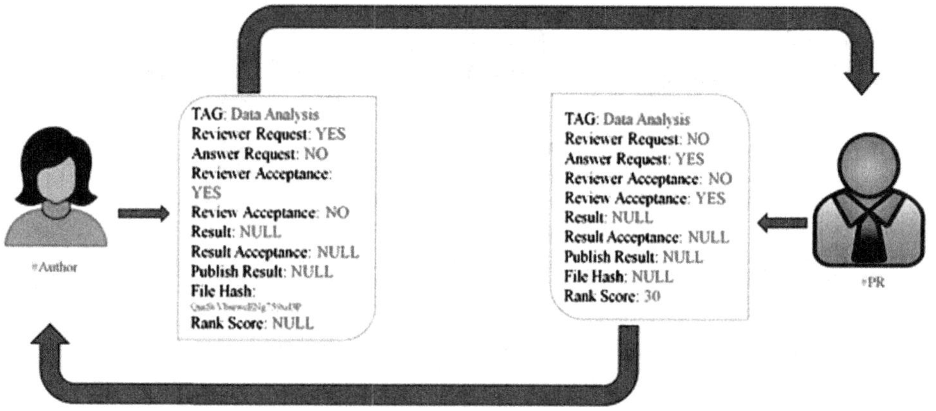

reviewing. To avoid this situation, the system proposes what it can be called as "Two-step verification process".

As it has been mentioned earlier there could be three (3) different roles a user can play –

- Author (#Author)
- Primary Reviewer (#PR)
- Secondary Reviewer (#SR)

Here, a #Author submits an article for peer-reviewing. #PR reviews the article. Any user other than #Author and #PR will go through the previously mentioned TAG matching process and Reviewer ranking process. Top ranked reviewers will get the proposal of reviewing the review of #PR. First two (2) users that accept the proposal will be selected as #SR. #SR will then review the reviewing or rating submitted by #PR.

This way there will be a two-tier or two-step peer-reviewing and if the submitted article should be published or not, gets verified through this two-step verification process.

Primary Review: Review of the Submitted Article

After #PR is selected through TAG matching and Reviewer selection process described earlier, #Author can see the list of three (3) finally selected #PRs who accepted the request of reviewing the article.

IPFS then takes the address of the article can create a hash. The system then encrypts the address hash with the public key of a #PR. Then #Author share the encrypted hash with the #PR. #PR decrypts the article with his private key (see figure: 13). After decrypting he uses the decrypted address hash to download the article from IPFS. This process is repeated for all three (3) selected #PRs.

#Author will initiate a transaction with the #PR to send the hash of the article.

This transaction happens each time #Author sends a hash of his article to a #PR. After #PR gets the hash, he then decrypts the hash using his private key. After the decryption, he gets the hash that is generated from the address or location of the article in #Author's directory by IPFS that #Author wants him to review. He then uses it to download the file through IPFS.

Figure 13. #Author sending Article to #PR using IPFS

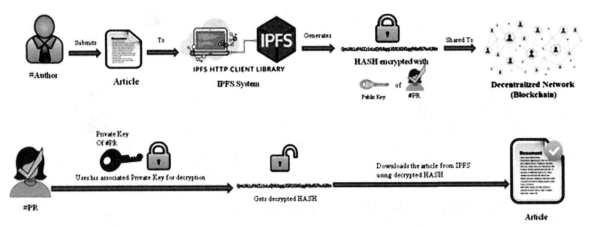

Figure 14. #Author sending hash of the article created by IPFS to #PR within a transaction

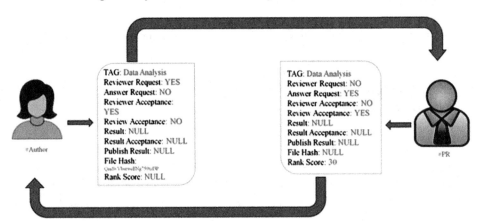

After reviewing the article #PR creates a file that includes the rating decision (A/MAR/MIR/R) and comments regarding the submitted article. This review file is then sent to #SR with the main submitted article.

Secondary Review: Review of the Primary Review

The job of a secondary reviewer is to make sure that the primary reviewer completes his job correctly. Secondary reviewer or #SR is selected from the users excluding the #Author and three #PR. #SR selection process is the same as the selection process of #PR. At first, TAG is matched. Then eligible reviewers are ranked based on their rank score. After that they are asked to be #SR based on their rank on a descending manner. The user with best rank score is asked first, then second best, then third best and so on. This process is same as the #PR selection process described above.

First two (2) eligible reviewers who agree to the review request become secondary reviewer or #SR.

After #PR downloads, decrypts and reviews the article submitted by the #Author; he writes down his review, comments and the rating (A/MAR/MIR/R) he has given to the submitted article and creates a doc file or pdf file. Then he keeps both his review file and the submitted article in a folder. Then #PR uploads the folder to IPFS. IPFS then generates a hash of the address of this folder. Then the system encrypts the hash with the public key of a #SR. Then the encrypted address hash of the folder is shared with the #SR. This process is repeated for both #SR. #SR then decrypts the encrypted address hash, and then he uses the decrypted hash to download the folder from IPFS. After downloading is completed he collects both file; the submitted article and the review file. For better understanding please see figure 15.

After collecting both files #SR will review the primary review and the article. Then he will produce

Figure 15. #PR sending hash of the combined article and review file created by IPFS to #PR within a transaction

a binary decision, the primary review is TRUE, or the primary review is FALSE. The decision being TRUE means, the review of the primary reviewer is accepted, if FALSE it means the review of the primary reviewer is rejected. As there will be two #SR, a primary review will be considered true only if both #SR gives the decision "TRUE". And a primary review will be considered false only if both #SR gives the decision "FALSE".

There can be three possible situations-

1. If the primary review was "A" meaning "Accepted" and the secondary reviewer gives the binary decision TRUE, then the submitted article will be published.
2. If the primary review was "MAR" or "MIR" or "R" and the secondary reviewer gives the binary decision TRUE, then the author will be notified and the submitted article won't get published at that time.
3. If the secondary review is "FALSE" then the primary review will become void. The primary reviewer will be notified, and his reputation point will decrease as a penalty for being biased, unethical and unprofessional. The whole process will re-initiate automatically until the review process is completed rightfully.

For better understanding of how the decision will be sent as transaction, take a look at figure 16.

Once, #PR gives "A" rating to the submitted article and #SR gives the decision "TRUE"; the submitted article will get published and added to the proposed system.

Figure 16. #SR sending final decision to #Author

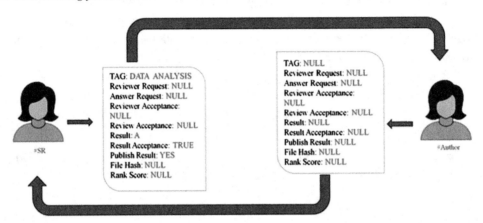

This two-step verification process ensures that the submitted article is being reviewed correctly without any kind of biasness. It does so because of following reasons-

1. All of three (3) primary reviewers don't know the #Author. It will be a blind review process.
2. None of the primary reviewers will be sluggish and give wrong or biased review of the submitted article because their review will be reviewed by the #SR. And if any primary reviewer gives wrong review, his reputation point will be decreased as penalty.
3. There will be two (2) #SR and the final decision will be taken only if both of the #SR gives the same decision. So, there is no chance that the final decision will be biased or wrong.

REPUTATION POINT - BASED ON THE IDEA OF CRYPTO CURRENCY

Reputation Point or RP can be denoted as a form of reward gained each time a reviewer successfully completes a review process. RP cannot be used as any form of currency, it cannot be transferred; however, one can earn RP through completing an authentic and correct review of a submitted paper. If the review is rejected because of its questionable character, then the primary reviewer that made the review will lose RP because of his/her questionable reviewing on the submitted paper. Thus, Reputation Point acknowledges a researcher's expertise as a reviewer.

Primary reviewers will earn RP by giving authenticate review of Author's submitted paper. Secondary reviewers will earn RP by reviewing the reviews previously given by the primary reviewers.

So, a high-ranking reviewer (primary and secondary) will have a high number of published works as well as a high number of Reputation Points indicating the reviewer's expertise as a reviewer.

Reputation Point: Crypto Reward

Reputation Point or RP plays a vital role in the proposed system. It is a variation of crypto currency which holds only abstract value. It has no monetary value.

Primary reviewer (#PR) and Secondary reviewer (#SR) both get selected on the basis of the number of publication and Reputation Point or RP.

This Reputation Point will act as a token of gratitude. The information of total amount of Reputation Point a user has will always be public. The more Reputation Points reflects a better reviewer. This can also be viewed as a certificate given by publishers to the reviewer. Unbiased, authentic and rightful or fair review will earn a reviewer some Reputation Points. Failing to do so will result in penalty and Reputation Point will be deducted from the reviewer.

Whenever, a #PR completes an authentic and rightful article review process, he will be rewarded with, for example 10 Reputation Points. This Reputation Points will be awarded to the #PR for giving an authentic review by the system itself.

#SR will be reviewing the primary review produced by the #PR. For completing the secondary review process, #SR will be awarded with, for example 5 Reputation Points.

For better understanding of matter, please see figure 17.

If a #PR gives a review that is biased, wrong or unethical; then, for example 6 Reputation Point will be reduced as a penalty from his current amount of Reputation Points. #SR will not lose any Reputation Points because he will only be reviewing the primary review that #PR produced. And also, as the final decision will be taken only when both of two #SR agrees on the decision, the secondary review, has a very less chance of being biased. This is why #SR won't be penalized here.

#SR will have a very little amount of Reputation Point gain from the review process, but there is no penalty for him. #PR will have a much higher gain of Reputation Point than the #SR but will be penalized if found guilty of giving wrong review.

For better understanding of matter, please see figure 18.

As it can be observed that there is a strong relation between review and Reputation Point. Higher amount of Reputation Points indicate that the user is a good reviewer who is unbiased and does rightful reviews of scientific articles. Lower amount of Reputation Points indicate that the user is not up to par as a reviewer. That means, the more Reputation Points a user has, the more eligible and better reviewer he is. It should be mentioned here that; higher and lower amount is relative. Having 15 Reputation Points

Figure 17. Gaining reputation points in case of primary and secondary reviewer

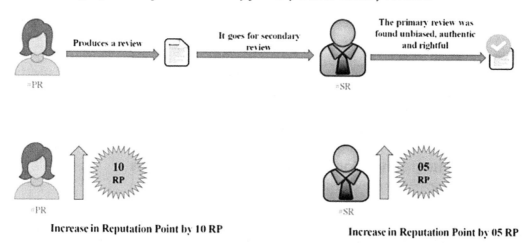

Figure 18. Loosing reputation points in case of primary reviewer

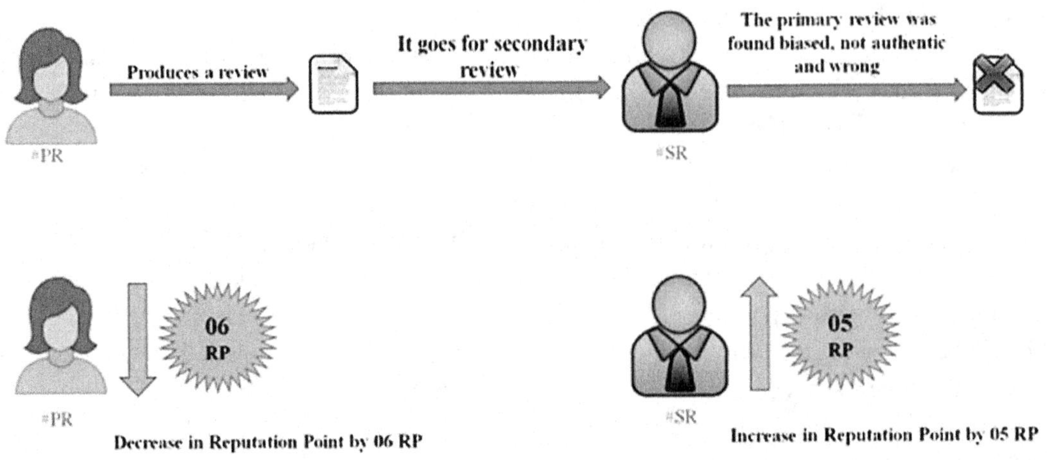

can be considered as high amount, if other users of the system have lower than 15 Reputation Points. On other hand, having 100 Reputation Points can be considered as a lower amount if others have more than 100 Reputation Points.

Validating Transactions: Another Use of Reputation Points as Crypto Reward

There is a fourth role a user of the system can act on. This role is not a part of the whole review process but a part of the Blockchain who will act indirectly to maintain the reliability of the system.

In existing Blockchain based systems, there is a type of users called miner. Miners deal with validating transactions and building new adding new block to the Blockchain (Ellervee, Matulevičius & Mayer, 2017). Fundamentally, a Blockchain operator is a miner, because miner's tasks in a Blockchain environment are to create new blocks, sign them, validate them and submit them to the Blockchain (Ellervee et al., 2017). Usually mining a block gets a miner some crypto currency that he can spend. But as all of our users will be from scientific and researcher community, there is a significant amount of probability that the miner validating the blocks of the proposed peer-reviewing system based on Blockchain will also come from the same community. As in the proposed system infrastructure, a miner is helping the review process by validating the transactions, he will be rewarded with a minimal amount of Reputation Point for his contribution.

Reputation Point, in all means will not act as a traditional crypto currency; but a crypto reward based on the idea of crypto currency. As Reputation Point holds no monetary value and cannot be transferred from one account to another, there is a less chance of bribery and corruption. But as it holds an abstract value, it will help identifying a user as a better reviewer and a better contributor to the field of research.

Challenges of Integrating Blockchain and Smart Contracts in Scientific Paper Peer Reviewing System

There are several challenges of implementing the proposed system along with the limitations of Blockchain technology discussed in earlier section. The challenges are discussed below.

- **Human Interaction:** As it is sure that there is no sufficient technology which can review or evaluate a scientific paper, therefore, this proposed system must have some interaction with human. This brings a possibility that can potentially corrupt the system. But, as the system integrates smart contracts that control the behavior of the stakeholders of the system, the possibility is less and also any aberrant behavior can be traced back through the data stored on the blockchain. However, this system still struggles to maintain human interaction with the system.

- **File Storage:** Authors will submit their paper through IPFS, and other reviewers are supposed to download and seed the file. But it is imminent that no one wants to waste their storage for seeding other files. This makes a challenge for the proposed system that how the file will be stored. Initially, the author must seed his own file. But to circulate the file efficiently through system it is necessary that some other users also seed the same file. This problem can be eliminated through offering rewards or crypto-currency to store files. Already, Filecoin is in its development phase which provides the user with some crypto-currency to host other people's files.

- **Proper Reviewing Rules or Criteria:** As there are no ground rules for reviewing a paper, it sometimes may get confusing whether a paper is reviewed correctly or not. Though the secondary review process is integrated into the system, it is not sure that the quality is impeccable. However, if this system is maintained by an organization that sets some ground rules then this problem may not exist.

- **Implementing the Flow of Cryptocurrency:** Another important fact that should not go unnoticed that the flow of reputation point, and cryptocurrency play a big role to the system. Though, it is also a debatable topic that whether a reviewer should get crypto-currency in exchange of his or her review. This problem can also be eliminated if a single organization adopt the system and set ground rules for biasfree reviewing of scientific papers.

- **Immutability of Smart Contracts:** Smart contracts are immutable by definition. This system cannot assure that the rules will remain same forever. So, it is challenging to maintain or upgrade smart contracts. Though, there are ways to upgrade a smart contract by using an intermediate contract where the active smart contract's address will be saved. There are some security risks to upgrade smart contracts that cannot be overlooked. So, this is also a challenge to maintain smart contracts of the proposed system.

IMPLEMENTATION

A prototype has been prepared to validate the above given proposed system. Distributions of article using IPFS, finding eligible reviewers, giving review – these parts have been successfully implemented. The system was implemented using Ethereum's test network. Backend was developed using Solidity and frontend was developed with ReactJS. Currently "Two-step verification" and "Reputation Point" are being worked on and will be added to the system as soon as possible.

SIMILAR WORK

Recently, Digital Science and Katalysis have launched a pilot project to implement blockchain technology to test the peer review process. This project aims to discover the practical solutions to enhance distributed

Figure 19. Implemented parts of the proposed system

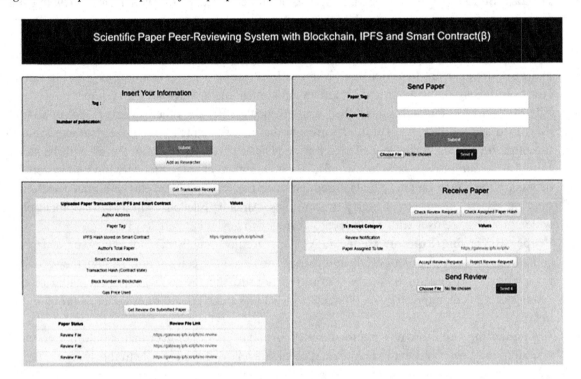

registry and smart contracts which are the elements of Blockchain technology. The initiative is divided into three (3) parts namely Pilot Phase, Minimal Viable Product Phase and Advanced Development. Participation is almost closed for the first phase as of Feb 01, 2019. (Blockchain Peer Review Project)

CONCLUSION

Recently, the decentralized applications (DApp) based on Blockchain technology are gaining attention to the developer and researcher communities. In this paper an anonymous scientific paper reviewing system based on Blockchain and IPFS technology has been proposed. However, the scalability of this system is needed to be observed. Researches can improve the scalability of this system.

Reputation Point of this system does not hold any monetary value. The integration of monetary system in peer reviewing system is a debatable topic. So, researches in this area could unearth whether peer reviewing should be done by exchanging cryptocurrency or not. Again, access to the published paper could also be monetized. This system presently does not integrate any monetary system. So, feasibility of integrating money exchange in this system needs more study.

Design of the smart contracts can be of different forms, so more precise contracts formation may emerge. So, the evaluation of different contracts can be analyzed and ensure efficiency of this system.

In this proposed system, the users of the network store the files, but they are not provided anything in return. So, to ensure that the published papers are held by maximum number of users, cryptocurrency can be provided to the holders of scientific papers in the network.

REFERENCES

Ahram, T., Sargolzaei, A., Sargolzaei, S., Daniels, J., & Amaba, B. (2017). *Blockchain technology innovations. In 2017 IEEE Technology & Engineering Management Conference.* TEMSCON. doi:10.1109/temscon.2017.7998367

Allison, I. (2016, October 13). *Juan Benet of IPFS talks about Filecoin.* Retrieved October 27, 2018, from https://www.ibtimes.co.uk/juan-benet-ipfs-talks-about-filecoin-1586122

Arora, J. (n.d.). *How EOS can solve the Blockchain scaling problems.* Retrieved August 5, 2018, from https://itsblockchain.com/eos-scaling/

Blockchain Council. (2018, July 10). *How is blockchain verifiable by public and yet anonymous?* Retrieved January 29, 2019 from https://www.blockchain-council.org/blockchain/how-is-blockchain-verifiable-by-public-and-yet-anonymous/

Blockchain on AWS. (n.d.). Retrieved October 26, 2018 from https://aws.amazon.com/blockchain/

Blockchain Peer Review Project. (n.d.). Retrieved February 01, 2019 from https://www.blockchainpeer-review.org

Chaum, D. (1997). David Chaum on Electronic Commerce How much do you trust Big Brother? *IEEE Internet Computing, 1*(6), 8–16. doi:10.1109/MIC.1997.643931

Chen, W., Ma, M., Ye, Y., Zheng, Z., & Zhou, Y. (2018). IoT Service Based on JointCloudBlockchain: The Case Study of Smart Traveling. *2018 IEEE Symposium on Service-Oriented System Engineering (SOSE).* 10.1109/SOSE.2018.00036

Crypto Celebrities. (n.d.). Retrieved October 29, 2018, from https://cryptocelebrities.co/

CryptoKitties. (n.d.). Retrieved October 29, 2018, from https://www.cryptokitties.co/

Csiszar, A. (2016). Peer review: Troubled from the start. *Nature, 532*(7599), 306–308. doi:10.1038/532306a PMID:27111616

Dey, T., Jaiswal, S., Sunderkrishnan, S., & Katre, N. (2017). HealthSense: A medical use case of Internet of Things and blockchain. *2017 International Conference on Intelligent Sustainable Systems (ICISS).* 10.1109/ISS1.2017.8389459

Ehsani, F. (2016, December 21). *Blockchain in Finance: From Buzzword to Watchword in 2016.* Retrieved October 26, 2018 from https://www.coindesk.com/blockchain-finance-buzzword-watchword-2016/

Ekin, A., & Unay, D. (2018). Blockchain applications in healthcare. *2018 26th Signal Processing and Communications Applications Conference (SIU).* doi:10.1109iu.2018.8404275

Ellervee, A., Matulevičius, R., & Mayer, N. (n.d.). *A Comprehensive Reference Model for Blockchain-based Distributed Ledger Technology.* Retrieved October 27, 2018, from http://ceur-ws.org/Vol-1979/paper-09.pdf

Etherbots. (n.d.). Retrieved October 29, 2018, from https://etherbots.io/

Feld, S., Schönfeld, M., & Werner, M. (2014). Analyzing the Deployment of Bitcoins P2P Network under an AS-level Perspective. *Procedia Computer Science, 32*, 1121–1126. doi:10.1016/j.procs.2014.05.542

Filesystem in Userspace. (2018, October 22). Retrieved October 27, 2018, from https://en.wikipedia.org/wiki/Filesystem_in_Userspace

Finley, K. (2016, June 20). *The Inventors of the Internet Are Trying to Build a Truly Permanent Web.* Retrieved October 26, 2018 from https://www.wired.com/2016/06/inventors-internet-trying-build-truly-permanent-web/

Hay, S. (2018, January 02). *What is the Bitcoin Lightning Network? A Beginner's Explanation.* Retrieved October 26, 2018 from https://99bitcoins.com/what-is-the-bitcoin-lightning-network-a-beginners-explanation/

Hjalmarsson, F. P., Hreioarsson, G. K., Hamdaqa, M., & Hjalmtysson, G. (2018). Blockchain-Based E-Voting System. *2018 IEEE 11th International Conference on Cloud Computing (CLOUD).* doi:10.1109/cloud.2018.00151

Hojat, M., Gonnella, J. S., & Caelleigh, A. S. (2003). Impartial Judgment by the "Gatekeepers" of Science: Fallibility and Accountability in the Peer Review Process. *Advances in Health Sciences Education: Theory and Practice, 8*(1), 75–96. doi:10.1023/A:1022670432373 PMID:12652170

Hyperledger: Blockchain collaboration changing the business world. (n.d.). Retrieved October 26, 2018 from https://www.ibm.com/blockchain/hyperledger

Infographic. (2018, October 4). *A history of academic peer review.* Retrieved October 26, 2018 from https://www.editage.com/insights/a-history-of-academic-peer-review

IPFS is the Distributed Web. (n.d.). Retrieved October 27, 2018, from https://ipfs.io/#how

Ipfs/README.md. (n.d.). Retrieved October 27, 2018, from https://github.com/ipfs/ipfs/blob/master/README.md#who-designed-it

Jordan, R. (2018, January 10). *How to Scale Ethereum: Sharding Explained – Prysmatic Labs – Medium.* Retrieved October 26, 2018 from https://medium.com/prysmatic-labs/how-to-scale-ethereum-sharding-explained-ba2e283b7fce

Kalodner, H., Carlsten, M., Ellenbogen, P., Bonneau, J., & Narayanan, A. (2015). *An empirical study of Namecoin and lessons for decentralized namespace design.* Retrieved October 26, 2018, from http://randomwalker.info/publications/namespaces.pdf

Kiyomoto, S., Rahman, M. S., & Basu, A. (2017). On blockchain-based anonymized dataset distribution platform. *2017 IEEE 15th International Conference on Software Engineering Research, Management and Applications (SERA).* doi:10.1109era.2017.7965711

Koshy, P., Koshy, D., & McDaniel, P. (2014) An Analysis of Anonymity in Bitcoin Using P2P Network Traffic. In Lecture Notes in Computer Science: Vol. 8437. Financial Cryptography and Data Security. Springer. doi:10.1007/978-3-662-45472-5_30

Kronick, D. A. (1990). Peer Review in 18th-Century Scientific Journalism. *Journal of the American Medical Association, 263*(10), 1321. doi:10.1001/jama.1990.03440100021002 PMID:2406469

Kshetri, N., & Voas, J. (2018). Blockchain-Enabled E-Voting. *IEEE Software, 35*(4), 95–99. doi:10.1109/MS.2018.2801546

Lerback, J., & Hanson, B. (2017). Journals invite too few women to referee. *Nature, 541*(7638), 455–457. doi:10.1038/541455a PMID:28128272

Litecoin. (n.d.). Retrieved October 26, 2018, from https://en.wikipedia.org/wiki/Litecoin

Loeliger, J., & McCullough, M. (2012). *Version control with Git*. Sebastopol, CA: OReilly.

Mahoney, M. J. (1977). Publication prejudices: An experimental study of confirmatory bias in the peer review system. *Cognitive Therapy and Research, 1*(2), 161–175. doi:10.1007/BF01173636

Meiklejohn, S., & Orlandi, C. (2015). Privacy-Enhancing Overlays in Bitcoin. In M. Brenner, N. Christin, B. Johnson, & K. Rohloff (Eds.), Lecture Notes in Computer Science: Vol. 8976. *Financial Cryptography and Data Security. FC 2015*. Berlin: Springer. doi:10.1007/978-3-662-48051-9_10

Merton, R. K. (1968). The Matthew Effect in Science: The reward and communication systems of science are considered. *Science, 159*(3810), 56–63. doi:10.1126cience.159.3810.56

Mitra, R. (2017, December 4). *Lightning Protocol &The Raiden Network: A Beginner's Guide*. Retrieved October 26, 2018 from https://blog.springrole.com/lightning-protocol-the-raiden-network-a-beginners-guide-c9d7bc702748

Mulligan, A., Hall, L., & Raphael, E. (2012). Peer review in a changing world: An international study measuring the attitudes of researchers. *Journal of the American Society for Information Science and Technology, 64*(1), 132–161. doi:10.1002/asi.22798

Nakamoto, S. (n.d.). *Bitcoin: A Peer-to-Peer Electronic Cash System*. Retrieved October 26, 2018 from https://bitcoin.org/bitcoin.pdf

Niya, S. R., Shupfer, F., Bocek, T., & Stiller, B. (2018). Setting up flexible and light weight trading with enhanced user privacy using smart contracts. *NOMS 2018 - 2018 IEEE/IFIP Network Operations and Management Symposium*. doi:10.1109/noms.2018.8406112

Peer Reviewed Medical Journals. (n.d.). Retrieved October 26, 2018 from https://www.omicsonline.org/peer-reviewed-medical-journals.php

Ratnasamy, S., Francis, P., Handley, M., Karp, R., & Schenker, S. (2001). A scalable content-addressable network. *Proceedings of the 2001 Conference on Applications, Technologies, Architectures, and Protocols for Computer Communications - SIGCOMM 01*. doi:10.1145/383059.383072

Rowland, F. (2002). The peer-review process. *Learned Publishing, 15*(4), 247–258. doi:10.1087/095315102760319206

Schwartz, D., Youngs, N., & Britto, A. (2014). *The Ripple Protocol Consensus Algorithm*. Retrieved October 26, 2018, from https://ripple.com/files/ripple_consensus_whitepaper.pdf

Sharp, D. W. (1990). What Can and Should Be Done to Reduce Publication Bias? *Journal of the American Medical Association*, *263*(10), 1390. doi:10.1001/jama.1990.03440100102015 PMID:2304218

Shema, H. (2014, April 19). *The Birth of Modern Peer Review*. Retrieved October 26, 2018 from https://blogs.scientificamerican.com/information-culture/the-birth-of-modern-peer-review/

Spier, R. (2002). The history of the peer-review process. *Trends in Biotechnology*, *20*(8), 357–358. doi:10.1016/S0167-7799(02)01985-6 PMID:12127284

Stoye, E. (2017, June 19). *Studies flag signs of gender bias in peer review*. Retrieved October 26, 2018 from https://www.chemistryworld.com/news/studies-flag-signs-of-gender-bias-in-peer-review/3007593.article

Szabo, N. (1996). *Smart Contracts: Building Blocks for Digital Markets*. Retrieved October 26, 2018, from http://www.fon.hum.uva.nl/rob/Courses/InformationInSpeech/CDROM/Literature/LOTwinterschool2006/szabo.best.vwh.net/smart_contracts_2.html

Tapscott, D., & Tapscott, A. (2016). *Blockchain revolution how the technology behind Bitcoin is changing money, business and the world*. Portfolio/Penguin.

Tenorio-Fornés, A., Hassan, S., & Pavón, J. (2018). Open Peer-to-Peer Systems over Blockchain and IPFS. *Proceedings of the 1st Workshop on Cryptocurrencies and Blockchains for Distributed Systems - CryBlock18*. 10.1145/3211933.3211937

The Linux Foundation. (2015, December 17). *Linux Foundation Unites Industry Leaders to Advance BlockchainTechnology* [Press release]. Retrieved October 26, 2018 from https://www.linuxfoundation.org/press-release/2015/12/linux-foundation-unites-industry-leaders-to-advance-blockchain-technology/

Thomas, L., Long, C., Burnap, P., Wu, J., & Jenkins, N. (2017). Automation of the supplier role in the GB power system using blockchain-based smart contracts. *CIRED - Open Access Proceedings Journal*, *2017*(1), 2619-2623. doi:10.1049/oap-cired.2017.0987

Valenta, L., & Rowan, B. (2015). Blindcoin: Blinded, Accountable Mixes for Bitcoin. In M. Brenner, N. Christin, B. Johnson, & K. Rohloff (Eds.), Lecture Notes in Computer Science: Vol. 8976. *Financial Cryptography and Data Security. FC 2015*. Berlin: Springer. doi:10.1007/978-3-662-48051-9_9

Wood, G. (2014). *ETHEREUM: A Secure Decentralized Generalized Transaction Ledger EIP-150 REVISION*. Retrieved October 26, 2018, from https://gavwood.com/paper.pdf

Yli-Huumo, J., Ko, D., Choi, S., Park, S., & Smolander, K. (2016). Where Is Current Research on Blockchain Technology? A Systematic Review. *PLoS One*, *11*(10), e0163477. doi:10.1371/journal.pone.0163477 PMID:27695049

Young, J. (2016, September 24). *IPFS Protocol Selects Ethereum Over Bitcoin, Prefers Ethereum Dev Community*. Retrieved October 27, 2018, from https://cointelegraph.com/news/ipfs-protocol-selects-ethereum-over-bitcoin-prefers-ethereum-dev-community

Zhang, P., Walker, M. A., White, J., Schmidt, D. C., & Lenz, G. (2017). Metrics for assessing blockchain-based healthcare decentralized apps. *2017 IEEE 19th International Conference on E-Health Networking, Applications and Services (Healthcom)*. doi:10.1109/healthcom.2017.8210842

Zhao, J. L., Fan, S., & Yan, J. (2016). Overview of business innovations and research opportunities in blockchain and introduction to the special issue. *Financial Innovation*, 2(1), 28. doi:10.118640854-016-0049-2

Chapter 11
Bank Data Certification and Repurposing Using Blockchain

Usha B. Ajay
BMS Institute of Technology and Management, India

Sangeetha K. Nanjundaswamy
Jagadguru Sri Shivarathreeshwara Academy of Technical Education, India

ABSTRACT

Privacy protection is one of the basic needs for supporting a good interaction in a globally interconnected society. It is important not just for business and government but also to a huge and increasing body of electronic or online societies. In such situations, a traditional digital ledger storage systems seems more centralized. Security of traditional digital ledger system has always been a greater concern when considered for implementing at a huge scale. When such sensitive data is at stake, there should be nothing doubtable about the system's strength to secure data and withhold itself against any potential attacks. Blockchain is one way through which such potential security issues can be solved. A blockchain, actually block chain, is basically a continuously increasing list of records, which are called blocks; these blocks are linked and secured mainly using cryptography. Every block typically has a cryptographic hash of the block previous to it, along with a timestamp and data of the transaction.

INTRODUCTION

Since its inception, the blockchain technology has shown promising application prospects. From the initial cryptocurrency to the current smart contract, blockchain has been applied to many fields. Although there are some studies on the security and privacy issues of blockchain, there lacks a systematic examination on the security of blockchain systems (Thomas, 2017). Since the debut of Bitcoin in 2009, its underlying technique, blockchain, has shown promising application prospects and attracted lots of attentions from academia and industry. Being the first cryptocurrency, Bitcoin was rated as the top performing currency in 2015 and the best performing commodity in 2016, and has more than 300K confirmed transactions daily in May, 2017. At the same time, the blockchain technique has been applied to many fields, including medicine economics, Internet of things, software engineering and so on. With the decentralized

DOI: 10.4018/978-1-5225-9257-0.ch011

consensus mechanism of blockchain, smart contracts allow mutually distrusted users to complete data exchange or transaction without the need of any third-party trusted authority. Ethereum is now (May of 2017) the most widely used blockchain supporting smart contracts, where there are already 317,506 smart contracts and more than 75,000 transactions happened daily.

A BlockChain, an actually block chain, is basically a continuously increasing list of records, which is termed as blocks, these blocks are linked and secured mainly using cryptography. Every block typically has a cryptographic hash of the block previous to it, along with a timestamp and data of the transaction. The design of the BlockChain is such that it is basically resistant to modification of its transaction data (Mahdi H et al., 2018).

BlockChain is an open, distributed ledger which records transactions between any two clients efficiently and in such a manner that those transactions are verifiable and are permanent. BlockChain is usually maintained by a peer-to-peer network which collectively adheres to a protocol for communication between nodes and validating new blocks (Xiaoqi Lia et al., 2018). After a transaction is recorded it is not possible to alter the data in any given block without changing all previous blocks, which requires high computational power.

As Bitcoin (Fangfang Dai et al., 2017) emerged in 2009 with it BlockChain gained prominence and though it now exists for almost a decade, people are still not able to fully understand the potential of it. Experimental solutions that are beyond crypto-currencies like Ethereum, Bitcoin show a future for elementally changing society and with such innovations right now we may look at the dawn of cryptographically secured and trust-free transactions economy.

"The trust machine" that was the term coined by The Economist recently, which indicates that blockchain has potential for taking care of trust issues, which in turn frees people from implementing a method to show or convey trust. With similar words, the implemented system is working without any trust concerns, making the transactions "trust free", once it makes an impression as agreement in blockchain. Bitcoin blockchain showed us that it was just a beginning, as the availability of generic blockchains and self-programmable blockchains increased, like the once provided by Ethereum, blockchains are now being used in areas beyond crypto-currencies. These features trust-free, highly secure and transparent nature of blockchain paved the way for utilizing it in other application areas. For example, Samsung and IBM plan to experiment with blockchain to produce IOT solutions.

State of Art Development

In this section, studies were conducted, different techniques were studied and evolved, and most of the research carried out was to exploit BlockChain advantages.

In (Orcutt et al., 2017), Studies carried out give a full detail and knowledge of Zero-Knowledge proof. The idea of zero-knowledge proofs has been known to developers for a very long time, but it wasn't until recently that researchers figured out what the technology actually holds: It's a mathematical concept that lets users share data with any users without actually revealing the contents of the data. In other words, the user can only prove that he is the owner of the data without revealing a single bit of information to the verifying party.

In (Beck et al., 2016), author discusses about the vast advantages of BlockChain and briefly explains the way they can be used in industry; the scopes of article basically involves how by incorporating a trustless system that is decentralized, a number of centrally controlled third party agencies can be replaced and hence provide an efficient application based on proof of concept.

In (Wu et al., 2014) author analyses the principles of non-interactive zero knowledge proof system and provides a solution to NP systems. It shows a practical approach to include a zero-knowledge proof system to an application using concepts of cryptography. Also, the author describes how verifying the applications built using zero knowledge proof is a lot easier using cryptography although making it harder for the miners of blockchain to validate the entries on the blockchain at the same time making it easier to verify.

In (Bahsoun et al., 2015) author discusses about fault tolerance of existing systems, Fault tolerance is extremely essential especially in distributed and decentralized environment as the full nodes are communicating with each other via a peer to peer network thus any down time on one node should be immune to the other node, thus maintaining the integrity of the network involved. Failure to do so may result in overwriting Consensus protocols and loss of user data.

In (Devi, 2013), the principle point is to give a broad review of system security and cryptography, with specific regard to digitized marks. System security and cryptography is a subject too wide to scope about how to ensure data protection and to give security services. However, the author discusses about various algorithms providing an overview of network security and cryptography.

In (T. Bamert et al., 2013), The authors describe how increasing common malicious attacks and software errors are these days in the cyber space. Each full node of blockchain is replicated to other nodes in a peer to peer manner such that they all arrive at consensus. However, the nodes if prone to attack must not affect the state of the other. The problem is called byzantine generals' problem and the author discusses how blockchain should be running practical Byzantine fault tolerance algorithms which was first introduced in the bitcoin blockchain.

In (Sompolinsky and Zohar. 2015), the author describes the cheat free nature of blockchain. The blockchain uses a number of game theory concepts to achieve the cheat free, prominent among which is the Nash algorithm. It avoids miners of full nodes mining on top of an invalid transaction or adding new block to the chain without passing the consensus algorithm. These are avoided using Nash algorithm.

In (Yves-Alexandre de Montjoye et al., 2013), the author describes the use of Merkle Tree and Merkle Root in building the blockchain. Blockchain are tamper proof and the transactions are transparent. This is because internally for every transaction Merkle tree structure is followed which makes these transactions tamper proof and also uses fewer resources for storing transaction details. Verifying a transaction on the blockchain becomes easy with the use of Merkle tree as it removes the need to download the entire blockchain to verify a transaction.

In (Mukund R et al., 2015), author mainly focuses on concepts of how to protect data transmission and network over a wireless network. It also emphasizes on secure data transmission over an unreliable network. Varieties of computer networks are used in day-today life which must be considered for network security. Also, in (Mukund R et al., 2015), Paper focuses on providing network security using advanced cryptographic techniques. Network security is vital in information security as it is responsible for securing information passed through network systems.

In (Yves-Alexandre de Montjoye et al., 2014), author describes in detail about blockchain, how blockchain was invented, advantages of using the technology and how different it is from existing technologies. It also describes how hash is used in blockchain with providing a minimalist implementation using python.

In (Sumedha Kaushik et al., 2012), the author describes the self-governance property of blockchain. The author also discusses how the entire system is trust-less and can be trusted upon by proving mathematically. The amount of resources required to falsify a transaction on the blockchain would be equivalent to that of a hundred of supercomputers put together, and since the Ethereum blockchain is a public ledger; such malicious attempts will be visible to every other node on the network.

Above survey emphasis on how important data is today's world and how data can be misused. They also throw light on current existing methods like zero-knowledge proof, which are in picture since few decades but aren't used industrially and how such concepts when used along with BlockChain result in strong data protection methods.

Motivation

The current model of storing and collecting data is questioned with increase in reported incidents of security and surveillance breaches of user's private and sensitive data. The quantity of data in the present world is increasing at rapid rates. According to a recent report, 20% of the total data present was collected in the recent past few years. Facebook, one of the largest social-media networks, approximately collected around 300 petabytes of private data since its start- which is 100 times the quantity of data collected by Library of congress in over a period of 200 years. In this era of Big Data, data is continuously collected, manipulated and processed, leading to growth of economy and innovation. Organizations and companies use the data collected to optimize corporate decision making, personalize services and guess future trends and many more. In today's scenario data is an asset that is valued very high in the economy. In the financial space Bitcoin (Massimo, 2017) has shown that audit-able and trusted processing is possible making use of decentralized system of companions joined by a single public ledger.

Problem Statement

Throughout this project, it addresses the privacy issues (Juan, Aggelos & Nikos, **2015**) that users commonly face when using third party services that are highly centralized. Here it mainly focuses on Bank data where users provide sensitive data to a bank (Ashwin Machanavajjhala et al., 2007). The bank is centralized, and it is wholly responsible for controlling of data.

- Traditional ledger system is highly Centralized and expensive.
- Traditional data ledger system is often subjected to manipulation and is not transparent to the users.
- 72% of the consumers believe data breaches have serious implications for their security.
- By forming a distributed network for validation and immutable data storage process we propose to overcome the above issues.

Objective

The main objective of this project is to implement system which has following features:

- Retaining anonymity of the user's identity and the data created.
- Demonstrate data ownership without revealing actual data.
- Document time-stamping and immutable recording.
- Provide a means to hold a token of monetary value in return for the data provided.

- Real time validation and certification of consumer data.
- Provide a user-friendly ownership validation and storage system and cut the cost of any central authority.

Methodology

The problem is addressed by introducing a platform, which takes the user data and produces a hash. Hash is produced using SHA-29 technique. The hash produced in the first step is used to make entry in the BlockChain ledger (Beck, et al., 2015). A Smart-Contract defined previously make sure the data is valid and how these transactions should be shown. These entries are immutable and time-stamped. Here instead of getting the entire block to the local system platform uses MetaMask an open source platform for making Ethereum transactions. Each of these transactions has a monetary value after their successful completion.

Proposed platform also provides a method for checking the transactions and user validity. At the other end if another bank needs to check the validity, then user gives the hash he has produced to the bank. The hash can then be used to check the transaction entry in the ledger and see the details of the transaction without actually having access to the original data. The transactions can be searched using both signers address and the hash value produced. Signers address is a Hexadecimal number that each user gets after registering in Ethereum through MetaMask.

Section Summary

This section starts with the introduction of the topic. Research study materials are reviewed for similar kinds of techniques. It also discusses about the motivation, problem statement, objectives, scope and methodology of the project.

OVERVIEW OF BLOCKCHAIN AND SMART CONTRACT

The blockchain is an incorruptible digital ledger of economic transactions that can be programmed to record not just financial transactions but virtually everything of value.

Blockchain

A blockchain is a digitized, decentralized, public ledger of all crypto currency transactions. Constantly growing as 'completed' blocks (the most recent transactions) are recorded and added to it in chronological order, it allows market participants to keep track of digital currency transactions without central record-keeping. Each node (a computer connected to the network) gets a copy of the blockchain, which is downloaded automatically (James Ball, 2013).

Originally developed as the accounting method for the virtual currency Bitcoin, blockchains – which use what's known as distributed ledger technology (DLT) – are appearing in a variety of commercial applications today. Currently, the technology is primarily used to verify transactions, within digital currencies though it is possible to digitize, code and insert practically any document into the blockchain.

Doing so creates an indelible record that cannot be changed; furthermore, the record's authenticity can be verified by the entire community using the blockchain instead of a single centralized authority.

A block is the 'current' part of a blockchain, which records some or all of the recent transactions. Once completed, a block goes into the blockchain as a permanent database. Each time a block gets completed, a new one is generated. There is a countless number of such blocks in the blockchain, connected to each other (like links in a chain) in proper linear, chronological order. Every block contains a hash of the previous block. The blockchain has complete information about different user addresses and their balances right from the genesis block to the most recently completed block.

The blockchain was designed so these transactions are immutable, meaning they cannot be deleted. The blocks are added through cryptography, ensuring that they remain meddle-proof: The data can be distributed, but not copied. However, the ever-growing size of the blockchain is considered by some to be a problem, creating issues of storage and synchronization (Don Johnson et al., 2001)

Distributed Ledgers

A distributed ledger is a database that is consensually shared and synchronised across network spread across multiple sites, institutions or geographies. It allows transactions to have public "witnesses," thereby making a cyber-attack more difficult. The participant at each node of the network can access the recordings shared across that network and can own an identical copy of it. Further, any changes or additions made to the ledger are reflected and copied to all participants in a matter of seconds or minutes.

A distributed ledger can be depicted as a ledger of any transactions or contracts maintained in decentralized form across various locations and individuals, taking out the need of a central authority to keep a check against manipulation. All the information on it is securely and precisely stored using cryptography and can be accessed using keys and cryptographic signatures. Once the information is stored, it becomes an immutable database and is administrated by the rules of the network. While centralized ledgers are inclined to cyber-attack, distributed ledgers are characteristically harder to attack because all the distributed copies need to be attacked at the same time for an attack to be successful. Further, these records are impervious to malevolent changes by a single party.

Smart Contract

Smart contracts are self-executing contracts with the terms of the understanding amongst buyer and seller being directly written into lines of code. The code and the agreements contained therein exist across a distributed, decentralized blockchain network. Smart contracts allow trusted transactions and agreements to be done among different, anonymous parties without the requirement for a central authority, lawful framework, or external enforcement mechanism. They render transactions traceable, straightforward, and irreversible. Smart contracts were first proposed in 1994 by Nick Szabo, an American computer scientist who designed a virtual currency called "Bit Gold" in 1998, completely 10 years before the creation of Bitcoin. Indeed, Szabo is often rumored to be the genuine Satoshi Nakamoto, the mysterious designer of Bitcoin, which he has denied.

Smart contracts are complex, and their potential goes past the simple transfer of assets -- they can execute exchanges in an extensive variety of fields, from lawful procedures to insurance premiums to crowd-funding agreements to financial subsidiaries. Smart contracts can possibly dis-intermediate the legal and financial fields; specifically, by simplifying and robotizing normal and repetitive procedures for which individuals currently pay legal advisors and banks sizeable charges.

The smart contract deployment process involves the triggering of the smart contract based on a predefined event. The deployed contract is visible on the public ledger and is easily verifiable using blockchain explorers which is shown in Figure 1

Blockchain is perfect for storing smart contracts because of the technology's security and immutability. Smart contract data is encoded on a shared ledger, making it difficult, almost impossible to lose the information stored in the blocks.

Another preferred standpoint of blockchain technology being incorporated into smart contracts is adaptability. Developers can store almost any type of data inside a blockchain, and they have a wide variety of transaction choices to choose from during smart contract deployment.

- **Cost-Effectiveness:** Smart contracts remove numerous operational costs and save assets, including the staff expected to monitor their progress.
- **Processing Speed:** Smart contracts run on automated procedures and, in most cases, can eliminate human association, increasing the speed of business exchanges stipulated in the agreement.
- **Autonomy:** Smart contracts are performed naturally by the network, removing the need and related risk of a third party being engaged in smart contract deployment.
- **Reliability:** Data entered in the blockchain can't be changed or erased. On the off chance that one gathering does not finish its commitments, the other will be ensured by the states of the smart contract. The automated transactions also eliminate the potential for human blunder and guarantee accuracy when executing the contracts Cost-effectiveness. Smart contracts remove numerous operational costs and save assets, including the staff expected to monitor their progress.

Section Summary

This section gives a brief introduction of BlockChain and Smart Contracts. It includes brief explanation of how BlockChain came into existence, how it can be implemented and how it works along with explaining how well smart contract go in hand with BlockChain with its advantages.

SOFTWARE REQUIREMENTS SPECIFICATION OF BANK DATA CERTIFICATION AND REPURPOSING USING BLOCKCHAIN

A Software Requirements Specification (SRS) is a document that gives the details of the project, operating system and software used. It provides number of guidelines to write the document that follows

Figure 1. Smart contract generation and deployment

according to software requirements specification that is already defined. This specification includes the topic like motivation, problem statement, constraints, functional and non-functional requirements, user characteristics, dependencies and also hardware and software requirements etc.

Overall Description

This section describes the general factors which affects system and the requirements. The software developed should provide means to configure order assignment generate master files with required restrictions and must handle concurrent assignment of orders to reconciliation specialists. This section also deals with user characteristics, constraints on using the system and dependencies of the system on other applications.

Product Perspective

The system should be versatile and easy to use. It should be flexible and the response time should be quick. The system is composed of several modules performing different tasks and they must be well coordinated. The system developed should be easy to deploy and maintain. The intended end users for this are mostly normal bank end users who are not well versed with technical knowledge. The system must be directive so as to inform the end users in case of common mistakes made in inputs and to allow comprehensive usage of the feature.

Product Functions

There are three functions that this system is responsible for, the primary one being producing the hash when the file is uploaded. The other one being checking, whether the user data is valid using the hash or the signer address. Both of which are unique to file and user respectively. Platform also provides detailed information about the used technologies.

User Characteristics

The end users of the system are mainly bank users, normal people. Since they are not technical specialists, the user interface is expected to be directive and easy to use. The other users are bank staff who are technically familiar and need little graphical support.

Constraints and Dependencies

System has some dependencies since it runs on Ethereum (Buterin, V, 2014), to make all the transactions it requires continuous internet, active running of MetaMask is required.

Specific Requirements

In this section, it gives brief description of the requirements that are used to carry out the project. It includes performance, functional, hardware and software requirements etc.

Functional Requirements

Functional requirement is one of the requirements which are used to check whether the project is running according to the specified functionality that is given in the project. It provides the basic flow on how the project has to be executed, what might go wrong or what necessary actions are taken if the module is not working as per the defined functionality. This kind of requirements is checked in functional requirements.

Performance Requirements

For each of transactions we make through the platform, we make sure that such transactions make entry in the blockchain. These transactions are heavy process and require little time. The generation of hash has to be optimal and faster. Even in case of validating the user for credibility, the searching of particular transactions using hash value and the signer address should be optimal and faster.

Supportability

The system is web based. Thus, it should work with all standard browsers without much difference in appearance of the interface.

Software Requirements

- Windows or Linux
- React 16.2
- MetaMask version 4.4.4 and above

Hardware Requirements

- 3 GB RAM.
- 8 GB Hard Disk.
- Optical Mouse.
- Keyboard, etc.

Section Summary

This section gives a complete software requirement specification required for the project. It specifies product functionality, constraints and dependencies and also specific requirements like functional, performance, software and hardware requirements are also specified in this section.

HIGH LEVEL DESIGN OF BANK DATA CERTIFICATION AND REPURPOSING USING BLOCKCHAIN

Design is significant phase in development of software. It is basically a creative procedure which includes the description of the system Organization, establishes that it satisfies the functional and non-functional system requirements. Larger systems divided down into smaller sub-systems contain services that are related to each other. The output in design phase describes the architecture of software to be used for the development of the common endpoint service. This section depicts the issues that are required to be covered or resolved before attempting to devise a complete design solution. The detailed design includes an explanation for all the modules. It throws light on the purpose, functionality, input and output. The software specification requirements have been studied to design appropriate and efficient software to handle a multitude of users belonging to different user groups simultaneously accessing the system.

Design Considerations

There are several design consideration issues that need to be fixed before designing a solution for the system to be implemented. The following sections describe constraints that have heavy impact on the software, a method or approach used for the development and the architectural strategies. It also describes the overview of the system design:

General Constraints

General constraints which need to be considered to use the system are listed below:

- The user should be entitled to use the system, in the sense that the user has to belong to a particular user group to be able to access group-specific functionalities.
- The user should have knowledge of the required inputs and the formats of the inputs
- The files input by the user have to be valid and within the formats specified
- Details of the transactions must be available

Development Methods

The design method employed is highlighted in this chapter. The data flow model has been the design method employed for development of the system. A data flow model is modelling system based on data transformation that takes place as the data is being processed. The notations used represent functional processing and data stores. Data flow models gives the better understanding of how data is associated with the particular process by tracking and providing the documentation

Architectural Strategies

Architecture strategy translates business strategy into objectives for building, enhancing, or replacing business and system capabilities together with an implementation roadmap, all-the-while maintaining resilience to change as a key architectural objective.

Programming Language

The system involves two major segments, the frontend and backend which are built using react.js and Solidity respectively.

For front end purposes, React (sometimes React.js or ReactJS) is a JavaScript has been used. React has been widely used for designing single page applications. These applications are lighter and reduce server load also saving bandwidth which is essential for blockchain applications since the space available for serving the applications cannot be subjected to redundancy in terms of data storage.

Solidity is a contract-oriented programming language for writing smart contracts. It is used for implementing smart contracts on various blockchain platforms. Solidity is a statically-typed programming language designed for developing smart contracts that run on the EVM. Solidity is compiled to byte code that is executable on the EVM. Thus, providing way to write feasible smart contracts.

User Interface Paradigm

The GUI of the system is a multi-tabbed single window system. Each of the modules has a tab to represent its functionality. React js framework provides required functionality which helps to automatically set the main tabs available to a user and helps to seamlessly switch between tabs and redirect to different pages as required

Error Detection and Recovery

There is no much scope for any error as the project mainly focuses on producing hash and making those transactions visible on ledger. Exceptions may occur, if the user enters incompatible data. An occurrence of error also triggers a warning message to the required developers who would immediately look into and fix any errors.

Data Storage Management

Data storage management is an important aspect of the implemented project. Most of the data is stored with the user, the hash produced out of the data becomes the transaction data. That makes an impression in the blockchain ledger.

System Architecture

The system architecture which is shown in Figure 2 depicts the overall model that defines the structure, behavior, and more views of a system. This architecture description is a formal description and representation of a system, organized in a way that supports the representation of different models and their connections.

The System architecture consists of five different blocks. User interface is where user interacts with the system for inputs or to view displayed outputs. This interface is connected to switches and hosts which connects to controller. The SDN controller controls the network and also the database updating the data into it. The detection and mitigation system comprises of continuous entropy calculation and alarms he system if there is an attack. Also, mitigation process is initiated necessarily if there is an attack.

Figure 2. System architecture for bank data certification and repurposing using blockchain

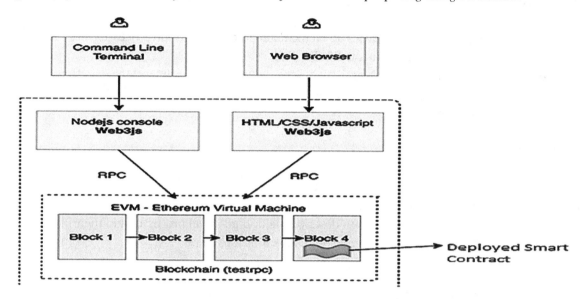

Data Flow Diagram

A data flow diagram (DFD) is a graphical representation which describes the flow of the data through its incremental steps. A DFD is usually used to give overall description of the project rather than giving complete detail of the project.

A DFD gives the information about the input and output of the system in each of the DFD level. It also shows how these inputs are processing inside the components and also produce the expected output for the given information. But it does not show the information on how these data are processed or the information on how much time it takes to process for the particular inputs. DFD divides the flow of the information into some levels where each level is interconnected.

Data Flow Diagram Level 0

A level 0 data flow diagram (DFD), also known as a context diagram, shows a data system as a whole and emphasizes the way it interacts with external entities.

In reference with Figure 3, the DFD level 0 shows the overall data functionality of the system. System here for a user takes an input file and when the other end user tests the validity of such user gets a validation result along with the validating transaction details.

Figure 3. DFD level 0 for bank data certification and repurposing system

Data Flow Diagram Level 1

A level 1 data flow diagram (DFD) breaks down the main processes into sub processes that can then be analysed and improved on a more intimate level.

In reference with Figure 4, in DFD level 1 it describes how each at each level the data flows. In case of generation of hash, making that hash as a transaction in the ledger and retrieval of those transactions and validating those transactions.

Section Summary

The above data models depict how data is processed by the system. This constitutes the analysis level. The notations applied above represent functional processing, data stores and data movement amongst the functions. The purpose of chapter is to describe major high- level processes and their interrelation in the system. All the above mentioned levels of DFDs illustrate these.

DETAILED DESIGN OF BANK DATA CERTIFICATION AND REPURPOSING USING BLOCKCHAIN

Detailed design is the phase where the detailed description along with the functional modules is explained in this section. It also gives details about the software, techniques and methods that are included in the project. This chapter consists of Structure chart and functional description of modules.

State Chart Diagram

State chart diagram is one of the UML diagrams that is used to describe the dynamic nature of the system. It includes states which define the functionality of the state. It also contains transitions from one state to another or also self-loop. Whenever particular functionality has to be executed, event is created and sent to the state it changes the transition to the state which has the functionality that can be achieved to the given events.

Figure 4. DFD level 1 for bank data certification and repurposing system

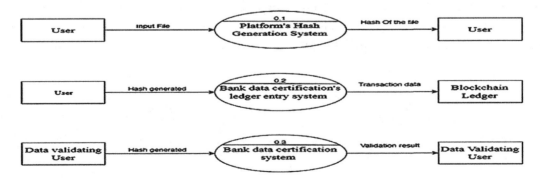

State chart diagram which is shown in Figure 5 describes the flow of steps from one state to another state. States are well-defined as a condition in which an object exists and it changes when some event is triggered. The most important purpose of State chart diagram is to model lifetime of an object from creation to termination.

Functional Description of Modules

Each functional module built are explained briefly in this section with reference to the above state chart diagram (Figure 5) mentioned earlier. In this state chart diagram, there are five functional modules:

1. **Input File:** File contains details of the user, data is sensitive or may not be, but its anonymity is to be protected, and validated without disclosing.
2. **File Validation:** File need to be checked before it is uploaded or used for hash generation.
3. **Hash Generation:** The process where file is hashed so that it is protected and doesn't leave the user or not centrally stored with a third party.
4. **Making Ledger Entry:** The produced hash is used to make entry into the Ethereum BlockChain Ledger, these transactions are permanent once done cannot be revoked.
5. **Searching:** Once the user makes entry in the blockchain for his data, in such cases user can use the hash produced by the file for further verification and validation of his bank data. Platform developed here provides with functions to make such searches.

Figure 5. State chart for bank data certification and repurposing system

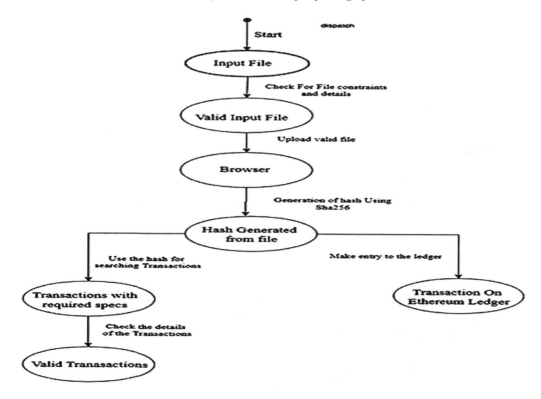

Section Summary

This section gives a very detailed of each functional module with its flow using state chart diagram. Each module in explained briefly in the section of functional description of module.

IMPLEMENTATION OF BANK DATA CERTIFICATION AND REPURPOSING USING BLOCKCHAIN

In this section, the programming language used and its respective code conventions that should be followed are briefed. Also, platforms selected to perform this experiment is also mentioned in this section.

Programming Language Selection

Solidity is a java script derivative that is used to write smart contracts. It was designed to help developers write decentralized applications better. It has been widely accepted among the developer community for this purpose. It has been programmed to target Ethereum virtual machine (EVM). The programming language is influenced by C++ and python as-well. It's a high level and contract-oriented language.

For front end and GUI purposes React Js has been used. It's a Java Script library that is used for building user interfaces. It is used to build single page applications. This means that the entire site contents and routes are loaded at once at the start of the site request and for every new view there is no need for repeated requests being sent to servers every-time. This has many advantages mainly faster load times and data security.

Platform Selection

Ethereum is an open blockchain platform and thus anyone can run their application on it. However to test the smart contract before deploying a virtual machine call Ethereum virtual machine was introduced. Since there needs to be mutual exclusion for applications hosted and any failure in an application should not affect the entire network, which is very much probable to occur in centralized systems. Thus for testing the application before deploying on the main-net, Ethereum virtual machine was made use of. It is free and every Ethereum node in the network runs their own EVM.

Users that host these main-net full nodes of Ethereum perform mining operations that help validate the transactions on the platform. They are rewarded in terms of Crypto currency, which motivates more users to host such instances.

Code Conventions

Code Conventions is a standard that is defined for each programming language. It follows some rules for defining of variable, classes, constructs, namespace, comments, conditions and some of the programming practices etc. It makes the program more readable and understandable.

- It helps to maintain the code throughout its lifetime
- It is impractical to maintain the code only by its original author.

- It improve the readability of the software, thus provides engineers to understand new code more quickly and thoroughly.

Naming Conventions

Naming conventions is used for making programs more understandable to read. It gives information on how the packages, classes, interfaces, variables, methods etc., thus providing better readability of code. The following conventions are followed in solidity:

- Packages names are declared in lower-case ASCII letters
- Classes and Interface names are declared with first letter capitalizing and it should be noun. It should be simple and descriptive.
- Methods and variables should be verbs, in mixed case with the first letter lowercase, with the first letter of each internal word capitalized.
- The constants should be in uppercase by separating with underscore between the words.

File Organizations

Structuring code, both among and within files is essential to making it understandable. Thoughtful partitioning and ordering, increases the value of the code. In our code following conventions are followed

- Files should consist of less than 2000 lines of code. If the file is more than 2000 it leads to ambiguity and readability of code is difficult.
- File should be separated and for every function there should be a comment describing about the functionality.
- The public class should be defined first in the file.
- The Program is well modularized.
- A function in one file interacts with other code through input and output arguments and global variables.

Declaration

There are declarations of classes, functions and variables in the implemented program. The class is declared by giving a class name. The class names are all in capital case. The function names are given appropriate access specifiers and are named in camel case fashion. The function name describes its functionality. The variables are all named in small case and relevant of the values they hold.

Comment

Comments are used to understand the code. The purpose of comments is to add information to the code. Typical uses for comments are to explain usage, provide reference information, to justify decisions, to describe limitations, to mention needed improvements. Experience indicates that it is better to write comments at the same time as the code rather than to intend to add comments later. Solidity has three types of comments

- Single Line Comment (//): It is used to comment one line
- Multi Line Comment (/*......*/):It is used to comment multiple line
- Documentation Comment (/**.......*/):The documentation comment is used to create documentation API.

Section Summary

This section deals with briefing the programming language used in implementation of this project which is Solidity. It also briefs about development environment and platform selection. It explains the different code conventions and declaration that is followed while coding. It also explains about comment section i.e., how comments are to be given while coding in java programming language.

SOFTWARE TESTING OF BANK DATA CERTIFICATION AND REPURPOSING USING BLOCKCHAIN

Testing a decentralized application that is run on a blockchain is a lot different from the traditional applications. The entire source code (smart contract) is embedded into the blockchain and replicated for every instance of the blockchain, thus the code should work on a distributed and decentralized network run by a peer to peer (p2p) environment.

The application has been deployed on testnet provided by Ethereum called Ropsten and was tested accordingly. Since the application is decentralized and distributed it is essential to make sure that the same behavior is exhibited on all platforms and devices, also the outcome of each module is tested to produce a consistent output.

Test Environment

A testing environment is a setup of software package and hardware for the testing teams to execute test cases. In different words, it supports test execution with hardware, software package and network organized. Test bed or test environment is organized as per the requirement of the applying under Test.

The test environment that we have used for deploying and testing our application is Ethereum reposten. The environment is a testnet for the actual Ethereum network that allows for deploying final Dapps. The test environment instance that we have made use of was hosted on an operating system macOS high Sierra 10.13.4 and npm 6.0.1 for serving the application locally.

Unit Testing of Main Modules

Unit testing is a software testing method by which individual units of source code, sets of one or more computer program modules together with associated control data, usage procedures, and operating procedures, are tested to determine whether they are fit for use which is shown in Table 1 and Table 2 respectively.

Table 1 explains unit testing for generation of hash for each file as a test case.

Table 2 explains unit testing for querying of certification entries using signers address and optionally document hash as-well.

Table 1. Hash generation test

Sl. No of test case	1
Name of the test case	Generation of Hash
Feature being tested	Hash for every file uploaded
Description	Unique hash generation for each file, and same hash needs to be generated if the file contents are the same
Sample input	Any hash-able data (ex: pdf, xls, txt, etc)
Sample output	Unique hash for each file
Actual output	Unique hash generation for each file
Remarks	Test case passed

Integration Testing of Modules

Integration testing is the phase in software testing in which individual software modules are combined and tested as a group. It occurs after unit testing and before validation testing. This testing takes as its input modules that have been unit tested, groups them in larger aggregates, applies tests defined, and delivers as its output the integrated system ready for system testing which is shown in Table 3 and Table 4 respectively.

Table 3 which explains unit testing for checking network connectivity with the blockchain as a test case.

Table 2. Signer address query test

Sl. No of test case	2
Name of the test case	Signer address query
Feature being tested	Query for details using Signer address
Description	Certification details are Queried using Signer address
Sample input	Signer address
Sample output	Search results for given signer address
Actual output	Details of for Entries using signer address
Remarks	Test case passed

Table 3. Checking network connectivity test

Sl. No of test case	1
Name of the test case	Checking network connectivity
Feature being tested	Network connectivity with the blockchain
Description	After logging in using MetaMask the client's private keys gets connected to the blockchain
Sample input	Clients public and private keys
Sample output	Displays a list of entries from blockchain
Actual output	Displays a list of entries from blockchain
Remarks	Test case passed

Table 4 which explains unit testing for transaction through MetaMask containing parameters such as input, output and its description of this test case.

System Testing

System testing of software or hardware is testing conducted on a complete, integrated system to evaluate the system's compliance with its specified requirements. System testing falls within the scope of black-box testing, and as such, should require no knowledge of the inner design of the code or logic which is shown in Table 5 and Table 6 respectively.

Table 5 which explains unit testing for new entries test case.

Table 6 which explains unit testing for certification validation test case that helps verify if an entry on the blockchain is actually valid or not.

Section Summary

This section deals with testing of the application. Initially each module is tested individually. The tested modules are grouped and an integrated testing of modules was carried out. Finally with all the modules in picture the entire system as a whole was tested and the results are recorded as shown above. No abnormal behavior was recorded.

Table 4. Transaction through MetaMask

Sl. No of test case	2
Name of the test case	Transaction through MetaMask
Feature being tested	Transaction status and entry
Description	The feature tested here is to ensure that each transaction goes through successfully and its status and entry are shown on the blockchain.
Sample input	Hash generated from file
Sample output	Transaction status and entry
Actual output	Transaction status and entry
Remarks	Test case passed

Table 5. New entry test

Sl. No of test case	1
Name of the test case	New entry test
Feature being tested	Make a new entry to the blockchain
Description	After hash is generated for a file a transaction is made with the blockchain that makes an entry.
Sample input	Hash-able file for certification.
Sample output	Displays the entry on blockchain on after transaction succeeds.
Actual output	Displays the entry on blockchain on after transaction succeeds.
Remarks	Test case passed

Table 6. Certification verification test

Sl. No of test case	2
Name of the test case	Certification verification test
Feature being tested	Verification of an existing entry
Description	On uploading a file, if a hash is present on the blockchain, will return the details of the existing entry.
Sample input	File upload or hash entry
Sample output	Search results from blockchain entry
Actual output	Search results from blockchain entry
Remarks	Test case passed

EXPERIMENTAL RESULTS AND ANALYSIS OF BANK DATA CERTIFICATION AND REPURPOSING USING BLOCKCHAIN

Although the application may remain the same, the underlying blockchain on which it is deployed makes a lot of difference. Thus the same application may produce different performance related results for different blockchain platforms. We have compared the basic parameters of Ethereum with other available platforms such as hyper-ledger fabric and sawtooth which are also under constant development.

Evaluation Metric

Metrics considered for the project valuation are given below
Performance criteria:

- Transactions submitted per second (in milliseconds)
- Transactions committed per second (in milliseconds)
- Transaction latency (in milliseconds)

Functional criteria:

- Byzantine Fault Tolerance
- Configurable/pluggable consensus

Subjective criteria:

- Ease of Platform Implementation
- Ease of Transaction Logic Development

Experimental Dataset

A large number of file formats were considered as datasets. It was observed that formats such as pdf, xls, txt, docx were commonly used to store data by the banking institutions, along with custom database file formats such as ending in (*.db).

It is essential to note that the file format does not matter for the application, in other words the server end of the application is blind to what the file content and the format is. Thus, adding to the better privacy protection of user content.

The application has been tested for all the above mentioned file formats and has succeeded in producing the expected results. The application is designed to accept one file at a time as input even when multiple files have been selected. Also, it was verified that any modifications or additions made to an already hashed file produces a unique hash every time changes were made to the file thus making sure there is no way that a file's content be manipulated to produce the same hash again.

Performance Analysis

The performance analysis is represented using two graphs namely transactions per second versus platform used and transmission latency versus platform used to evaluate the scalability and other performance of the application.

In the transactions submitted and committed versus platform used graph which is shown in Figure 6, can be inferred that there are other platforms like sawtooth which have a larger number of processing transactions and committing them on the blockchain.

In the Transmission latency versus platform used graph which is shown in Figure 7 can be inferred that the latency is considerably low for Ethereum.

Figure 6. Transactions submitted and committed versus platform used graph

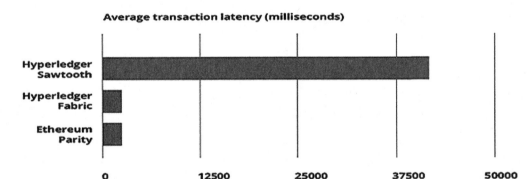

Figure 7. Transmission latency versus platform used graph

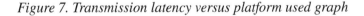
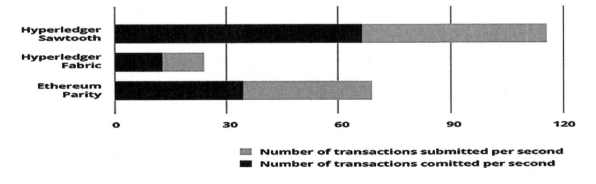

Section Summary

This section deals with the performance analysis of the bank data certification and repurposing using blockchain. Along with performance, results that are obtained are also mentioned and are graphed to provide a better representation of Ethereum platform being used. Dataset used for experiment is same for all the platforms.

CONCLUSION AND FUTURE ENHANCEMENT

Since the blockchain adoption to the mainstream is still in its early stages there's a lot of scope for future enhancement. This having said the existing blockchain isn't free from imperfections although many platforms are ready for developer adoption and deployment.

Since open, complete autonomy and censorship-free environment is what blockchain has always been highlighted for, this also drags a lot of government attraction. As a number of ethical questions are raised starting with the use of a peer to peer (p2p) network for operation, the need for a central authority is removed, which is both an advantage and also a disadvantage at times. This situation is the same which was faced by the bit-torrent protocol when initially torrents were introduced for file sharing. Complete anonymity is something the Internet might not be ready for yet.

Limitations

The current application is efficient and meets the requirements that are discussed in the testing phase, however there are certain areas which the application might not meet the expected standards although not failing altogether. Some of these limitations of the project are:

- Hash generation for files of large size is not supported.
- Higher cost per byte of data that is stored beyond the default for each transaction.
- Transaction validation and verification on the blockchain takes longer than traditional database systems.
- Risk of a 51% attack on the consensus protocol thus affecting entire blockchain.
- High GPU hungry resources required for blockchain mining.

Future Enhancements

One of the most challenging aspects of deploying an application on blockchain is scalability. Since the blockchain is a distributed ledger and typically works in a peer to peer network each node in the blockchain has to host an instance of the entire blockchain. Thus the amount of data that can be stored in the blockchain has to be minimal without introducing the need for redundant storage issues. The existing Ethereum blockchain also has the issue of scalability. One of the biggest issues that the consensus based blockchains have to face is to scale the magnitude to support a large number of transactions on top of the blockchain at any given time. This has to be attained at a low cost without the need for addition expense of hardware as well. This can be attained by introducing new consensus mechanisms that govern the core functioning of the blockchain.

Currently the most widely accepted consensus protocol is the proof of work protocol. This algorithm requires a lot of computational power for block validation and verification which is also known as mining. Recently another protocol called proof of stake was introduced which uses significantly less GPU hungry resources and is efficient. The scope of future enhancement is thus to enable highly scalable and efficient blockchain application deployment platform where any decentralized application can be deployed and run seamlessly in a censorship free environment.

Section Summary

This section gives a conclusion of the project and briefly states the limitation of the project and the future enhancements to grow and overcome the limitations of the system built during the course of the project. In particular this chapter describes how consensus protocols are the key factor in deciding the adoption of such decentralized applications to the masses.

REFERENCES

Bahsoun & Shoker. (2015). *A Parallel and Distributed Processing Symposium (IPDPS).* IEEE.

Ball, J. (2013). Nsa's prism surveillance program: how it works and what it can do. *The Guardian.*

Bamert, T., Decker, C., Elsen, L., Wattenhofer, R., & Welten, S. (2013). Have a snack pay with bitcoins. *Proceedings of the 13th IEEE International Conference on Peer-to-Peer Computing*, 1-5.

Beck, R., Avital, M., Rossi, M., & Thatcher, J. B. (2017). Blockchain technology in business and information systems research. Business and Information Systems Engineering, 59(6), 381–384.

Beck, R., Czepluch, S., & Jacob, L. (2016). Blockchain – The Gateway to Trust-Free Cryptographic Transactions. Academic Press.

Buterin, V. (2014). *Ethereum Development Tutorial.* Available at: https://github.com/ethereum/wiki/wiki/Ethereum-Development-Tutorial

Dai, F., Shi, Y., Meng, N., Wei, L., & Ye, Z. (2017). From Bitcoin to cybersecurity: A comparative study of blockchain application and security issues. *4th International Conference on Systems and Informatics (ICSAI)*, 975 – 979. 10.1109/ICSAI.2017.8248427

De Montjoye, Y. A., Shmueli, E., & Samuel, S. (2014). Openpds: Protecting the privacy of metadata through safeanswers. *PLoS One, 7*(9).

Devi, T. R. (2013). Importance of Cryptography In network Security. *Communication Systems and Network Technologies (CSNT), in International Conference.*

Di Pierro. (2017). What Is the Blockchain? *IEEE Computer Society American Institute of Physics, Computing in Science & Engineering, 19*(5).

Don Johnson, A. M., & Vanstone, S. (2001). The elliptic curve digital signature algorithm. *International Journal of Information Security, 1*(1), 36–63. doi:10.1007102070100002

Garay, J., Kiayias, A., & Leonardos, N. (2015). The bitcoin backbone protocol: Analysis and applications. *Annual International Conference on the Theory and Applications of Cryptographic Techniques*, 281-310. 10.1007/978-3-662-46803-6_10

Joshi & Karkade. (2015, January). Network Security with Cryptography. *International Journal of Computer Science and Mobile Computing*.

Kaushik & Singhal. (2012). Network Security Using Cryptographic Techniques. *International Journal of Advanced Research in Computer Science and Software Engineering, 2012*(12).

Keenan, T. P. (2017). Alice in Blockchains: Surprising Security Pitfalls in PoW and PoS Blockchain Systems. *15th Annual Conference on Privacy, Security and Trust (PST)*, 400–402. 10.1109/PST.2017.00057

Lia, Peng, Chenb, Luoa, & Wenc. (2018). *A Survey on the Security of Blockchain Systems*. Department of Computing, The Hong Kong Polytechnic University.

Machanavajjhala, Kifer, Gehrke, & Venkitasubramaniam. (2007). l-diversity: Privacy beyond kanonymity. *ACM Transactions on Knowledge Discovery from Data, 1*(1), 3.

Miraz, M. H., & Ali, M. (2018, January). Applications of Blockchain Technology beyond Cryptocurrency. *International Association of Educators and Researchers, 2*(1), 1–6.

Orcutt, M. (2017). *A mind-bending cryptographic trick promises to take blockchains mainstream. MIT Technology Review*.

Sompolinsky, Y., & Zohar, A. (2015). Secure high-rate transaction processing in bitcoin. *Financial Cryptography and Data Security – 19th International Conference*, 507-527. 10.1007/978-3-662-47854-7_32

Wu, H., & Wang, F. (2014). A Survey of Noninteractive Zero Knowledge Proof System and Its Applications. *The Scientific World Journal*. PMID:24883407

Yves-Alexandre, D. M., C'esar A Hidalgo, M. V., & Vincent, D. (2013). Unique in the crowd: The privacy bounds of human mobility. *Scientific Reports*.

Chapter 12
Data Confidentiality, Integrity, and Authentication

Dhanalakshmi Senthilkumar

https://orcid.org/0000-0003-0363-5370

Malla Reddy Engineering College (Autonomous), India

ABSTRACT

Blockchain has been created in the process of development in bitcoin. It's a singly linked list of block, with each block containing a number of transactions and each list in the blocks using with crypto-graphic functions. The cryptographic hash function contains the hash of the previous block, timestamp, and transaction ID. Blockchain services include the authentication, confidentiality, integrity, data and resource provenance, and privacy and access control lists technologies. The authentication provider authenticates decentralized database with transactions in private-public key pair. This key-pair is used in the transport layer security with the entire network. The network legitimizes the transaction after that and adds the transaction to the blockchain. A sequence of blocks in blockchain holds the complete record of transactions like a public ledger. The integrity data written in the blockchain cannot be altered subsequently. By limiting access to the information in confidentiality, only authorized users can access the information, so that information is also protected.

INTRODUCTION

Bitcoin and its underlying Blockchain technology were first conceptualized by Satoshi Nakamoto in 2008 but implemented in 2009, as a core of peer-to-peer version of electronic cash systems, these cash systems allows online payments to send directly from one party to another party without central trusted authorities like bank systems or payment services (Nakamoto, 2008). The digital currency i.e., Bitcoin components support for these transactions. Blockchain could be regarded as a public ledger for all committed transactions stored in list of blocks, are new blocks are appended to it continuously, and it resolved by double spend problem together with peer-to-peer technology with cryptographic tools. So that linking every transaction to the transaction preceding it in a tamper proof resistant manner. Blockchain is an open distributed ledger technology that can record the transactions between two par-

DOI: 10.4018/978-1-5225-9257-0.ch012

ties efficiently and in a verifiable and permanent way (Marco and Karim, 2017). The Blockchain can be specified that different requirements or keywords; the first requirement is open (whatever information inside the Blockchain, that information should be accessible to all i.e. Everyone will be able to validate and use that particular information), second one is distributed ledger or decentralized (no single party control – who are in the platform and their communicating with each other), third one is efficiently (need to ensure the efficiency of the information, efficiency of the protocol, so that the protocol need to be fast and scalable), the next one is verifiable(verifiable is important key in Blockchain, who are in the network they should be able to check the validity of the information and final one is permanent (inside the information in Blockchain, that information is persistent).So that once you have inserted information into the Blockchain, then you will not be able to change or update that information in future time, that means the information is persistent, its otherwise called tamper proof, so these are the important properties of Blockchain environment. The requirements said that, any alternation of any block cannot be done without alternation of all subsequent blocks which makes the system permanent, efficient and verifiable. When Bitcoin cryptocurrency introduced that time Blockchain technology used. Blockchain was born with Bitcoin. Bitcoin most commonly used application in Blockchain technology, the entire Bitcoin network it supports Blockchain, and Blockchain works as a fundamental building block with behind the development of Bitcoin. Which is emerged as a digital currency, many people believe that Blockchain could revolutionize many fields, such as finance, accounting, management, and law leading. It's a decentralized digital currency payment system with public transaction ledger. Bitcoin uses public key infrastructure (PKI) mechanism. The user of PKI has pair of public and private keys. The private key is authentication of user and the public key is address of the user in Bitcoin wallet (Yli-Huumo, KO, Choj and Park, 2016).

The evolution of Blockchain technology namely; Blockchain 1.0 – it's the decentralization of money and payments, basically used for cryptocurrencies, Blockchain 2.0 used for digital finance and industries (In Blockchain 2.0 smart contract was first introduced the way to verify assets, properties, products and services), and Blockchain 3.0 is the decentralization of digital society and its used for applications of IoT, health and government, it offers more security as compared to Blockchain 1.0 and 2.0, and it's used for various industries, arts health, media and many government institutions (Supriya and Kulkarani, 2017).

Blockchain technology is the sharing and storing of information in a single block, each block has many transactions, storing of information is permanent in the block; blocks are connected with each other. block chain has been created in the process of development is bit coin, is growing list of records with linked list manners, each list in the blocks using with cryptographic functions. Both users sharing the documents and also simultaneously edit the documents. One problem to be raised in centralized systems for single point of failure; to load the data in Google doc do not have enough bandwidth, not able to edit the documents. In centralized systems single point is not safe vs. decentralized systems can have multiple points of coordination's vs. distributed systems can have each one executes the job. Blockchain is a type of database that is duplicated on many systems or nodes. Every node, the node maintains local copy of global data sheet. All the nodes have the same information's for to access the transactions, the information is stored on blocks, but cannot change or delete a transaction from the Blockchain.

Each block has multiple transactions, with each transaction having a unique reference number, time stamp and points to previous transactions. Each node to access to all previous blocks. The last block in the Blockchain contains the latest executed transactions, so that the Blockchain is continuously growing. A decentralized database system ensures that strong consistency support with local copy of data; every node is identical based on the global information local copies of data always updated. The cryptographic hash functions any string as input and fixed size output, secure hash algorithm that generate 256 bits in Blockchain. Hash function performs the collision-free, hiding and puzzle-friendly. In cryptographic hash pointer stored hash of the information, retrieve the information and check the information, but the checked information has not been modified.

BACKGROUND IN BLOCKCHAIN TECHNOLOGY

Blocks

Blockchain came from the chained list of blocks in data structure. The chained blocks distribute over a peer to peer network, every node maintain the latest version, in which each block can contain information about transactions. The structure of block consists of two fields; every block has header field and body field (Mahdi and Maaruf, 2018). Structure of block Header shows the header and body fields of Figure 1. The block has two components block header (A block, in a Blockchain is a collection of data recording the transaction) and list of transaction. (A transaction in a Blockchain represents the action triggered by the participant).

The block header contains the previous block hash, version, time, bits, nonce, mining and Merkle tree root (Zheng, Xie, Dai and Wang, 2018). The metadata every block inherits from previous block, previous block's hash to create the new block's hash make the tamper proof, to generate the hash for Bitcoin mining and Merkle tree is root of all transactions, Blockchain design structure organized and used to construct

Figure 1. Blockchain design structure of block header

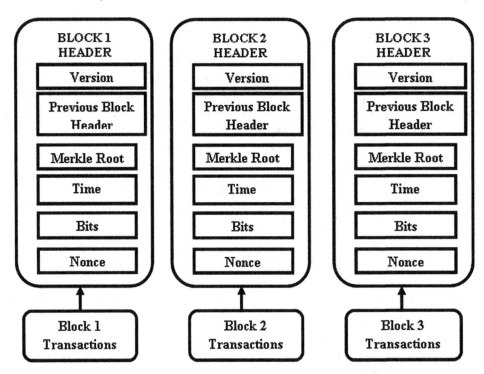

Table 1. Field description with size in block header

Field	Description	Size (BYTES)
Version	Block Version Number	4
Previous Block Header	Hash of Previous Header	32
Merkle Root	Tx Merkle Root Hash	32
Time	Unix Time Stamp	4
Bits	Current Difficulty	4
Nonce	Allows Miners Search	4

the block hash, if change any transaction in the header then need to change all subsequent blocks hash and finally all transaction will result change at the block header. The headers of all subsequent blocks are connected in a chain. The Blockchain network maintains the local copy of Blockchain. The block header in typical metadata contains; block version, previous block header hash, Merkle root, timestamp, Bits, and Nonce (Zheng, Xie, Dai and Wang, 2017).

It represents that; *Version-* current version of the block structure, indicates which set of block validation rule to follow, *Previous Block Header-* the reference of block parent block, link of a block to its previous one in the chain, the previous block information will be inputted to hash function to get the value, *Merkle Root -* cryptographic hash value of all the transactions in the block, *Time -* current time as seconds in universal time, the time that this block was created, *Bits -* target threshold of a valid block hash (current difficulty that was used to create this block), and *Nonce -* it's an 4-byte field, which usually starts with 0 and increases for every hash calculation, number of attempts to find the target value (Zheng et al, 2018). The Table 1 shows that field description with size in Blockchain header.

These fields constitute the block header, rest of a block contains transactions, and users create transactions and submit to the network. The block body is composed of a transaction counter and transactions. The maximum number of transactions that a block can contain depends on the block size and the size of each transaction. Blockchain uses an asymmetric cryptography mechanism to validate the authentication of transactions. Blocks are chained together with previous blocks header. The Blockchains are probabilistic systems, as a block is created and set around the network, then each node processes the block and decides to fit in the current overarching Blockchain ledger. The Blockchain can either be public or private, the public Blockchain enables all the users with read and write permissions, but in private Blockchain limits the access to selected trusted participants only. Bitcoin is a public Blockchain, it was designed to be completely open, decentralized and permissionless, that means anyone can access it. The transaction counter and transaction are two parts of block body. Each block depends on block size and size of each transaction. In Blockchain technology, to support and confirm the transaction authentication cryptographic mechanism is used. A digital signature based on asymmetric cryptography is used in an untrustworthy environment.

Building the blocks in Blockchain are maintained database, many participants keep copies of the ledger/database and also simultaneously update databases for verification. Three characteristics for underlie Blockchain technology; secure identity – secured the private key cryptography and digital identity, Verification – verify distributed network in consensus mechanism, and Protocol – systems of rules in Blockchain, service the network transactions and security.

Blockchain Architecture

Blockchain technology is a data structure used to create a decentralized ledger in serialized manner (Zheng et al 2018). Blockchain is a Singly Linked List of blocks, with each block containing several transactions. It's a decentralized and information sharing platform, not trust with multiple domains, users can be shared the block and record all the transactions, each transaction can be easily queried. block chain has been created in the process of development is bit coin, is growing list of records with linked list manners, each list in the blocks using with cryptographic functions (Noe, Longzhi, Fei and Yi, 2018). The cryptographic hash function contains the hash of the previous block, timestamp and transaction id, multiple authoritative domains of decentralized computation and information sharing platform to collaborate, cooperate and coordinate in decision making process, both users can share the information and also simultaneously edit the information in Google documents, one problem to be raised in centralized systems for single point of failure, to load the data in Google doc do not have sufficient bandwidth, not able to edit the documents. Figure 2 represents those Blockchain systems of centralized vs. decentralized vs. distributed systems techniques. In centralized network; the nodes directly send the central node to the recipient. Opposed of the centralized systems, the decentralized model of distributed network of centralized networks system without central node. A decentralized system is referred that without intermediary party data is propagated onto the entire network, that is the system does not rely upon single server with single point of failure. These Blockchain technology works on the concept of decentralized database where these databases exist in multiple computers and every copy of these databases are identical. These structures maintain their data in centralized database with decentralized structure of Blockchain, the Blockchain as a tamper proof technology and considered as a peer to peer network (Sandi and Kyung-Hyune, 2018).

Blockchain technology has three components or three layers; the components are applications, decentralized ledger and peer-to-peer network. The first components are application layer; it contains the application software of the Blockchain, and it's performed the Bitcoin wallet and provides a human

Figure 2. Centralized vs. Decentralized vs. Distributed

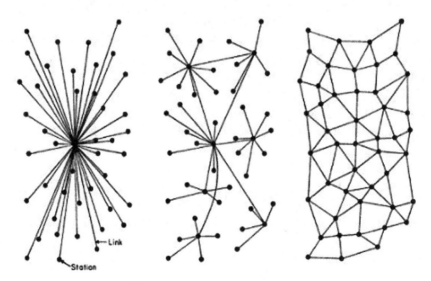

readable interface where users can keep track of their transactions. Middle components are the decentralized ledger in Blockchain technology, that confirms a tamper proof and transactions are grouped into blocks with linked to one another, then the decentralized ledger is performing tokens, validations, proof of work, mining, consensus, transaction and Blockchain. The bottom one is the peer-to-peer network, a peer refer that the way to connect each other and it's also performing multiple tasks together in the network. It provides broadcasting information to the entire node in the same network, and the connection with other peers thro IP address with TCP protocol. So that the peer maintains up to 8 outgoing connections with the other peers.

Digital Signature

Signatures generated on the Blockchain are referred as digital, digital signature is a particular type of electronic signature that encrypts the signed document. Digital signature is a digital code which included with an electronically transmitted document, with this digital code you can verify first of all whether the content of the document is authenticated or not (digitally sign the data so that no one can deny their own activities). So, it works like a sign say whenever you are sending a document or say a physical document from one person to another person in an administrative domain you need to physically sign the document and then send it which works as verification that the physical document is the authenticated document, so it's used for making tamper proof. It refers to encryption/decryption technology to build with electronic signature solution; these encryptions secure the associated data with signed document and verify authenticity of a signed record (Johnson, Menezes and Vanstone, 2001).

Digital signatures have some characteristics;

- Based on public-key cryptography
- Accepted as legal evidence
- During transfer of document from one digital space to another they provide authenticity
- Do not prove the identity of signatory and its provide authentication of document's bit stream, so that public key encrypted by sender and private key decrypts with receiver
- Private key is linked with bit stream authentications

The purpose of digital signature is that only the signing authority can sign a document, but everyone can verify the signature, signature is associated with the particular document which helps in proving the authenticity of the documents, so that signature of one document cannot be transferred to another document. In that way the digital signature should provide the authenticity of the document and it also provides identity of the origin of particular document. The important factor of digital signature is public key cryptography or asymmetric key cryptography. In these cryptographic systems two keys are used, one key is called pubic key (public key, which is public to everyone) and another one key is called private key (private key is the key, which only knows the particular user). Public key cryptography concept where the public key is used to encrypt the message then anyone can encrypt the data and the private key is used to decrypt the message then the decryption key is kept secret with only the intended receiver can decrypt the data.

Types of Blockchains

Generally, types of Blockchains depending on managed data, availability of data and what actions can be performed by the user. In Blockchain technologies divided into three types. Public Blockchain, Private Blockchain and Consortium Blockchain (El-Din and Mahmoud Khalifa, 2018).

1. **Public Blockchain:** In Public Blockchain has no single owner, all the data in the Public Blockchain is accessible and visible to anyone; their consensus process is open to all. It Public Blockchain can receive and send transactions from anybody in the world, but everyone can check and verify the transaction, also participate the process of getting consensus. In a Public Blockchain anyone is able to join the Blockchain without any approval and can act as a simple node or as a miner (node), but they are not only decentralized, but fully distributed. It is easy to detect fraud on the chain (Karim, Ubar and Rubina, 2018). These types of Blockchains are usually given an economic incentive, such as in cryptocurrency networks. Examples of Public Blockchain Bitcoin, Ethereum, Monero, Dash, Litecoin etc.,

2. **Private Blockchain:** Node will be restricted, not every node can participate this Blockchain, and only enables chosen nodes to join the network, and data can be access on strict authority management. It's a distributed yet centralized network. They are managed by one organization in trusted party then it's used for private purposes. Each transaction can be writes and verify the transactions on private Blockchain completely faster and allows much greater efficiency. It uses privileges to control who can read from and write to the Blockchain, it also called permissioned (Karim, Umar and Rubina, 2018). Hyperledger fabric and ripple are examples of private Blockchain networks.

3. **Consortium Blockchain:** Consortium Blockchain is part private, part public. It means the only selected group of nodes to participate in the consensus process, which had the authority, can be choose in advance (Emmanuelle, 2018). On consortium Blockchain, a pre-selected group of nodes control the consensus process, but the other nodes may be allowed to participate in creating new transactions / reviewing it. Its hybrid between the 'low-trust' provided by public Blockchains and 'single highly-trusted entity' model of private Blockchains. It can be established in like business to business, financial sector, insurance companies, government institutions, the data in Blockchain can be open or private, can be seen as Partly Decentralized. Like Hyperledger and R3 (Banks), EWF (Energy), B3i (Insurance), Corda, are both consortium Blockchains. The Table 2 represents those properties with different Blockchain. Public Blockchains are when no central entity is available to verify a transaction, and full decentralization is needed. Private and consortium Blockchains, which allows defining different permissions on different user on the network. The advantages of private and consortium Blockchains are; Such as lower validation costs and shorter validation times (given the fact that, because of the smaller number of nodes, the mathematical problem can be simplified), reduced risk of attacks (since nodes that validate transactions are known) and increased privacy (as read permissions could be granted only to selected nodes).

Table 2. Different properties of blockchain type

Properties	Public Blockchain	Private Blockchain	Consortium Blockchain
Efficiency	Low	High	High
Consensus Process	Permission-less	Permissioned	Permissioned
Centralized	No	Yes	Partial
Access	Public	Restricted	Restricted
Determination	Miners	One Organization	Selected set of nodes
Network	Decentralized	Distributed	Traditional centralized systems
Example	Bitcoin, Ethereum	Hyperledger Fabric, Ripple	Corda, R3, B3i
Speed	Slower	Faster	Medium

TECHNICAL ASPECTS OF BLOCKCHAIN METHODOLOGY

Characteristics of Blockchain

Blockchain is mean to store and record Bitcoin transaction, but not everything that can record and store transactions are labelled Blockchain (Zheng et al, 2018).

1. **Immutable:** It's a permanent record of transactions, which is unchangeable record, once the state is created, it cannot be modified. Once the block is added, it cannot be altered. It is interlinked with security, then the properties of confidentiality, integrity and availability (CIV). The data can be replicated in many different locations, once established the data cannot be easily changed. The transaction has been recorded on the ledger, no participant can modify a transaction, if an error occurs on the transactions, a new transaction must be used to reverse the error, once the error is rectified, and both transactions are visible in the ledger (Karim et al, 2018).
2. **Transparency and Provenance:** Blockchain is an open file, any participants can access and read the transactions, this Blockchain transactions are linked to an identifier, but the Blockchain transactions cannot be decoded and tracked. In provenance, each asset must be traceable, so that the participants know that, in overtime how the ownership has changed and where the asset came from. Blockchain technology provides an indisputable mechanism to verify that the data, so that transaction has existed at specific time. Each block is specified that chain format, the chain contains some information about previous block; position and ownership of block data, each block is automatically authenticated but cannot be altered.
3. **Consensus Driven:** Each block on the Blockchain is verified independently with consensus models, the transaction to be accepted and recorded on Blockchain, to provide the rules for validating a block, so that all participants must agree to follow the same rules. it is referred to as mining process, if a transaction violates one of the rules in network, the transaction will be considered as invalid, so that each participant to trust the network (Karim et al, 2018). This mechanism works without the use of a central authority (trust verification).
4. **Decentralized:** A Blockchain is stored in a file that can be accessed and copied at any node on the given network. It creates decentralizations, then it ensures that all participating nodes using scal-

ability and robustness techniques, if not using this technique i.e., any problem will occur, to solve problem of single point of failure. In conventional centralized transaction systems, each transaction validates through central trusted agency at the central servers, and the transaction conducted between any two P2P without authentication by central agency (Karim et al, 2018).

5. **Consistent:** It's consistent, accurate, complete, widely and timely available for Blockchain data.
6. **Digital Signature:** Its mainly focus on two keys, public and private keys, in public keys are decryption code with codes are known to everyone on the network and private keys are encryption keys only owner to create proof of ownership. The main purpose is to avoiding fraud in managing record.
7. **Anonymity:** In Blockchain anonymity provides the efficient way of hiding the identity of users and maintains their identities private (Zheng et al, 2017).
8. **Security:** No Single Point of Failure in Blockchain technology, so that it's providing better security.
9. **Capacity Increased:** In Blockchain Technology, the entire network capacity to be increased, then the thousands of computers working together, but few centralized servers having greater power.

Consensus Algorithms

Consensus is a problem in distributed computing concept; it has been used in Blockchain to provide the single version of truth by all peers on the Blockchain network.

Nodes within the system must reach an agreement to give the presence of faulty processes or deceptive nodes, all Blockchain nodes have agreement in same message, make sure that the latest blocks have been added to the chain correctly, and also confirm that the message stored by node was same one, even can protect from malicious attacks. By reaching consensus protocols it works out two problems among all nodes and reaches the consensus more efficiently and correctly to issue the technology in Blockchain. The two problems are Byzantine Generals Problem (BGP) and Byzantine Fault Tolerance (BFT). The first problem is described concerning communication failure, the generals are far apart, then able to communicate through messengers, which may not successfully deliver their messages and actively attempt to deceive the others. The BFT is a replication algorithms category, then to solve the problem reaching consensus, nodes can generate arbitrary data, can also guarantee that safety and liveness of a system (Supriya and Kulkarani, 2017).

Proof-of-Work (PoW)

PoW is Proof-of-Work, is the original and the very first implementation of a distributed & trustless consensus algorithm in Blockchain network is called PoW algorithm. It is a piece of data which is difficult to produce but easy to verify and satisfy certain requirements. This algorithm is used to confirm transactions and produce new blocks to the chain. These mechanisms prove the credibility of the data to solve the solution of puzzle, the proving mechanisms is usually hard but easily verifiable the problem for that puzzle. The created in the block, then it must resolve a PoW puzzle. After resolved a PoW Puzzle, it will broadcast to other nodes. The other nodes to verify puzzle then to achieve the consensus mechanisms.

So the PoW consensus mechanisms require that to compute the puzzle, then miners to solve complex cryptographic puzzles, they can add a block to the Blockchain, each block is added to the Blockchain, then you must follow the certain set of consensus rules, the block do not follow that consensus rules, it will be rejected by network nodes. The synthesis of PoW consensus algorithms and consensus rules produce a reliable network, and then shared state of Blockchain can be achieved (Sandi and Kyung-Hyune, 2018).

Proof-of-Stake (PoS)

The Proof of Work method will cause a lot of electricity power and computing power be wasted, but Proof of Stake does not need expensive computing power. This method might provide increased protection from malicious attack on the network. PoS are Proof-of-Stake in consensus algorithms used by cryptocurrencies to validate blocks. The purpose is similar to proof of work, but different way to verify and validate the transactions or blocks. Once the user is selected to validate the block and accurately verify all transactions in that block, then they are rewarded a certain amount of digital currency for their work. The first idea was proof of stake is Bitcoin talk in 2011, but the first PoS based currency was PeerCoin in 2012, further it together with ShadowCash, Nxt, BlackCoin, NuShares/NuBits, Qors and Nav Coin. This approach works through for calculating the weight of a node according to its currency staking or holding only, which means more power and electricity saving. These two approaches, proof of work and proof of stake can be used for any cryptocurrency. PoS method to solve the energy demand problem in current Blockchain protocols, such as Bitcoin and Ethereum. This method does not use too much computing power; it's more cost than PoW method (King and Nadal, 2012).

Delegated Proof-of-Stake (DPoS)

Delegated Proof-of-Stake (DPoS) is a new consensus algorithm based on PoW and PoS to guarantee the security of digital currency network. It's similar to PoS then the miners get their priority to generate the blocks according to their stake, then it's a fast, excellent, decentralized and convenient consensus model, and it's also to solve the consensus problems in reasonable manner. Stakeholders elect their delegates to generate and validate a block (Zheng et al, 2017). This process is termed as very reliable and most efficient consensus algorithms in Blockchain networks, and it's a method for validating transactions and adding shared ledger of systems in Blockchain network. DPoS often described as representative democratic, but PoS described as direct democratic. Using reputation algorithms and real-time voting the Stakeholders elect their delegates to generate and validate a block. With significantly fewer nodes to validate the block, delegates validate blocks in random order, if one says no; the choice goes to next randomly chosen delegate. Then the block and making the transactions confirmed quickly. And also tuned parameters of the block size and block intervals, users do not need to worry about the dishonest delegates because the delegates could be voted out easily. DPOS has already been implemented and is the backbone of Bitshares. DPoS more efficient algorithm than PoS algorithms. DPoS, the delegated users quickly remove bad actors and sanction bad behavior. Delegated Proof of Stake (DPoS) cryptocurrencies are Bit Shares (BTS), EOS, STEEM, LSK, OXY and ARK. Backbone of Delegated Proof of Stake (DPoS) algorithm is Bitshares.

Practical Byzantine Fault Tolerance (PBFT)

It is an algorithm for solving the problem of low efficiency in Original Byzantine Fault Tolerance algorithm, it's a message-based consistency method, to run on three phase protocol; pre-prepare, prepare and commit (Zheng et al, 2018). A client send the request from one peers to other peers for pre-prepare messages in turn of broadcast channels; in the next stage of prepare, a prepare message is multicasted to other nodes; when replica receives prepare message and it also matches with the pre-prepare message, once the message is matched it changes the state to committed and executes in message operation. Then the message is executed, reply information is sent to client. So PBFT method, for before reaching agreement depends on three stage for exchanging message (Zheng et al 2017).

Ripple Protocol Consensus Algorithm (RPCA)

Ripple Protocol is a consensus algorithm used by ripple cryptocurrency, Ripple is decentralized, Blockchain based real-time gross settlement systems (RTGS), currency exchange and remittance network. It allows banking institutions to transfer large amounts of money freely and without delays on distributed network. It's first developed in 2004 by Ryan Fugger, wanted to create monetary system in decentralized manner and effectively create their own money & allow for individuals and communities. It's the first open standard internet protocol-based technology for Payment Service Providers (PSPs) to clear and settle transactions in distributed network.

Stellar Consensus Protocol (SCP)

Stellar consensus protocol is a decentralized consensus protocol, nodes within the network do not need to trust with the entire network, but the ability to choose which nodes they trust, so that the group of nodes which trust each is called quorum slice, that means set of nodes to reach an agreement. It's a decentralized hybrid Blockchain platform with open membership running on global network that is anyone can join this network run a stellar node and they can be a participant in this network, execute transactions and store the state of payments or accounts in this network. The Table 3 represents that Consensus Algorithms with Currency Name, they have a cryptocurrency called lumens that is native assets on which trading happens on the stellar network. It is the protocol, they have a Federated Byzantine Agreement (FBA) protocol, and it is an open membership where anybody can join in this protocol.

Table 3. Consensus algorithms with currency name

Currency Name	Consensus Algorithm
Bitcoin	Proof of Work
Ethereum	Proof of Work
EOS	Delegated Proof of Stake
NEM	Proof of Importance
Ripple	Ripple Protocol Consensus Algorithm
Cash Stellar	Delegated Byzantine Fault Tolerance
Litecoin	Proof of Work
Stellar Consensus Protocol	Stellar Consensus Protocol
Cardano	Proof of Stake
Bitcoin Cash	Proof of Work

Classifications of Blockchain

Blockchain networks can be categorized, and it's based on their two models; permissioned model and permissionless model. If the transactions can be made or anyone can publish a new block and its verified by the network this Blockchain said to be permissionless Blockchain; if the transactions can be made verified by predetermined authorized entities, that is only particular user can publish blocks, this Blockchain is said to be permissioned Blockchain (Dylan, Peter, Nik and Karen, 2018).

Permissionless Blockchain

In Permissionless Blockchain, this Blockchain is public, which means anyone can participate and contribute in the chain; it's a decentralized ledger platform to anyone publishing blocks, without need permission from any authority. It's an open source software platform to anyone download them and anyone right to publish blocks. It works based on Proof-of-Work system, in which each block contains hash, a unique identifier of the data contained in the block. This system allows the timestamp server's implementation of P2P network; this network can read and write to the ledger. This permissionless Blockchain networks utilize the multiparty agreement or consensus system that require the users to expand or maintain resources, for attempting to publish blocks. The permissioned Blockchains apply the concept of Smart Contract, but it does not apply the public Blockchain Proof of Work (Daniel, 2018).

The characteristics of permissionless models are;

- **Decentralization:** No central entity has the authority to edit the ledger
- **Digital Assets:** Presence of a financial system on the network
- **Anonymity:** The users does not require submitting personal information or transactions, but as user identity is indirectly tied to the addresses, they have the private keys of.
- **Transparency:** This network needs to freely give users access all information apart from private keys.

Permissioned Blockchain

Permissioned Blockchains act as closed ecosystems, the users are not freely able to join the network, have the special permission to access the chain, and also check the record history or own issue transactions. It's preferred by centralized or decentralized organizations, where users publishing blocks must be authorized by some authority. Since only authorized users are maintaining the Blockchain, then its restricted read access and also restricts who can issue transactions, they may restrict this access only to authorized individuals it's maintained and instantiated using open source or closed source software. The permissioned Blockchains also likely to private Blockchains, this Blockchains to securely record transactions and exchange information one another. Permissioned Blockchains used by organizations, that wish to work together, protect their Blockchains, how much they trust one another and invite business partners to record their transactions on a shared distributed ledger (Daniel, 2018).

The characteristics of permissionless models are;

- **Varying Decentralization:** For private Blockchain, it is entirely accepted if they are fully centralized or partially decentralized
- **Transparency and Anonymity:** Private Blockchains not required to be transparent, but they can choose to do freely, depending on the inner organizations of the businesses.
- **Governance:** In permissioned Blockchains, the governance is decided by members of the business network.

The Table 4 indicates that difference between permissionless and permissioned systems. Similarities of Permissionless Blockchains and Permissioned Blockchains; both Blockchains are decentralized and P2P, share the same copy of append only ledger of transactions, synchronize the network through consensus, and try to provide a certain level of immutability of the shared ledger.

Smart Contracts

Smart Contract is the recent development of Blockchain technology, dates 1994 defined by Nick Szabo, a computerized transaction protocol that executes the terms of a contract. Smart contract is an agreement whose execution is both automatable and enforceable. Automatable by computer, although some parts may require human input and control. Enforceable by either legal enforcement of rights and obligations or tamperproof execution. The main objectives of smart contract to satisfy common contractual conditions, such as confidentiality, terms if payment and enforcement, and also minimize the need for trusted intermediaries. Smart contracts are pieces of software that extend Blockchains utility from simply keeping a record of financial transaction entries to automatically implementing terms of multi-party agreements. It's a collection of code and data, deployed in cryptographically signed transactions on the Blockchain network. The nodes are executed within the Blockchain network, and the results of execution are recorded on the Blockchain. The smart contract code is written in high-level languages such as Solidity and Python for Ethereum applications. Smart contract enabled permissionless Blockchain networks; Ethereum is preferred technologies for the development of smart contract, the design and implementation of Ethereum are totally independently on cryptocurrency Bitcoin. The software code is executed on virtual machine referred to as the Ethereum Virtual Machine (EVM)

Table 4. Comparison of permissionless and permissioned systems

	Permissionless	**Permissioned**
Access	Open read/write access to the database	Permissioned read/write access to database
Scale	Large number of nodes, but not in transaction throughput	Scale in terms of transaction throughput but not too many nodes
Consensus	Proof of Work/Proof of Stake	Closed membership consensus algorithms
Identity	Anonymous or pseudonymous	Identities of nodes are known, but transaction identities can be private or anonymous or pseudonymous
Assets	Native assets	Data/state
Central Party	No central owner or administrator	External administration or control
Examples	Bitcoin, Ethereum	Hyperledger Fabric

Blockchain Components

The Blockchain components are ledger, smart contract, peer network, membership, events, systems management, and wallet and system integration. Ledger – it is a channels chain and current state data, so that every node in the Blockchain network is going to maintain ledger of all transactions and also maintain state of data to be stored on Blockchain network. Smart contract – running on a ledger, encode business logic code transaction for modifying the assets, Peer Network – the entire transaction, serves to generates an agreement on the order and to confirm correctness of the set of transactions for constituting a block, Membership – it provide service authenticates, authorizes, and manages identities on a permissioned Blockchain network, Events – the events creates notification of significant operations on the Blockchain, Systems Management – The systems management provides that ability to create, change and monitor Blockchain components, Wallet –users manages security credentials, and Systems Integration – it's the responsibility for integrating Blockchain bi-directionally with external systems, but it is not part of the Blockchain, but used in it.

Benefits of Blockchain

1. **Distributed and Sustainable:** The ledger is shared, updated with every transaction and selectively replicated among participants in near real-time.
2. **Secure and Indelible:** Cryptography authenticates and verifies transactions, maintains privacy and allows participants to see only the parts of the ledger that are relevant to them. Once conditions are agreed to, participants can't tamper with a record of the transaction. Errors can only be reversed with new transactions.
3. **Transparent and Auditable:** Because participants in a transaction have access to the same records, they can validate transactions, and verify identities or ownership without the need for third-party intermediaries (e.g. clearing house, broker, escrow, etc.)
4. **Consensus-Based and Asset-Centric:** All relevant network participants must agree that a transaction is valid. This is achieved by using consensus algorithms.
5. **Orchestrated and Flexible:** business rules and Smart Contracts that execute based on one or more conditions can be built into the platform, Blockchain business networks can evolve as they mature to support end-to-end business processes and a wide range of activities.

IMPACTS OF DATA INTEGRITY, DATA STORAGE, AUTHENTICATION, CONFIDENTIALITY, AND SMART CONTRACT SYSTEMS IN BLOCKCHAIN TECHNOLOGY

Blockchain Data Integrity

Data integrity in Blockchain technology, the data is a key asset; key assets are stored in the cloud. This data integrity services ensure that application developers and end users confirm that data assets to be stored on the cloud using Keyless Signature Infrastructure (KSI). It assured by using two hands, one is for cryptographic tools, and other hand is data replication strategies. The cryptographic tools used to sign the single pieces of data via cryptographic sign violations

The application users perform to generate non-reversible signature for their data, extend the signature and verify that since it was signed current version of data asset has not been altered. Once the service to be used and ensure that, data configurations and firmware have not been tampered, and to provide evidence and proof of legal to the Blockchain technology. It's a client Software Development Kit (SDK), software developers write the applications for easier and faster, and then a developer communicates with data integrity assurance. Blockchain data integrity functions to perform and allow application developers and a set of APIs, Application Programming Interface contains software development kits, this integrity functions with signing data verifying and extending signatures from client-side applications. Once integrity is compromised, no way to restore original data. Data integrity on public and private Blockchains intact and keep the cryptographic hashing and Merkle trees. Hashing is a function or operation, searching the key value in to the table, easy to perform. The most hash functions are MD5, SHA-1, and SHA-256. Merkle trees are a part of Blockchain technology, efficient and secure verification of content in very large body of data.

Secure Sensitive Data Storage in Blockchain

Normally every user store data, files and research documents etc., using cloud storage, excess storage capacity seeking to expand their decentralized networks, in secured data used for encryption technique, the encryption keys are stored cloud service provider, data is generally not encrypted meanwhile transmission, the problem of cloud storage. Block chain is faster and more secure than cloud storage. Signed and encrypted transactions verified by the peers that they are authorized user can only view the information on ledger, it's a database or ledger, the ledger is encrypted data shared across a network, documents cannot be manipulated but the records are shared in the data storage. The data is break into small blocks, these blocks are encrypted and uploaded onto Blockchain, even if part of the network is breakdown the data distributed into all blocks and all files are available on the blocks. Block is a container data structure in series of transaction; contain more than 500 transactions, average size is 1MB to 8MB. Large number of transactions for large blocks. Change transactions in block hash, all subsequent blocks also change.

The data is shared and encrypted; it's much more secure, unaltered, cheaper filer storage capacity, potentially allowing millions of users to store data securely. Basically, the files are stored on Bitcoin's Blockchain, but hashes of the files are being stored in Bitcoin transaction, very compact block header that can be secured for all transactions in the block, data can be store the document/ PDF / audio in the hexadecimal format. It's a distributed database system that systems maintain the all transactions, data records and secured from the cryptographic transactions. For securing data storage, the Blockchain technology discovered two new products like Storj and Sia technologies. This diagram represents that Figure 3 Even billion of users to store the data more secure and stable for Blockchain storage technology. Storj (Storage) secure the files and not viewed by unauthorized users, the users connected with secure P2P networks and decentralized systems to provide the encrypted cloud storage. Sia storage technology is decentralized storage platform, more reliable and low cost than other cloud storage providers, decentralized network for encrypts and distributes the file, its completely private, far more affordable, highly redundant, open source and compete for your business.

Secure data storage Figure 4 shows the data storage model of analytics with applications, In Secure data storage model in Blockchain technology secure distributed data storage model, third parties to transfer and store the data in way of data analytics methods, upload their data in encrypted form so the sensors generating/manipulating data from the encapsulation to the Blockchain service, this service

Figure 3. Scaling techniques in blockchain

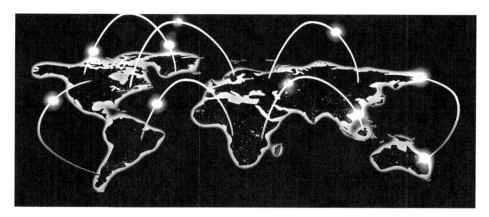

distributes a decentralized ledger of transactions, the network validate the transactions, finally data analytics approaches performs the generated big data is secured, valuable, immutable and high quality.

Smart Contract in Permissioned Blockchain

A self-executing contract in terms of the agreement between the buyer and seller is directly written into the lines of code. It's consistent of updating the information. User can access and see the information, that information sent and stored in concept is called smart contract, which contains transactions with some conditions and rule smart contract is implemented. It's clearly defined the functions and specifies

Figure 4. Secure data storage

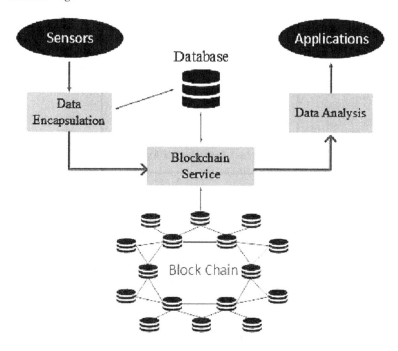

the way of work, performance of credible transactions without third parties. Smart contracts are core of Blockchain technologies, its self-verifying and self-executing agreements and address the Contract Lifecycle Management (CLM). Figure 5 specify the exchange of money with assets. In smart contract techniques using the scripts, it can extend the script to ensure Bitcoin smart contract execute, only certain condition is satisfied for executing the transactions, seller exchange the money with buyer but ensure that with ownership of assets is verified, make buyer with seller some contract in assets in the form of digital currency, fixed or limited number of buyer and seller is available in markets, all buyers and sellers is registered in the central portals, so that everyone know that details of smart contracts techniques in Blockchain concepts.

Malicious activities are preventing in the form of Blockchain systems. In smart contract the systems are executed in sequential order of transactions and executed in the same order. In certain contract take huge time to execute, other contract will not be able to execute previous contract has been executed, then only later contract to be execute, must maintain the sequential order of executing the transactions. Smart contract execution always needs to be deterministic, so that the systems implement on Domain Specific Language (DSL). In nondeterministic execution platforms use the language for go long, iteration over a data structure map to produce key with value, the map specifies the string with value in different key for different order of executions. Finally, the smart contract systems use for domain specific language with Ethereum platform. Ether is the currency of Ethereum, decentralized platforms that runs on smart contracts. Ethereum that modifies its state costs can be easily converted to other traditional currencies through crypto exchanges.

Confidentiality and Privacy: Public vs. Private Blockchain

To prevent transaction from other participants from certain facts or details about the transactions. Privacy challenges on the public Blockchain systems and private Blockchain systems. The public Blockchain

Figure 5. Exchange with digital currency

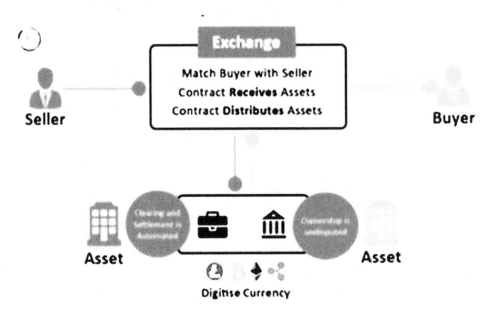

systems are permissionless, these systems open to anyone and users generate to represent their transactions, transaction details are clear and available on the public ledger of the systems. In public Blockchain systems decentralized systems has control over the network, anyone wants to read, write, and once validated on the Blockchain the data can't be changed. Public Blockchain dealing with cryptocurrency for buying and selling concepts, it can also require extensive computing power then large number of users can join public systems.

The private Blockchain systems are permissioned networks as an alternative to public ones, restricted and allows only authorized user can access these systems, it shared among a number of collaborating business partners, confidential transactions only visible to certain collaborators. It operates like centralized database systems that limits access to certain users, and then control the network for one or multiple entries.

Public and private Blockchain offer a new technology is hyperledger fabric. Its released version 1.0 in July 2017, large no. of organizations involved in hyperledger fabric i.e., 159 developers from 27 organizations, IBM is one of largest contributor of code, IP and development effort for hyperledger fabric is IBM. Figure 6 represents that hyperledger composer, it's the abstractions for business networks is high level applications hyperledger composer, composer is open source, quick solution creation for business centric, reduce risk and increase understanding, flexibility, it's part of Linux foundation hyperledger. Hyperledger composer supports for hyperledger fabric, its extensive, open development toolset and developing Blockchain applications easier, main goal of composer is accelerate time to value, applications invoke transactions to interact with business network and integrate existing system with record for Blockchain applications.

Hyperledger fabric is committed by all peers in the consistent network in the transactions; specify the membership services in identity of digital certificate, certificate authority is optional in services, external and fabric certificates authority provide with public key infrastructure (PKI), transaction to be signed and submitted to Blockchain, private key and public key associated with user, public and certificate authority recognized by network in user, public-private key pair authenticated with Blockchain, client application written in any language, SDK interact with Blockchain in HFC of endorser (Hyperledger Fabric Client) available with multiple language of java, python etc.. Blockchain has multiple components, peer is the

Figure 6. Hyperledger composer

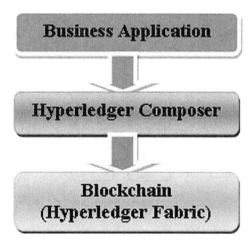

main components one organization run to multiple peer or multiple organizations run to one peer in the network. Ordering service also run multiple or one peer, it's totally ordering different transactions, decentralized service to the network. The Figure 7 represents that Hyperledger Fabric Architecture, Peer having the notions of endorser, committer, ledger, chain code and events. Peer is maintaining ledger, ledger is specifying the transaction of all state's information stored in it, Chaincode is code of smart contract running on Blockchain every node in the network to be executed. Event to be integrate on the transactions. Each Peer node have one or two functions of endorser and composer, peer sign is an endorser, the endorser execute the chain code, the copy of chaincode its responsible signing in output of chaincode, its identity of peer transaction, after executing its placed into ordering service, ordering service communicate with endorser and committer peer node, does not hold ledger.

The committer is separate function of Blockchain, executed transaction to be placed in ordering services, that service to be placed in committer functions, committer not executing the any transaction, but maintain the ledger and state. Hyperledger Fabric, consensus is achieved using the transaction flow of endorse, order and validate. Peers executing the transaction, signed transaction to be stored in endorser, collecting all the transactions to be placed to order parts, that order to be arranged the transaction in ordering wise, simultaneously modify the state that performs validation parts. Finally eliminate non deterministic transactions.

Authentication Transaction on Certificate Authority

Authentication is major concern in all around the world because identify theft and data leaks increased, one person accessing the data, but claim for another one. Perform secure payments enable the cryptocurrency concepts with decentralized database, which records all transactions in start from the Bitcoin, it's basically public-private key pairs are used in Transport Layer Security (TLS), which allows them to send and receive money in Bitcoin network, users want to pay certain amount to someone of Bitcoin,

Figure 7. Hyperledger fabric architecture

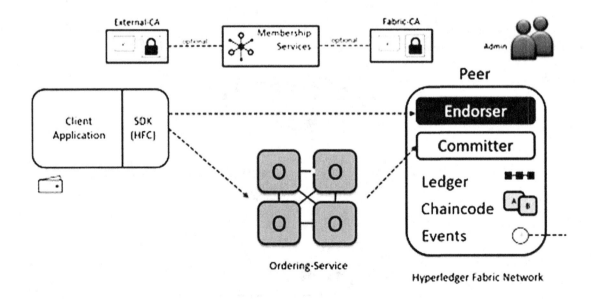

you broadcast the transaction over entire network and sign with private key. After the network validates the transaction then transaction to be added to Blockchain technology, when transaction is included in Blockchain technology, the process is to be completed. The Blockchain platforms developed various features and handle the identity management of transaction authentication in certificate authority, to the managed devices of hyperledger fabric channel, transaction authentication mechanism support for Ethereum platform.

This mechanism author signed by the transaction and it's secured by private key then generates hash. Authentication in certificate authority setup, the user provides the number of certificate services to the Blockchain, these services specify the enrollment, transaction invoked in the Blockchain, between users or components of the Blockchain secured connection between the TSL. New users to register with Blockchain network Secured. Individual users can participate in distributed ledger must be authenticated using highly secured, each transaction can be trusted in the network, then ensure that the transactions are valid in distributed network with secured of cryptographic keys, these keys are vulnerable. Transaction hash secure the key for transaction authentication process, then signed transaction can be executed and hash can be generated, for sharing purpose smart contract added on the hash transaction.

These transactions automatically happen with built-in verification systems. It executes in self manner then according to the given guidelines, without process of middleman. The Figure 8 shows the Blockchain authentication transaction system. Sender initiates the transaction to Blockchain application, the Blockchain application author signs the transaction with secret key and generates, executes the transaction hash,

Figure 8. Transaction authentication systems

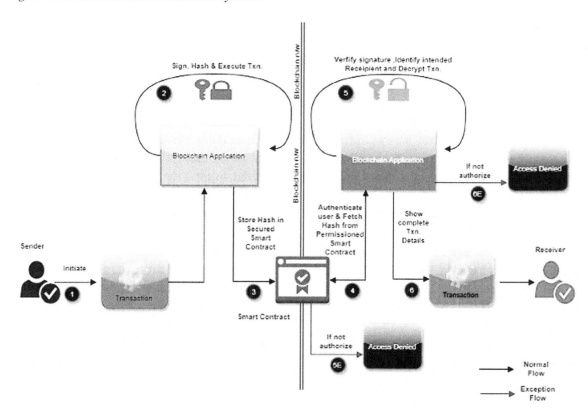

the application of executed hash functions secured in the form of smart contract, the smart contract push to transaction hash of encrypted function with permissioned Blockchain for intended recipients, these intended recipients verify the signature and decrypt the transaction hash, after decrypting of transaction decode the signed transaction for verification of authentication process, display the complete transaction process. Finally, the transaction is authenticated. This diagram represents that sender initiate the transaction and receiver receive the transaction in the form of encode/encrypt the transaction to decode/decrypt the transactions i.e., plaintext to cipher text, the entire process ensures transaction authentication secured way of hash functioning systems.

BLOCKCHAIN TECHNOLOGY USE CASES AND ITS VARIOUS REVOLUTION SYSTEMS

The first technology of Blockchain offers a way to fully manage digital assets in trusted, traceable, automated and predictable way. It's that each block is linked and secured using cryptography, and then the Bitcoin was famous application for managing digital assets. Next of Blockchain is smart contracts, where the contracts can be maintained and managed entirely digitally between participants. So that Blockchain technology otherwise called as distributed ledger technology, this technology allows that peer-to-peer transfer of assets refer to protocol, it's responsible for verifying and validating transactions online. The core functionality depends on creation of immutable ledger of all activity in peer-to-peer transaction. The usage of Blockchain platform to enable transfer of Bitcoin, public Blockchain is known as Bitcoin Blockchain. The Bitcoin is the initial transfer of Blockchain, have been created for multiple Blockchains. These Blockchains split into two main categories: Permissioned and Permissionless.

Blockchain in Business Systems

The Blockchain use cases were primarily concerned with payments. Many Industry people think that Blockchain; it is going to be completely transformative, looking at Blockchain for all sorts of applications it a financial service, supply chain, insurance, retail, media, healthcare etc. Most of the industries are looking forward how Blockchain would make a difference for them. For identifying good Blockchain use case, what are the common occupants of a Blockchain in use case; it is not always be easy. The Blockchain use case, a business problem that needs to be solved, to solve the problem do not try to solve it using Blockchain, has to be in business problem; that people are willing to spend money on spend time to have it soft, that cannot be more efficiently solved with other technologies, has to be solved using Blockchain. Other technologies can be used to solve that problem; then must identify business network, so that the participants having some information are exchanging with each other but modify this information in some other way. To solve that a business problem, must be need for trust, if there is no need for trust and everyone in this network, to share all information and all transactions with single person to perform. It must involve with multiple parties, do not trust with each other, so that need Blockchain technology; to install trust. A need for trust, use the notation of consensus, immutability, finality and provenance of the information. To solve small problem for the organizations or set of organizations, define the scope for that problem, specify the vision of building for an entire industry and also specify Moto rates i.e. start small and grow fast.

- **Understanding Business Problem:** Scope the business challenge, understand current systems and areas for improvement, and specific aspects of business problem will be addressed
- **Understanding Participants**: Understand who the participants in business networks are, they are involved in their business network, what are their job roles, and understand the key users in business network and how they interact with each other.
- **Identities:** Participants need to know their identities, but in Bitcoin pseudo anonymous identities were created. In most business use-cases, some form identity is required, public Blockchains could provide some information sources to linked to a trusted database that is the sources can collect from governments, financial institutions or utility providers, and private Blockchains gateway or controller or consortium determines the identities of entities is verified before credentials issued to the user.
- **Understanding Assets and Transactions:** What is the key information associated with assets, what information is going to get exchanged, and what assets are associated with transactions.
- **Defining Transactions**: In Blockchain network, what type of transactions process need to take, the transactions are to be recorded on the Blockchain, is called invoked transactions, the invoked transactions are add, delete, update, change and transfer ownership.
- **Accessing Business Value:** Succeed in setting up the Blockchain network to grow it.

Blockchain in Financial Services

The Blockchain is an incorruptible digital ledger of economic transactions that can be programmed to record not just financial transactions but virtually everything of value. The financial sector parties have a grasp concept of Bitcoins and other cryptocurrencies, these concepts work on the Blockchain technology, which is a digital, distributed transaction ledger with identical copies maintained on the network. The Blockchain in financial service use cases are compliance, cross border payments, financial trade, smart contract and other industries etc.,

Financial Service in Compliance: KYC and AML

Compliance is the next component of financial services in Blockchain technology, there is process in compliance called KYC (Know Your Customer Process), KYC processes are generally repetitive, inconsistent, and duplicated, leading to high administrative overheads and costs. In KYC process if you have opened a bank account or if you have login on any recharge account first you must open with Gmail account/face book account after that, the recharge account asked that KYC process. This process is regulatory requirement, and it is a mandatory requirement, so that the person working with any places, for any online relevant places where apply for KYC is applied, it is a regulated requirement to ensure that knowledge for customers and every organizations, and its useful that the information to help prevent fraud or money laundering. Main part of KYC process is collecting personal information. The KYC documents are currently specified that:

- Stored and collect the internal information using document management system in the format of database.
- Shared the database with multiple external agencies for validation on an individual basis.

- Updated, all these processes are there guidelines the regulatory authority will provide to the banks, and collection database details with their repository for successful validation and reported to central agencies.
- Banking consortiums and government bodies have led to an upsurge in the number of KYC registries.
- These registries act as centralized repositories that store all documents and information related to KYC compliance, whereas the central registry stores digitized data tagged to a unique identification number for each customer.
- Every bank and financial institution must perform the KYC process individually and upload the validated information and documents to the central registry. By using the unique ID, banks can access the stored data to perform due diligence whenever customers request for a new service within the same banking relationship or from another bank.

So, that the whole KYC process once done, there is a lot of processes that happen for AML, AML is anti-money laundering, there is a whole lot of due diligence that is done for every transaction, an anti-money laundering set of processes that happen to make sure you are not doing something suspicious or fraudulent right.

Financial Service in Mortgage Process

Mortgage Process into a slick, secure and fast end-to-end solution connecting all elements of the home loan chain. Blockchain technology radically alter the process through which consumers buy a home, way of financial institutions handles mortgages, i.e., complex processes with multiple intermediaries and duplication of data entry. The current points in mortgage process are;

1. **Mortgage Orientation:** The mortgage originator work with homeowners to generate mortgage loans
2. **Loan Servicing:** Loan servicers will engage with homeowners for the duration of the loan, serving institution will collect payments for the loans and distribute to investors, and will also negotiate loan modifications, conduct foreclosures, provide tax & insurance payments etc.,
3. **Mortgage Securitization:** Majority of loans sold to government sponsored entities to generate agency
4. **Friction and Delays**: Multiple parties interact with manual updates throughout transaction lifecycle (example. Exchange of contracts and Release of funds)
5. **Fraud:** Blockchain could reduce the odds of mortgage fraud, when bad actors falsify documents or pretend to own assets everyone suffers
6. **Servicing**: Blockchain could increase data accuracy, availability and streamlining

Financial Service in Cross Border Payments

The transfer of value has always been expensive and slow process, but the blockchain technology is able to speed up and simplify this process and reduces costs significantly, so that can improve many processes within the financial sector in the Blockchain technology is called cross border payments. If a person wants to transfer money from India to their family in the Euro, who have an account with a local bank, it takes several banks (and currencies) before the money can be collected. Some of the properties satisfy for them to be accepted as a currency.

- **Medium of Exchange:** Merchants are willing to accept the currency in exchange for goods and services (seller is selling a set of goods or services to a buyer and the buyer pays in terms of this currency right)
- **Unit of Account:** Measure the real values of goods and services (I want to by computer, the price would be say 10000 rupees, the value of 10000 is Indian rupee itself, so that Indian rupee the three are exchange markets that would price the Indian rupee with various other currencies, instance conversion of INR with some other Currency either Euro or USD, the value of rupee keeps fluctuating, the real value of goods and service is unit of account)
- **Store of Value:** A mode of investment

Financial Service in Share Trading / Trade Finance

In Blockchain technology has the potential to improve many processes in financial sector, including share trading. Buying and selling in stocks and shares always involve many middlemen, such as brokers and the stock exchange. Decentralized and secure ledger process in Blockchain technology specify that every party say the validation of transaction, speeds up the settlement process, greater trade accuracy and some of the middlemen cut out, changing the others.

The trade finance business includes multiple trading partners and huge amounts of manual records handling, checking and paperwork. This creates delays, duplication and fraud and high levels of inefficiency. It is a sector ripe for a Blockchain revolution. Now overall over 14 trillion dollars of trade is being financed, the overall amount of trade it takes up to 3 weeks for documents to be verified, actual shipment it will takes less than 10 days to go over ship. So that by applying Blockchain technology to trade finance, new emergent players such Trade IX, a technology infrastructure company is able to reduce the complexity and increase efficiency. The key benefits of Blockchain technology in Trade Finance are; Traceability, Efficiency, Collaboration, Security, Transparency and Audit ability.

Blockchain in Other Industries

Blockchain industry looks at that health care, important factors in health care use cases; patient consent & health data exchange, payment & claims, pharma supply chain provenance & traceability, and Rethinking clinical trial management. In health data exchange means, the hospital people can talk to each other and able to exchange information about the patient with each other, all information are private, has to be highly secure and needs to be audited, and the patient also have feel secure that information regarded, they have right to disclose their information, second use cases very closed related to health care insurance (large portion of payment will come from insurance company directly), the third use case pharma supply chain, these aspects are compliance aspects, how pharmaceutical codes have to be transported and have to be refrigerated, so that verify and scan it across an entry in the pharmaceutical company that produced good. The last use case clinical trial management, information getting exchanged between multiple entities on clinical trials

Blockchain in Banking Sectors

Blockchain has functions that improve the efficiency of the financial systems. These have been implemented in various industries with great success, due to their wide-ranged application. In the case of banking, several spheres of Blockchain are compatible with financial services, them being a network of information, ledger accounting, and transaction system. Majority of third-party financial transactions in the banking industry consume lots of time, this time could range from few days to even weeks, and transaction via Blockchain will take only few seconds to complete. The impacts of Blockchain in banking sectors; fast-paced financial transactions – eliminate third party gateways, lower cost of financial transactions – fast-paced transaction and eliminating payment gateways will result in low financial transaction cost, reduction of fraud – Blockchain systems to mitigate financial fraud, establish smart contract – Blockchain technology has the ability to store enormous digital information, and helps eliminate fraud in trading platforms – use of Blockchain on these platforms will reduce cost and improve system efficiency. So that the Blockchain impact can revolutionize Banking Sector (Supriya and Kulkarani, 2017).

Blockchain in Government

Government can utilize, this Blockchain platform particularly useful, you have multiple organization or multiple institution with different authorities' domains they want to share certain data or certain information's, so that government need to maintain daily operations & activities, government assets, details of people, records of people and business transactions. Government can get benefited by utilization of Blockchain technology; to make the tax management simplified and can be utilized for digital land record management. The first use case is, processing of tax payment in Good and Service Tax (GST), it is an indirect tax which covers various goods and services provided by different kind of service providers or vendors, during the production and the service stages. So, this GST is levied on different goods or services that procuring, the GST has broadly classified two components; SGST (State GST) and CGST (Central GST). Entire workflow of GST collection and management is very complex, its managing entire tax with help of decentralized ledger platform. The collected GST is also distributed among state government (SGST) and central government (CGST), whatever tax amount is being collected from entire GST procedure that need to be distributed among multiple states and central government, so that the entire procedure very complicated.

Without Blockchain Environment how GST payment works (going to purchase certain things at that time).

- A GST invoice issued to the seller
- Buyer pays that bill with GST
- Information about GST is entered by seller to GST portal, the amount of GST collected over fortnight, Seller pays this entire collected amount to the government, at the same time seller actually working as production house, which is purchasing multiple raw materials

- Whenever they are purchasing raw materials, the seller pays the certain tax GST to the suppliers
- Finally, collected and get it distributed among central government and state government
- Additional payment is adjusted

So, this entire adjustment is done by the government employees who are connected with this tax department, this government tax department they have to manually do this entire calculation or with the help of certain software's, after complete the calculation they may adjust the amount of GST at individual production stages, and the entire final amount which is being collected that gets distributed among the state government and the central government. The tax officers their task is to calculate all these things and then adjust it accordingly, then this entire process, there are multiple authorities or administrative domains who are getting connected, need to have a trust relationship that whatever additional amount you are paying, that you are giving the tax to the government at the same time you have giving certain tax whenever you are purchasing the raw materials, if you are giving the tax to the government then whatever tax you have used or you have paid for purchasing the raw materials that will come back to buyers. The simplification of this entire tax payment process will be done with help of smart contract.

With Blockchain Environment, how the entire process simplified with help of Blockchain, how the GST payment works;

- Similarly, the GST invoice is issued by the seller
- Buyer pays the bill with GST
- Seller pays to the suppliers
- All these payments are done with smart contract platform, Smart contract in Blockchain environment, the smart contract platform it automatically calculates this tax; smart contract adjusts the tax calculation during the payment. Now this smart contract it can automatically do all the adjustments.
- During the payment for good or service, the Blockchain smart contracts can calculate invoice based on tax amount that is already levied during the production process
- Smart contract directly transfers the tax amount to tax authority either CGST or SGCT, Final tax goes to the government
- The refund, if any is directly paid to the customer's account

CONCLUSION

Blockchain technology concepts and features applied to wide variety of situations, not for every situation, but each situation understands the factors, characteristics and benefits of Blockchain technology for transforming the possibility space for future world; the future indicates both centralized and decentralized models. On strengthen the use of Blockchain technology horizontally across in use cases, financial sectors, banking sectors and many industries, but some innovation to improve performance and scalability. The mainstream of Blockchain technology is consensus mechanisms. In Blockchain based smart contracts systems allow automatic execution of commercial transaction and agreements, have more security than traditional contracts. The potential of financial services, many financial institutions are willing to explore Blockchain technology, it has the highest potential for eliminating the occurrence of fraud in financial transactions, and it's more securely done by using cards with contactless interface with higher security level. They provide user-controlled and unauthorized access to cryptographic keys. In Blockchain technology can bridge the gap of missing security and transparency in daily transactions.

REFERENCES

Buterin, V. (2013). *Ethereum White Paper: A next-generation smart contract and decentralized application platform*. Academic Press.

Chuen, L. K. D. (2015). Handbook of Digital Currency: Bitcoin Innovation, Financial Instruments, and Big Data. Elsevier.

Daniel, D. (2018). *Permissioned vs. Permissionless Blockchains: Understanding the Differences*. Retrieved July 17, 2018 from https://blockonomi.com/permissioned-vs-permissionless-blockchains/

Dylan, Y., Peter, M., Nik, R., & Karen, S. (2018). *Blockchain Technology Overview*. Retrieved October 2018, from National Institute of Standards and Technology, U.S. Department of Commerce: https://nvlpubs.nist.gov/nistpubs/ir/2018/NIST.IR.8202.pdf

El-Din, D. M., & Mahmoud Khalifa, N. E. (2018). A Blockchain Technology Evolution between Business Process Management (BPM) and Internet-of-Things (IoT). *International Journal of Advanced Computer Science and Applications*, 9(8), 442–450.

Emmanuelle, G. (2018). *Can Blockchain Revolutionize International Trade? Switcherland*. World Trade Organization.

Johnson, D., Menezes, A., & Vanstone, S. (2001). The elliptic curve digital signature algorithm (ECDSA). *International Journal of Information Security*, 1(1), 36–63. doi:10.1007102070100002

Karim, S., Umar, R., & Rubina, L. (2018). *Conceptualizing Blockchains Characteristics & Applications*. 11th IADIS International Conference Information Systems 2018, Lisbon, Portugal.

King, S., & Nadal, S. (2012). *PPcoin: Peer-to-Peer Crypto-Currency with Proof-of-Stake*. Academic Press.

Lamport, L., Shostak, R., & Pease, M. (1982). The Byzantine Generals' Problem. *ACM Transactions on Programming Languages and Systems*, 4(3), 382–401. doi:10.1145/357172.357176

Mahdi, H. M., & Maaruf, A. (2018). Applications of Blockchain Technology beyond Cryptocurrency. *Annals of Emerging Technologies in Computing*, 2(1), 1–6. doi:10.33166/AETiC.2018.01.001

Marco, L., & Karim, R. L. (2017). The Truth about Blockchain -. *Harvard Business Review*.

Mauro, C., Sandeep Kumar, E., Chhagan, L., & Sushmita, R. (2017). *A Survey on Security and Privacy Issues of Bitcoin.* Academic Press.

Nakamoto, S. (2008). Bitcoin: A peer-to-peer electronic cash system. Academic Press.

Noe, E., Longzhi, Y., Fei, C., & Yi, C. (2018). A Framework of Blockchain-based secure and privacy-preserving E-government system. *Wireless Networks*, 1-11.

Sandi, R., & Kyung-Hyune, R. (2018). Blockchain Technology for providing an architecture model of decentralized personal health information. *International Journal of Engineering Business Management*, *10*, 1–12.

Supriya, T. A., & Kulkarani, V. (2017). Blockchain and Its Applications – A Detailed Survey. *International Journal of Computers and Applications*, *180*(3), 29–35. doi:10.5120/ijca2017915994

Swan, M. (2017). Anticipating the Economic Benefits of Blockchain. *Technology Innovation Management Review*, *7*(10), 6–13. doi:10.22215/timreview/1109

Yli-Huumo, J., Ko, D., Choi, S., Park, S., & Smolander, K. (2016). Where is Current Research on Blockchain Technology? -A Systematic Review. *PLoS One*, *11*(10), e0163477. doi:10.1371/journal.pone.0163477 PMID:27695049

Zheng, Z., Xie, S., Dai, H. N., & Wang, H. (2017). An Overview of Blockchain Technology: Architecture, Consensus, and Future Trends. *IEEE 6th International Congress on Big Data Congress*.

Zheng, Z., Xie, S., Dai, H. N., & Wang, H. (2018). Blockchain challenges and opportunities: A Survey. *International Journal of Web and Grid Services*, *14*(4), 352–375. doi:10.1504/IJWGS.2018.095647

KEY TERMS AND DEFINITIONS

Digital Signature: It is a mathematical scheme for presenting the authenticity of digital messages or documents; it uses public and private keys to encrypt and decrypt the data.

Distributed ledger: It's a decentralized technology to eliminate the need for a central authority or intermediary to process, validate, or authenticate transactions or other types of data exchanges.

Hyderledger Fabric: Hyperledger fabric is responsible for ordering a sequence of transactions into blocks, and it is going to deliver these sequences of totally ordered transactions to all the pairs in the network.

Merkle Tree: Merkle tree is a tree structure where the leaf nodes will contain the hash of the document, and every individual node or intermediate node will contain the hash of the combination of the left child under a right child.

Permission-Less Blockchain: Here anyone can join the network, participate in the process of block verification to create consensus and also create smart contracts. Permissioned blockchains do not have to use the computing power-based mining to reach a consensus since all the actors are known.

Permissioned Blockchain: Its works in open environment and large network of participants, so the participants do not need to reveal their own identity. The users do not need to reveal their own identity to other peers. It's something called private model. In a permissioned blockchain, only a restricted set of users have the rights to validate the block transactions.

Private Blockchain: A blockchain controlled by someone or something such as a company.

Public Blockchain: A blockchain that anyone can read.

Smart Contracts: Its basically provide a decentralized platform that can be utilized to avoid the intermediately in a contract. It's an automated computerized protocol used for digitally facilitating, verifying, or enforcing the negotiation or performance of a legal contract by avoiding intermediates and directly validating the contract.

Compilation of References

Ahmed, S., & Broek, N. (2017). Food Supply: Blockchain could boost food security. *Nature, 550*(7674), 43. doi:10.1038/550043e PMID:28980633

Ahram, T., Sargolzaei, A., Sargolzaei, S., Daniels, J., & Amaba, B. (2017). *Blockchain technology innovations. In 2017 IEEE Technology & Engineering Management Conference.* TEMSCON. doi:10.1109/temscon.2017.7998367

Akins, W., Chapman, J. L., & Gordon, J. M. (2013). *A whole new world: Income tax considerations of the bitcoin economy.* Available: https://ssrn.com/abstract=2394738

Alabi, K. (2017). Digital blockchain networks appear to be following Metcalfe's Law. *Electronic Commerce Research and Applications, 24*, 23–29. doi:10.1016/j.elerap.2017.06.003

Alavi, H. (2016). Mitigating the Risk of Fraud in Documentary Letters of Credit. *Baltic Journal of European Studies, 6*(1), 139–156. doi:10.1515/bjes-2016-0006

Alexander, N. A., & Kim, H. (2017). Adequacy by any other name: A comparative look at educational spending in the United States and the Republic of Korea. *Journal of Education Finance, 43*(1), 65–83.

Ali, M., Nelson, J. C., Shea, R., & Freedman, M. J. (2016). Blockstack: A Global Naming and Storage System Secured by Blockchains. *USENIX Annual Technical Conference*, 181-194.

Alketbi, A., Nasir, Q., & Talib, M. A. (2018). Blockchain for government services—Use cases, security benefits and challenges. In *Learning and Technology Conference (L&T), 2018 15th* (pp. 112-119). IEEE. 10.1109/LT.2018.8368494

Allen, D. (2017). *Discovering and developing the blockchain cryptoeconomy.* Academic Press.

Allison, I. (2016, October 13). *Juan Benet of IPFS talks about Filecoin.* Retrieved October 27, 2018, from https://www.ibtimes.co.uk/juan-benet-ipfs-talks-about-filecoin-1586122

Altenergymag. (2018). Retrieved from https://www.altenergymag.com/news/2018/01/15/bax--company-co-develop-first-large-scale-peer-to-peer-energy-market-in-nl/27712/

AlterNet. (2011). Retrieved from https://www.alternet.org/story/151921/chomsky%3A_public_education_under_massive_corp orate_assault_%E2%80%94_what%27s_next

Andersen, N. (2016). *Blockchain Technology A game-changer in accounting?* Deloitte.

Andersen, T. G., & Bollerslev, T. (2018). *Volatility*. Edward Elgar Publishing Limited.

Andoni, M., Robu, V., Flynn, D., Abram, S., Geach, D., Jenkins, D., ... Peacock, A. (2019). Blockchain technology in the energy sector: A systematic review of challenges and opportunities. *Renewable & Sustainable Energy Reviews, 100,* 143–174. doi:10.1016/j.rser.2018.10.014

Anonymous. (2015, October 31). The trust machine - the promise of the blockchain. *The Economist*.

Anonymous. (2017). Blockchain Technology Innovations. *IIE Annual Conference Proceedings, 49-54*.

Antle, R., & Demski, J. (1989). Revenue recognition. *Contemporary Accounting Research, 5*(2), 423–451. doi:10.1111/j.1911-3846.1989.tb00713.x

Arora, J. (n.d.). *How EOS can solve the Blockchain scaling problems*. Retrieved August 5, 2018, from https://itsblockchain.com/eos-scaling/

Arruñada & Garicano. (2018). *Blockchain: The birth of decentralized governance*. Academic Press.

Aste, T., Tasca, P., & Di Matteo, T. (2017). Blockchain technologies: The foreseeable impact on society and industry. *Computer, 50*(9), 18–28. doi:10.1109/MC.2017.3571064

Atzei, N., Bartoletti, M., & Cimoli, T. (2017). A survey of attacks on ethereum smart contracts (sok). In Principles of Security and Trust (pp. 164-186). Springer.

Atzori, M. (2015). *Blockchain technology and decentralized governance: Is the state still necessary?* Academic Press.

Atzori, M. (2015). Blockchain technology and decentralized governance: Is the state still necessary? In *The Layman's Guide to Bitcoin: What it is, How it works, and why it matters*. Brutsch.

Aud, S., Hussar, W., Planty, M., Snyder, T., Bianco, K., Fox, M. A., . . . Drake, L. (2010). *The condition of education* (NCES 2010-028). Retrieved from https://eric.ed.gov/?id=ED509940

Azar & Raouf. (2017). Sustainability issues in the GCC. In *Sustainability in the Gulf* (pp. 27–30). Routledge.

Bach, L. M., Mihaljevic, B., & Zagar, M. (2018). Comparative analysis of blockchain consensus algorithms. *41st International Convention on Information and Communication Technology, Electronics and Microelectronics (MIPRO),* 1545-1550. 10.23919/MIPRO.2018.8400278

Baden-Fuller, C., & Haefliger, S. (2013). Business models and technological innovation. *Long Range Planning, 46*(6), 419–426. doi:10.1016/j.lrp.2013.08.023

Bahsoun & Shoker. (2015). *A Parallel and Distributed Processing Symposium (IPDPS)*. IEEE.

Balcilar, M., Bouri, E., Gupta, R., & Roubaud, D. (2017). Can volume predict Bitcoin returns and volatility? A quantiles-based approach. *Economic Modelling, 64,* 74–81. doi:10.1016/j.econmod.2017.03.019

Ball, J. (2013). Nsa's prism surveillance program: how it works and what it can do. *The Guardian.*

Ball, R., & Brown, P. (1969). Portfolio theory and accounting. *Journal of Accounting Research, 7*(2), 300–323. doi:10.2307/2489972

Bamert, T., Decker, C., Elsen, L., Wattenhofer, R., & Welten, S. (2013). Have a snack pay with bitcoins. *Proceedings of the 13th IEEE International Conference on Peer-to-Peer Computing,* 1-5.

Banerjee, L., Lee, J., & Choo, K.-K. R. (2018). A blockchain future for internet of things security: A position paper. *Digital Communications and Networks, 4*(3), 149–160. doi:10.1016/j.dcan.2017.10.006

Barabási, A.-L. (2016). *Network science.* Cambridge University Press.

Barr, N. (2003). Financing higher education: Comparing the options. London School of Economics and Political Sciences, 10.

Barr, N. (2017). Funding post-compulsory education. In G. Johnes, J. Johnes, T. Agasisti, & L. López-Torres (Eds.), Handbook on the Economics of Education. Academic Press. doi:10.4337/9781785369070.00021

Barrat, M. (2004). Understanding the meaning of collaboration in the supply chain. *Supply Chain Management, 9*(1), 30–42. doi:10.1108/13598540410517566

Barr, M. J., & McClellan, G. S. (2018). *Budgets and Financial Management in Higher Education* (3rd ed.). San Francisco: Jossey-Bass.

Barr, M. J., & McClellan, G. S. (2018). *Budgets and financial management in higher education.* Somerset, NJ: John Wiley & Sons.

Barr, N. (1993). Alternative funding resources for higher education. *Economic Journal (London), 103*(418), 718–728. doi:10.2307/2234544

Barr, N. (2001). Funding higher education: Policies for access and quality. *House of Commons Education and Skills Committee, Post-16 student support. Session, 2,* 24.

Barr, N. (2004). Higher education funding. *Oxford Review of Economic Policy, 20*(2), 264–283. doi:10.1093/oxrep/grh015

Basden, J., & Cottrell, M. (2017). How utilities are using blockchain to modernize the grid. *Harvard Business Review.*

Batsaikhan, U. (2017). *Cryptoeconomics - the opportunities and challenges of blockchain.* IDEAS Working Paper Series from RePEc, St. Loius.

Baur, D. G., Dimpfl, T., & Kuck, K. (2018). Bitcoin, gold and the US dollar: A replication and extension. *Finance Research Letters, 25,* 103–110. doi:10.1016/j.frl.2017.10.012

Beaver, W., Kettler, P., & Scholes, M. (1970). The association between market determined and accounting determined risk measures. *The Accounting Review, 45*(4), 654–682.

Beck & Müller-Bloch. (2017). *Blockchain as radical innovation: a framework for engaging with distributed ledgers as incumbent organization*. Academic Press.

Beck, R., Avital, M., Rossi, M., & Thatcher, J. B. (2017). Blockchain technology in business and information systems research. Business and Information Systems Engineering, 59(6), 381–384.

Beck, R., Czepluch, J. S., Lollike, N., & Malone, S. (2016). Blockchain-the Gateway to Trust-Free Cryptographic Transactions. ECIS.

Beck, R., Czepluch, S., & Jacob, L. (2016). Blockchain – The Gateway to Trust-Free Cryptographic Transactions. Academic Press.

Beck, R. (2018). Beyond Bitcoin: The Rise of Blockchain World. *Computer, 51*(2), 54–58. doi:10.1109/MC.2018.1451660

Beck, R., Avital, M., Rossi, M., & Thatcher, J. B. (2017). Blockchain technology in business and information systems research. *Business & Information Systems Engineering, 59*(6), 381–384. doi:10.100712599-017-0505-1

Bentov, I., Gabizon, A., & Mizrahi, A. (2016). Cryptocurrencies without proof of work. In *International Conference on Financial Cryptography and Data Security* (pp. 142-157). Springer. 10.1007/978-3-662-53357-4_10

Berger, A. N., Frame, W. S., & Ioannidou, V. (2011). Tests of ex-ante versus ex-post theories of collateral using private and public information. *Journal of Financial Economics, 100*(1), 85–97. doi:10.1016/j.jfineco.2010.10.014

Bergstra, J. A. (2014). *Bitcoin: not a currency-like informational commodity*. Informatics.

Biktimirov, M., Domashev, R., Cherkashin, A., & Shcherbakov, V. (2017). Blockchain Technology: Universal Structure and Requirements. *Automatic Documentation and Mathematical Linguistics, 51*(6), 235–238. doi:10.3103/S0005105517060036

Birkhead, N. A. (2016). *State Budgetary Delays in an Era of Party Polarization*. State and Local. doi:10.1177/0160323X16687813

Blau, B. M. (2017, October). Price dynamics and speculative trading in Bitcoin. *Research in International Business and Finance, 43*, 493–499. doi:10.1016/j.ribaf.2017.05.010

Blockchain Council. (2018, July 10). *How is blockchain verifiable by public and yet anonymous?* Retrieved January 29, 2019 from https://www.blockchain-council.org/blockchain/how-is-blockchain-verifiable-by-public-and-yet-anonymous/

Blockchain on AWS. (n.d.). Retrieved October 26, 2018 from https://aws.amazon.com/blockchain/

Blockchain Peer Review Project. (n.d.). Retrieved February 01, 2019 from https://www.blockchainpeer-review.org

Bolero. (2018). *Company Overview*. Retrieved from http://www.bolero.net/home/company-overview/

Bollerslev, T., Engle, R. F., & Wooldridge, J. M. (1988). A capital asset pricing model with time-varying covariances. *Journal of Political Economy, 96*(1), 116–131. doi:10.1086/261527

Bolton, P., Freixas, X., & Shapiro, J. (2012). The credit ratings game. *The Journal of Finance, 67*(1), 85–111. doi:10.1111/j.1540-6261.2011.01708.x

Booth, P. (2015). Crowdfunding: A Spimatic application of digital fandom. *New Media & Society, 17*(2), 149–166. doi:10.1177/1461444814558907

Borthick, A. F., & Pennington, R. R. (2017). When Data Become Ubiquitous, What Becomes of Accounting and Assurance? *Journal of Information Systems, 31*(3), 1–4. doi:10.2308/isys-10554

Bowen, W. M., & Qian, H. (2017). State spending for higher education: Does it improve economic performance? *Regional Science Policy & Practice, 9*(1), 7–23. doi:10.1111/rsp3.12086

Boyd, M., & Medjao, M. (2016). Banking APIs: State of the Market. *Axway*. Retrieved from https://static.openbankproject.com/bnpp/BANKING-APIS-2016.pdf

Boz, G., Menéndez-Plans, C., & Orgaz-Guerrero, N. (2015). The Systematic-Risk Determinants of the European Accommodation and Food Services Industry in the Period 2003-2011. *Cornell Hospitality Quarterly, 56*(1), 41–57. doi:10.1177/1938965514559047

Broens, H. (2014). *The Impact of the Financial Crisis of 2008 on Corporate Trade Finance*. Academic Press.

Bryant, C., & Camerinelli, E. (2012). *Supply chain finance*. Academic Press.

Bryzek, P. (2018). *A quick glimpse of Blockchain and its Revolutionary Applications*. Academic Press.

Burniske, C., & White, A. (2017). *Bitcoin: Ringing the bell for a new asset class* (White paper). Ark Invest. Retrieved from https://research. Ark-invest.com/hubfs/1_Download_Files_ARK-Invest/White_Papers/Bitcoin-Ringing-The-Bell-For-A-New-Asset-Class. pdf

Burniske, C., & White, A. (2017). *Bitcoin: Ringing the bell for a new asset class*. Retrieved from https://research.ark-invest.com/hubfs/1_Download_Files_ARK-Invest/White_Papers/Bitcoin-Ringing-The-Bell-For-A-New-Asset-Class.pdf

Burniske, C., & Tatar, J. (2017). *Cryptoassets: The Innovative Investor's Guide to Bitcoin and Beyond*. New York: McGraw Hill Professional.

Burniske, C., & Tatar, J. (2018). *Cryptoassets: The innovative investor's guide to bitcoin and beyond*. New York, NY: McGraw-Hill.

Burrell, J. (2016). How the machine 'thinks': Understanding opacity in machine learning algorithms. *Big Data & Society, 3*(1). doi:10.1177/2053951715622512

Buterin, V. (2013). *Ethereum White Paper: A next-generation smart contract and decentralized application platform*. Academic Press.

Buterin, V. (2014). *A next-generation smart contract and decentralized application platform* (white paper). Academic Press.

Buterin, V. (2014). *Ethereum Development Tutorial*. Available at: https://github.com/ethereum/wiki/wiki/Ethereum-Development-Tutorial

Buterin, V. (2015). *On public and private blockchains*. Available: https://blog.ethereum.org/2015/08/07/on-public-and-private-blockchains/

Byrne, P. J., & Heavey, C. (2006). The impact of information sharing and forecasting in capacitated industrial supply chains: A case study. *International Journal of Production Economics, 103*(1), 420–437. doi:10.1016/j.ijpe.2005.10.007

Byun, S. J., Jeon, B. H., Min, B., & Yoon, S.-J. (2015). The role of the variance premium in Jump GARCH option pricing models. *Journal of Banking & Finance, 59*, 38–56. doi:10.1016/j.jbankfin.2015.05.009

Calatayud, A., Carlan, V., Sys, C., & Vanelslander, T. (2018). *Digital Innovation in Maritime Supply Chains: Experiences from Northwestern Europe* (No. IDB-DP-00577). Inter-American Development Bank.

Camarinha-Matos, L. M. (2001). Execution system for distributed business processes in a virtual enterprise. *Future Generation Computer Systems, 17*(8), 1009–1021. doi:10.1016/S0167-739X(01)00044-9

Cannella, S. (2014). Order-up-to policies in information exchange supply chains. *Applied Mathematical Modelling, 38*(23), 5553–5561. doi:10.1016/j.apm.2014.04.029

Carey, P., Simnett, R., & Tanewski, G. (2000). Voluntary demand for internal and external auditing by family businesses. *Auditing, 19*(Supplement), 36–51. doi:10.2308/aud.2000.19.supplement.37

Carlozo, L. (2017). What is blockchain? *Journal of Accountancy, 224*(1), 29.

Carson, B., Romanelli, G., Walsh, P., & Zhumaev, A. (2018). Blockchain beyond the hype: What is the strategic business value? McKinsey & Company.

Casey & Vigna. (2018). In blockchain we trust. *MIT Technology Review*.

Casey, M. J., & Wong, P. (2017, March). Global supply chains are about to get better, thanks to blockchain. *Harvard Business Review*, 13.

Chalaemwongwan, N., & Kurutach, W. (2018). State of the art and challenges facing consensus protocols on blockchain. *International Conference on Information Networking (ICOIN)*, 957-962. 10.1109/ICOIN.2018.8343266

Chan, R. Y. (2016). Understanding the purpose of higher education: An analysis of the economic and social benefits for completing a college degree. *Journal of Education Policy, Planning and Administration, 6*(5), 1–40.

Chan, R. Y. (2017). The future of accessibility in higher education: Making college skills and degrees more accessible. In H. C. Alphin Jr, J. Lavine, & R. Y. Chan (Eds.), *Disability and Equity in Higher Education Accessibility* (pp. 1–45). Hershey, PA: IGI Global. doi:10.4018/978-1-5225-2665-0.ch001

Chaum, D. (1997). David Chaum on Electronic Commerce How much do you trust Big Brother? *IEEE Internet Computing*, *1*(6), 8–16. doi:10.1109/MIC.1997.643931

Chen, R. (2018). A traceability chain algorithm for artificial neural networks using T–S fuzzy cognitive maps in blockchain. *Future Generation Computer Systems*, *80*, 198–210. doi:10.1016/j.future.2017.09.077

Chen, W., Ma, M., Ye, Y., Zheng, Z., & Zhou, Y. (2018). IoT Service Based on JointCloudBlockchain: The Case Study of Smart Traveling. *2018 IEEE Symposium on Service-Oriented System Engineering (SOSE)*. 10.1109/SOSE.2018.00036

Chen, Y. (2018). Blockchain tokens and the potential democratization of entrepreneurship and innovation. *Business Horizons*, *61*(4), 567–575. doi:10.1016/j.bushor.2018.03.006

Chesbrough, H. (2010). Business model innovation: Opportunities and barriers. *Long Range Planning*, *43*(2-3), 354–363. doi:10.1016/j.lrp.2009.07.010

Chomsky N. (2011). *Public Education Under Massive Corporate Assault—What's Next?* Academic Press.

Christensen, C. M., Horn, M. B., Soares, L., & Caldera, L. (2011). *Disrupting college: How disruptive innovation can deliver quality and affordability to postsecondary education*. Retrieved from https://www.americanprogress.org/issues/economy/reports/2011/02/08/9034/disrupting-college/

Christensen, J. (2010). *Conceptual frameworks of accounting from an information perspective*. Academic Press.

Christensen, C. M., & Eyring, H. J. (2011). *The Innovative University: Changing the DNA of Higher Education from the Inside Out*. San Francisco: Jossey-Bass.

Christensen, C. M., & Eyring, H. J. (2011). *The innovative university: Changing the DNA of higher education from the inside out*. Somerset, NJ: John Wiley & Sons.

Christensen, C. M., Horn, M. B., Caldera, L., & Soares, L. (2011). *Disrupting college: How disruptive innovation can deliver quality and affordability to postsecondary education*. Washington, DC: Center for American Progress. Retrieved from https://files.eric.ed.gov/fulltext/ED535182.pdf

Christensen, C. M., Raynor, M. E., & McDonald, R. (2015). What is disruptive innovation. *Harvard Business Review*, *93*, 44–53. PMID:17183796

Christidis, K., & Devetsikiotis, M. (2016). Blockchains and smart contracts for the internet of things. *IEEE Access: Practical Innovations, Open Solutions*, *4*, 2292–2303. doi:10.1109/ACCESS.2016.2566339

Christman, D. E. (2000). Multiple realities: Characteristics of loan defaulters at a two-year public institution. *Community College Review*, *27*(4), 16–32. doi:10.1177/009155210002700402

Chuen, L. K. D. (2015). Handbook of Digital Currency: Bitcoin Innovation, Financial Instruments, and Big Data. Elsevier.

Chu, J., Chan, S., Nadarajah, S., & Osterrieder, J. (2017). GARCH modelling of cryptocurrencies. *J. Risk Financ. Manage.*, *10*(4), 17. doi:10.3390/jrfm10040017

Church, Z. (2017). Blockchain, explained. *MIT Digital Blog.* Retrieved from http://ide.mit.edu/news-blog/blog/blockchain-explained

Civelek, M.E., & Özalp, A. (2018). *Blockchain Technology and Final Challenges for Paperless Foreign Trade.* Academic Press.

Civelek, M.E., Uca, N., & Çemberci, M. (2015). *eUCP and electronic commerce investments: e-signature and paperless foreign trade.* Academic Press.

Clemes, M. D., Hu, B., & Li, X. (2016). Services and economic growth in China: An empirical analysis. *Journal of the Asia Pacific Economy*, *21*(4), 612–627. doi:10.1080/13547860.2016.1190492

Coase, R. H. (1937). The nature of the firm. *Economica*, *4*(16), 386–405. doi:10.1111/j.1468-0335.1937.tb00002.x

Cocco, L., Pinna, A., & Marchesi, M. (2017). Banking on Blockchain: Costs Savings Thanks to the Blockchain Technology. *Future Internet*, *9*(3).

Cohn, A., West, T., & Parker, C. (2017). Smart After All: Blockchain, Smart Contracts, Parametric Insurance, and Smart Energy Grids. *Georgetown Law Technology Review*, *1*(2), 273–304.

Cong, L. W., & He, Z. (2018). *Blockchain disruption and smart contracts.* National Bureau of Economic Research. doi:10.3386/w24399

Conn, J. (2016). Could blockchain help cure health IT's security woes? *Modern Healthcare*, *46*(45).

Conte de Leon, D., Stalick, A. Q., Jillepalli, A. A., Haney, M. A., & Sheldon, F. T. (2017). Blockchain: Properties and misconceptions. *Asia Pacific Journal of Innovation and Entrepreneurship*, *11*(3), 286–300. doi:10.1108/APJIE-12-2017-034

Council for Aid to Education. (2018) *Colleges and universities raised $43.60 billion in 2017.* Retrieved from https://cae.org/images/uploads/pdf/VSE-2017-Press-Release.pdf

Crane, A., & Ruebottom, T. (2011). Stakeholder theory and social identity: Rethinking stakeholder identification. *Journal of Business Ethics*, *102*(S1), 77–87. doi:10.100710551-011-1191-4

Crosby, M., Pattanayak, P., & Verma, S. (2016). Applied Innovation Review. *Applied Innovation Review*, (2).

Crosby, M., Nachiappan Pattanayak, P., Verma, S., & Kalyanaraman, V. (2016). Blockchain technology: Beyond bitcoin. *Appl Innov Rev*, *2*, 6–19.

Crosby, M., Pattanayak, P., Verma, S., & Kalyanaraman, V. (2016). Blockchain technology: Beyond bitcoin. *Applied Innovation*, *2*, 6–10.

Crypto Celebrities. (n.d.). Retrieved October 29, 2018, from https://cryptocelebrities.co/

CryptoKitties. (n.d.). Retrieved October 29, 2018, from https://www.cryptokitties.co/

Csiszar, A. (2016). Peer review: Troubled from the start. *Nature*, *532*(7599), 306–308. doi:10.1038/532306a PMID:27111616

Dai, F., Shi, Y., Meng, N., Wei, L., & Ye, Z. (2017). From Bitcoin to cybersecurity: A comparative study of blockchain application and security issues. *4th International Conference on Systems and Informatics (ICSAI)*, 975 – 979. 10.1109/ICSAI.2017.8248427

Dai, J., & Vasarhelyi, M. A. (2017). Toward blockchain-based accounting and assurance. *Journal of Information Systems*, *31*(3), 5–21. doi:10.2308/isys-51804

Daniel, D. (2018). *Permissioned vs. Permissionless Blockchains: Understanding the Differences*. Retrieved July 17, 2018 from https://blockonomi.com/permissioned-vs-permissionless-blockchains/

Davis, J. H., Schoorman, F. D., & Donaldson, R. (1997). Toward a stewardship theory of management. *Academy of Management Review*, *22*(1), 20–47. doi:10.5465/amr.1997.9707180258

De Montjoye, Y. A., Shmueli, E., & Samuel, S. (2014). Openpds: Protecting the privacy of metadata through safeanswers. *PLoS One*, *7*(9).

DeAngelo, L. E. (1981). Auditor size and audit quality. *Journal of Accounting and Economics*, *3*(3), 183–199. doi:10.1016/0165-4101(81)90002-1

Debreceny, R., Rahman, A., & Wang, T. (2017). Corporate network centrality score: Methodologies and informativenes. *Journal of Information Systems*, *31*(3), 23–43. doi:10.2308/isys-51797

Decker, C., & Wattenhofer, R. (2013, September). Information propagation in the bitcoin network. In *Peer-to-Peer Computing (P2P), 2013 IEEE Thirteenth International Conference on* (pp. 1-10). IEEE. 10.1109/P2P.2013.6688704

Deethman, S. (2016). *Bitcoin could consume as much electricity as Denmark by 2020*. Retrieved from http://motherboard.vice.com/read/bitcoin-could-consume-as-much-electricity-as-denmark-by-2020 on September 20, 2018

Del Castillo, M. (2018). *Big Blockchain: The 50 Largest Public Companies Exploring Blockchain*. Retrieved from https://www.forbes.com/sites/michaeldelcastillo/2018/07/03/big-blockchain-the-50-largest-public-companies-exploring-blockchain/#11f70c6d2b5b

Demski, J. S., & Feltham, G. A. (1976). *Cost determination: a conceptual approach. Iowa*. Ames, IA: State University Press.

Devi, T. R. (2013). Importance of Cryptography In network Security. *Communication Systems and Network Technologies (CSNT), in International Conference.*

Dey, T., Jaiswal, S., Sunderkrishnan, S., & Katre, N. (2017). HealthSense: A medical use case of Internet of Things and blockchain. *2017 International Conference on Intelligent Sustainable Systems (ICISS).* 10.1109/ISS1.2017.8389459

Di Pierro. (2017). What Is the Blockchain? *IEEE Computer Society American Institute of Physics, Computing in Science & Engineering, 19*(5).

Dijkstra, M. (2017). *Blockchain: Towards disruption in the real estate sector. In An Exploration on the Impact of Blockchain Technology in the Real Estate Management Process.* Delft: University of Delft.

Dillon, E., & Carey, K. (2009). *Drowning in Debt: The Emerging Student Loan Crisis.* Washington, DC: Education Sector.

Dinh, T. T. A., Liu, R., Zhang, M., Chen, G., Ooi, B. C., & Wang, J. (2018). Untangling blockchain: A data processing view of blockchain. *IEEE Transactions on Knowledge and Data Engineering, 30*(7), 1366–1385. doi:10.1109/TKDE.2017.2781227

Diosdado, B. (2017, June 22). The price of vacancy: The cost of unfilled technology jobs [blog post]. Forbes Community Voice. Retrieved from https://www.forbes.com/sites/forbestechcouncil/2017/06/22/the-price-of-vacancy-the-cost-of-unfilled-technology-jobs/#5849a6c85747

Dixon, M., Glasson, B., & Network, E. C. (1999). Electronic Payment Systems for International Trade. *Western Australian Workshop on Information Systems Research.*

Dogru, Mody, & Leonardi. (2018). *Blockchain Technology & its Implications for the Hospitality Industry.* Academic Press.

Dolvin, S. D. (2012, November 28). Student loan debt [blog post]. Butler University. Retrieved from https://digitalcommons.butler.edu/jmdallchapters/49/

Dolwick, J. S. (2009). 'The social' and beyond: Introducing actor-network theory. *Journal of Maritime Archaeology, 4,* 21-49.

Don Johnson, A. M., & Vanstone, S. (2001). The elliptic curve digital signature algorithm. *International Journal of Information Security, 1*(1), 36–63. doi:10.1007102070100002

Dorri, A., Kanhere, S. S., & Jurdak, R. (2016). *Blockchain in internet of things: challenges and solutions.* arXiv preprint arXiv:1608.05187

Duran, R. E. (2013). *Financial Services Technology: Processes, Architecture, and Solutions.* Cengage Learning.

Duranti, L., & Rogers, C. (2012). Trust in digital records: An increasingly cloudy legal area. *Computer Law & Security Review, 28*(5), 522–531. doi:10.1016/j.clsr.2012.07.009

Dyhrberg, A. H. (2016). Bitcoin, gold and the dollar–A GARCH volatility analysis. *Finance Research Letters*, *16*, 85–92. doi:10.1016/j.frl.2015.10.008

Dylan, Y., Peter, M., Nik, R., & Karen, S. (2018). *Blockchain Technology Overview*. Retrieved October 2018, from National Institute of Standards and Technology, U.S. Department of Commerce: https://nvlpubs.nist.gov/nistpubs/ir/2018/NIST.IR.8202.pdf

Dynarski, M. (1994). Who defaults on student loans? Findings from the national postsecondary student aid study. *Economics of Education Review*, *13*(1), 55–68. doi:10.1016/0272-7757(94)90023-X

Economist. (2015). The great chain of being sure about things. *Economist*. Retrieved from https://www.economist.com/briefing/2015/10/31/the-great-chain-of-being-sure-about-things

Efanov, D., & Roschin, P. (2018). The All-Pervasiveness of the Blockchain Technology. *Procedia Computer Science*, *123*, 116–121. doi:10.1016/j.procs.2018.01.019

Ehsani, F. (2016, December 21). *Blockchain in Finance: From Buzzword to Watchword in 2016*. Retrieved October 26, 2018 from https://www.coindesk.com/blockchain-finance-buzzword-watchword-2016/

Ekin, A., & Unay, D. (2018). Blockchain applications in healthcare. *2018 26th Signal Processing and Communications Applications Conference (SIU)*. doi:10.1109iu.2018.8404275

El-Din, D. M., & Mahmoud Khalifa, N. E. (2018). A Blockchain Technology Evolution between Business Process Management (BPM) and Internet-of-Things (IoT). *International Journal of Advanced Computer Science and Applications*, *9*(8), 442–450.

El-Hawary, M. E. (2014). The smart grid—State-of-the-art and future trends. *Electric Power Components and Systems*, *42*(3-4), 239–250. doi:10.1080/15325008.2013.868558

Ellervee, A., Matulevi˘cius, R., & Mayer, N. (n.d.). *A Comprehensive Reference Model for Blockchain-based Distributed Ledger Technology*. Retrieved October 27, 2018, from http://ceur-ws.org/Vol-1979/paper-09.pdf

Emdin, C. (2006). Beyond coteaching: Power dynamics, cosmopolitanism and the psychoanalytic dimension. *Forum Qualitative Social Research*, *7*(4). doi:10.17169/fqs-7.4.189

Emdin, C. (2010). *Urban Science Education for the Hip-Hop Generation*. Boston: Sense.

Emdin, C., & Lehner, E. (2006). Situating cogenerative dialogue in a cosmopolitan ethic. *Forum Qualitative Social Research*, *7*(2). doi:10.17169/fqs-7.2.125

Emdin, C., & Lehner, E. (2006, March). Situating cogenerative dialogue in a cosmopolitan ethic. *Forum Qualitative Sozialforschung/Forum: Qualitative Social Research*, *7*(2).

Emmanuelle, G. (2018). *Can Blockchain Revolutionize International Trade? Switcherland*. World Trade Organization.

Engle, R. F., & Bollerslev, T. (1986). Modelling the persistence of conditional variances. *Econometric Reviews*, *5*(1), 1–50. doi:10.1080/07474938608800095

English, M., Auer, S., & Domingue, J. (2016). Block chain technologies & the semantic web: a framework for symbiotic development. In J. Lehmann, H. Thakkar, L. Halilaj, & R. Asmat (Eds.), *Computer Science Conference for University of Bonn Students* (pp. 47–61). Academic Press.

Etherbots. (n.d.). Retrieved October 29, 2018, from https://etherbots.io/

Extance, A. (2017). Could Bitcoin technology help science? *Nature, 552*(7685), 301–302. doi:10.1038/d41586-017-08589-4 PMID:29293234

FASB. (1978). *Concepts Statement No. 1: Objectives of Financial Reporting by Business Enterprises.* Financial Accounting Standards Board.

Fassin, Y. (2009). The stakeholder model refined. *Journal of Business Ethics, 84*(1), 113–135. doi:10.100710551-008-9677-4

Feld, S., Schönfeld, M., & Werner, M. (2014). Analyzing the Deployment of Bitcoins P2P Network under an AS-level Perspective. *Procedia Computer Science, 32*, 1121–1126. doi:10.1016/j.procs.2014.05.542

Feltham, G., & Ohlson, J. (1995). Valuation and clean surplus accounting for operating and financial activities. *Contemporary Accounting Research, 11*(2), 689–731. doi:10.1111/j.1911-3846.1995.tb00462.x

Filesystem in Userspace. (2018, October 22). Retrieved October 27, 2018, from https://en.wikipedia.org/wiki/Filesystem_in_Userspace

Findlay, C. (2015). Decentralised and inviolate: the blockchain and its uses for digital archives. *Recordkeeping Roundtable.* Available at https://rkroundtable.org/2015/01/23/decentralised-and-inviolate-the-blockchain-and-its-uses-for-digital-archives/

Finley, K. (2016, June 20). *The Inventors of the Internet Are Trying to Build a Truly Permanent Web.* Retrieved October 26, 2018 from https://www.wired.com/2016/06/inventors-internet-trying-build-truly-permanent-web/

Foroglou, G., & Tsilidou, A-L. (2015). *Further applications of the blockchain.* Academic Press.

Garay, J., Kiayias, A., & Leonardos, N. (2015). The bitcoin backbone protocol: Analysis and applications. *Annual International Conference on the Theory and Applications of Cryptographic Techniques*, 281-310. 10.1007/978-3-662-46803-6_10

Gehrke, F. (2001). *New Attempts at Electronic Documentation in Transport Bolero–The end of the experiment, the beginning of the future* (Unpublished Masters Dissertation). University of Cape Town.

Gertchev, N. (2013). *The moneyness of bitcoin. Mises Daily.* Auburn: Ludwig von Mises.

Giancaspro, M. (2017). Is a "smart contract" really a smart idea? Insights from a legal perspective. *Computer Law & Security Review.*

Gilbert, D. U., & Rasche, A. (2008). Opportunities and problems of standardized ethics initiatives: A stakeholder theory perspective. *Journal of Business Ethics, 82*(3), 755–773. doi:10.100710551-007-9591-1

Gilchrist, H. (2018). *Higher education as a human right*. Retrieved from https://ssrn.com/abstract=3100852

Giroux, H., Giroux, S. S., & White. (2018). *Sport and the neoliberal university: Profit, politics, and pedagogy*. New Brunswick, NJ: Rutgers University Press.

Gittleson, K., & Usher, B. (2017). Higher education for refugees. *Stanford Soc. Innov. Rev.* Retrieved from https://ssir.org/articles/entry/higher_education_for_refugees

Gladieux, L. (1995). Federal student aid policy: A history and an assessment. In *Financing Postsecondary Education: The Federal Role*. Retrieved from http://www2.ed.gov/offices/OPE/PPI/FinPostSecEd/gladieux.html

Gladieux, L., & Perna, L. (2005). *Borrowers who drop out: A neglected aspect of the college student loan trend*. Retrieved from http://www.highereducation.org/reports/borrowing/index.shtml

Gomez-Sanz, J. J., Garcia-Rodriguez, S., Cuartero-Soler, N., & Hernandez-Callejo, L. (2014). Reviewing microgrids from a multi-agent systems perspective. *Energies*, *7*(5), 3355–3382. doi:10.3390/en7053355

Goranović, A., Meisel, M., Fotiadis, L., Wilker, S., Treytl, A., & Sauter, T. (2017). Blockchain applications in microgrids an overview of current projects and concepts. In *Industrial Electronics Society, IECON 2017-43rd Annual Conference of the IEEE* (pp. 6153-6158). IEEE. 10.1109/IECON.2017.8217069

Governatori, G., Idelberger, F., Milosevic, Z., Riveret, R., Sartor, G., & Xu, X. (2018). On legal contracts, imperative and declarative smart contracts, and blockchain systems. *Artificial Intelligence and Law*, *26*(4), 377–409. doi:10.100710506-018-9223-3

Gramoli, V. (2017). From blockchain consensus back to Byzantine consensus. *Future Generation Computer Systems*.

Greenwood, D. J., & Levin, M. (2005). Reform of the social sciences and of universities through action research. The Sage handbook of qualitative research, 3, 43-64.

Greenwood, D. J. (2008). Theoretical research, applied research, and action research. In C. R. Hale (Ed.), *Engaging Contradictions: Theory, Politics, and Methods of Activist Scholarship* (pp. 319–340). Berkeley, CA: University of California Press.

Greenwood, J. D., & Levin, M. (2011). *Introduction to Action Research* (2nd ed.). Thousand Oaks, CA: Sage.

Greer, R. J. (1997). What is an asset class, anyway? *The Journal of Portfolio.*

Greiner, U., Lippe, S., Kahl, T., Ziemann, J., & Jäkel, F. W. (2007). Designing and implementing cross-organizational business processes-description and application of a modelling framework. In *Enterprise Interoperability* (pp. 137–147). London: Springer. doi:10.1007/978-1-84628-714-5_13

Gronwald, M. (2014). *The economics of bitcoins: Market characteristics and price jumps*. Retrieved from https://ideas.repec.org/p/ces/ceswps/_5121.html

Guba, E. G., & Lincoln, Y. S. (1989). *Fourth generation evaluation.* Thousand Oaks, CA: Sage.

Gumport, P. J. (1997). In search of strategic perspective: A tool for mapping the market in postsecondary education. *Change: The Magazine of Higher Learning, 29*(6), 23–38. doi:10.1080/00091389709602344

Gurkaynak, G., Yilmaz, I., Yesilaltay, B., & Bengi, B. (2018). Intellectual property law and practice in the blockchain realm. *Computer Law & Security Review, 34*(4), 847–862. doi:10.1016/j.clsr.2018.05.027

Hacker, P. (2017). *Corporate Governance for Complex Cryptocurrencies? A Framework for Stability and Decision Making in Blockchain-Based Monetary Systems.* Academic Press.

Hagström, L., & Dahlquist, O. (2017). *Scaling blockchain for the energy sector.* Uppsala: University of Uppsala.

Harackiewicz, J. M., & Priniski, S. J. (2018). Improving student outcomes in higher education: The science of targeted intervention. *Annual Review of Psychology, 69*(1), 409–435. doi:10.1146/annurev-psych-122216-011725 PMID:28934586

Harwick, C. (2014). *Crypto-Currency and the Problem of Intermediation.* Available at SSRN. doi:10.2139srn.2523771

Hassanzadeh, A., Jafarian, A., & Amiri, M. (2013). Modeling and analysis of the causes of bullwhip effect in centralized and decentralized supply chain using response surface method. *Applied Mathematical Modelling, 38*(9-10), 2353–2365. doi:10.1016/j.apm.2013.10.051

Hassink, H., Meuwissen, R., & Bollen, L. (2010). Fraud detection, redress, and reporting by auditors. *Managerial Auditing Journal, 25*(9), 861–881. doi:10.1108/02686901011080044

Hawlitschek, N., Notheisen, B., & Teubner, T. (2018). The limits of trust-free systems: A literature review on blockchain technology and trust in the sharing economy. *Electronic Commerce Research and Applications, 29*, 50–63. doi:10.1016/j.elerap.2018.03.005

Hay, S. (2018, January 02). *What is the Bitcoin Lightning Network? A Beginner's Explanation.* Retrieved October 26, 2018 from https://99bitcoins.com/what-is-the-bitcoin-lightning-network-a-beginners-explanation/

Hayes, A. (2015). *What factors give cryptocurrencies their value: An empirical analysis.* Retrieved from https://papers.ssrn.com/sol3/papers.cfm?abstract_id=2579445

Hayes, A. S. (2017). Cryptocurrency value formation: An empirical study leading to a cost of production model for valuing bitcoin. *Telematics and Informatics, 34*(7), 1308–1321. doi:10.1016/j.tele.2016.05.005

Heber, D., & Groll, M. (2017, August). Towards a digital twin: How the blockchain can foster E/E-traceability in consideration of model-based systems engineering. In *DS 87-3 Proceedings of the 21st International Conference on Engineering Design (ICED 17) Vol 3: Product, Services and Systems Design, Vancouver, Canada, 21-25.08. 2017* (pp. 321-330). Academic Press.

Henry, R., Herzberg, A., & Kate, A. (2018). Blockchain Access Privacy: Challenges and Directions. *Security & Privacy, IEEE, 16*(4), 38–45. doi:10.1109/MSP.2018.3111245

Henshall, A. (2018). *An Introduction to Blockchain: The Potential for Process Management and Beyond.* Retrieved from https://www.process.st/introduction-to-blockchain/

Herman, E., & Stefanescu, D. (2017). Can higher education stimulate entrepreneurial intentions among engineering and business students? *Educational Studies, 43*(3), 312–327. doi:10.1080/03055698.2016 .1277134

Herrera-Joancomartí, J., & Pérez-Solà, C. (2016, September). Privacy in bitcoin transactions: new challenges from blockchain scalability solutions. In *Modeling Decisions for Artificial Intelligence* (pp. 26–44). Cham: Springer. doi:10.1007/978-3-319-45656-0_3

Herzog, E., & Benartzi, G. (2017). *Bancor protocol-white paper.* Retrieved from: https://website-bancor. storage.googleapis.com/2018/04/01ba8253-bancor_protocol_whitepaper_en.pdf

Hess, A. (2017). Harvard Business School professor: Half of American colleges will be bankrupt in 10 to 15 years. *CNBC.* Retrieved from https://www.cnbc.com/2017/11/15/hbs-professor-half-of-us-colleges-will-be-bankrupt-in-10-to-15-years.html

Hillman, N. W. (2014). *College on credit: A multilevel analysis of student loan default* (37th ed.). Rev. High.

Hjalmarsson, F. P., Hreioarsson, G. K., Hamdaqa, M., & Hjalmtysson, G. (2018). Blockchain-Based E-Voting System. *2018 IEEE 11th International Conference on Cloud Computing (CLOUD).* doi:10.1109/cloud.2018.00151

Hojat, M., Gonnella, J. S., & Caelleigh, A. S. (2003). Impartial Judgment by the "Gatekeepers" of Science: Fallibility and Accountability in the Peer Review Process. *Advances in Health Sciences Education: Theory and Practice, 8*(1), 75–96. doi:10.1023/A:1022670432373 PMID:12652170

Hölmstrom, B. (1979). Moral hazard and observability. *The Bell Journal of Economics, 10*(1), 74–91. doi:10.2307/3003320

Holweg, M., Disney, S. M., Holmstrom, J., & Smaros, J. (2005). Supply chain collaboration: Making sense of the strategy continuum. *European Management Journal, 23*(3), 170–181. doi:10.1016/j. emj.2005.02.008

Horngren, C., Foster, G., & Datar, S. (2003). *Cost Accounting: A Managerial Emphasis.* Prentice-Hall.

Ho, S. C., Wang, W. Y. C., Pauleen, D. J., & Ting, P. H. (2011). Perspectives on the performance of supply chain systems: The effects of attitude and assimilation. *International Journal of Information Technology & Decision Making, 10*(4), 635–658. doi:10.1142/S021962201100449X

HSBC. (2018). *HSBC and ING execute groundbreaking live trade finance transaction on R3's Corda Blockchain platform.* Retrieved from https://www.hsbc.com/news-and-insight/media-resources/media-releases/2018/hsbc-trade-blockchain-transaction-press-release

Huang & Chiang. (2017). *RegTech Evolution: The TrustChain*. Academic Press.

Huckle, B., Bhattacharya, R., White, M., & Beloff, N. (2016). Internet of Things, Blockchain and Shared Economy Applications. *Procedia Computer Science*, *98*(C), 461–466. doi:10.1016/j.procs.2016.09.074

Hutcheson, P. A., & Kidder, R. D. (2011). In the national interest: The college and university in the United States in the post-World War II era. In *Higher education: Handbook of theory and research* (pp. 221–264). Springer. doi:10.1007/978-94-007-0702-3_6

Hyperledger project. (2015). Available: https://www.hyperledger.org/

Hyperledger: Blockchain collaboration changing the business world. (n.d.). Retrieved October 26, 2018 from https://www.ibm.com/blockchain/hyperledger

Hyvärinen, H., Risius, M., & Friis, G. (2017). A Blockchain-Based Approach Towards Overcoming Financial Fraud in Public Sector Services. *Business & Information Systems Engineering*, *59*(6), 441–456. doi:10.100712599-017-0502-4

IASB. (2018). *Conceptual Framework for Financial Reporting*. IASB.

IASC. (1989). *Framework for the Preparation and Presentation of Financial Statements*. Published by the International Accounting Standards Committee Board (IASC Board) in July 1989 and adopted by the International Accounting standards Board (IASB) in April 2001. Currently available in the annual volume of IFRS published by the IASB.

Indera, N. I., Yassin, I. M., Zabidi, A., & Rizman, Z. I. (2017). Non-linear autoregressive with exogeneous input (NARX) Bitcoin price prediction model using PSO-optimized parameters and moving average technical indicators. *Rev. Sci. Fondam. Appl.*, *9*(3S), 791–808. doi:10.4314/jfas.v9i3s.61

Infographic. (2018, October 4). *A history of academic peer review*. Retrieved October 26, 2018 from https://www.editage.com/insights/a-history-of-academic-peer-review

Inganäs, O., & Sundström, V. (2016). Solar energy for electricity and fuels. *Ambio*, *45*(1), 15–23. doi:10.100713280-015-0729-6 PMID:26667056

Inter PARES. (2015). *Terminology database*. Available at: http://arstweb.clayton.edu/interlex/

IPFS is the Distributed Web. (n.d.). Retrieved October 27, 2018, from https://ipfs.io/#how

Ipfs/README.md. (n.d.). Retrieved October 27, 2018, from https://github.com/ipfs/ipfs/blob/master/README.md#who-designed-it

Ireland, R. & Crum, C. (2005). *Supply Chain Collaboration*. J Ross Publishing.

IRENA. (2018). *Renewable Energy Policies in a Time of Transition*. Retrieved from https://www.irena.org/publications/2018/Apr/Renewable-energy-policies-in-a-time-of-transition

Ishan, P. B., & Rai, G. (2018). Analysis of Cryptographic Hash in Blockchain for Bitcoin Mining Process. *International Conference on Advances in Computing and Communication Engineering (ICACCE)*, 105-110. 10.1109/ICACCE.2018.8441688

Islam, S., & Ahamed, S. (2008). *Preventing Letter of Credit Fraud*. Academic Press.

Ivarsson, M. (2012). *World Wide Trade, a manual affair. A study of the current position of the electronic bill of lading*. Academic Press.

Jacobovitz, O. (2016). *Blockchain for identity management*. The Lynne and William Frankel Center for Computer Science Department of Computer Science, Ben-Gurion University.

Jäger, K. D., Isabella, O., Smets, A. H., van Swaaij, R. A., & Zeman, M. (2016). *Solar Energy: Fundamentals, Technology and Systems*. UIT Cambridge.

Jaradat, M., Jarrah, M., Bousselham, A., Jararweh, Y., & Al-Ayyoub, M. (2015). The internet of energy: Smart sensor networks and big data management for smart grid. *Procedia Computer Science*, *56*, 592–597. doi:10.1016/j.procs.2015.07.250

Jayachandran, P. (2017). The difference between public and private blockchain. *IBM Blockchain Blog*. Retrieved from https://www.ibm.com/blogs/blockchain/2017/05/the-difference-between-public-and-private-blockchain/

Jemielniak, D., & Greenwood, D. J. (2015). Wake up or perish: Neo-liberalism, the social sciences, and salvaging the public university. *Cultural Studies? Critical Methodologies*, *15*(1), 72–82. doi:10.1177/1532708613516430

Jensen, M. C., & Meckling, W. H. (1976). Theory of the firm: Managerial behavior, agency costs and ownership structure. *Journal of Financial Economics*, *3*(4), 305–360. doi:10.1016/0304-405X(76)90026-X

Jessel, B., & DiCaprio, A. (2018). Can blockchain make trade finance more inclusive? *Journal of Financial Transformation*, *47*, 35–50.

Jordan, R. (2018, January 10). *How to Scale Ethereum: Sharding Explained – Prysmatic Labs – Medium*. Retrieved October 26, 2018 from https://medium.com/prysmatic-labs/how-to-scale-ethereum-sharding-explained-ba2e283b7fce

Joshi & Karkade. (2015, January). Network Security with Cryptography. *International Journal of Computer Science and Mobile Computing*.

Jun, M. (2018). Blockchain government-a next form of infrastructure for the twenty-first century. *Journal of Open Innovation: Technology, Market, and Complexity*, *4*(1), 7. doi:10.118640852-018-0086-3

Jutila, L. (2017). *The blockchain technology and its applications in the financial sector*. Available at: https://aaltodoc.aalto.fi/bitstream/handle/123456789/27209/bachelor_Jutila_Laura_2017.pdf;jsessionid=EB73ECF52889104CB772C6FA3B968EF7?sequence=1

Kalodner, H., Carlsten, M., Ellenbogen, P., Bonneau, J., & Narayanan, A. (2015). *An empirical study of Namecoin and lessons for decentralized namespace design*. Retrieved October 26, 2018, from http://randomwalker.info/publications/namespaces.pdf

Kaplan, A. M., & Haenlein, M. (2016). Higher education and the digital revolution: About MOOCs, SPOCs, social media, and the Cookie Monster. *Business Horizons*, *59*(4), 441–450. doi:10.1016/j.bushor.2016.03.008

Karamitsos, I., Papadaki, M., & Al Barghuthi, N. B. (2018). Design of the Blockchain Smart Contract: A Use Case for Real Estate. *Journal of Information Security*, *9*(03), 177–190. doi:10.4236/jis.2018.93013

Karim, S., Umar, R., & Rubina, L. (2018). *Conceptualizing Blockchains Characteristics & Applications.* 11th IADIS International Conference Information Systems 2018, Lisbon, Portugal.

Katsiampa, P. (2017). Volatility estimation for Bitcoin: A comparison of GARCH models. *Economics Letters*, *158*, 3–6. doi:10.1016/j.econlet.2017.06.023

Kaushik & Singhal. (2012). Network Security Using Cryptographic Techniques. *International Journal of Advanced Research in Computer Science and Software Engineering, 2012*(12).

Kaushik, A., Choudhary, A., Ektare, C., Thomas, D., & Akram, S. (2017). Blockchain — Literature survey. *2nd IEEE International Conference on Recent Trends in Electronics, Information & Communication Technology (RTEICT)*, 2145-2148.

Kavassalis, P., Stieber, H., Breymann, W., Saxton, K., & Gross, F. J. (2018). An innovative RegTech approach to financial risk monitoring and supervisory reporting. *The Journal of Risk Finance*, *19*(1), 39–55. doi:10.1108/JRF-07-2017-0111

Kazin, M. (2016). Trump and American populism: Old whine, new bottles. *Foreign Affairs*, *95*, 17.

Keay, A. (2017). Stewardship theory: Is board accountability necessary? *International Journal of Law and Management*, *59*(6), 1292–1314. doi:10.1108/IJLMA-11-2016-0118

Keenan, T. P. (2017). Alice in Blockchains: Surprising Security Pitfalls in PoW and PoS Blockchain Systems. *15th Annual Conference on Privacy, Security and Trust (PST)*, 400–402. 10.1109/PST.2017.00057

Keller, K. R. (2006). Investment in primary, secondary, and higher education and the effects on economic growth. *Contemporary Economic Policy*, *24*(1), 18–34. doi:10.1093/cep/byj012

Kincheloe, J. L., McLaren, P., Steinberg, S. R., & Monzó, L. D. (2017). *Critical pedagogy and qualitative research: Advancing the Bricolage.* Thousand Oaks, CA: Sage.

Kincheloe, J. L., & Tobin, K. (2009). The much exaggerated death of positivism. *Cultural Studies of Science Education*, *4*(3), 513–528. doi:10.100711422-009-9178-5

King, S., & Nadal, S. (2012). *PPcoin: Peer-to-Peer Crypto-Currency with Proof of-Stake.* Academic Press.

King, S., & Nadal, S. (2012). Ppcoin: Peer-to-peer crypto-currency with proof-of-stake. Self-Published Paper.

Kiyomoto, S., Rahman, M. S., & Basu, A. (2017). On blockchain-based anonymized dataset distribution platform. *2017 IEEE 15th International Conference on Software Engineering Research, Management and Applications (SERA)*. doi:10.1109era.2017.7965711

Klen, A. A. P., Rabelo, R. J., Ferreira, A. C., & Spinosa, L. M. (2001). Managing distributed business processes in the virtual enterprise. *Journal of Intelligent Manufacturing, 12*(2), 185–197. doi:10.1023/A:1011256711648

Kluvers, R., & Tippett, J. (2011). An exploration of stewardship theory in a not-for-profit organisation. *Accounting Forum, 35*(4), 275–284. doi:10.1016/j.accfor.2011.04.002

Konashevych, O. I. (2016). Advantages and current issues of Blockchain use in Microgrids. *Electronic Modelling, 38*(2), 94–103.

Kosba, Miller, Shi, Wen, & Papamanthou. (2016). Hawk: The blockchain model of cryptography and privacy-preserving smart contracts. *Proceedings of IEEE Symposium on Security and Privacy (SP)*, 839–858. 10.1109/SP.2016.55

Koshy, P., Koshy, D., & McDaniel, P. (2014) An Analysis of Anonymity in Bitcoin Using P2P Network Traffic. In Lecture Notes in Computer Science: Vol. 8437. Financial Cryptography and Data Security. Springer. doi:10.1007/978-3-662-45472-5_30

Kronick, D. A. (1990). Peer Review in 18th-Century Scientific Journalism. *Journal of the American Medical Association, 263*(10), 1321. doi:10.1001/jama.1990.03440100021002 PMID:2406469

Kshetri, N. (2017). Blockchain's roles in strengthening cybersecurity and protecting privacy. *Telecommunications Policy, 41*(10), 1027–1038. doi:10.1016/j.telpol.2017.09.003

Kshetri, N. (2018). 1 Blockchain's roles in meeting key supply chain management objectives. *International Journal of Information Management, 39*, 80–89. doi:10.1016/j.ijinfomgt.2017.12.005

Kshetri, N., & Voas, J. (2018). Blockchain in Developing Countries. *IT Professional, 20*(2), 11–14. doi:10.1109/MITP.2018.021921645

Kshetri, N., & Voas, J. (2018). Blockchain-Enabled E-Voting. *IEEE Software, 35*(4), 95–99. doi:10.1109/MS.2018.2801546

KuoChuen, L. (Ed.). (2015). *Handbook of Digital Currency*. Elsevier. Available: http://EconPapers. repec.org/RePEc:eee:monogr:9780128021170

Kuppuswamy, V., & Bayus, B. L. (2018). Crowdfunding creative ideas: The dynamics of project backers. In The Economics of Crowdfunding (pp. 151-182). Springer.

Kwon, J. (2014). *Tendermint: Consensus without mining*. Retrieved from http://tendermint. com/docs/ tendermint v04. pdf

Lagemann, E. C., & Lewis, H. (2012). Renewing the civic mission of American higher education. In E. C. Lagemann & H. Lewis (Eds.), *What is college for? The public purpose of higher education* (pp. 9–45). New York, NY: Teachers College Press.

Lamoureux, J.F., & Evans, T. (2011). *Supply chain finance: a new means to support the competitiveness and resilience of global value chains*. Academic Press.

Lamport, L., Shostak, R., & Pease, M. (1982). The byzantine generals problem. *ACM Transactions on Programming Languages and Systems, 4*(3), 382–401. doi:10.1145/357172.357176

Leachman, M., Masterson, K., & Wallace, M. (2016). *After nearly a decade, school investments still way down in some states*. Washington, DC: Center on Budget and Policy Priorities.

Lederman, D. (2017, April 28). Clay Christensen, doubling down. *Inside Higher Ed*. Retrieved from https://www.insidehighered.com/digital-learning/article/2017/04/28/clay-christensen-sticks-predictions-massive-college-closures

Lee, I. (2017). Big data: Dimensions, evolution, impacts, and challenges. *Business Horizons, 60*(3), 293–303. doi:10.1016/j.bushor.2017.01.004

Lehner, E., & Finley, K. (2016). *Should the New England education research organization start a journal in the age of audit culture? Reflections on academic publishing, metrics, and the new academy*. CUNY Academic Work. Retrieved from https://academicworks.cuny.edu/cgi/viewcontent.cgi?article=1017&context=bx_pubs

Lehner, E., & Finley, K. (2016). *Should the New England Education Research Organization start a journal in the age of audit culture? Reflections on academic publishing, metrics, and the new academy*. Retrieved from https://academicworks.cuny.edu/bx_pubs/15/

Lehner, E., Hunzeker, D., & Ziegler, J. R. (2017). Funding science with science: Cryptocurrency and independent academic research funding. *Ledger, 2*. Retrieved from https://ledger.pitt.edu/ojs/index.php/ledger/article/view/108

Lehner, E. (2007). Describing students of the African Diaspora: Understanding micro and meso level science learning as gateways to standards based discourse. *Cultural Studies of Science Education, 2*(2), 441–473. doi:10.100711422-007-9062-0

Lehner, E., Hunzeker, D., & Ziegler, J. R. (2017). Funding science with science: Cryptocurrency and independent academic research funding. *Ledger, 2*, 65–76. doi:10.5195/LEDGER.2017.108

Lehner, E., Thomas, K., Shaddai, J., & Hernen, T. (2017). Measuring the effectiveness of critical literacy as an instructional method. *Journal of College Literacy and Learning, 43*(1), 26–53.

Lemieux, V. L. (2016). Trusting records: Is Blockchain technology the answer? *Records Management Journal, 26*(2), 110–139. doi:10.1108/RMJ-12-2015-0042

Lerback, J., & Hanson, B. (2017). Journals invite too few women to referee. *Nature, 541*(7638), 455–457. doi:10.1038/541455a PMID:28128272

Letourneau, K. B., & Whelan, S. T. (2017). Blockchain: Staying Ahead of Tomorrow. *The Journal of Equipment Lease Financing (Online), 35*(2), 1–6.

Levin, M., & Greenwood, D. J. (2017). *Creating a New Public University and Reviving Democracy.* New York: Berghahn.

Levy, J. (2014). I love the Blockchain, just not bitcoin. *CoinDesk.* Available at: www.coindesk. com/love-blockchain-just-bitcoin/

Lia, Peng, Chenb, Luoa, & Wenc. (2018). *A Survey on the Security of Blockchain Systems.* Department of Computing, The Hong Kong Polytechnic University.

Li, C. (2013). Controlling the bullwhip effect in a supply chain system with constrained information flows. *Applied Mathematical Modelling, 37*(4), 1897–1909. doi:10.1016/j.apm.2012.04.020

Lietaer, B. (2013). *The future of money.* Random House.

Lietaer, B. A., & Dunne, J. (2013). *Rethinking money: How new currencies turn scarcity into prosperity.* Oakland, CA: Berrett-Koehler Publishers.

Li, J., & Chen, L. (2017). A survey on the security of blockchain systems. *Future Generation Computer Systems.* doi:10.1016/j.future.2017.08.020

Li, J., Greenwood, D., & Kassem, M. (2018). *Blockchain in the built environment: analysing current applications and developing an emergent framework.* Diamond Congress Ltd.

Lincoln, Y. S., & Guba, E. (1985). *Naturalistic inquiry.* Beverly Hills, CA: Sage. doi:10.1016/0147-1767(85)90062-8

Lin, I. C., & Liao, T. C. (2017). A Survey of Blockchain Security Issues and Challenges. *International Journal of Network Security, 19*(5), 653–659.

Litecoin. (n.d.). Retrieved October 26, 2018, from https://en.wikipedia.org/wiki/Litecoin

Li, Z., Kang, J., Yu, R., Ye, D., Deng, Q., & Zhang, Y. (2018). Consortium blockchain for secure energy trading in industrial internet of things. *IEEE Transactions on Industrial Informatics, 14*(8), 3690–3700.

Loeliger, J., & McCullough, M. (2012). *Version control with Git.* Sebastopol, CA: OReilly.

Lopez, C. (2015). *Trade Finance: A Catalyst for Asian Growth.* Academic Press.

Luke, D. A., Sarli, C. C., Suiter, A. M., Carothers, B. J., Combs, T. B., Allen, J. L., ... Evanoff, B. A. (2018). The translational science benefits model: A new framework for assessing the health and societal benefits of clinical and translational sciences. *Clinical and Translational Science, 11*(1), 77–84. doi:10.1111/cts.12495 PMID:28887873

Lyall, A., Mercier, P., & Gstettner, S. (2018). The death of supply chain management. *Harvard Business Review*, (June): 15.

Machanavajjhala, Kifer, Gehrke, & Venkitasubramaniam. (2007). l-diversity: Privacy beyond kanonymity. *ACM Transactions on Knowledge Discovery from Data, 1*(1), 3.

Mackay, M. E. (2015). *Solar energy: An introduction.* OUP UK. doi:10.1093/acprof:oso/9780199652105.001.0001

Mahdi, H. M., & Maaruf, A. (2018). Applications of Blockchain Technology beyond Cryptocurrency. *Annals of Emerging Technologies in Computing, 2*(1), 1–6. doi:10.33166/AETiC.2018.01.001

Mahoney, M. J. (1977). Publication prejudices: An experimental study of confirmatory bias in the peer review system. *Cognitive Therapy and Research, 1*(2), 161–175. doi:10.1007/BF01173636

Mainelli, M., & Smith, M. (2015). *Sharing ledgers for sharing economies: an exploration of mutual distributed ledgers (aka blockchain technology).* Academic Press.

Ma, J., Jiang, M., Gao, H., & Wang, Z. (2018). Blockchain for digital rights management. *Future Generation Computer Systems, 89*, 746–764. doi:10.1016/j.future.2018.07.029

Marco, L., & Karim, R. L. (2017). The Truth about Blockchain -. *Harvard Business Review*.

Mattila, J. (2016). *The blockchain phenomenon.* Berkeley Roundtable of the International Economy.

Mattila, J. (2016). *The blockchain phenomenon–the disruptive potential of distributed consensus architectures (No. 38).* The Research Institute of the Finnish Economy.

Mauro, C., Sandeep Kumar, E., Chhagan, L., & Sushmita, R. (2017). *A Survey on Security and Privacy Issues of Bitcoin.* Academic Press.

Mazieres, D. (2015). *The stellar consensus protocol: A federated model for internet-level consensus.* Stellar Development Foundation.

McMahon, W. W. (2009). *Higher learning, greater good: The private and social benefits of higher education.* Baltimore, MD: JHU Press.

McMahon, W. W. (2009). *Higher Learning, Greater Good: The Private and Social Benefits of Higher Education.* Baltimore, MD: Johns Hopkins University.

McMahon, W. W. (2015). Financing education for the public good: A new strategy. *Journal of Education Finance, 40*(4), 414–437.

McMahon, W. W., & Oketch, M. (2013). Education's effects on individual life chances and development: An overview. *British Journal of Educational Studies, 61*(1), 79–107. doi:10.1080/00071005.2012.756170

McMyn, A., & Sim, M. (2017). *R3 Reports with Hogan Lovells.* Academic Press.

Mead, W. R. (2017). The Jacksonian revolt: American populism and the liberal order. *Foreign Affairs, 96*, 2.

Meiklejohn, S., & Orlandi, C. (2015). Privacy-Enhancing Overlays in Bitcoin. In M. Brenner, N. Christin, B. Johnson, & K. Rohloff (Eds.), Lecture Notes in Computer Science: Vol. 8976. *Financial Cryptography and Data Security. FC 2015.* Berlin: Springer. doi:10.1007/978-3-662-48051-9_10

Meinel, C., Gayvoronskaya, T., & Schnjakin, M. (2018). Blockchain: Hype or Innovation. *Hasso-Plattner-Institute, Prof.-Dr.-Helmert-Straffe*, 2-3.

Mendling, J., Weber, I., Aalst, W. V. D., Brocke, J. V., Cabanillas, C., Daniel, F., ... Dustdar, S. (2018). Blockchains for business process management-challenges and opportunities. *ACM Transactions on Management Information Systems*, *9*(1), 4. doi:10.1145/3183367

Merkle, R. C. (1980, April). Protocols for public key cryptosystems. In *Security and Privacy, 1980 IEEE Symposium on* (pp. 122-122). IEEE. 10.1109/SP.1980.10006

Merton, R. K. (1968). The Matthew Effect in Science: The reward and communication systems of science are considered. *Science*, *159*(3810), 56–63. doi:10.1126cience.159.3810.56

Metcalfe, B. (2013). Metcalfe's law after 40 years of ethernet. *Computer*, *46*(12), 26–31. doi:10.1109/MC.2013.374

Mettler, M. (2016, September). Blockchain technology in healthcare: The revolution starts here. In *e-Health Networking, Applications and Services (Healthcom), 2016 IEEE 18th International Conference on* (pp. 1-3). IEEE.

Miers, I., Garman, C., Green, M., & Rubin, A. D. (2013, May). Zerocoin: Anonymous distributed e-cash from bitcoin. In *Security and Privacy (SP), 2013 IEEE Symposium on* (pp. 397-411). IEEE.

Miguel, C., & Barbara, L. (1999). Practical byzantine fault tolerance. *Proceedings of the Third Symposium on Operating Systems Design and Implementation*, 99, 173–186.

Miles, S. (2017). Stakeholder Theory Classification: A Theoretical and Empirical Evaluation of Definitions. *Journal of Business Ethics*, *142*(3), 437–459. doi:10.100710551-015-2741-y

Mingxiao, D., Xiaofeng, M., Zhe, Z., Xiangwei, W., & Qijun, C. (2017). A review on consensus algorithm of blockchain. *IEEE International Conference on Systems, Man, and Cybernetics (SMC)*, 2567-2572. 10.1109/SMC.2017.8123011

Miraz, M. H., & Ali, M. (2018, January). Applications of Blockchain Technology beyond Cryptocurrency. *International Association of Educators and Researchers*, *2*(1), 1–6.

Mitra, R. (2017, December 4). *Lightning Protocol &The Raiden Network: A Beginner's Guide.* Retrieved October 26, 2018 from https://blog.springrole.com/lightning-protocol-the-raiden-network-a-beginners-guide-c9d7bc702748

Montemayor, L., & Boersma, T. (2018). *Comprehensive Guide to Companies involved in Blockchain& Energy Blockchain Business.* Retrieved from https://ipci.io/wp-content/uploads/2017/12/Energy-Blockchain-Report.compressed.pdf

Moore, G. (2014). The nature of the firm - 75 years later. In *Reinventing the company in the digital age.* Madrid: BBVA.

Mougayar, W. (2016). *The Business Blockchain: Promise, Practice, and Application of the Next Internet Technology.* Wiley.

Mukhopadhyay, D. (2017). Cryptography: Advanced Encryption Standard (AES). Encyclopedia of Computer Science and Technology, 279.

Müller-Bloch, C., & King, J. L. (2018). Governance in the Blockchain Economy: A Framework and Research Agenda. *Journal of the Association for Information Systems, 19,* 2–36.

Mulligan, A., Hall, L., & Raphael, E. (2012). Peer review in a changing world: An international study measuring the attitudes of researchers. *Journal of the American Society for Information Science and Technology, 64*(1), 132–161. doi:10.1002/asi.22798

Nakamoto, S. (2008). *Bitcoin: A peer-to-peer electronic cash system.* Academic Press.

Nakamoto, S. (2008). *Bitcoin: A Peer-to-Peer Electronic Cash System.* Retrieved from https://bitcoin.org/bitcoin.pdf

Nakamoto, S. (2009). *Bitcoin: A Peer-to-Peer Electronic Cash System.* Available at: https://bitcoin.org/bitcoin.pdf

Nakamoto, S. (n.d.). *Bitcoin: A Peer-to-Peer Electronic Cash System.* Retrieved October 26, 2018 from https://bitcoin.org/bitcoin.pdf

Nakamoto, S. (2008). *Bitcoin: a peer-to-peer electronic cash system.* Retrieved from www.bitcoin.org

Nehaï, Z., & Guerard, G. (2017). Integration of the Blockchain in a smart grid model. In *The 14th International Conference of Young Scientists on Energy Issues (CYSENI)* (pp. 127-134). Academic Press.

Neher, C., Patterson, D., Duffield, J. W., & Harvey, A. (2017). Budgeting for the future: The long-term impacts of short-term thinking in Alabama K-12 education funding. *Journal of Education Finance, 42*(4), 448–470.

Neville, R. C. (1995). *Solar energy conversion: the solar cell.* Elsevier.

Nguyen, Q. K. (2016, November). Blockchain-a financial technology for future sustainable development. In *Green Technology and Sustainable Development (GTSD), International Conference on* (pp. 51-54). IEEE. 10.1109/GTSD.2016.22

Niya, S. R., Shupfer, F., Bocek, T., & Stiller, B. (2018). Setting up flexible and light weight trading with enhanced user privacy using smart contracts. *NOMS 2018 - 2018 IEEE/IFIP Network Operations and Management Symposium.* doi:10.1109/noms.2018.8406112

Noe, E., Longzhi, Y., Fei, C., & Yi, C. (2018). A Framework of Blockchain-based secure and privacy-preserving E-government system. *Wireless Networks,* 1-11.

Nowiński, W., & Kozma, M. (2017). How Can Blockchain Technology Disrupt the Existing Business Models? *Entrepreneurial Business and Economics Review, 5*(3), 173–188. doi:10.15678/EBER.2017.050309

Noyes. (2016). *Bitav: Fast anti-malware by distributed blockchain consensus and feedforward scanning.* arXiv preprint arXiv:1601.01405

O'Leary, D. E. (2017). Configuring blockchain architectures for transaction information in blockchain consortiums: The case of accounting and supply chain systems. *Intelligent Systems in Accounting, Finance & Management, 24*(4), 138–147. doi:10.1002/isaf.1417

Ogiela, M. R., & Majcher, M. (2018). Security of Distributed Ledger Solutions Based on Blockchain Technologies. *IEEE 32nd International Conference on Advanced Information Networking and Applications (AINA),* 1089-1095. 10.1109/AINA.2018.00156

Ølnes, S., Ubacht, J., & Janssen, M. (2017). *Blockchain in government: Benefits and implications of distributed ledger technology for information sharing.* Elsevier.

Onder, I., & Treiblmaier, H. (2018). Blockchain and tourism: Three research propositions. *Annals of Tourism Research, 72,* 180–182. doi:10.1016/j.annals.2018.03.005

Orcutt, M. (2017). *A mind-bending cryptographic trick promises to take blockchains mainstream. MIT Technology Review.*

Ovenden, J. (2017). Will blockchain render accountants irrelevant? *The Innovation Enterprise.* Retrieved from http://www.iicpa.com/articles/Will%20Blockchain%20Render%20Accountants%20Irrelevant.pdf

Pandian, D. R. (2013). An analysis of effective financial supply chain management. *International Journal of Advanced Research in Management and Social Sciences, 2,* 18.

Parham, R. (2017). *The predictable cost of Bitcoin.* Retrieved from https://papers.ssrn.com/sol3/papers.cfm?abstract_id=3080586

Parry, G. C., Brax, S. A., Maull, R. S., & Ng, I. C. L. (2016). Operationalising IoT for reverse supply: The development of use-visibility measures. *Supply Chain Management, 21*(2), 228–244. doi:10.1108/SCM-10-2015-0386

Peasnell, K. V. (1982). Some formal connections between economic values and yields and accounting numbers. *Journal of Business Finance & Accounting, 9*(3), 361–381. doi:10.1111/j.1468-5957.1982.tb01001.x

Peck, M. E. (2017). Blockchain world-Do you need a blockchain? This chart will tell you if the technology can solve your problem. *IEEE Spectrum, 54*(10), 38–60. doi:10.1109/MSPEC.2017.8048838

Peer Reviewed Medical Journals. (n.d.). Retrieved October 26, 2018 from https://www.omicsonline.org/peer-reviewed-medical-journals.php

Perez, R., & Perez, M. (2009). A fundamental look at energy reserves for the planet. *IEA SHC Solar Update.* Retrieved from http://www.asrc.cestm.albany.edu/perez/Kit/pdf/a-fundamental-lookat%20the-planetary-energy-reserves.pdf

Peters, G., Panayi, E., & Chapelle, A. (2015). Trends in crypto-currencies and blockchain technologies: A monetary theory and regulation perspective. *Online (Bergheim)*. doi:10.2139srn.2646618

Peters, M. A. (2018). The end of neoliberal globalisation and the rise of authoritarian populism. *Educational Philosophy and Theory*, 50(4), 323–325. doi:10.1080/00131857.2017.1305720

Peterson, J., & Krug, J. (2015). *Augur: a decentralized, open-source platform for prediction markets.* arXiv preprint arXiv:1501.01042

Peterson, T. (2018). Metcalfe's Law as a model for Bitcoin's value. *Alternative Investment Analyst Review*, 7(2), 9–18. doi:10.2139srn.3078248

Pike, K. L. (1967). *Language in Relation to a Unified Theory of the Structure of Human Behavior* (2nd rev. ed.). The Hague, The Netherlands: Mouton. doi:10.1515/9783111657158

Pilkington, M. (2016). 11 Blockchain technology: principles and applications. *Research handbook on digital transformations*, 225.

Porru, S., Pinna, A., Marchesi, M., & Tonelli, R. (2017, May). Blockchain-oriented software engineering: challenges and new directions. In *Proceedings of the 39th International Conference on Software Engineering Companion* (pp. 169-171). IEEE Press. 10.1109/ICSE-C.2017.142

Preston, J. D., Preston, D. A., Vance, T. M., Simpson, B. C., Madakson, P. A., & Rieger, W. R. (2018). *Systems and methods for using smart contracts to control the trade, supply, manufacture, and distribution of commodities.* US Patent App. 15/675,697.

PwC. (2018). *How blockchain technology could improve the tax system.* Retrieved from https://www.pwc.co.uk/issues/futuretax/how-blockchain-technology-could-improve-tax-system.html

Ramayah, T., & Omar, R. (2010). Information exchange and supply chain performance. *International Journal of Information Technology & Decision Making*, 9(1), 35–52. doi:10.1142/S0219622010003658

Rathnayaka, A. J. D., Potdar, V. M., & Kuruppu, S. J. (2012). Design of smart grid prosumer communities via online social networking communities. *International Journal for Infonomics*, 5(1/2), 544–556. doi:10.20533/iji.1742.4712.2012.0062

Ratnasamy, S., Francis, P., Handley, M., Karp, R., & Schenker, S. (2001). A scalable content-addressable network. *Proceedings of the 2001 Conference on Applications, Technologies, Architectures, and Protocols for Computer Communications - SIGCOMM 01*. doi:10.1145/383059.383072

Reed, D. P. (2001). The law of the pack. *Harvard Business Review*, 79(2), 23. PMID:11213694

Reheul, A.-M., Van Caneghem, T., & Verbruggen, S. (2014). Financial reporting lags in the non-profit sector: An empirical analysis. *Voluntas*, 25(2), 352–377. doi:10.100711266-012-9344-3

Reid, F., & Harrigan, M. (2013). An analysis of anonymity in the bitcoin system. In *Security and privacy in social networks* (pp. 197–223). New York, NY: Springer. doi:10.1007/978-1-4614-4139-7_10

Reiss, D. (2017). *What You Should Know About Dividend Reinvestment Plans.* Academic Press.

Reiss, D. (2017, January 12). What you should know about dividend reinvestment plans. *U.S. News & World Report*. Retrieved from https://money.usnews.com/investing/articles/2017-01-12/what-you-should-know-about-dividend-reinvestment-plans

Richardson, L. & Amundsen, M. (2013). *RESTful Web APIs: Services for a Changing World*. O'Reilly Press.

Rickman, D. S., & Wang, H. (2018). Two tales of two US states: Regional fiscal austerity and economic performance. *Regional Science and Urban Economics*, *68*, 46–55. doi:10.1016/j.regsciurbeco.2017.10.008

Roger, J., & Baum, R. C. (2017). Student loans: This economic bubble will wreak havoc when it bursts. *Fortune*. Retrieved from http://fortune.com/2017/07/10/higher-education-student-loans-economic-bubble-federal//

Roth, W. M. (2010). *Language, learning, context: Talking the talk*. Routledge. doi:10.4324/9780203853177

Rowland, F. (2002). The peer-review process. *Learned Publishing*, *15*(4), 247–258. doi:10.1087/095315102760319206

Saarikko, T., Westergren, U. H., & Blomquist, T. (2017). The Internet of Things: Are you ready for what's coming? *Business Horizons*, *60*(5), 667–676. doi:10.1016/j.bushor.2017.05.010

Saberi, S., Kouhizadeh, M., Sarkis, J., & Shen, L. (2018). Blockchain technology and its relationships to sustainable supply chain management. *International Journal of Production Research*, 1–19.

Salman, A., & Razzaq, M. G. A. (2018). Bitcoin and the World of Digital Currencies. In *Financial Management from an Emerging Market Perspective*. InTech. doi:10.5772/intechopen.71294

Salman, T., Zolanvari, M., Erbad, A., Jain, R., & Samaka, M. (2016). Security Services Using Blockchains: A State-of-the-Art Survey. *IEEE Communications Surveys and Tutorials*.

Samaniego, M., & Deters, R. (2016, December). Blockchain as a Service for IoT. In *Internet of Things (iThings) and IEEE Green Computing and Communications (GreenCom) and IEEE Cyber, Physical and Social Computing (CPSCom) and IEEE Smart Data (SmartData), 2016 IEEE International Conference on* (pp. 433-436). IEEE. 10.1109/iThings-GreenCom-CPSCom-SmartData.2016.102

Sandi, R., & Kyung-Hyune, R. (2018). Blockchain Technology for providing an architecture model of decentralized personal health information. *International Journal of Engineering Business Management*, *10*, 1–12.

Sankar, L. S., Sindhu, M., & Sethumadhavan, M. (2017). Survey of consensus protocols on blockchain applications. *4th International Conference on Advanced Computing and Communication Systems (ICACCS)*, 1-5. 10.1109/ICACCS.2017.8014672

Schmitt, A. J., Sun, S. A., Snyder, L. V., & Shen, Z.-J. M. (2015). Centralization versus decentralization: Risk pooling, risk diversification, and supply chain disruptions. *Omega*, *52*, 201–212. doi:10.1016/j.omega.2014.06.002

Schwartz, D., Youngs, N., & Britto, A. (2014). *The Ripple Protocol Consensus Algorithm.* Retrieved October 26, 2018, from https://ripple.com/files/ripple_consensus_whitepaper.pdf

Schwartz, Youngs, & Britto. (2014). *The ripple protocol consensus algorithm.* Ripple Labs Inc White Paper.

Scott, S. V., & Zachariadis, M. (2014). SWIFT. Routledge Press.

Selingo, J. J. (2013). *College (un) bound: The future of higher education and what it means for students.* Boston, MA: Houghton Mifflin Harcourt.

Shankararaman, V., & Megargel, A. (2013). Enterprise Integration: Architectural Approaches". 01/2013. In *Service-driven Approaches to Architecture and Enterprise Integration.* Hershey, PA: Information Science Reference.

Sharp, D. W. (1990). What Can and Should Be Done to Reduce Publication Bias? *Journal of the American Medical Association, 263*(10), 1390. doi:10.1001/jama.1990.03440100102015 PMID:2304218

Sharples, M., & Domingue, J. (2015). The blockchain and kudos: A distributed system for educational record, reputation and reward. *Proceedings of 11th European Conference on Technology Enhanced Learning (EC-TEL 2015),* 490–496.

Shema, H. (2014, April 19). *The Birth of Modern Peer Review.* Retrieved October 26, 2018 from https://blogs.scientificamerican.com/information-culture/the-birth-of-modern-peer-review/

Shore, C. (2008). Audit culture and illiberal governance: Universities and the politics of accountability. *Anthropological Theory, 8*(3), 278–298. doi:10.1177/1463499608093815

Singhal, B., Dhameja, G., & Panda, P. S. 2018. Blockchain Application Development. In Beginning Blockchain (pp. 267-317). Springer. doi:10.1007/978-1-4842-3444-0_5

Singh, S., & Singh, N. (2016*).* Blockchain: Future of financial and cyber security. *2nd International Conference on Contemporary Computing and Informatics (IC3I),* 463-467. 10.1109/IC3I.2016.7918009

Skybakmoe, T. (2011). *What MFT Is, and How It Applies to You. Gartner Report, June 2011, ID G00214111.* Gartner.

Sompolinsky, Y., & Zohar, A. (2015). Secure high-rate transaction processing in bitcoin. *Financial Cryptography and Data Security – 19th International Conference,* 507-527. 10.1007/978-3-662-47854-7_32

Spier, R. (2002). The history of the peer-review process. *Trends in Biotechnology, 20*(8), 357–358. doi:10.1016/S0167-7799(02)01985-6 PMID:12127284

Steijvers, T., & Voordeckers, W. (2009). Collateral and credit rationing: A review of recent empirical studies as a guide for future research. *Journal of Economic Surveys, 23*(5), 924–946. doi:10.1111/j.1467-6419.2009.00587.x

Stoney, C., & Winstanley, D. (2001). Stakeholding: Confusion or Utopia? Mapping the conceptual terrain. *Journal of Management Studies, 38*(5), 603–626. doi:10.1111/1467-6486.00251

Stout, L. (2003). On the proper motives of corporate directors (or why you don't want to invite homo economicus to join your board). *Delaware Journal of Corporate Law, 28*(1).

Stoye, E. (2017, June 19). *Studies flag signs of gender bias in peer review.* Retrieved October 26, 2018 from https://www.chemistryworld.com/news/studies-flag-signs-of-gender-bias-in-peer-review/3007593. article

Summers, R. (2017). *The Everything Bubble: The Endgame for Central Bank Policy.* Random.

Sundaram, S., Schwarz, A., Jones, E., & Chin, W. W. (2007). Technology use on the front line: How information technology enhances individual performance. *Journal of the Academy of Marketing Science, 35*(1), 101–112. doi:10.100711747-006-0010-4

Sun, Q., Ge, X., Liu, L., Xu, X., Zhang, Y., Niu, R., & Zeng, Y. (2011). Review of smart grid comprehensive assessment systems. *Energy Procedia, 12*, 219–229. doi:10.1016/j.egypro.2011.10.031

Supriya, T. A., & Kulkarani, V. (2017). Blockchain and Its Applications – A Detailed Survey. *International Journal of Computers and Applications, 180*(3), 29–35. doi:10.5120/ijca2017915994

Swaminathan, G., & Umashankar, S. (2012, November). Influence of Solar Power in Smart Grids. *Energetica India Magazine*, 52-53.

Swan, M. (2015). *Blockchain: Blueprint for a new economy.* O'Reilly Media, Inc.

Swan, M. (2017). Anticipating the Economic Benefits of Blockchain. *Technology Innovation Management Review, 7*(10), 6–13. doi:10.22215/timreview/1109

Szabo, N. (1996). *Smart Contracts: Building Blocks for Digital Markets.* Retrieved October 26, 2018, from http://www.fon.hum.uva.nl/rob/Courses/InformationInSpeech/CDROM/Literature/LOTwinterschool2006/szabo.best.vwh.net/smart_contracts_2.html

Szabo, N. (2005). *Secure Property Titles with Owner Authority.* Available at: http://szabo.best.vwh.net/securetitle.html

Tabak, J. (2009). *Solar and geothermal energy.* Infobase Publishing.

Taleb, N. N. (2018). Foreword. In S. Ammous (Ed.), *The Bitcoin Standard: The Decentralized Alternative to Central Banking.* Hoboken, NJ: Wiley.

Tan, B. S., & Low, K. Y. (2017). Bitcoin – Its Economics for Financial Reporting. *Australian Accounting Review, 27*(2), 220–227. doi:10.1111/auar.12167

Tapscott, A., & Tapscott, D. (2017). How blockchain is changing finance. *Harvard Business Review*, 1.

Tapscott, D., & Tapscott, A. (2016). *Blockchain revolution how the technology behind Bitcoin is changing money, business and the world.* Portfolio/Penguin.

Tasatanattakool, P., & Techapanupreeda, C. (2018). Blockchain: Challenges and applications. *International Conference on Information Networking (ICOIN)*, 473-475.

Tasca, P., Aste, T., Pelizzon, L., & Perony, N. (Eds.), *Banking Beyond Banks and Money. New Economic Windows*. Cham: Springer.

Tayeb, S. (2018). *Blockchain Technology: Between High Hopes and Challenging Implications*. Academic Press.

Taylor, B. (2018). Triple-Entry Accounting And Blockchain: A Common Misconception. *Forbes*. Available at: https://www.forbes.com/sites/forbesfinancecouncil/2017/11/28/triple-entry-accounting-and-blockchain-a-common-misconception/#47b1820c190f

Teece, D. J. (2010). Business models, business strategy and innovation. *Long Range Planning*, *43*(2-3), 172–194. doi:10.1016/j.lrp.2009.07.003

Tenorio-Fornés, A., Hassan, S., & Pavón, J. (2018). Open Peer-to-Peer Systems over Blockchain and IPFS. *Proceedings of the 1st Workshop on Cryptocurrencies and Blockchains for Distributed Systems - CryBlock18*. 10.1145/3211933.3211937

The Belmont Report (1979). Retrieved from https://www.hhs.gov/ohrp/regulations-and-policy/belmont-report/read-the-belmont-report/index.html

The Linux Foundation. (2015, December 17). *Linux Foundation Unites Industry Leaders to Advance BlockchainTechnology* [Press release]. Retrieved October 26, 2018 from https://www.linuxfoundation.org/press-release/2015/12/linux-foundation-unites-industry-leaders-to-advance-blockchain-technology/

The National Task Force. (2012). A crucible moment: College learning and democracy's future. Washington, DC: Association of American Colleges and Universities (AAC&U).

The Pew Charitable Trusts. (2015, June 11). *Federal and state funding of higher education: A changing landscape*. Retrieved from http://www.pewtrusts.org/en/research-and-analysis/issue-briefs/2015/06/federal-and-state-funding-of-higher-education

Thelin, J. R. (2011). *A history of American higher education*. Baltimore, MD: JHU Press.

Thomas, L., Long, C., Burnap, P., Wu, J., & Jenkins, N. (2017). Automation of the supplier role in the GB power system using blockchain-based smart contracts. *CIRED - Open Access Proceedings Journal*, *2017*(1), 2619-2623. doi:10.1049/oap-cired.2017.0987

Thomson Reuters. (2018). *Thomson Reuters Knowledge Direct API*. Retrieved from https://financial.thomsonreuters.com/content/dam/openweb/documents/pdf/financial/knowledge-direct-digital-solutions.pdf

Tobin, K. (2010). Tuning in to others' voices: Beyond the hegemony of mono-logical narratives. value. *Applied Economics Letters*, *26*(7), 554–560.

Tosh, D. K., Shetty, S., Liang, X., Kamhoua, C., & Njilla, L. (2017). Consensus protocols for blockchain-based data provenance: Challenges and opportunities. *IEEE 8th Annual Ubiquitous Computing, Electronics and Mobile Communication Conference (UEMCON)*, 469-474.

Trapero, J. R., Kourentzes, N., & Fildes, R. (2012). Impact of information exchange on supplier forecasting performance. *Omega*, *40*(6), 738–747. doi:10.1016/j.omega.2011.08.009

Treiblmaier, H. (2018). The impact of the blockchain on the supply chain: A theory-based research framework and a call for action. *Supply Chain Management*, *23*(6), 545–559. doi:10.1108/SCM-01-2018-0029

Tschorsch, F., & Scheuermann, B. (2016). Bitcoin and beyond: A technical survey on decentralized digital currencies. *IEEE Communications Surveys and Tutorials*, *18*(3), 2084–2123. doi:10.1109/COMST.2016.2535718

Turk & Klinc. (2017). Potentials of Blockchain Technology for Construction Management. *Procedia Engineering*, *196*, 638-645.

Turrisi, M., Bruccoleri, M., & Cannella, S. (2013). Impact of reverse logistics on supply chain performance. *International Journal of Physical Distribution & Logistics Management*, *43*(7), 564–585. doi:10.1108/IJPDLM-04-2012-0132

UN. (2018). *Report of the World Commission on Environment and Development: Our Common Future.* Retrieved from http://www.un-documents.net/wced-ocf.htm

Underwood, S. (2016). Blockchain beyond bitcoin. *Communications of the ACM*, *59*(11), 15–17. doi:10.1145/2994581

Valenta, L., & Rowan, B. (2015). Blindcoin: Blinded, Accountable Mixes for Bitcoin. In M. Brenner, N. Christin, B. Johnson, & K. Rohloff (Eds.), Lecture Notes in Computer Science: Vol. 8976. *Financial Cryptography and Data Security. FC 2015.* Berlin: Springer. doi:10.1007/978-3-662-48051-9_9

Van Slyke, M. (2006). Agents or stewards: Using theory to understand the government nonprofit social service contracting relationship. *Journal of Public Administration: Research and Theory*, *17*(2), 157–187. doi:10.1093/jopart/mul012

Van Vliet, B. (2018). (Forthcoming). An Alternative Model of Metcalfe's Law for Valuing Bitcoin. *Economics Letters.* doi:10.2139srn.3087398

Veuger, J. (2018). Trust in a viable real estate economy with disruption and blockchain. *Facilities*, *36*(1/2), 103–120. doi:10.1108/F-11-2017-0106

Vijayapriya, T., & Kothari, D. P. (2011). Smart grid: An overview. *Smart Grid and Renewable Energy*, *2*(04), 305–311. doi:10.4236gre.2011.24035

Vilanova, L. (2007). Neither Shareholder nor Stakeholder Management: What Happens When Firms are Run for their Short-term Salient Stakeholder? *European Management Journal*, *25*(2), 146–162. doi:10.1016/j.emj.2007.01.002

Vovchenko, N. G., Andreeva, A. V., Orobinskiy, A. S., & Filippov, Y. M. (2017). Competitive Advantages of Financial Transactions on the Basis of the Blockchain Technology in Digital Economy. *European Research Studies*, *XX*(3), 193–212.

Vukoli'c, M. (2015). The quest for scalable blockchain fabric: Proof-of-work vs. bft replication. *International Workshop on Open Problems in Network Security*, 112–125.

Wall, F., & Greiling, D. (2011). Accounting information for managerial decision-making in shareholder management versus stakeholder management. *Review of Managerial Science*, 5(2-3), 91–135. doi:10.100711846-011-0063-8

Walther, T., Klein, T., & Thu, H. P. (2018). Bitcoin is not the new gold: A comparison of volatility, correlation, and portfolio performance. *International Review of Financial Analysis*, 59, 105–116. doi:10.1016/j.irfa.2018.07.010

Wang, P., Liu, X., Chen, J., Zhan, Y., & Jin, Z. (2018). QoS-aware service composition using blockchain-based smart contracts. In *Proceedings of the 40th International Conference on Software Engineering: Companion Proceeedings* (pp. 296-297). ACM. 10.1145/3183440.3194978

Wang, R., Lin, Z., & Luo, H. (2018). Blockchain, bank credit and SME financing. *Quality & Quantity*, 1–14.

Wang, Y., Cai, S., Lin, C., Chen, Z., Wang, T., Gao, Z., & Zhou, C. (2019). Study of Blockchains's Consensus Mechanism Based on Credit. *IEEE Access: Practical Innovations, Open Solutions*, 7, 10224–10231. doi:10.1109/ACCESS.2019.2891065

Wasfi, M. (2011, February). Solar Energy and Photovoltaic Systems. *Cyber Journals: Journal of Selected Areas in Renewable and Sustainable Energy*, 1(2), 1–8.

Watts, R., & Zimmerman, J. (1976). *Positive accounting theory*. Englewood Cliffs, NJ: Prentice Hall.

Wild, J., Arnold, M., & Stafford, P. (2015). Technology: banks seek the key to blockchain. *Financial Times*. Available at: http://on.ft.com/1NiyWWs

Winters, J. V. (2013b, December). *STEM graduates, human capital externalities, wages in the US*. IZA Discussion Paper No. 7830. Retrieved from http://ftp.iza.org/dp7830.pdf

Winters, J. V. (2013a). Human capital externalities and employment differences across metropolitan areas of the USA. *Journal of Economic Geography*, 13(5), 799–822. doi:10.1093/jeg/lbs046

Wood, G. (2014). *ETHEREUM: A Secure Decentralized Generalized Transaction Ledger EIP-150 REVISION*. Retrieved October 26, 2018, from https://gavwood.com/paper.pdf

Wood, G. (2014). *Ethereum: A secure decentralisedgeneralised transaction ledger*. Ethereum Project Yellow Paper.

Woodside, J. M., Augustine, F. K. Jr, & Giberson, W. (2017). Blockchain technology adoption status and strategies. *Journal of International Technology and Information Management*, 26(2), 65–93.

Wright, A., & De Filippi, P. (2015). *Decentralized blockchain technology and the rise of lexcryptographia*. Academic Press.

Wu, H., & Wang, F. (2014). A Survey of Noninteractive Zero Knowledge Proof System and Its Applications. *The Scientific World Journal*. PMID:24883407

Wust, K., & Gervais, A. (2017). Do you need a Blockchain? *IACR Cryptology ePrint Archive, 2017*, 375.

Xiarchos, I. M., & Vick, B. (2011). *Solar energy use in US agriculture: Overview and policy issues*. US Department of Agriculture, Office of the Chief Economist, Office of Energy Policy and New Uses.

Xu, X., Pautasso, C., Zhu, L., Gramoli, V., Ponomarev, A., Tran, A. B., & Chen, S. (2016). The blockchain as a software connector. In *2016 13th Working IEEE/IFIP Conference on Software Architecture (WICSA)* (pp. 182-191). IEEE. 10.1109/WICSA.2016.21

Xu, L., Chen, L., Gao, Z., Xu, S., & Shi, W. (2018). Efficient Public Blockchain Client for Lightweight Users. *EAI Endorsed Transactions on Security and Safety, 4*(13), 1–8.

Yeo, G. (2013). Trust and context in cyberspace. *Architectural Record, 34*(2), 214–234. doi:10.1080/23257962.2013.825207

Yermack, D. (2015). Is Bitcoin a real currency? An economic appraisal. In Handbook of digital currency. Academic Press. doi:10.1016/B978-0-12-802117-0.00002-3

Yermack, D. (2017). Corporate governance and blockchains. *Review of Finance, 21*, 7–31.

Yli-Huumo, J., Ko, D., Choi, S., Park, S., & Smolander, K. (2016). Where is current research on blockchain technology? A systematic review. *PLoS One, 11*(10), e0163477. doi:10.1371/journal.pone.0163477 PMID:27695049

Yoon, K., Hoogduin, L., & Zhang, L. (2015). Big Data as complementary audit evidence. *Accounting Horizons, 29*(2), 431–438. doi:10.2308/acch-51076

Young, J. (2016, September 24). *IPFS Protocol Selects Ethereum Over Bitcoin, Prefers Ethereum Dev Community*. Retrieved October 27, 2018, from https://cointelegraph.com/news/ipfs-protocol-selects-ethereum-over-bitcoin-prefers-ethereum-dev-community

Young, S. (2018). Changing Governance Models by Applying Blockchain Computing. *Catholic University Journal of Law and Technology, 26*, 4.

Yuan, Y., & Wang, F. (2018). Blockchain and Cryptocurrencies: Model, Techniques, and Applications. *IEEE Transactions on Systems, Man, and Cybernetics. Systems, 48*(9), 1421–1428. doi:10.1109/TSMC.2018.2854904

Yves-Alexandre, D. M., C'esar A Hidalgo, M. V., & Vincent, D. (2013). Unique in the crowd: The privacy bounds of human mobility. *Scientific Reports*.

Zalan, T. (2018). Born global on blockchain. *Review of International Business and Strategy, 28*(1), 19–34. doi:10.1108/RIBS-08-2017-0069

Zhang, P., Walker, M. A., White, J., Schmidt, D. C., & Lenz, G. (2017). Metrics for assessing blockchain-based healthcare decentralized apps. *2017 IEEE 19th International Conference on E-Health Networking, Applications and Services (Healthcom)*. doi:10.1109/healthcom.2017.8210842

Zhang, Y., & Wen, J. (2015). An iot electric business model based on the protocol of bitcoin. *Proceedings of 18th International Conference on Intelligence in Next Generation Networks (ICIN)*, 184–191. 10.1109/ICIN.2015.7073830

Zhao, J. L., Fan, S., & Yan, J. (2016). Overview of business innovations and research opportunities in blockchain and introduction to the special issue. *Financial Innovation*, *2*(1), 28. doi:10.118640854-016-0049-2

Zheng, Z., Xie, S., Dai, H. N., & Wang, H. (2017). An Overview of Blockchain Technology: Architecture, Consensus, and Future Trends. *IEEE 6th International Congress on Big Data Congress*.

Zheng, Z., Xie, S., Dai, H., Chen, X., & Wang, H. (2017). An Overview of Blockchain Technology: Architecture, Consensus, and Future Trends. *IEEE International Congress on Big Data (BigData Congress)*, 557-564.

Zheng, Z., Xie, S., Dai, H., Chen, X., & Wang, H. (2017, June). An overview of blockchain technology: Architecture, consensus, and future trends. In *Big Data (BigData Congress), 2017 IEEE International Congress on* (pp. 557-564). IEEE.

Zheng, Z., Xie, S., Dai, H. N., & Wang, H. (2016). Blockchain challenges and opportunities: A survey. *Work Pap*.

Zheng, Z., Xie, S., Dai, H. N., & Wang, H. (2018). Blockchain challenges and opportunities: A Survey. *International Journal of Web and Grid Services*, *14*(4), 352–375. doi:10.1504/IJWGS.2018.095647

Zhu, H., & Zhou, Z. Z. (2016). Analysis and outlook of applications of blockchain technology to equity crowdfunding in China. *Financial Innovation*, *2*(1), 29. doi:10.118640854-016-0044-7

Zook, M. A., & Blankenship, J. (2018). New spaces of disruption? The failures of Bitcoin and the rhetorical power of algorithmic governance. *Geoforum*, *96*, 248–255. doi:10.1016/j.geoforum.2018.08.023

Related References

To continue our tradition of advancing information science and technology research, we have compiled a list of recommended IGI Global readings. These references will provide additional information and guidance to further enrich your knowledge and assist you with your own research and future publications.

Aasi, P., Rusu, L., & Vieru, D. (2017). The Role of Culture in IT Governance Five Focus Areas: A Literature Review. *International Journal of IT/Business Alignment and Governance, 8*(2), 42-61. doi:10.4018/IJITBAG.2017070103

Abdrabo, A. A. (2018). Egypt's Knowledge-Based Development: Opportunities, Challenges, and Future Possibilities. In A. Alraouf (Ed.), *Knowledge-Based Urban Development in the Middle East* (pp. 80–101). Hershey, PA: IGI Global. doi:10.4018/978-1-5225-3734-2.ch005

Abu Doush, I., & Alhami, I. (2018). Evaluating the Accessibility of Computer Laboratories, Libraries, and Websites in Jordanian Universities and Colleges. *International Journal of Information Systems and Social Change, 9*(2), 44–60. doi:10.4018/IJISSC.2018040104

Adeboye, A. (2016). Perceived Use and Acceptance of Cloud Enterprise Resource Planning (ERP) Implementation in the Manufacturing Industries. *International Journal of Strategic Information Technology and Applications, 7*(3), 24–40. doi:10.4018/IJSITA.2016070102

Adegbore, A. M., Quadri, M. O., & Oyewo, O. R. (2018). A Theoretical Approach to the Adoption of Electronic Resource Management Systems (ERMS) in Nigerian University Libraries. In A. Tella & T. Kwanya (Eds.), *Handbook of Research on Managing Intellectual Property in Digital Libraries* (pp. 292–311). Hershey, PA: IGI Global. doi:10.4018/978-1-5225-3093-0.ch015

Adhikari, M., & Roy, D. (2016). Green Computing. In G. Deka, G. Siddesh, K. Srinivasa, & L. Patnaik (Eds.), *Emerging Research Surrounding Power Consumption and Performance Issues in Utility Computing* (pp. 84–108). Hershey, PA: IGI Global. doi:10.4018/978-1-4666-8853-7.ch005

Afolabi, O. A. (2018). Myths and Challenges of Building an Effective Digital Library in Developing Nations: An African Perspective. In A. Tella & T. Kwanya (Eds.), *Handbook of Research on Managing Intellectual Property in Digital Libraries* (pp. 51–79). Hershey, PA: IGI Global. doi:10.4018/978-1-5225-3093-0.ch004

Agarwal, R., Singh, A., & Sen, S. (2016). Role of Molecular Docking in Computer-Aided Drug Design and Development. In S. Dastmalchi, M. Hamzeh-Mivehroud, & B. Sokouti (Eds.), *Applied Case Studies and Solutions in Molecular Docking-Based Drug Design* (pp. 1–28). Hershey, PA: IGI Global. doi:10.4018/978-1-5225-0362-0.ch001

Ali, O., & Soar, J. (2016). Technology Innovation Adoption Theories. In L. Al-Hakim, X. Wu, A. Koronios, & Y. Shou (Eds.), *Handbook of Research on Driving Competitive Advantage through Sustainable, Lean, and Disruptive Innovation* (pp. 1–38). Hershey, PA: IGI Global. doi:10.4018/978-1-5225-0135-0.ch001

Alsharo, M. (2017). Attitudes Towards Cloud Computing Adoption in Emerging Economies. *International Journal of Cloud Applications and Computing*, 7(3), 44–58. doi:10.4018/IJCAC.2017070102

Amer, T. S., & Johnson, T. L. (2016). Information Technology Progress Indicators: Temporal Expectancy, User Preference, and the Perception of Process Duration. *International Journal of Technology and Human Interaction*, 12(4), 1–14. doi:10.4018/IJTHI.2016100101

Amer, T. S., & Johnson, T. L. (2017). Information Technology Progress Indicators: Research Employing Psychological Frameworks. In A. Mesquita (Ed.), *Research Paradigms and Contemporary Perspectives on Human-Technology Interaction* (pp. 168–186). Hershey, PA: IGI Global. doi:10.4018/978-1-5225-1868-6.ch008

Anchugam, C. V., & Thangadurai, K. (2016). Introduction to Network Security. In D. G., M. Singh, & M. Jayanthi (Eds.), Network Security Attacks and Countermeasures (pp. 1-48). Hershey, PA: IGI Global. doi:10.4018/978-1-4666-8761-5.ch001

Anchugam, C. V., & Thangadurai, K. (2016). Classification of Network Attacks and Countermeasures of Different Attacks. In D. G., M. Singh, & M. Jayanthi (Eds.), Network Security Attacks and Countermeasures (pp. 115-156). Hershey, PA: IGI Global. doi:10.4018/978-1-4666-8761-5.ch004

Anohah, E. (2016). Pedagogy and Design of Online Learning Environment in Computer Science Education for High Schools. *International Journal of Online Pedagogy and Course Design*, 6(3), 39–51. doi:10.4018/IJOPCD.2016070104

Anohah, E. (2017). Paradigm and Architecture of Computing Augmented Learning Management System for Computer Science Education. *International Journal of Online Pedagogy and Course Design*, 7(2), 60–70. doi:10.4018/IJOPCD.2017040105

Anohah, E., & Suhonen, J. (2017). Trends of Mobile Learning in Computing Education from 2006 to 2014: A Systematic Review of Research Publications. *International Journal of Mobile and Blended Learning*, 9(1), 16–33. doi:10.4018/IJMBL.2017010102

Assis-Hassid, S., Heart, T., Reychav, I., & Pliskin, J. S. (2016). Modelling Factors Affecting Patient-Doctor-Computer Communication in Primary Care. *International Journal of Reliable and Quality E-Healthcare*, 5(1), 1–17. doi:10.4018/IJRQEH.2016010101

Bailey, E. K. (2017). Applying Learning Theories to Computer Technology Supported Instruction. In M. Grassetti & S. Brookby (Eds.), *Advancing Next-Generation Teacher Education through Digital Tools and Applications* (pp. 61–81). Hershey, PA: IGI Global. doi:10.4018/978-1-5225-0965-3.ch004

Balasubramanian, K. (2016). Attacks on Online Banking and Commerce. In K. Balasubramanian, K. Mala, & M. Rajakani (Eds.), *Cryptographic Solutions for Secure Online Banking and Commerce* (pp. 1–19). Hershey, PA: IGI Global. doi:10.4018/978-1-5225-0273-9.ch001

Baldwin, S., Opoku-Agyemang, K., & Roy, D. (2016). Games People Play: A Trilateral Collaboration Researching Computer Gaming across Cultures. In K. Valentine & L. Jensen (Eds.), *Examining the Evolution of Gaming and Its Impact on Social, Cultural, and Political Perspectives* (pp. 364–376). Hershey, PA: IGI Global. doi:10.4018/978-1-5225-0261-6.ch017

Banerjee, S., Sing, T. Y., Chowdhury, A. R., & Anwar, H. (2018). Let's Go Green: Towards a Taxonomy of Green Computing Enablers for Business Sustainability. In M. Khosrow-Pour (Ed.), *Green Computing Strategies for Competitive Advantage and Business Sustainability* (pp. 89–109). Hershey, PA: IGI Global. doi:10.4018/978-1-5225-5017-4.ch005

Basham, R. (2018). Information Science and Technology in Crisis Response and Management. In M. Khosrow-Pour, D.B.A. (Ed.), Encyclopedia of Information Science and Technology, Fourth Edition (pp. 1407-1418). Hershey, PA: IGI Global. doi:10.4018/978-1-5225-2255-3.ch121

Batyashe, T., & Iyamu, T. (2018). Architectural Framework for the Implementation of Information Technology Governance in Organisations. In M. Khosrow-Pour, D.B.A. (Ed.), Encyclopedia of Information Science and Technology, Fourth Edition (pp. 810-819). Hershey, PA: IGI Global. doi:10.4018/978-1-5225-2255-3.ch070

Bekleyen, N., & Çelik, S. (2017). Attitudes of Adult EFL Learners towards Preparing for a Language Test via CALL. In D. Tafazoli & M. Romero (Eds.), *Multiculturalism and Technology-Enhanced Language Learning* (pp. 214–229). Hershey, PA: IGI Global. doi:10.4018/978-1-5225-1882-2.ch013

Bennett, A., Eglash, R., Lachney, M., & Babbitt, W. (2016). Design Agency: Diversifying Computer Science at the Intersections of Creativity and Culture. In M. Raisinghani (Ed.), *Revolutionizing Education through Web-Based Instruction* (pp. 35–56). Hershey, PA: IGI Global. doi:10.4018/978-1-4666-9932-8.ch003

Bergeron, F., Croteau, A., Uwizeyemungu, S., & Raymond, L. (2017). A Framework for Research on Information Technology Governance in SMEs. In S. De Haes & W. Van Grembergen (Eds.), *Strategic IT Governance and Alignment in Business Settings* (pp. 53–81). Hershey, PA: IGI Global. doi:10.4018/978-1-5225-0861-8.ch003

Bhatt, G. D., Wang, Z., & Rodger, J. A. (2017). Information Systems Capabilities and Their Effects on Competitive Advantages: A Study of Chinese Companies. *Information Resources Management Journal*, *30*(3), 41–57. doi:10.4018/IRMJ.2017070103

Bogdanoski, M., Stoilkovski, M., & Risteski, A. (2016). Novel First Responder Digital Forensics Tool as a Support to Law Enforcement. In M. Hadji-Janev & M. Bogdanoski (Eds.), *Handbook of Research on Civil Society and National Security in the Era of Cyber Warfare* (pp. 352–376). Hershey, PA: IGI Global. doi:10.4018/978-1-4666-8793-6.ch016

Boontarig, W., Papasratorn, B., & Chutimaskul, W. (2016). The Unified Model for Acceptance and Use of Health Information on Online Social Networks: Evidence from Thailand. *International Journal of E-Health and Medical Communications*, 7(1), 31–47. doi:10.4018/IJEHMC.2016010102

Brown, S., & Yuan, X. (2016). Techniques for Retaining Computer Science Students at Historical Black Colleges and Universities. In C. Prince & R. Ford (Eds.), *Setting a New Agenda for Student Engagement and Retention in Historically Black Colleges and Universities* (pp. 251–268). Hershey, PA: IGI Global. doi:10.4018/978-1-5225-0308-8.ch014

Burcoff, A., & Shamir, L. (2017). Computer Analysis of Pablo Picasso's Artistic Style. *International Journal of Art, Culture and Design Technologies*, 6(1), 1–18. doi:10.4018/IJACDT.2017010101

Byker, E. J. (2017). I Play I Learn: Introducing Technological Play Theory. In C. Martin & D. Polly (Eds.), *Handbook of Research on Teacher Education and Professional Development* (pp. 297–306). Hershey, PA: IGI Global. doi:10.4018/978-1-5225-1067-3.ch016

Calongne, C. M., Stricker, A. G., Truman, B., & Arenas, F. J. (2017). Cognitive Apprenticeship and Computer Science Education in Cyberspace: Reimagining the Past. In A. Stricker, C. Calongne, B. Truman, & F. Arenas (Eds.), *Integrating an Awareness of Selfhood and Society into Virtual Learning* (pp. 180–197). Hershey, PA: IGI Global. doi:10.4018/978-1-5225-2182-2.ch013

Carlton, E. L., Holsinger, J. W. Jr, & Anunobi, N. (2016). Physician Engagement with Health Information Technology: Implications for Practice and Professionalism. *International Journal of Computers in Clinical Practice*, 1(2), 51–73. doi:10.4018/IJCCP.2016070103

Carneiro, A. D. (2017). Defending Information Networks in Cyberspace: Some Notes on Security Needs. In M. Dawson, D. Kisku, P. Gupta, J. Sing, & W. Li (Eds.), Developing Next-Generation Countermeasures for Homeland Security Threat Prevention (pp. 354-375). Hershey, PA: IGI Global. doi:10.4018/978-1-5225-0703-1.ch016

Cavalcanti, J. C. (2016). The New "ABC" of ICTs (Analytics + Big Data + Cloud Computing): A Complex Trade-Off between IT and CT Costs. In J. Martins & A. Molnar (Eds.), *Handbook of Research on Innovations in Information Retrieval, Analysis, and Management* (pp. 152–186). Hershey, PA: IGI Global. doi:10.4018/978-1-4666-8833-9.ch006

Chase, J. P., & Yan, Z. (2017). Affect in Statistics Cognition. In *Assessing and Measuring Statistics Cognition in Higher Education Online Environments: Emerging Research and Opportunities* (pp. 144–187). Hershey, PA: IGI Global. doi:10.4018/978-1-5225-2420-5.ch005

Chen, C. (2016). Effective Learning Strategies for the 21st Century: Implications for the E-Learning. In M. Anderson & C. Gavan (Eds.), *Developing Effective Educational Experiences through Learning Analytics* (pp. 143–169). Hershey, PA: IGI Global. doi:10.4018/978-1-4666-9983-0.ch006

Chen, E. T. (2016). Examining the Influence of Information Technology on Modern Health Care. In P. Manolitzas, E. Grigoroudis, N. Matsatsinis, & D. Yannacopoulos (Eds.), *Effective Methods for Modern Healthcare Service Quality and Evaluation* (pp. 110–136). Hershey, PA: IGI Global. doi:10.4018/978-1-4666-9961-8.ch006

Cimermanova, I. (2017). Computer-Assisted Learning in Slovakia. In D. Tafazoli & M. Romero (Eds.), *Multiculturalism and Technology-Enhanced Language Learning* (pp. 252–270). Hershey, PA: IGI Global. doi:10.4018/978-1-5225-1882-2.ch015

Cipolla-Ficarra, F. V., & Cipolla-Ficarra, M. (2018). Computer Animation for Ingenious Revival. In F. Cipolla-Ficarra, M. Ficarra, M. Cipolla-Ficarra, A. Quiroga, J. Alma, & J. Carré (Eds.), *Technology-Enhanced Human Interaction in Modern Society* (pp. 159–181). Hershey, PA: IGI Global. doi:10.4018/978-1-5225-3437-2.ch008

Cockrell, S., Damron, T. S., Melton, A. M., & Smith, A. D. (2018). Offshoring IT. In M. Khosrow-Pour, D.B.A. (Ed.), Encyclopedia of Information Science and Technology, Fourth Edition (pp. 5476-5489). Hershey, PA: IGI Global. doi:10.4018/978-1-5225-2255-3.ch476

Coffey, J. W. (2018). Logic and Proof in Computer Science: Categories and Limits of Proof Techniques. In J. Horne (Ed.), *Philosophical Perceptions on Logic and Order* (pp. 218–240). Hershey, PA: IGI Global. doi:10.4018/978-1-5225-2443-4.ch007

Dale, M. (2017). Re-Thinking the Challenges of Enterprise Architecture Implementation. In M. Tavana (Ed.), *Enterprise Information Systems and the Digitalization of Business Functions* (pp. 205–221). Hershey, PA: IGI Global. doi:10.4018/978-1-5225-2382-6.ch009

Das, A., Dasgupta, R., & Bagchi, A. (2016). Overview of Cellular Computing-Basic Principles and Applications. In J. Mandal, S. Mukhopadhyay, & T. Pal (Eds.), *Handbook of Research on Natural Computing for Optimization Problems* (pp. 637–662). Hershey, PA: IGI Global. doi:10.4018/978-1-5225-0058-2.ch026

De Maere, K., De Haes, S., & von Kutzschenbach, M. (2017). CIO Perspectives on Organizational Learning within the Context of IT Governance. *International Journal of IT/Business Alignment and Governance, 8*(1), 32-47. doi:10.4018/IJITBAG.2017010103

Demir, K., Çaka, C., Yaman, N. D., İslamoğlu, H., & Kuzu, A. (2018). Examining the Current Definitions of Computational Thinking. In H. Ozcinar, G. Wong, & H. Ozturk (Eds.), *Teaching Computational Thinking in Primary Education* (pp. 36–64). Hershey, PA: IGI Global. doi:10.4018/978-1-5225-3200-2.ch003

Deng, X., Hung, Y., & Lin, C. D. (2017). Design and Analysis of Computer Experiments. In S. Saha, A. Mandal, A. Narasimhamurthy, S. V, & S. Sangam (Eds.), Handbook of Research on Applied Cybernetics and Systems Science (pp. 264-279). Hershey, PA: IGI Global. doi:10.4018/978-1-5225-2498-4.ch013

Denner, J., Martinez, J., & Thiry, H. (2017). Strategies for Engaging Hispanic/Latino Youth in the US in Computer Science. In Y. Rankin & J. Thomas (Eds.), *Moving Students of Color from Consumers to Producers of Technology* (pp. 24–48). Hershey, PA: IGI Global. doi:10.4018/978-1-5225-2005-4.ch002

Devi, A. (2017). Cyber Crime and Cyber Security: A Quick Glance. In R. Kumar, P. Pattnaik, & P. Pandey (Eds.), *Detecting and Mitigating Robotic Cyber Security Risks* (pp. 160–171). Hershey, PA: IGI Global. doi:10.4018/978-1-5225-2154-9.ch011

Dores, A. R., Barbosa, F., Guerreiro, S., Almeida, I., & Carvalho, I. P. (2016). Computer-Based Neuropsychological Rehabilitation: Virtual Reality and Serious Games. In M. Cruz-Cunha, I. Miranda, R. Martinho, & R. Rijo (Eds.), *Encyclopedia of E-Health and Telemedicine* (pp. 473–485). Hershey, PA: IGI Global. doi:10.4018/978-1-4666-9978-6.ch037

Doshi, N., & Schaefer, G. (2016). Computer-Aided Analysis of Nailfold Capillaroscopy Images. In D. Fotiadis (Ed.), *Handbook of Research on Trends in the Diagnosis and Treatment of Chronic Conditions* (pp. 146–158). Hershey, PA: IGI Global. doi:10.4018/978-1-4666-8828-5.ch007

Doyle, D. J., & Fahy, P. J. (2018). Interactivity in Distance Education and Computer-Aided Learning, With Medical Education Examples. In M. Khosrow-Pour, D.B.A. (Ed.), Encyclopedia of Information Science and Technology, Fourth Edition (pp. 5829-5840). Hershey, PA: IGI Global. doi:10.4018/978-1-5225-2255-3.ch507

Elias, N. I., & Walker, T. W. (2017). Factors that Contribute to Continued Use of E-Training among Healthcare Professionals. In F. Topor (Ed.), *Handbook of Research on Individualism and Identity in the Globalized Digital Age* (pp. 403–429). Hershey, PA: IGI Global. doi:10.4018/978-1-5225-0522-8.ch018

Eloy, S., Dias, M. S., Lopes, P. F., & Vilar, E. (2016). Digital Technologies in Architecture and Engineering: Exploring an Engaged Interaction within Curricula. In D. Fonseca & E. Redondo (Eds.), *Handbook of Research on Applied E-Learning in Engineering and Architecture Education* (pp. 368–402). Hershey, PA: IGI Global. doi:10.4018/978-1-4666-8803-2.ch017

Estrela, V. V., Magalhães, H. A., & Saotome, O. (2016). Total Variation Applications in Computer Vision. In N. Kamila (Ed.), *Handbook of Research on Emerging Perspectives in Intelligent Pattern Recognition, Analysis, and Image Processing* (pp. 41–64). Hershey, PA: IGI Global. doi:10.4018/978-1-4666-8654-0.ch002

Filipovic, N., Radovic, M., Nikolic, D. D., Saveljic, I., Milosevic, Z., Exarchos, T. P., ... Parodi, O. (2016). Computer Predictive Model for Plaque Formation and Progression in the Artery. In D. Fotiadis (Ed.), *Handbook of Research on Trends in the Diagnosis and Treatment of Chronic Conditions* (pp. 279–300). Hershey, PA: IGI Global. doi:10.4018/978-1-4666-8828-5.ch013

Fisher, R. L. (2018). Computer-Assisted Indian Matrimonial Services. In M. Khosrow-Pour, D.B.A. (Ed.), Encyclopedia of Information Science and Technology, Fourth Edition (pp. 4136-4145). Hershey, PA: IGI Global. doi:10.4018/978-1-5225-2255-3.ch358

Fleenor, H. G., & Hodhod, R. (2016). Assessment of Learning and Technology: Computer Science Education. In V. Wang (Ed.), *Handbook of Research on Learning Outcomes and Opportunities in the Digital Age* (pp. 51–78). Hershey, PA: IGI Global. doi:10.4018/978-1-4666-9577-1.ch003

García-Valcárcel, A., & Mena, J. (2016). Information Technology as a Way To Support Collaborative Learning: What In-Service Teachers Think, Know and Do. *Journal of Information Technology Research*, *9*(1), 1–17. doi:10.4018/JITR.2016010101

Gardner-McCune, C., & Jimenez, Y. (2017). Historical App Developers: Integrating CS into K-12 through Cross-Disciplinary Projects. In Y. Rankin & J. Thomas (Eds.), *Moving Students of Color from Consumers to Producers of Technology* (pp. 85–112). Hershey, PA: IGI Global. doi:10.4018/978-1-5225-2005-4.ch005

Garvey, G. P. (2016). Exploring Perception, Cognition, and Neural Pathways of Stereo Vision and the Split–Brain Human Computer Interface. In A. Ursyn (Ed.), *Knowledge Visualization and Visual Literacy in Science Education* (pp. 28–76). Hershey, PA: IGI Global. doi:10.4018/978-1-5225-0480-1.ch002

Ghafele, R., & Gibert, B. (2018). Open Growth: The Economic Impact of Open Source Software in the USA. In M. Khosrow-Pour (Ed.), *Optimizing Contemporary Application and Processes in Open Source Software* (pp. 164–197). Hershey, PA: IGI Global. doi:10.4018/978-1-5225-5314-4.ch007

Ghobakhloo, M., & Azar, A. (2018). Information Technology Resources, the Organizational Capability of Lean-Agile Manufacturing, and Business Performance. *Information Resources Management Journal*, *31*(2), 47–74. doi:10.4018/IRMJ.2018040103

Gianni, M., & Gotzamani, K. (2016). Integrated Management Systems and Information Management Systems: Common Threads. In P. Papajorgji, F. Pinet, A. Guimarães, & J. Papathanasiou (Eds.), *Automated Enterprise Systems for Maximizing Business Performance* (pp. 195–214). Hershey, PA: IGI Global. doi:10.4018/978-1-4666-8841-4.ch011

Gikandi, J. W. (2017). Computer-Supported Collaborative Learning and Assessment: A Strategy for Developing Online Learning Communities in Continuing Education. In J. Keengwe & G. Onchwari (Eds.), *Handbook of Research on Learner-Centered Pedagogy in Teacher Education and Professional Development* (pp. 309–333). Hershey, PA: IGI Global. doi:10.4018/978-1-5225-0892-2.ch017

Gokhale, A. A., & Machina, K. F. (2017). Development of a Scale to Measure Attitudes toward Information Technology. In L. Tomei (Ed.), *Exploring the New Era of Technology-Infused Education* (pp. 49–64). Hershey, PA: IGI Global. doi:10.4018/978-1-5225-1709-2.ch004

Grace, A., O'Donoghue, J., Mahony, C., Heffernan, T., Molony, D., & Carroll, T. (2016). Computerized Decision Support Systems for Multimorbidity Care: An Urgent Call for Research and Development. In M. Cruz-Cunha, I. Miranda, R. Martinho, & R. Rijo (Eds.), *Encyclopedia of E-Health and Telemedicine* (pp. 486–494). Hershey, PA: IGI Global. doi:10.4018/978-1-4666-9978-6.ch038

Gupta, A., & Singh, O. (2016). Computer Aided Modeling and Finite Element Analysis of Human Elbow. *International Journal of Biomedical and Clinical Engineering*, 5(1), 31–38. doi:10.4018/IJBCE.2016010104

H., S. K. (2016). Classification of Cybercrimes and Punishments under the Information Technology Act, 2000. In S. Geetha, & A. Phamila (Eds.), *Combating Security Breaches and Criminal Activity in the Digital Sphere* (pp. 57-66). Hershey, PA: IGI Global. doi:10.4018/978-1-5225-0193-0.ch004

Hafeez-Baig, A., Gururajan, R., & Wickramasinghe, N. (2017). Readiness as a Novel Construct of Readiness Acceptance Model (RAM) for the Wireless Handheld Technology. In N. Wickramasinghe (Ed.), *Handbook of Research on Healthcare Administration and Management* (pp. 578–595). Hershey, PA: IGI Global. doi:10.4018/978-1-5225-0920-2.ch035

Hanafizadeh, P., Ghandchi, S., & Asgarimehr, M. (2017). Impact of Information Technology on Lifestyle: A Literature Review and Classification. *International Journal of Virtual Communities and Social Networking*, 9(2), 1–23. doi:10.4018/IJVCSN.2017040101

Harlow, D. B., Dwyer, H., Hansen, A. K., Hill, C., Iveland, A., Leak, A. E., & Franklin, D. M. (2016). Computer Programming in Elementary and Middle School: Connections across Content. In M. Urban & D. Falvo (Eds.), *Improving K-12 STEM Education Outcomes through Technological Integration* (pp. 337–361). Hershey, PA: IGI Global. doi:10.4018/978-1-4666-9616-7.ch015

Haseski, H. İ., Ilic, U., & Tuğtekin, U. (2018). Computational Thinking in Educational Digital Games: An Assessment Tool Proposal. In H. Ozcinar, G. Wong, & H. Ozturk (Eds.), *Teaching Computational Thinking in Primary Education* (pp. 256–287). Hershey, PA: IGI Global. doi:10.4018/978-1-5225-3200-2.ch013

Hee, W. J., Jalleh, G., Lai, H., & Lin, C. (2017). E-Commerce and IT Projects: Evaluation and Management Issues in Australian and Taiwanese Hospitals. *International Journal of Public Health Management and Ethics*, 2(1), 69–90. doi:10.4018/IJPHME.2017010104

Hernandez, A. A. (2017). Green Information Technology Usage: Awareness and Practices of Philippine IT Professionals. *International Journal of Enterprise Information Systems*, 13(4), 90–103. doi:10.4018/IJEIS.2017100106

Hernandez, A. A., & Ona, S. E. (2016). Green IT Adoption: Lessons from the Philippines Business Process Outsourcing Industry. *International Journal of Social Ecology and Sustainable Development*, 7(1), 1–34. doi:10.4018/IJSESD.2016010101

Hernandez, M. A., Marin, E. C., Garcia-Rodriguez, J., Azorin-Lopez, J., & Cazorla, M. (2017). Automatic Learning Improves Human-Robot Interaction in Productive Environments: A Review. *International Journal of Computer Vision and Image Processing*, 7(3), 65–75. doi:10.4018/IJCVIP.2017070106

Horne-Popp, L. M., Tessone, E. B., & Welker, J. (2018). If You Build It, They Will Come: Creating a Library Statistics Dashboard for Decision-Making. In L. Costello & M. Powers (Eds.), *Developing In-House Digital Tools in Library Spaces* (pp. 177–203). Hershey, PA: IGI Global. doi:10.4018/978-1-5225-2676-6.ch009

Hossan, C. G., & Ryan, J. C. (2016). Factors Affecting e-Government Technology Adoption Behaviour in a Voluntary Environment. *International Journal of Electronic Government Research*, *12*(1), 24–49. doi:10.4018/IJEGR.2016010102

Hu, H., Hu, P. J., & Al-Gahtani, S. S. (2017). User Acceptance of Computer Technology at Work in Arabian Culture: A Model Comparison Approach. In M. Khosrow-Pour (Ed.), *Handbook of Research on Technology Adoption, Social Policy, and Global Integration* (pp. 205–228). Hershey, PA: IGI Global. doi:10.4018/978-1-5225-2668-1.ch011

Huie, C. P. (2016). Perceptions of Business Intelligence Professionals about Factors Related to Business Intelligence input in Decision Making. *International Journal of Business Analytics*, *3*(3), 1–24. doi:10.4018/IJBAN.2016070101

Hung, S., Huang, W., Yen, D. C., Chang, S., & Lu, C. (2016). Effect of Information Service Competence and Contextual Factors on the Effectiveness of Strategic Information Systems Planning in Hospitals. *Journal of Global Information Management*, *24*(1), 14–36. doi:10.4018/JGIM.2016010102

Ifinedo, P. (2017). Using an Extended Theory of Planned Behavior to Study Nurses' Adoption of Healthcare Information Systems in Nova Scotia. *International Journal of Technology Diffusion*, *8*(1), 1–17. doi:10.4018/IJTD.2017010101

Ilie, V., & Sneha, S. (2018). A Three Country Study for Understanding Physicians' Engagement With Electronic Information Resources Pre and Post System Implementation. *Journal of Global Information Management*, *26*(2), 48–73. doi:10.4018/JGIM.2018040103

Inoue-Smith, Y. (2017). Perceived Ease in Using Technology Predicts Teacher Candidates' Preferences for Online Resources. *International Journal of Online Pedagogy and Course Design*, *7*(3), 17–28. doi:10.4018/IJOPCD.2017070102

Islam, A. A. (2016). Development and Validation of the Technology Adoption and Gratification (TAG) Model in Higher Education: A Cross-Cultural Study Between Malaysia and China. *International Journal of Technology and Human Interaction*, *12*(3), 78–105. doi:10.4018/IJTHI.2016070106

Islam, A. Y. (2017). Technology Satisfaction in an Academic Context: Moderating Effect of Gender. In A. Mesquita (Ed.), *Research Paradigms and Contemporary Perspectives on Human-Technology Interaction* (pp. 187–211). Hershey, PA: IGI Global. doi:10.4018/978-1-5225-1868-6.ch009

Jamil, G. L., & Jamil, C. C. (2017). Information and Knowledge Management Perspective Contributions for Fashion Studies: Observing Logistics and Supply Chain Management Processes. In G. Jamil, A. Soares, & C. Pessoa (Eds.), *Handbook of Research on Information Management for Effective Logistics and Supply Chains* (pp. 199–221). Hershey, PA: IGI Global. doi:10.4018/978-1-5225-0973-8.ch011

Jamil, G. L., Jamil, L. C., Vieira, A. A., & Xavier, A. J. (2016). Challenges in Modelling Healthcare Services: A Study Case of Information Architecture Perspectives. In G. Jamil, J. Poças Rascão, F. Ribeiro, & A. Malheiro da Silva (Eds.), *Handbook of Research on Information Architecture and Management in Modern Organizations* (pp. 1–23). Hershey, PA: IGI Global. doi:10.4018/978-1-4666-8637-3.ch001

Janakova, M. (2018). Big Data and Simulations for the Solution of Controversies in Small Businesses. In M. Khosrow-Pour, D.B.A. (Ed.), Encyclopedia of Information Science and Technology, Fourth Edition (pp. 6907-6915). Hershey, PA: IGI Global. doi:10.4018/978-1-5225-2255-3.ch598

Jha, D. G. (2016). Preparing for Information Technology Driven Changes. In S. Tiwari & L. Nafees (Eds.), *Innovative Management Education Pedagogies for Preparing Next-Generation Leaders* (pp. 258–274). Hershey, PA: IGI Global. doi:10.4018/978-1-4666-9691-4.ch015

Jhawar, A., & Garg, S. K. (2018). Logistics Improvement by Investment in Information Technology Using System Dynamics. In A. Azar & S. Vaidyanathan (Eds.), *Advances in System Dynamics and Control* (pp. 528–567). Hershey, PA: IGI Global. doi:10.4018/978-1-5225-4077-9.ch017

Kalelioğlu, F., Gülbahar, Y., & Doğan, D. (2018). Teaching How to Think Like a Programmer: Emerging Insights. In H. Ozcinar, G. Wong, & H. Ozturk (Eds.), *Teaching Computational Thinking in Primary Education* (pp. 18–35). Hershey, PA: IGI Global. doi:10.4018/978-1-5225-3200-2.ch002

Kamberi, S. (2017). A Girls-Only Online Virtual World Environment and its Implications for Game-Based Learning. In A. Stricker, C. Calongne, B. Truman, & F. Arenas (Eds.), *Integrating an Awareness of Selfhood and Society into Virtual Learning* (pp. 74–95). Hershey, PA: IGI Global. doi:10.4018/978-1-5225-2182-2.ch006

Kamel, S., & Rizk, N. (2017). ICT Strategy Development: From Design to Implementation – Case of Egypt. In C. Howard & K. Hargiss (Eds.), *Strategic Information Systems and Technologies in Modern Organizations* (pp. 239–257). Hershey, PA: IGI Global. doi:10.4018/978-1-5225-1680-4.ch010

Kamel, S. H. (2018). The Potential Role of the Software Industry in Supporting Economic Development. In M. Khosrow-Pour, D.B.A. (Ed.), Encyclopedia of Information Science and Technology, Fourth Edition (pp. 7259-7269). Hershey, PA: IGI Global. doi:10.4018/978-1-5225-2255-3.ch631

Karon, R. (2016). Utilisation of Health Information Systems for Service Delivery in the Namibian Environment. In T. Iyamu & A. Tatnall (Eds.), *Maximizing Healthcare Delivery and Management through Technology Integration* (pp. 169–183). Hershey, PA: IGI Global. doi:10.4018/978-1-4666-9446-0.ch011

Kawata, S. (2018). Computer-Assisted Parallel Program Generation. In M. Khosrow-Pour, D.B.A. (Ed.), Encyclopedia of Information Science and Technology, Fourth Edition (pp. 4583-4593). Hershey, PA: IGI Global. doi:10.4018/978-1-5225-2255-3.ch398

Khanam, S., Siddiqui, J., & Talib, F. (2016). A DEMATEL Approach for Prioritizing the TQM Enablers and IT Resources in the Indian ICT Industry. *International Journal of Applied Management Sciences and Engineering*, 3(1), 11–29. doi:10.4018/IJAMSE.2016010102

Khari, M., Shrivastava, G., Gupta, S., & Gupta, R. (2017). Role of Cyber Security in Today's Scenario. In R. Kumar, P. Pattnaik, & P. Pandey (Eds.), *Detecting and Mitigating Robotic Cyber Security Risks* (pp. 177–191). Hershey, PA: IGI Global. doi:10.4018/978-1-5225-2154-9.ch013

Khouja, M., Rodriguez, I. B., Ben Halima, Y., & Moalla, S. (2018). IT Governance in Higher Education Institutions: A Systematic Literature Review. *International Journal of Human Capital and Information Technology Professionals*, 9(2), 52–67. doi:10.4018/IJHCITP.2018040104

Kim, S., Chang, M., Choi, N., Park, J., & Kim, H. (2016). The Direct and Indirect Effects of Computer Uses on Student Success in Math. *International Journal of Cyber Behavior, Psychology and Learning*, 6(3), 48–64. doi:10.4018/IJCBPL.2016070104

Kiourt, C., Pavlidis, G., Koutsoudis, A., & Kalles, D. (2017). Realistic Simulation of Cultural Heritage. *International Journal of Computational Methods in Heritage Science*, 1(1), 10–40. doi:10.4018/IJC-MHS.2017010102

Korikov, A., & Krivtsov, O. (2016). System of People-Computer: On the Way of Creation of Human-Oriented Interface. In V. Mkrttchian, A. Bershadsky, A. Bozhday, M. Kataev, & S. Kataev (Eds.), *Handbook of Research on Estimation and Control Techniques in E-Learning Systems* (pp. 458–470). Hershey, PA: IGI Global. doi:10.4018/978-1-4666-9489-7.ch032

Köse, U. (2017). An Augmented-Reality-Based Intelligent Mobile Application for Open Computer Education. In G. Kurubacak & H. Altinpulluk (Eds.), *Mobile Technologies and Augmented Reality in Open Education* (pp. 154–174). Hershey, PA: IGI Global. doi:10.4018/978-1-5225-2110-5.ch008

Lahmiri, S. (2018). Information Technology Outsourcing Risk Factors and Provider Selection. In M. Gupta, R. Sharman, J. Walp, & P. Mulgund (Eds.), *Information Technology Risk Management and Compliance in Modern Organizations* (pp. 214–228). Hershey, PA: IGI Global. doi:10.4018/978-1-5225-2604-9.ch008

Landriscina, F. (2017). Computer-Supported Imagination: The Interplay Between Computer and Mental Simulation in Understanding Scientific Concepts. In I. Levin & D. Tsybulsky (Eds.), *Digital Tools and Solutions for Inquiry-Based STEM Learning* (pp. 33–60). Hershey, PA: IGI Global. doi:10.4018/978-1-5225-2525-7.ch002

Lau, S. K., Winley, G. K., Leung, N. K., Tsang, N., & Lau, S. Y. (2016). An Exploratory Study of Expectation in IT Skills in a Developing Nation: Vietnam. *Journal of Global Information Management*, 24(1), 1–13. doi:10.4018/JGIM.2016010101

Lavranos, C., Kostagiolas, P., & Papadatos, J. (2016). Information Retrieval Technologies and the "Realities" of Music Information Seeking. In I. Deliyannis, P. Kostagiolas, & C. Banou (Eds.), *Experimental Multimedia Systems for Interactivity and Strategic Innovation* (pp. 102–121). Hershey, PA: IGI Global. doi:10.4018/978-1-4666-8659-5.ch005

Lee, W. W. (2018). Ethical Computing Continues From Problem to Solution. In M. Khosrow-Pour, D.B.A. (Ed.), Encyclopedia of Information Science and Technology, Fourth Edition (pp. 4884-4897). Hershey, PA: IGI Global. doi:10.4018/978-1-5225-2255-3.ch423

Lehto, M. (2016). Cyber Security Education and Research in the Finland's Universities and Universities of Applied Sciences. *International Journal of Cyber Warfare & Terrorism*, 6(2), 15–31. doi:10.4018/IJCWT.2016040102

Lin, C., Jalleh, G., & Huang, Y. (2016). Evaluating and Managing Electronic Commerce and Outsourcing Projects in Hospitals. In A. Dwivedi (Ed.), *Reshaping Medical Practice and Care with Health Information Systems* (pp. 132–172). Hershey, PA: IGI Global. doi:10.4018/978-1-4666-9870-3.ch005

Lin, S., Chen, S., & Chuang, S. (2017). Perceived Innovation and Quick Response Codes in an Online-to-Offline E-Commerce Service Model. *International Journal of E-Adoption*, 9(2), 1–16. doi:10.4018/IJEA.2017070101

Liu, M., Wang, Y., Xu, W., & Liu, L. (2017). Automated Scoring of Chinese Engineering Students' English Essays. *International Journal of Distance Education Technologies*, 15(1), 52–68. doi:10.4018/IJDET.2017010104

Luciano, E. M., Wiedenhöft, G. C., Macadar, M. A., & Pinheiro dos Santos, F. (2016). Information Technology Governance Adoption: Understanding its Expectations Through the Lens of Organizational Citizenship. *International Journal of IT/Business Alignment and Governance, 7*(2), 22-32. doi:10.4018/IJITBAG.2016070102

Mabe, L. K., & Oladele, O. I. (2017). Application of Information Communication Technologies for Agricultural Development through Extension Services: A Review. In T. Tossy (Ed.), *Information Technology Integration for Socio-Economic Development* (pp. 52–101). Hershey, PA: IGI Global. doi:10.4018/978-1-5225-0539-6.ch003

Manogaran, G., Thota, C., & Lopez, D. (2018). Human-Computer Interaction With Big Data Analytics. In D. Lopez & M. Durai (Eds.), *HCI Challenges and Privacy Preservation in Big Data Security* (pp. 1–22). Hershey, PA: IGI Global. doi:10.4018/978-1-5225-2863-0.ch001

Margolis, J., Goode, J., & Flapan, J. (2017). A Critical Crossroads for Computer Science for All: "Identifying Talent" or "Building Talent," and What Difference Does It Make? In Y. Rankin & J. Thomas (Eds.), *Moving Students of Color from Consumers to Producers of Technology* (pp. 1–23). Hershey, PA: IGI Global. doi:10.4018/978-1-5225-2005-4.ch001

Mbale, J. (2018). Computer Centres Resource Cloud Elasticity-Scalability (CRECES): Copperbelt University Case Study. In S. Aljawarneh & M. Malhotra (Eds.), *Critical Research on Scalability and Security Issues in Virtual Cloud Environments* (pp. 48–70). Hershey, PA: IGI Global. doi:10.4018/978-1-5225-3029-9.ch003

McKee, J. (2018). The Right Information: The Key to Effective Business Planning. In *Business Architectures for Risk Assessment and Strategic Planning: Emerging Research and Opportunities* (pp. 38–52). Hershey, PA: IGI Global. doi:10.4018/978-1-5225-3392-4.ch003

Mensah, I. K., & Mi, J. (2018). Determinants of Intention to Use Local E-Government Services in Ghana: The Perspective of Local Government Workers. *International Journal of Technology Diffusion*, 9(2), 41–60. doi:10.4018/IJTD.2018040103

Mohamed, J. H. (2018). Scientograph-Based Visualization of Computer Forensics Research Literature. In J. Jeyasekar & P. Saravanan (Eds.), *Innovations in Measuring and Evaluating Scientific Information* (pp. 148–162). Hershey, PA: IGI Global. doi:10.4018/978-1-5225-3457-0.ch010

Moore, R. L., & Johnson, N. (2017). Earning a Seat at the Table: How IT Departments Can Partner in Organizational Change and Innovation. *International Journal of Knowledge-Based Organizations*, *7*(2), 1–12. doi:10.4018/IJKBO.2017040101

Mtebe, J. S., & Kissaka, M. M. (2016). Enhancing the Quality of Computer Science Education with MOOCs in Sub-Saharan Africa. In J. Keengwe & G. Onchwari (Eds.), *Handbook of Research on Active Learning and the Flipped Classroom Model in the Digital Age* (pp. 366–377). Hershey, PA: IGI Global. doi:10.4018/978-1-4666-9680-8.ch019

Mukul, M. K., & Bhattaharyya, S. (2017). Brain-Machine Interface: Human-Computer Interaction. In E. Noughabi, B. Raahemi, A. Albadvi, & B. Far (Eds.), *Handbook of Research on Data Science for Effective Healthcare Practice and Administration* (pp. 417–443). Hershey, PA: IGI Global. doi:10.4018/978-1-5225-2515-8.ch018

Na, L. (2017). Library and Information Science Education and Graduate Programs in Academic Libraries. In L. Ruan, Q. Zhu, & Y. Ye (Eds.), *Academic Library Development and Administration in China* (pp. 218–229). Hershey, PA: IGI Global. doi:10.4018/978-1-5225-0550-1.ch013

Nabavi, A., Taghavi-Fard, M. T., Hanafizadeh, P., & Taghva, M. R. (2016). Information Technology Continuance Intention: A Systematic Literature Review. *International Journal of E-Business Research*, *12*(1), 58–95. doi:10.4018/IJEBR.2016010104

Nath, R., & Murthy, V. N. (2018). What Accounts for the Differences in Internet Diffusion Rates Around the World? In M. Khosrow-Pour, D.B.A. (Ed.), Encyclopedia of Information Science and Technology, Fourth Edition (pp. 8095-8104). Hershey, PA: IGI Global. doi:10.4018/978-1-5225-2255-3.ch705

Nedelko, Z., & Potocan, V. (2018). The Role of Emerging Information Technologies for Supporting Supply Chain Management. In M. Khosrow-Pour, D.B.A. (Ed.), Encyclopedia of Information Science and Technology, Fourth Edition (pp. 5559-5569). Hershey, PA: IGI Global. doi:10.4018/978-1-5225-2255-3.ch483

Ngafeeson, M. N. (2018). User Resistance to Health Information Technology. In M. Khosrow-Pour, D.B.A. (Ed.), Encyclopedia of Information Science and Technology, Fourth Edition (pp. 3816-3825). Hershey, PA: IGI Global. doi:10.4018/978-1-5225-2255-3.ch331

Nozari, H., Najafi, S. E., Jafari-Eskandari, M., & Aliahmadi, A. (2016). Providing a Model for Virtual Project Management with an Emphasis on IT Projects. In C. Graham (Ed.), *Strategic Management and Leadership for Systems Development in Virtual Spaces* (pp. 43–63). Hershey, PA: IGI Global. doi:10.4018/978-1-4666-9688-4.ch003

Nurdin, N., Stockdale, R., & Scheepers, H. (2016). Influence of Organizational Factors in the Sustainability of E-Government: A Case Study of Local E-Government in Indonesia. In I. Sodhi (Ed.), *Trends, Prospects, and Challenges in Asian E-Governance* (pp. 281–323). Hershey, PA: IGI Global. doi:10.4018/978-1-4666-9536-8.ch014

Odagiri, K. (2017). Introduction of Individual Technology to Constitute the Current Internet. In *Strategic Policy-Based Network Management in Contemporary Organizations* (pp. 20–96). Hershey, PA: IGI Global. doi:10.4018/978-1-68318-003-6.ch003

Okike, E. U. (2018). Computer Science and Prison Education. In I. Biao (Ed.), *Strategic Learning Ideologies in Prison Education Programs* (pp. 246–264). Hershey, PA: IGI Global. doi:10.4018/978-1-5225-2909-5.ch012

Olelewe, C. J., & Nwafor, I. P. (2017). Level of Computer Appreciation Skills Acquired for Sustainable Development by Secondary School Students in Nsukka LGA of Enugu State, Nigeria. In C. Ayo & V. Mbarika (Eds.), *Sustainable ICT Adoption and Integration for Socio-Economic Development* (pp. 214–233). Hershey, PA: IGI Global. doi:10.4018/978-1-5225-2565-3.ch010

Oliveira, M., Maçada, A. C., Curado, C., & Nodari, F. (2017). Infrastructure Profiles and Knowledge Sharing. *International Journal of Technology and Human Interaction*, 13(3), 1–12. doi:10.4018/IJTHI.2017070101

Otarkhani, A., Shokouhyar, S., & Pour, S. S. (2017). Analyzing the Impact of Governance of Enterprise IT on Hospital Performance: Tehran's (Iran) Hospitals – A Case Study. *International Journal of Healthcare Information Systems and Informatics*, 12(3), 1–20. doi:10.4018/IJHISI.2017070101

Otunla, A. O., & Amuda, C. O. (2018). Nigerian Undergraduate Students' Computer Competencies and Use of Information Technology Tools and Resources for Study Skills and Habits' Enhancement. In M. Khosrow-Pour, D.B.A. (Ed.), Encyclopedia of Information Science and Technology, Fourth Edition (pp. 2303-2313). Hershey, PA: IGI Global. doi:10.4018/978-1-5225-2255-3.ch200

Özçınar, H. (2018). A Brief Discussion on Incentives and Barriers to Computational Thinking Education. In H. Ozcinar, G. Wong, & H. Ozturk (Eds.), *Teaching Computational Thinking in Primary Education* (pp. 1–17). Hershey, PA: IGI Global. doi:10.4018/978-1-5225-3200-2.ch001

Pandey, J. M., Garg, S., Mishra, P., & Mishra, B. P. (2017). Computer Based Psychological Interventions: Subject to the Efficacy of Psychological Services. *International Journal of Computers in Clinical Practice*, 2(1), 25–33. doi:10.4018/IJCCP.2017010102

Parry, V. K., & Lind, M. L. (2016). Alignment of Business Strategy and Information Technology Considering Information Technology Governance, Project Portfolio Control, and Risk Management. *International Journal of Information Technology Project Management*, 7(4), 21–37. doi:10.4018/IJITPM.2016100102

Patro, C. (2017). Impulsion of Information Technology on Human Resource Practices. In P. Ordóñez de Pablos (Ed.), *Managerial Strategies and Solutions for Business Success in Asia* (pp. 231–254). Hershey, PA: IGI Global. doi:10.4018/978-1-5225-1886-0.ch013

Patro, C. S., & Raghunath, K. M. (2017). Information Technology Paraphernalia for Supply Chain Management Decisions. In M. Tavana (Ed.), *Enterprise Information Systems and the Digitalization of Business Functions* (pp. 294–320). Hershey, PA: IGI Global. doi:10.4018/978-1-5225-2382-6.ch014

Paul, P. K. (2016). Cloud Computing: An Agent of Promoting Interdisciplinary Sciences, Especially Information Science and I-Schools – Emerging Techno-Educational Scenario. In L. Chao (Ed.), *Handbook of Research on Cloud-Based STEM Education for Improved Learning Outcomes* (pp. 247–258). Hershey, PA: IGI Global. doi:10.4018/978-1-4666-9924-3.ch016

Paul, P. K. (2018). The Context of IST for Solid Information Retrieval and Infrastructure Building: Study of Developing Country. *International Journal of Information Retrieval Research*, 8(1), 86–100. doi:10.4018/IJIRR.2018010106

Paul, P. K., & Chatterjee, D. (2018). iSchools Promoting "Information Science and Technology" (IST) Domain Towards Community, Business, and Society With Contemporary Worldwide Trend and Emerging Potentialities in India. In M. Khosrow-Pour, D.B.A. (Ed.), Encyclopedia of Information Science and Technology, Fourth Edition (pp. 4723-4735). Hershey, PA: IGI Global. doi:10.4018/978-1-5225-2255-3.ch410

Pessoa, C. R., & Marques, M. E. (2017). Information Technology and Communication Management in Supply Chain Management. In G. Jamil, A. Soares, & C. Pessoa (Eds.), *Handbook of Research on Information Management for Effective Logistics and Supply Chains* (pp. 23–33). Hershey, PA: IGI Global. doi:10.4018/978-1-5225-0973-8.ch002

Pineda, R. G. (2016). Where the Interaction Is Not: Reflections on the Philosophy of Human-Computer Interaction. *International Journal of Art, Culture and Design Technologies*, 5(1), 1–12. doi:10.4018/IJACDT.2016010101

Pineda, R. G. (2018). Remediating Interaction: Towards a Philosophy of Human-Computer Relationship. In M. Khosrow-Pour (Ed.), *Enhancing Art, Culture, and Design With Technological Integration* (pp. 75–98). Hershey, PA: IGI Global. doi:10.4018/978-1-5225-5023-5.ch004

Poikela, P., & Vuojärvi, H. (2016). Learning ICT-Mediated Communication through Computer-Based Simulations. In M. Cruz-Cunha, I. Miranda, R. Martinho, & R. Rijo (Eds.), *Encyclopedia of E-Health and Telemedicine* (pp. 674–687). Hershey, PA: IGI Global. doi:10.4018/978-1-4666-9978-6.ch052

Qian, Y. (2017). Computer Simulation in Higher Education: Affordances, Opportunities, and Outcomes. In P. Vu, S. Fredrickson, & C. Moore (Eds.), *Handbook of Research on Innovative Pedagogies and Technologies for Online Learning in Higher Education* (pp. 236–262). Hershey, PA: IGI Global. doi:10.4018/978-1-5225-1851-8.ch011

Radant, O., Colomo-Palacios, R., & Stantchev, V. (2016). Factors for the Management of Scarce Human Resources and Highly Skilled Employees in IT-Departments: A Systematic Review. *Journal of Information Technology Research*, 9(1), 65–82. doi:10.4018/JITR.2016010105

Rahman, N. (2016). Toward Achieving Environmental Sustainability in the Computer Industry. *International Journal of Green Computing*, 7(1), 37–54. doi:10.4018/IJGC.2016010103

Rahman, N. (2017). Lessons from a Successful Data Warehousing Project Management. *International Journal of Information Technology Project Management*, 8(4), 30–45. doi:10.4018/IJITPM.2017100103

Rahman, N. (2018). Environmental Sustainability in the Computer Industry for Competitive Advantage. In M. Khosrow-Pour (Ed.), *Green Computing Strategies for Competitive Advantage and Business Sustainability* (pp. 110–130). Hershey, PA: IGI Global. doi:10.4018/978-1-5225-5017-4.ch006

Rajh, A., & Pavetic, T. (2017). Computer Generated Description as the Required Digital Competence in Archival Profession. *International Journal of Digital Literacy and Digital Competence*, 8(1), 36–49. doi:10.4018/IJDLDC.2017010103

Raman, A., & Goyal, D. P. (2017). Extending IMPLEMENT Framework for Enterprise Information Systems Implementation to Information System Innovation. In M. Tavana (Ed.), *Enterprise Information Systems and the Digitalization of Business Functions* (pp. 137–177). Hershey, PA: IGI Global. doi:10.4018/978-1-5225-2382-6.ch007

Rao, Y. S., Rauta, A. K., Saini, H., & Panda, T. C. (2017). Mathematical Model for Cyber Attack in Computer Network. *International Journal of Business Data Communications and Networking*, 13(1), 58–65. doi:10.4018/IJBDCN.2017010105

Rapaport, W. J. (2018). Syntactic Semantics and the Proper Treatment of Computationalism. In M. Danesi (Ed.), *Empirical Research on Semiotics and Visual Rhetoric* (pp. 128–176). Hershey, PA: IGI Global. doi:10.4018/978-1-5225-5622-0.ch007

Raut, R., Priyadarshinee, P., & Jha, M. (2017). Understanding the Mediation Effect of Cloud Computing Adoption in Indian Organization: Integrating TAM-TOE- Risk Model. *International Journal of Service Science, Management, Engineering, and Technology*, 8(3), 40–59. doi:10.4018/IJSSMET.2017070103

Regan, E. A., & Wang, J. (2016). Realizing the Value of EHR Systems Critical Success Factors. *International Journal of Healthcare Information Systems and Informatics*, 11(3), 1–18. doi:10.4018/IJHISI.2016070101

Rezaie, S., Mirabedini, S. J., & Abtahi, A. (2018). Designing a Model for Implementation of Business Intelligence in the Banking Industry. *International Journal of Enterprise Information Systems*, 14(1), 77–103. doi:10.4018/IJEIS.2018010105

Rezende, D. A. (2016). Digital City Projects: Information and Public Services Offered by Chicago (USA) and Curitiba (Brazil). *International Journal of Knowledge Society Research*, 7(3), 16–30. doi:10.4018/IJKSR.2016070102

Rezende, D. A. (2018). Strategic Digital City Projects: Innovative Information and Public Services Offered by Chicago (USA) and Curitiba (Brazil). In M. Lytras, L. Daniela, & A. Visvizi (Eds.), *Enhancing Knowledge Discovery and Innovation in the Digital Era* (pp. 204–223). Hershey, PA: IGI Global. doi:10.4018/978-1-5225-4191-2.ch012

Riabov, V. V. (2016). Teaching Online Computer-Science Courses in LMS and Cloud Environment. *International Journal of Quality Assurance in Engineering and Technology Education*, 5(4), 12–41. doi:10.4018/IJQAETE.2016100102

Ricordel, V., Wang, J., Da Silva, M. P., & Le Callet, P. (2016). 2D and 3D Visual Attention for Computer Vision: Concepts, Measurement, and Modeling. In R. Pal (Ed.), *Innovative Research in Attention Modeling and Computer Vision Applications* (pp. 1–44). Hershey, PA: IGI Global. doi:10.4018/978-1-4666-8723-3.ch001

Rodriguez, A., Rico-Diaz, A. J., Rabuñal, J. R., & Gestal, M. (2017). Fish Tracking with Computer Vision Techniques: An Application to Vertical Slot Fishways. In M. S., & V. V. (Eds.), Multi-Core Computer Vision and Image Processing for Intelligent Applications (pp. 74-104). Hershey, PA: IGI Global. doi:10.4018/978-1-5225-0889-2.ch003

Romero, J. A. (2018). Sustainable Advantages of Business Value of Information Technology. In M. Khosrow-Pour, D.B.A. (Ed.), Encyclopedia of Information Science and Technology, Fourth Edition (pp. 923-929). Hershey, PA: IGI Global. doi:10.4018/978-1-5225-2255-3.ch079

Romero, J. A. (2018). The Always-On Business Model and Competitive Advantage. In N. Bajgoric (Ed.), *Always-On Enterprise Information Systems for Modern Organizations* (pp. 23–40). Hershey, PA: IGI Global. doi:10.4018/978-1-5225-3704-5.ch002

Rosen, Y. (2018). Computer Agent Technologies in Collaborative Learning and Assessment. In M. Khosrow-Pour, D.B.A. (Ed.), Encyclopedia of Information Science and Technology, Fourth Edition (pp. 2402-2410). Hershey, PA: IGI Global. doi:10.4018/978-1-5225-2255-3.ch209

Rosen, Y., & Mosharraf, M. (2016). Computer Agent Technologies in Collaborative Assessments. In Y. Rosen, S. Ferrara, & M. Mosharraf (Eds.), *Handbook of Research on Technology Tools for Real-World Skill Development* (pp. 319–343). Hershey, PA: IGI Global. doi:10.4018/978-1-4666-9441-5.ch012

Roy, D. (2018). Success Factors of Adoption of Mobile Applications in Rural India: Effect of Service Characteristics on Conceptual Model. In M. Khosrow-Pour (Ed.), *Green Computing Strategies for Competitive Advantage and Business Sustainability* (pp. 211–238). Hershey, PA: IGI Global. doi:10.4018/978-1-5225-5017-4.ch010

Ruffin, T. R. (2016). Health Information Technology and Change. In V. Wang (Ed.), *Handbook of Research on Advancing Health Education through Technology* (pp. 259–285). Hershey, PA: IGI Global. doi:10.4018/978-1-4666-9494-1.ch012

Ruffin, T. R. (2016). Health Information Technology and Quality Management. *International Journal of Information Communication Technologies and Human Development*, 8(4), 56–72. doi:10.4018/IJICTHD.2016100105

Ruffin, T. R., & Hawkins, D. P. (2018). Trends in Health Care Information Technology and Informatics. In M. Khosrow-Pour, D.B.A. (Ed.), Encyclopedia of Information Science and Technology, Fourth Edition (pp. 3805-3815). Hershey, PA: IGI Global. doi:10.4018/978-1-5225-2255-3.ch330

Safari, M. R., & Jiang, Q. (2018). The Theory and Practice of IT Governance Maturity and Strategies Alignment: Evidence From Banking Industry. *Journal of Global Information Management, 26*(2), 127–146. doi:10.4018/JGIM.2018040106

Sahin, H. B., & Anagun, S. S. (2018). Educational Computer Games in Math Teaching: A Learning Culture. In E. Toprak & E. Kumtepe (Eds.), *Supporting Multiculturalism in Open and Distance Learning Spaces* (pp. 249–280). Hershey, PA: IGI Global. doi:10.4018/978-1-5225-3076-3.ch013

Sanna, A., & Valpreda, F. (2017). An Assessment of the Impact of a Collaborative Didactic Approach and Students' Background in Teaching Computer Animation. *International Journal of Information and Communication Technology Education, 13*(4), 1–16. doi:10.4018/IJICTE.2017100101

Savita, K., Dominic, P., & Ramayah, T. (2016). The Drivers, Practices and Outcomes of Green Supply Chain Management: Insights from ISO14001 Manufacturing Firms in Malaysia. *International Journal of Information Systems and Supply Chain Management, 9*(2), 35–60. doi:10.4018/IJISSCM.2016040103

Scott, A., Martin, A., & McAlear, F. (2017). Enhancing Participation in Computer Science among Girls of Color: An Examination of a Preparatory AP Computer Science Intervention. In Y. Rankin & J. Thomas (Eds.), *Moving Students of Color from Consumers to Producers of Technology* (pp. 62–84). Hershey, PA: IGI Global. doi:10.4018/978-1-5225-2005-4.ch004

Shahsavandi, E., Mayah, G., & Rahbari, H. (2016). Impact of E-Government on Transparency and Corruption in Iran. In I. Sodhi (Ed.), *Trends, Prospects, and Challenges in Asian E-Governance* (pp. 75–94). Hershey, PA: IGI Global. doi:10.4018/978-1-4666-9536-8.ch004

Siddoo, V., & Wongsai, N. (2017). Factors Influencing the Adoption of ISO/IEC 29110 in Thai Government Projects: A Case Study. *International Journal of Information Technologies and Systems Approach, 10*(1), 22–44. doi:10.4018/IJITSA.2017010102

Sidorkina, I., & Rybakov, A. (2016). Computer-Aided Design as Carrier of Set Development Changes System in E-Course Engineering. In V. Mkrttchian, A. Bershadsky, A. Bozhday, M. Kataev, & S. Kataev (Eds.), *Handbook of Research on Estimation and Control Techniques in E-Learning Systems* (pp. 500–515). Hershey, PA: IGI Global. doi:10.4018/978-1-4666-9489-7.ch035

Sidorkina, I., & Rybakov, A. (2016). Creating Model of E-Course: As an Object of Computer-Aided Design. In V. Mkrttchian, A. Bershadsky, A. Bozhday, M. Kataev, & S. Kataev (Eds.), *Handbook of Research on Estimation and Control Techniques in E-Learning Systems* (pp. 286–297). Hershey, PA: IGI Global. doi:10.4018/978-1-4666-9489-7.ch019

Simões, A. (2017). Using Game Frameworks to Teach Computer Programming. In R. Alexandre Peixoto de Queirós & M. Pinto (Eds.), *Gamification-Based E-Learning Strategies for Computer Programming Education* (pp. 221–236). Hershey, PA: IGI Global. doi:10.4018/978-1-5225-1034-5.ch010

Sllame, A. M. (2017). Integrating LAB Work With Classes in Computer Network Courses. In H. Alphin Jr, R. Chan, & J. Lavine (Eds.), *The Future of Accessibility in International Higher Education* (pp. 253–275). Hershey, PA: IGI Global. doi:10.4018/978-1-5225-2560-8.ch015

Smirnov, A., Ponomarev, A., Shilov, N., Kashevnik, A., & Teslya, N. (2018). Ontology-Based Human-Computer Cloud for Decision Support: Architecture and Applications in Tourism. *International Journal of Embedded and Real-Time Communication Systems*, 9(1), 1–19. doi:10.4018/IJERTCS.2018010101

Smith-Ditizio, A. A., & Smith, A. D. (2018). Computer Fraud Challenges and Its Legal Implications. In M. Khosrow-Pour, D.B.A. (Ed.), Encyclopedia of Information Science and Technology, Fourth Edition (pp. 4837-4848). Hershey, PA: IGI Global. doi:10.4018/978-1-5225-2255-3.ch419

Sohani, S. S. (2016). Job Shadowing in Information Technology Projects: A Source of Competitive Advantage. *International Journal of Information Technology Project Management*, 7(1), 47–57. doi:10.4018/IJITPM.2016010104

Sosnin, P. (2018). Figuratively Semantic Support of Human-Computer Interactions. In *Experience-Based Human-Computer Interactions: Emerging Research and Opportunities* (pp. 244–272). Hershey, PA: IGI Global. doi:10.4018/978-1-5225-2987-3.ch008

Spinelli, R., & Benevolo, C. (2016). From Healthcare Services to E-Health Applications: A Delivery System-Based Taxonomy. In A. Dwivedi (Ed.), *Reshaping Medical Practice and Care with Health Information Systems* (pp. 205–245). Hershey, PA: IGI Global. doi:10.4018/978-1-4666-9870-3.ch007

Srinivasan, S. (2016). Overview of Clinical Trial and Pharmacovigilance Process and Areas of Application of Computer System. In P. Chakraborty & A. Nagal (Eds.), *Software Innovations in Clinical Drug Development and Safety* (pp. 1–13). Hershey, PA: IGI Global. doi:10.4018/978-1-4666-8726-4.ch001

Srisawasdi, N. (2016). Motivating Inquiry-Based Learning Through a Combination of Physical and Virtual Computer-Based Laboratory Experiments in High School Science. In M. Urban & D. Falvo (Eds.), *Improving K-12 STEM Education Outcomes through Technological Integration* (pp. 108–134). Hershey, PA: IGI Global. doi:10.4018/978-1-4666-9616-7.ch006

Stavridi, S. V., & Hamada, D. R. (2016). Children and Youth Librarians: Competencies Required in Technology-Based Environment. In J. Yap, M. Perez, M. Ayson, & G. Entico (Eds.), *Special Library Administration, Standardization and Technological Integration* (pp. 25–50). Hershey, PA: IGI Global. doi:10.4018/978-1-4666-9542-9.ch002

Sung, W., Ahn, J., Kai, S. M., Choi, A., & Black, J. B. (2016). Incorporating Touch-Based Tablets into Classroom Activities: Fostering Children's Computational Thinking through iPad Integrated Instruction. In D. Mentor (Ed.), *Handbook of Research on Mobile Learning in Contemporary Classrooms* (pp. 378–406). Hershey, PA: IGI Global. doi:10.4018/978-1-5225-0251-7.ch019

Syväjärvi, A., Leinonen, J., Kivivirta, V., & Kesti, M. (2017). The Latitude of Information Management in Local Government: Views of Local Government Managers. *International Journal of Electronic Government Research*, 13(1), 69–85. doi:10.4018/IJEGR.2017010105

Tanque, M., & Foxwell, H. J. (2018). Big Data and Cloud Computing: A Review of Supply Chain Capabilities and Challenges. In A. Prasad (Ed.), *Exploring the Convergence of Big Data and the Internet of Things* (pp. 1–28). Hershey, PA: IGI Global. doi:10.4018/978-1-5225-2947-7.ch001

Teixeira, A., Gomes, A., & Orvalho, J. G. (2017). Auditory Feedback in a Computer Game for Blind People. In T. Issa, P. Kommers, T. Issa, P. Isaías, & T. Issa (Eds.), *Smart Technology Applications in Business Environments* (pp. 134–158). Hershey, PA: IGI Global. doi:10.4018/978-1-5225-2492-2.ch007

Thompson, N., McGill, T., & Murray, D. (2018). Affect-Sensitive Computer Systems. In M. Khosrow-Pour, D.B.A. (Ed.), Encyclopedia of Information Science and Technology, Fourth Edition (pp. 4124-4135). Hershey, PA: IGI Global. doi:10.4018/978-1-5225-2255-3.ch357

Trad, A., & Kalpić, D. (2016). The E-Business Transformation Framework for E-Commerce Control and Monitoring Pattern. In I. Lee (Ed.), *Encyclopedia of E-Commerce Development, Implementation, and Management* (pp. 754–777). Hershey, PA: IGI Global. doi:10.4018/978-1-4666-9787-4.ch053

Triberti, S., Brivio, E., & Galimberti, C. (2018). On Social Presence: Theories, Methodologies, and Guidelines for the Innovative Contexts of Computer-Mediated Learning. In M. Marmon (Ed.), *Enhancing Social Presence in Online Learning Environments* (pp. 20–41). Hershey, PA: IGI Global. doi:10.4018/978-1-5225-3229-3.ch002

Tripathy, B. K. T. R., S., & Mohanty, R. K. (2018). Memetic Algorithms and Their Applications in Computer Science. In S. Dash, B. Tripathy, & A. Rahman (Eds.), Handbook of Research on Modeling, Analysis, and Application of Nature-Inspired Metaheuristic Algorithms (pp. 73-93). Hershey, PA: IGI Global. doi:10.4018/978-1-5225-2857-9.ch004

Turulja, L., & Bajgoric, N. (2017). Human Resource Management IT and Global Economy Perspective: Global Human Resource Information Systems. In M. Khosrow-Pour (Ed.), *Handbook of Research on Technology Adoption, Social Policy, and Global Integration* (pp. 377–394). Hershey, PA: IGI Global. doi:10.4018/978-1-5225-2668-1.ch018

Unwin, D. W., Sanzogni, L., & Sandhu, K. (2017). Developing and Measuring the Business Case for Health Information Technology. In K. Moahi, K. Bwalya, & P. Sebina (Eds.), *Health Information Systems and the Advancement of Medical Practice in Developing Countries* (pp. 262–290). Hershey, PA: IGI Global. doi:10.4018/978-1-5225-2262-1.ch015

Vadhanam, B. R. S., M., Sugumaran, V., V., V., & Ramalingam, V. V. (2017). Computer Vision Based Classification on Commercial Videos. In M. S., & V. V. (Eds.), Multi-Core Computer Vision and Image Processing for Intelligent Applications (pp. 105-135). Hershey, PA: IGI Global. doi:10.4018/978-1-5225-0889-2.ch004

Valverde, R., Torres, B., & Motaghi, H. (2018). A Quantum NeuroIS Data Analytics Architecture for the Usability Evaluation of Learning Management Systems. In S. Bhattacharyya (Ed.), *Quantum-Inspired Intelligent Systems for Multimedia Data Analysis* (pp. 277–299). Hershey, PA: IGI Global. doi:10.4018/978-1-5225-5219-2.ch009

Vassilis, E. (2018). Learning and Teaching Methodology: "1:1 Educational Computing. In K. Koutsopoulos, K. Doukas, & Y. Kotsanis (Eds.), *Handbook of Research on Educational Design and Cloud Computing in Modern Classroom Settings* (pp. 122–155). Hershey, PA: IGI Global. doi:10.4018/978-1-5225-3053-4.ch007

Wadhwani, A. K., Wadhwani, S., & Singh, T. (2016). Computer Aided Diagnosis System for Breast Cancer Detection. In Y. Morsi, A. Shukla, & C. Rathore (Eds.), *Optimizing Assistive Technologies for Aging Populations* (pp. 378–395). Hershey, PA: IGI Global. doi:10.4018/978-1-4666-9530-6.ch015

Wang, L., Wu, Y., & Hu, C. (2016). English Teachers' Practice and Perspectives on Using Educational Computer Games in EIL Context. *International Journal of Technology and Human Interaction, 12*(3), 33–46. doi:10.4018/IJTHI.2016070103

Watfa, M. K., Majeed, H., & Salahuddin, T. (2016). Computer Based E-Healthcare Clinical Systems: A Comprehensive Survey. *International Journal of Privacy and Health Information Management, 4*(1), 50–69. doi:10.4018/IJPHIM.2016010104

Weeger, A., & Haase, U. (2016). Taking up Three Challenges to Business-IT Alignment Research by the Use of Activity Theory. *International Journal of IT/Business Alignment and Governance, 7*(2), 1-21. doi:10.4018/IJITBAG.2016070101

Wexler, B. E. (2017). Computer-Presented and Physical Brain-Training Exercises for School Children: Improving Executive Functions and Learning. In B. Dubbels (Ed.), *Transforming Gaming and Computer Simulation Technologies across Industries* (pp. 206–224). Hershey, PA: IGI Global. doi:10.4018/978-1-5225-1817-4.ch012

Williams, D. M., Gani, M. O., Addo, I. D., Majumder, A. J., Tamma, C. P., Wang, M., ... Chu, C. (2016). Challenges in Developing Applications for Aging Populations. In Y. Morsi, A. Shukla, & C. Rathore (Eds.), *Optimizing Assistive Technologies for Aging Populations* (pp. 1–21). Hershey, PA: IGI Global. doi:10.4018/978-1-4666-9530-6.ch001

Wimble, M., Singh, H., & Phillips, B. (2018). Understanding Cross-Level Interactions of Firm-Level Information Technology and Industry Environment: A Multilevel Model of Business Value. *Information Resources Management Journal, 31*(1), 1–20. doi:10.4018/IRMJ.2018010101

Wimmer, H., Powell, L., Kilgus, L., & Force, C. (2017). Improving Course Assessment via Web-based Homework. *International Journal of Online Pedagogy and Course Design, 7*(2), 1–19. doi:10.4018/IJOPCD.2017040101

Wong, Y. L., & Siu, K. W. (2018). Assessing Computer-Aided Design Skills. In M. Khosrow-Pour, D.B.A. (Ed.), Encyclopedia of Information Science and Technology, Fourth Edition (pp. 7382-7391). Hershey, PA: IGI Global. doi:10.4018/978-1-5225-2255-3.ch642

Wongsurawat, W., & Shrestha, V. (2018). Information Technology, Globalization, and Local Conditions: Implications for Entrepreneurs in Southeast Asia. In P. Ordóñez de Pablos (Ed.), *Management Strategies and Technology Fluidity in the Asian Business Sector* (pp. 163–176). Hershey, PA: IGI Global. doi:10.4018/978-1-5225-4056-4.ch010

Yang, Y., Zhu, X., Jin, C., & Li, J. J. (2018). Reforming Classroom Education Through a QQ Group: A Pilot Experiment at a Primary School in Shanghai. In H. Spires (Ed.), *Digital Transformation and Innovation in Chinese Education* (pp. 211–231). Hershey, PA: IGI Global. doi:10.4018/978-1-5225-2924-8.ch012

Yilmaz, R., Sezgin, A., Kurnaz, S., & Arslan, Y. Z. (2018). Object-Oriented Programming in Computer Science. In M. Khosrow-Pour, D.B.A. (Ed.), Encyclopedia of Information Science and Technology, Fourth Edition (pp. 7470-7480). Hershey, PA: IGI Global. doi:10.4018/978-1-5225-2255-3.ch650

Yu, L. (2018). From Teaching Software Engineering Locally and Globally to Devising an Internationalized Computer Science Curriculum. In S. Dikli, B. Etheridge, & R. Rawls (Eds.), *Curriculum Internationalization and the Future of Education* (pp. 293–320). Hershey, PA: IGI Global. doi:10.4018/978-1-5225-2791-6.ch016

Yuhua, F. (2018). Computer Information Library Clusters. In M. Khosrow-Pour, D.B.A. (Ed.), Encyclopedia of Information Science and Technology, Fourth Edition (pp. 4399-4403). Hershey, PA: IGI Global. doi:10.4018/978-1-5225-2255-3.ch382

Zare, M. A., Taghavi Fard, M. T., & Hanafizadeh, P. (2016). The Assessment of Outsourcing IT Services using DEA Technique: A Study of Application Outsourcing in Research Centers. *International Journal of Operations Research and Information Systems*, 7(1), 45–57. doi:10.4018/IJORIS.2016010104

Zhao, J., Wang, Q., Guo, J., Gao, L., & Yang, F. (2016). An Overview on Passive Image Forensics Technology for Automatic Computer Forgery. *International Journal of Digital Crime and Forensics*, 8(4), 14–25. doi:10.4018/IJDCF.2016100102

Zimeras, S. (2016). Computer Virus Models and Analysis in M-Health IT Systems: Computer Virus Models. In A. Moumtzoglou (Ed.), *M-Health Innovations for Patient-Centered Care* (pp. 284–297). Hershey, PA: IGI Global. doi:10.4018/978-1-4666-9861-1.ch014

Zlatanovska, K. (2016). Hacking and Hacktivism as an Information Communication System Threat. In M. Hadji-Janev & M. Bogdanoski (Eds.), *Handbook of Research on Civil Society and National Security in the Era of Cyber Warfare* (pp. 68–101). Hershey, PA: IGI Global. doi:10.4018/978-1-4666-8793-6.ch004

About the Contributors

NanSi Shi received his Ph.D. from University of South Australia in 1998 and M.E. from Nanyang Technological University Singapore in 1995. Dr. Shi has over 30 years of experience in Information Management and Systems field, including industry practice, academic research, doctoral supervisor and teaching. He has authored and edited several books in various areas, including the E-Commence technology, architectural of Web-enabled e-business, wireless communications and mobile commerce and applications, as well as IT governance. He is currently working as a principle consultant and interested in blockchain technology, Internet of Thing, 4th generation technology flatform and applications, IT Governance, strategy and quality management etc.

***

Usha B. Ajay is working as Associate Professor and Head of the Department in Information Science & Engineering, BMSIT&M, Bengaluru. She received her Ph.D in Computer Science from Visvesvaraya Technological University, Belagavi in the Year 2016. Her research interests include Information security, Image Processing, Compiler Design and Cognitive Science. She has published nearly 25 papers in reputed International Journal & Conferences. She serves as a reviewer of various renowned International Journals and Conferences.

Shamim Akhter is working as Associate Professor, Department of Computer Science and Engineering (CSE), East West University (EWU), Bangladesh. He received his Ph.D. in Information Processing from Tokyo Institute of Technology (TokyoTech), M.Sc. in Computer Science and Information Management from Asian Institute of Technology (AIT) and B.Sc. in Computer Science from American International University Bangladesh (AIUB) in 2009, 2005 and 2002 respectively. He was also a JSPS Post Doctoral Research Fellow in National Institute of Informatics (NII) from FY 2009-2011, Visiting Researcher in Tokyo Institute of Technology, Japan from FY 2009-2011, Research Associate at the RS and GIS FoS, Asian Institute of Technology, Thailand in 2005, Global COE Research Assistant from Sep 2007~ Aug 2009 in Tokyo Institute of Technology, Japan and full time contact faculty at Thompson Rivers University, CANADA in 2013. He was awarded "The Excellent Student of The Year, FY2008", Global COE Program, Photonics Integration-Core Electronics (PICE), Tokyo Institute of Technology, Japan and Magna-Cum Laude for academic excellence from American International University Bangladesh in 2002. Dr. Akhter has around 50 research publications in renowned journals and conferences. His research interests are Artificial Intelligent, Evolutionary Algorithms and Models for their Parallelization, Remote Sensing (RS) and GIS applications, High Performance Computing (HPC), Algorithm and Complexity Analysis. He is a senior member of IEEE, member of JARC-Net and a member of IEEE CS technical committee for intelligence informatics and parallel processing. He serves as a reviewer of various renowned journals and numerous international conferences.

Louis Carter is CEO/Founder of Best Practice Institute, a research consortium, leadership development, talent management consultancy and project management organization. Louis is author of over 11 books on leadership and management including Change Champion's Field Guide and In Great Company (McGraw Hill) and is voted as one of the Top 10 Organizational Culture gurus in the world by Global Gurus. http://www.louiscarter.com and http://www.bestpracticeinstitute.org.

M. Pilar Casado-Belmonte is an assistant professor of Accounting and Finance in the Department of Economics and Business at Almeria University, Spain. She is the coordinator of the Finance and Accounting degree at the University of Almería. Her research interests include accounting, family firms and corporate governance. She has published her latest research findings in international journals such International Journal of Entrepreneurship and Small Business, and Psychology.

Paul Griffin is in SMU teaching postgraduate and undergraduate students in IT and FinTech as an Associate Professor of Information Systems and Director of Financial Technology & Analytics. He gained a PhD at Imperial College London in 1997 on Quantum Well Solar Cells and Thermophotovoltaics and is now researching disruptive technologies applications and their impact. Prior to SMU he was leading application development on global, regional and local projects for over 15 years in the UK and Asia in the financial industry. During this time, as well as leading internal IT development teams, he worked on outsourcing, off-shoring projects and IT support using his Black Belt in Six Sigma. Paul has been advising companies on smart contracts since 2014 and is now teaching courses on blockchain and smart contracts as well as presenting at events, judging hackathons and moderating panel discussions on FinTech.

Rajalakshmi Krishnamurthi obtained her Ph. D in Computer Science and Engineering from Jaypee Institute of Information Technology Noida, India. She did her M. E (CSE), and B. E. (EEE) from Bharathiar University, Coimbatore, India. She is currently an Assistant Professor (Senior Grade) with the Department of Computer Science and Engineering, Jaypee Institute of Information Technology, Noida. Her current research interests include Mobile computing, Wireless networks, Cloud Computing, Pervasive Computing.

Edward Lehner is a seasoned research methodologist with extensive training in qualitative and quantitative frameworks. Currently, he is focused on blockchain applications combining data sciences and higher education. In particular, Edward centers his efforts on cryptocurrencies and their ability to fund education and science. To understand cryptocurrency valuation metrics, Edward combines qualitative methodologies with data science, a complex and heterodox space, where there is much to research.

Maria J. Martínez-Romero is an assistant professor of Accounting and Finance in the Economics and Business Department at the University of Almería, Spain. She collaborates with the Santander Family Business Chair at this University. Her primary research interests include family firm research focusing on emotional, innovative, finance and corporate governance aspects. She has published her latest research findings in international journals such as Small Business Economics, Review of Managerial Science, International Journal of Entrepreneurship and Small Business, Management Research: Journal of the Iberoamerican Academy of Management.

Alan Megargel is a Senior Lecturer of Information Systems (Practice) at Singapore Management University where he serves as Coordinator for the undergraduate Financial Technology Career Track. His current areas of specialization include; enterprise architecture in banking, service-oriented architecture (SOA), payments technology, and non-bank FinTech alternative financial services. Alan has 30 years of industry experience including; Chief Technology Officer at TIBCO Software Asia, Vice President and Head of SOA at OCBC Bank, and Senior Enterprise Architect at ANZ Bank. His banking technology experience covers; Retail & Corporate Banking, Basel II, Data Warehouse, Data Centre Operations and Technology Infrastructure. Alan holds a Doctor of Innovation from Singapore Management University, and a Master of Science in Software, Systems and Information Engineering from the University of Sheffield.

Mohamed Mohamed Taysir is a certified Blockchain Solutions Architect, Business Strategist, Angel Investor and an Entrepreneur since a young age starting in 2009. Mohamed has worked within multiple industries in different capacities including Banking, Advertising, Management Consulting, Wealth Management and Public Relations. Mohamed is also involved with the Start-Up community through mentoring in accelerator labs. Mohamed holds an MSc. in Real Estate Development from the University of Manchester and a BBA from the American University in Cairo, with a major in finance and a double minor in macroeconomics and political science international relations.

Yusuf Muratoğlu obtained his BSc from Dokuz Eylul University, MSc from Hitit University and PhD from Gazi University. His MSc thesis is about the relationship between economic growth and unemployment and testing of it in Turkey in the framework of Okun's Law. His PhD dissertation is about the private sector external debt and its effects on financial stability in emerging market economies. His academic interests are unemployment, income inequality, migration, environmental economics, international trade, financial stability, and stock markets. He is working in Hitit University, Department of Economics.

Arun N. Nambiar is an associate professor at California State University - Fresno. His main research interests include software systems as it applies to mass customization, lean principles and production scheduling. He also works in the areas of RFID and data analytics. He is currently working on the applications of big data in agriculture and manufacturing.

Sangeetha K. Nanjundaswamy is working as Assistant Professor in the Department of Electronics & Communication Engineering, JSSATE, Bengaluru. She received her M.Tech from Visvesvaraya Technological University, Belagavi. She is pursuing her research in the area of Information Security.

Sharfi Rahman is a student of Computer Science and Engineering at East West University. Her research interests are decentralized network, Blockchain, Machine learning and data mining.

Shantanu Kumar Rahut, born in 1995, has recently (December 2018) completed his graduation from East West University - Bangladesh with a bachelor degree in computer science and engineering. He has worked as an undergraduate teaching assistant and after his graduation, a graduate teaching assistant. His general research interest is in the area of Blockchain, Decentralized Applications, Machine Learning, Data mining, and Human-Computer Interaction. He is an ambivert as a person.

Dhanalakshmi Senthilkumar obtained her Ph.D Degree in Information and Communication Engineering, in Anna University, Chennai, India. She Completed her M.E Degree in Anna University, Coimbatore, India and B.E., Degree in Madurai Kamaraj University, India. Now currently working as Professor in Department of Computer Science and Engineering, Malla Reddy Engineering College (A), India. Her general research interests are in the areas of Image Processing, Blockchain, Compiler Design and Data Structures.

Venky Shankararaman is a Professor of Information Systems (Education) and Deputy Dean (Practice & Education) at the School of Information Systems, Singapore Management University. He holds a PhD in Engineering from the University of Strathclyde, Glasgow, UK. His current areas of specialization include business process management and analytics, enterprise systems architecture and integration, and education pedagogy. He has over 25 years of experience in the IT industry in various capacities as a researcher, academic faculty member, IT professional and industry consultant. Venky has designed and delivered professional courses for government and industry in areas such as business process management and analytics, enterprise architecture, technical architecture, and enterprise integration. He has published over 75 papers in academic journals and conferences.

Tuhina Shree is currently associated with Jaypee Institute of Information Technology, Noida, India.

Razwan Ahmed Tanvir is a graduate of the Computer Science and Engineering Department in East West University (EWU). He is currently working as a Graduate Teaching Assistant in his department. He is also an Executive member of EWU Computer Programming Club (EWUCoPC). His general research interest is in the area of Blockchain, Decentralized Applications and Machine Learning. He is an ambivert as a person.

Jorge Tarifa-Fernández is Research Fellow in the Department of Economics and Business at the University of Almería since 2014. He received the MBA Degree in 2012 from the University of Almería and the PhD in 2017 also in the University of Almería. His research interests include supply chain management, environmental management, strategy, and digital technologies.

Erginbay Uğurlu is an Assoc. Professor of Econometrics in the Department of Economics and Finance at the Istanbul Aydın University. Uğurlu received his B.A. in Econometrics from Marmara University in 2004. He has attended to İstanbul Technical University in 2004 and received M.Sc. in Economics in 2006. In the same year, he started his doctoral education at Gazi University. He had the Ph.D. degree in the field of Econometrics in 2011. He was carrying out research in Columbia University Department of Economics as a Visiting Scholar and The Columbia Consortium for Risk Management as a Post Doctoral Academic Researcher in 2013. Uğurlu's research interests include econometrics, time series econometrics, panel data econometrics and limited dependent variables on economics and finance.

Charu Virmani is working as a Professor in Department of Computer Science and Engineering at Manav Rachna International Institute of Research and studies, Faridabad, Haryana. She holds B.E in Information Technology, M.Tech in Computer Science from M.D.U., Rohtak & Ph.D in Computer Engineering from YMCA University of Science and Technology, Faridabad. She has 13 years of Teaching experience. She published 28 Research Papers in National, International conferences and Journals. She has attended and organized many workshops, Guest Lectures, seminars, national and International conferences. She has delivered workshops on cyber security, social network mining and design thinking. She is also associated with professional societies like ACM,CSI. Her guided project 'CAR PARKING SYSTEM' got first prize in FIA in the year 2014 and appreciated by Dr. APJ Abdul Kalam during the 61st General Body meeting and concluding ceremony of Diamond Jubilee celebration of FIA. She is the spokesperson for an Industrial-Academia collaboration with Japan based organisation. She is a reviewer for high indexed journals (IGI,TSII to name a few). Dr. Charu's research interests are cyber security, data mining, big data, machine learning, Artificial Intelligence.

John R. Ziegler is an Assistant Professor of English at Bronx Community College, City University of New York. He has published on early modern English literature, contemporary popular culture, and, as a co-author, education.

Index

A

accounting process 46
augur 182

B

Bitcoin 13, 29, 32, 47, 69-70, 73, 75-77, 80, 82-84, 86-87, 89, 91-95, 97-98, 103, 105, 124, 135, 146, 149, 161, 169-170, 179, 182-185, 196, 222-227, 246-250, 253, 255, 258, 260, 262, 264, 266
Blockchain 1-2, 10, 13-14, 26-35, 37-40, 45-50, 52-63, 69-74, 76-80, 82-84, 86-92, 94-98, 100-106, 110-111, 114-115, 117-122, 124-125, 128, 136, 167-176, 178-185, 189-190, 193-197, 199-202, 207-208, 214-216, 222-228, 230, 232-234, 236, 238-244, 246-274
Blockchain 3.0 47, 88, 97-98, 110, 247
blockchain technology 13-14, 29-30, 32-35, 37-38, 40, 45-50, 53-58, 60-63, 69-71, 73, 84, 86-88, 90-92, 95, 98, 101, 103-106, 110-111, 114-115, 119-122, 124-125, 167-168, 181, 184-185, 189-190, 193-196, 199-201, 214-216, 222, 228, 246-251, 258-260, 265-272
business process 1-5, 7, 9-10, 13-14, 16, 19-21, 23-24, 27

C

centralized control 3, 9, 26
confidentiality 9, 246, 258-259, 262
consensus 2, 13, 27, 32, 37, 48, 54-55, 69-71, 75-79, 82, 87, 104, 115, 117, 120-122, 124, 128, 136, 168, 170, 172, 175, 177, 183, 195, 223-224, 243-244, 249, 251, 254-258, 264, 266, 271, 273
cryptocurrency 29-30, 40, 70, 78, 84, 92, 104, 115, 124, 128-130, 133-138, 140, 145-146, 148-150, 158-161, 190, 216, 222, 247, 255-256, 258, 263-264
cryptography 26, 32, 47-48, 52, 70, 73, 87, 89, 105, 128, 135-136, 149, 179, 194, 196, 222-224, 227, 249, 251, 266
cybersecurity 29, 49-50

D

data security 3, 29, 32-33, 35, 40, 49, 96, 236
data sharing 197
decentralization 3, 14, 20-21, 37, 49-50, 95, 115, 196, 247
decentralized control 1, 9, 26, 183
decentralized ledger 27, 69, 84, 177, 197, 250-251, 257, 261, 270
Decentralized Ledger Technology (DLT) 27
decision-making process 46, 55, 60
digital signature 47-48, 103, 249, 251, 273
distributed ledger 2, 26, 29, 46, 56, 167, 180, 194, 196, 223, 226-227, 243, 246-247, 257, 265-266, 273
distributed process 1, 3, 9, 13, 24, 26-27, 78
Double Spending Problem 84

E

energy sector 110, 113-115, 119-122, 124-125
Ethereum 13, 29-30, 70, 76, 85, 95, 97, 100, 121, 182, 195-196, 215, 223, 225-226, 229, 236, 238, 241-243, 255, 258, 262, 265

F

FINTECH 86-88, 103, 105

G

GARCH 145, 149-150, 153, 155, 157-160

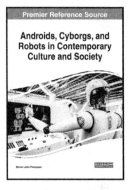

Ensure Quality Research is Introduced to the Academic Community

Become an IGI Global Reviewer for Authored Book Projects

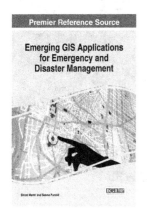
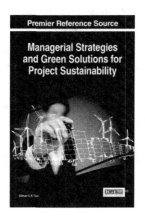

The overall success of an authored book project is dependent on quality and timely reviews.

In this competitive age of scholarly publishing, constructive and timely feedback significantly expedites the turnaround time of manuscripts from submission to acceptance, allowing the publication and discovery of forward-thinking research at a much more expeditious rate. Several IGI Global authored book projects are currently seeking highly qualified experts in the field to fill vacancies on their respective editorial review boards:

Applications may be sent to:
development@igi-global.com

Applicants must have a doctorate (or an equivalent degree) as well as publishing and reviewing experience. Reviewers are asked to write reviews in a timely, collegial, and constructive manner. All reviewers will begin their role on an ad-hoc basis for a period of one year, and upon successful completion of this term can be considered for full editorial review board status, with the potential for a subsequent promotion to Associate Editor.

If you have a colleague that may be interested in this opportunity,
we encourage you to share this information with them.

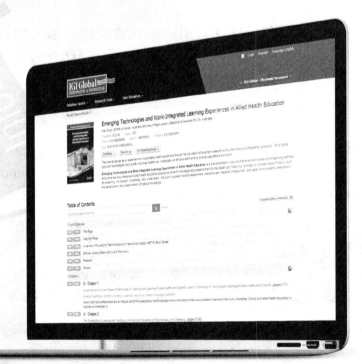

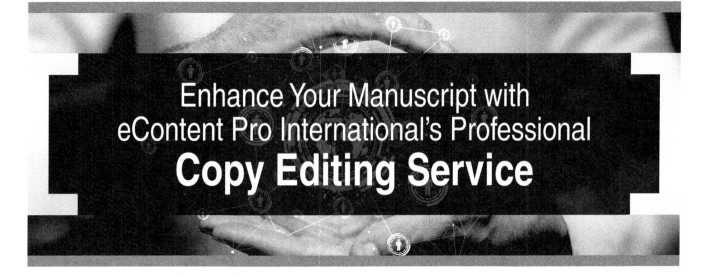

Printed in the United States
By Bookmasters